PUBLIC ADMINISTRATION AND PUBLIC POLICY

A Comprehensive Publication Program

Executive Editor

JACK RABIN

Graduate Program for Administrators
Rider College
Lawrenceville, New Jersey

1. Public Administration as a Developing Discipline (in two parts), *by Robert T. Golembiewski*
2. Comparative National Policies on Health Care, *by Milton I. Roemer, M.D.*
3. Exclusionary Injustice: The Problem of Illegally Obtained Evidence, *by Steven R. Schlesinger*
4. Personnel Management in Government: Politics and Process, *by Jay M. Shafritz, Walter L. Balk, Albert C. Hyde, and David H. Rosenbloom* (out of print)
5. Organization Development in Public Administration (in two parts), *edited by Robert T. Golembiewski and William B. Eddy* (Part two: out of print)
6. Public Administration: A Comparative Perspective. Second Edition, Revised and Expanded, *by Ferrel Heady*
7. Approaches to Planned Change (in two parts), *by Robert T. Golembiewski*
8. Program Evaluation at HEW (in three parts), *edited by James G. Abert*
9. The States and the Metropolis, *by Patricia S. Florestano and Vincent L. Marando*
10. Personnel Management in Government: Politics and Process. Second Edition, Revised and Expanded, *by Jay M. Shafritz, Albert C. Hyde, and David H. Rosenbloom*
11. Changing Bureaucracies: Understanding the Organization Before Selecting the Approach, *by William A. Medina*
12. Handbook on Public Budgeting and Financial Management, *edited by Jack Rabin and Thomas D. Lynch*

Making and Managing Policy

13. Encyclopedia of Policy Studies, *edited by Stuart S. Nagel*

14. Public Administration and Law: Bench v. Bureau in the United States, *by David H. Rosenbloom*

15. Handbook on Public Personnel Administration and Labor Relations, *edited by Jack Rabin, Thomas Vocino, W. Bartley Hildreth, and Gerald J. Miller*

16. Public Budgeting and Finance: Behavioral, Theoretical and Technical Perspectives, *edited by Robert T. Golembiewski and Jack Rabin*

17. Organizational Behavior and Public Management, *by Debra W. Stewart and G. David Garson*

18. The Politics of Terrorism. Second Edition, Revised and Expanded, *edited by Michael Stohl*

19. Handbook of Organization Management, *edited by William B. Eddy*

20. Organization Theory and Management, *edited by Thomas D. Lynch*

21. Labor Relations in the Public Sector, *by Richard C. Kearney*

22. Politics and Administration: Woodrow Wilson and American Public Administration, *edited by Jack Rabin and James S. Bowman*

23. Making and Managing Policy: Formulation, Analysis, Evaluation, *edited by G. Ronald Gilbert*

Other volumes in preparation

Making and Managing Policy

Formulation, Analysis, Evaluation

Edited by
G. Ronald Gilbert
College of Business Administration
Florida International University
Miami, Florida

MARCEL DEKKER, INC. New York and Basel

Library of Congress Cataloging in Publication Data
Main entry under title:

Making and managing policy.

(Public administration and public policy; 23)
Includes index.
1. Administrative agencies–United States–Evaluation–Addresses, essays, lectures. 2. Political planning–United States–Evaluation–Addresses, essays lectures. 3. Policy sciences–Addresses, essays, lectures. I. Gilbert, G. Ronald, 1939- . II. Series.
JK421.M3365 1984 353.07 84-1867

MARCEL DEKKER, INC.
270 Madison Avenue, New York, New York 10016

Current printing (last digit):
10 9 8 7 6 5 4 3 2 1

PRINTED IN THE UNITED STATES OF AMERICA

Preface

The purpose of this anthology is to make a statement about the processes and approaches which are used by public managers to make and guide public policy. It consists of three major sections: Policy Formulation, Policy Analysis, and Program Evaluation. It draws on examples from most of the major categories of public service, i.e. education, health, energy, environment, human services, transportation, defense and the like. It highlights landmark cases such as the passage of the Civil Service Reform Act of 1978 and the institutionalization of program evaluation in the U.S. General Accounting Office. Historical and definitional articles have been included as points from which future dialogue may occur about the practice and scope of public policy-making.

The chapters were specifically written for this text. Each chapter was reviewed by at least two members of the editorial board of the *Annals of Public Administration*, Policy Analysis and Evaluation section. Other outside reviewers were also included when their technical expertise was needed. The final decision to accept or reject each chapter was made by me.

The editorial board met three times over a two-year period. They worked diligently to create the framework used in this text. They developed a pool of national experts from which various articles could be requested. They strove to improve the quality of each author's contribution without jeopardizing the uniqueness of each. Collectively, they were brilliant, professionally committed to excellence, and dedicated to improved public management.

Robert F. Boruch, Walter D. Broadnax, Ross Clayton, Patrick J. Conklin, Howard E. Freeman, Sally Greenberg, Edward L. Hannon, David A. Hardcastle, Albert C. Hyde, N. Paul Loomba, William J. Page, Jr., Jay M. Shafritz, Carol H. Weiss, and Joseph S. Wholey were exceptionally helpful in the review process. Charles Nickerson, Leonardo Rodriguez and Enzo Valenzi provided me significant academic and administrative support for this endeavor. Special thanks to Estella Breitler, Jan Gilbert, Willabeth Jordan, Rosalind Knapp, Maria Martinez, Helen

Rodriguez, Maria Schottenheimer and Connie Waterhouse for their unique administrative contributions. Leonor Guerrero assumed a major coordinating role in this project. Her dedication, keen mind, and attention to detail kept me and this project on schedule.

Lastly my gratitude to Jack Rabin, editor, whose imagination, practical guidance and genuine interest in this field have made possible this contribution to public management.

G. Ronald Gilbert

Contents

Preface iii
Contributors ix

1 The Study of Policy Formulation and the Conduct of Policy Analysis and Evaluation
G. Ronald Gilbert 1

Part I Policy Formulation

2 Policy Formulation
John J. Kirlin 13

3 GAO and Evaluation: A Perspective from Elmer Staats
Patrick J. Conklin and Elmer Staats 25

4 The Congress and Evaluation
Harry S. Havens 43

5 Evaluating the Spatial Impacts of National Transportation Policies
A. C. Goodman and K. C. Lyall 57

6 The Passage of the Civil Service Reform Act of 1978: A Dialogue with Alan K. Campbell
Miriam Ershkowitz 67

Part II Policy Analysis

7 Policy Analysis
Stuart S. Nagel 87

8 Policy Analysis in Support of Congressional Oversight
Morton A. Myers 111

9 Policy Analysis in Long-Term Care
Sidney Katz and Joseph Papsidero 123

10 Analysis of Government Policies in Urban Transportation
Ronald F. Kirby 141

11 An Experiment in Federal Personnel Management: The Naval Laboratories Demonstration Project
Lloyd G. Nigro and Ross Clayton 153

12 Contributions of Evaluation Research and Analysis to Energy and Environmental Policy
E. J. Soderstrom and B. H. Bronfman 173

Part III Evaluation

13 Evaluation: Whose Questions Should Be Answered?
Thomas D. Cook 193

14 A Survey of the Program Evaluation and Evaluation Research Literature in Its Formative Stage
Albert C. Hyde 219

15 Evaluation on Demand: Two Congressionally Mandated Education Evaluations
Beryl A. Radin 239

16 Education Evaluations: More than Business as Usual
Lois-ellin Datta 257

17 Evaluation of Human Services
William J. Page, Jr. 269

18 Evaluating Defense Programs in an Era of Rising Expenditures
Grover Starling 289

19 The Evaluation of Social Action Programs Involving Minorities
David Lopez-Lee 309

20 Evaluation for the Training and Development Function
Enid F. Beaumont 327

21 Management of Evaluation: Implementing an Effective
Evaluation Program
Joseph S. Wholey 337

Index 347

Contributors

ENID F. BEAUMONT Academy for State and Local Government, Washington, D.C.

B. H. BRONFMAN* Bronfman Associates, Oak Ridge, Tennessee

ROSS CLAYTON, School of Public Administration, University of Southern California, Los Angeles, California

PATRICK J. CONKLIN Federal Executive Institute, Charlottesville, Virginia

THOMAS D. COOK Department of Psychology, Northwestern University, Evanston, Illinois

LOIS-ELLIN DATTA** National Institute of Education, United States Department of Education, Washington, D.C.

MIRIAM ERSHKOWITZ† Public Management Executive Development Institute, Temple University, Philadelphia, Pennsylvania

G. RONALD GILBERT College of Business Administration, Florida International University, Miami, Florida

A. C. GOODMAN Center for Metropolitan Planning and Research, The Johns Hopkins University, Baltimore, Maryland

HARRY S. HAVENS United States General Accounting Office, Washington, D.C.

ALBERT C. HYDE School of Business and Public Administration, University of Houston at Clear Lake, Houston, Texas

---

Present affiliations:
*Portland Operations, Evaluation Research Corporation, Portland, Oregon
**Institute for Program Evaluation, United States General Accounting Office, Washington, D.C.
†Center for Public Service, Texas Tech University, Lubbock, Texas

SIDNEY KATZ Department of Community Health, Brown University, Providence, Rhode Island

RONALD F. KIRBY Productivity and Economic Development Center, The Urban Institute, Washington, D.C.

JOHN J. KIRLIN School of Public Administration, University of Southern California, Sacramento, California

DAVID LOPEZ-LEE School of Public Administration, University of Southern California, Los Angeles, California

K. C. LYALL* Center for Metropolitan Planning and Research, The Johns Hopkins University, Baltimore, Maryland

MORTON A. MYERS** United States General Accounting Office, Boston, MA

STUART S. NAGEL Political Science Department, University of Illinois, Urbana, Illinois

LLOYD G. NIGRO Department of Political Science, Georgia State University, Atlanta, Georgia

WILLIAM J. PAGE, JR. Departments of Public Administration and Social Work, Florida State University, Tallahassee, Florida

JOSEPH PAPSIDERO Department of Community Health Science, Michigan State University, East Lansing, Michigan

BERYL A. RADIN Washington Public Affairs Center, University of Southern California, Washington, D.C.

E. J. SODERSTROM Oak Ridge National Laboratory, Oak Ridge, Tennessee

ELMER B. STAATS† Former Comptroller General of the United States, Washington, D.C.

GROVER STARLING School of Business and Public Administration, University of Houston at Clear Lake Houston, Texas

JOSEPH S. WHOLEY Washington Public Affairs Center, University of Southern California, Washington, D.C.

Present affiliations:
*The University of Wisconsin, Madison, Wisconsin
**United States General Accounting Office, Boston, Massachusetts
†President, Harry S. Truman Scholarship Foundation; corporate director; consultant, Washington, D.C.

Making and Managing Policy

1
The Study of Policy Formulation and the Conduct of Policy Analysis and Evaluation

G. Ronald Gilbert / *College of Business Administration, Florida International University, Miami, Florida*

POLICY MAKING AND THE PUBLIC ADMINISTRATOR

Government, in a positive constitutional democracy like ours, is guided by public policies. Some of these policies are found in natural law, others are more clearly defined by constitutional charters, agreements, and the like; other policies are established over time by precedent or situation. How and why public policies are created has been a subject of intense debate.

There is agreement that public policies are shaped by environmental factors, i.e., the influences, rationales, pressures and adjustments with political systems [1] but disagreement exists about the effects that groups [2] elites [3], processes [4], institutions [5], roles [6], and finally public administrators have on public policies.

We have energy policies, economic policies, policies for equal opportunities, civil liberties, health care, welfare, soil conservation, housing, defense, safety, science and technology, and agriculture, among others. These policies are rarely clear, rarely static, and rarely implemented in an identical manner from place to place, jurisdiction to jurisdiction.

Historically, this has led to an interesting and confusing role for public administrators. It has been argued on the one hand that the administrator's role is to develop and carry out the will of those who set policies (essentially maintaining the classic policy/administration dichotomy). On the other hand, there is recognition that administrators are actively involved as are other elites, interest groups and the like, in the making of policy in its formative as well as its implementation stages. In fact, in the regulatory area, the role of administrative agencies has been fused to the extent that administrators formulate, implement, and even adjudicate public policies. Public administrators are able to influence policy in its early formation stage through active campaigning, selective interpretation of technical information, and through their own program designs, strategies and tactics. They are often able to rearrange or modify the intent of legislative enactments as a program is formed and structured, or they can extend or reduce the policy terrain upon which their programs rest.

There is a unique professional interest among public administrators in the manner by which public policies are formed. Public administrators study policy formation to get better insight into the future, its implications for their work, and to recognize the degree to which a policy is representative of the pluralistic society in which they live, and, therefore, the degree to which a given policy initiative is potentially stable. Essentially, public administrators must be more knowledgable about the contextual environment of public policies and their own influence and power on that environment.

THE ADMINISTRATOR AS BUREAUCRAT OR MANAGER

There appear to be two role models of the professional public administrator. In the first role model, the administrator as "bureaucrat," emphasis is placed on administering resources in accord with grander policies set forth by government legislators and political executives. The public administrator reacts to policies articulated by others and acts to carry out such policies through sound administrative practices. The guidelines, rules, and regulations set forth by these administrators are subject to continued oversight and modification by others beyond their domain of control. Decisions they make are influenced by many and serve many means and ends. When the environment dominates, administrators tend to be incrementalists [7] emphasizing marginal changes, high policy continuity, and close attention to sunk costs and past investments.

In the second role model, as "manager," emphasis is placed on planning, organizing, and controlling processes to accomplish organizational goals through people. Here the administrator works in a more "emergent" environment where change, uncertainty, and instability abound. The manager model emphasizes the public administrator as policy maker within given legal guidelines. Contrary to the bureaucrat model, the manager would tend to lean more toward a rational decision making style as opposed to incremental decision making. Public managers are committed to making, enacting, and evaluating policy. However, such policies serve as rules, procedures, and guidelines to enable subordinate members of their organizations to make uniform decisions and conduct themselves in a manner that is consistent with the goals and objectives of the organization. They use policy guidelines as controls to assure that organizational performance will meet their expectations or standards.

Neither the public bureaucrat nor the public manager role models exist as pure types in reality. However, these role models help explain the kinds of conflicting role messages which presently exist within the profession. As one begins to address terms such as policy formulation, policy analysis, and program evaluation, it is important to give recognition to this perspective of the role of the bureaucrat/manager. In its best form, it means that while public administrators face severe challenges, they have a major opportunity to create "constructive" and "effective" governmental responses to societal problems. But in its worst form, it may signify a deadly form of ambivalence resulting in governmental non-policies, non-actions, and paralysis. Both roles–bureaucrats and managers–conceive of policy analysis and evaluation as important decision-driven techniques. However, the bureaucratic perspective sees analysis and evaluation to be more likely conducted by others external to the organization. Managers view these two functions to be integral parts of their decision domain, indeed, of their job. Bureaucrats view policy formation to be separate from their job, while managers view the making of policy to be central to their role, and it should occur as a result of strategic and operational planning.

POLICY MAKING IN PUBLIC AND PRIVATE ADMINISTRATION

Public administration has studied policy formulation differently than have their counter parts in business administration. While the tools and techniques used in public administration may be similar to those in business, policy making in public administration is more complex than in business. In general, business managers approach decision making with greater expectations for rationality than do public administrators whose literature is more heavily influenced by the incrementalism school. Steiner [8] states:

1. *Politics dominate the public sector* and that important policy decisions in government are made on the political anvil. This he views to be a fundamental difference between business and government, for in business, the great majority of decisions are dominated by economic considerations.
2. *Interest groups have a legal role to play in shaping policy* in the public sector, whereas in the private sector they play a role, but there is little legal compulsion to do so.
3. *Goals and objectives in public sector organizations are broader, more plentiful, and less likely to lend themselves to strategic plans* having long-range objectives than is the case in the business organizations. Thus, planning for policy formulation in the public sector is a more difficult and less realistic than it is for the manager in the private sector.

4. *Evaluation criteria in the public sector are less clear*, making them more difficult to use to assess alternatives and decisions than in the private sector. The criteria used in private sector analysis and evaluation are generally tied to return on investment, market share, profit, rates and margin, whereas in the public sector the basic criteria used are public interest, political efficiency and cost-benefit analysis. Both public interest and political efficiency are vague terms, not easily measured.
5. *Time horizons for public managers often differ from those of politicians* who play a key role in the formation of public policy. Thus for purposes of political expediency, politicians may legislate programs that deter strategic planning and analysis on the part of professional public managers.

Sutherland [9] suggests the private sectors' performance is more quantifiable (reflecting the nature of the outputs) and more objective, resulting in performance being evaluated using specific criteria generally known to the decision maker ahead of time—indeed, often emerging out of a bargaining process. Public sector performance is much more subjective. Public administrators are evaluated by criteria oftentimes unknown beforehand by those involved.

In the public sector, an outstanding manager can run an ineffective program, or conversely, an ineffective manager may run a very effective program. Even more ironic, a public manager may find that effective performance runs contrary to policy intentions, as a number of auditors and inspectors have found who reported program cost over-runs, for example, and lost favor and then their jobs as a result.

The private sector provides more legitimate opportunity for managers to redirect plans and management practices to achieve personal and organizational ends. Public administrators tend more to be bound to a wider range of policies which do not often lend themselves to change based solely on the initiative of the public administrator. "Social Regulations" or government regulations in such areas as Occupational Health and Safety, Equal Employment Opportunity, Minority Business Enterprise, and the like are "hints" to the business manager about what it is like to manage in the public sector where control of the organization's destiny is shared by many. Roy Ash, when director of the U.S. Office of Management and Budget, captured this difference between public and private management when he said: "Just imagine yourself as chief executive officer where your board of directors is made up of your employees, customers, suppliers, and competitors. How would you like to run that business and try to be effective?" [10].

Indeed, there are differences between public and business administration, with those in business having greater opportunity to form policy and plan, organize and control their resources to accomplish their policy objectives than do their counterparts in the public sector. The public administrator is required to have more skills in facilitating, interpreting, and implementing the formation of policies set by others. Public administrators do not run cities or governments; they administer them and manage programs within them. While city managers are viewed to be major policy shapers, they rarely are as much of an influence in the formation of policy as are their counterpart chief executive officers in the private sector. If public administrators act to form policies with the same autonomy as their private sector counterparts, they will likely be operating unconstitutionally or violating other laws or charters.

Because of these differences, the process of policy formulation is a more complex and significant area of concern for the public administrator, while in some contexts policy analysis and program evaluation may be quite similar in either the public or private sectors.

POLICY FORMULATION, POLICY ANALYSIS AND PROGRAM EVALUATION

The process of policy formulation in public administration has been described by Lasswell as having seven stages. Although Lasswell's policy making process model is one of a number of interpretations, it uses these seven stages to describe the decision-making process that occurs when public policy is formed [11]:

1. *Intelligence* addresses how information is processed by policy makers to formulate problems or alternatives.
2. *Promotion* deals with the processes by which agitation and other tactics are used to promote causes and self interests.
3. *Prescription* considers how general rules about a policy alternative are adopted or enacted and by whom.
4. *Invocation* describes how the application of the policy rules or laws are made and where the focus of power and authority to assure compliance with policy lie.
5. *Application* defines how laws or rules are applied by executives or enforcement officers.
6. *Termination* focuses on how the original rules or laws are terminated or modified or extended.
7. *Appraisal* labels the processes by which the success or failure of the operation of policies are appraised.

These stages have been labelled to help students and practitioners understand public intention and the responsibility of public administrators as they act as instruments to assure such policies are managed economically, efficiently, and effectively. As policy formulation helps public administrators better understand the nature, intention, and content of public policy, policy analysis and program evaluation help them manage public programs and projects. Thus, these are applied research areas. They constitute rational quantitative and qualitative methods, tools and techniques to identify manageable problems and organizational objectives within a broad policy context, to define and select alternative strategies, monitor activities, and assess results for program improvement. As such, they rely heavily on the academic disciplines of political science, psychology, sociology, anthropology, law, economics, operations research and evaluation research, to mention a few. Policy analysis is prospective in terms of program action while program evaluation is retrospective. That is, policy analysis is used to aid managers plan and design programs or projects while program evaluation is used to compare performance to standards and make realistic programmatic adjustments as well as identify intended and unintended results of policy efforts.

Figure 1 attempts to relate the processes of policy formulation and the practices of policy analysis and program evaluation to the decision-making process employed by public administrators.

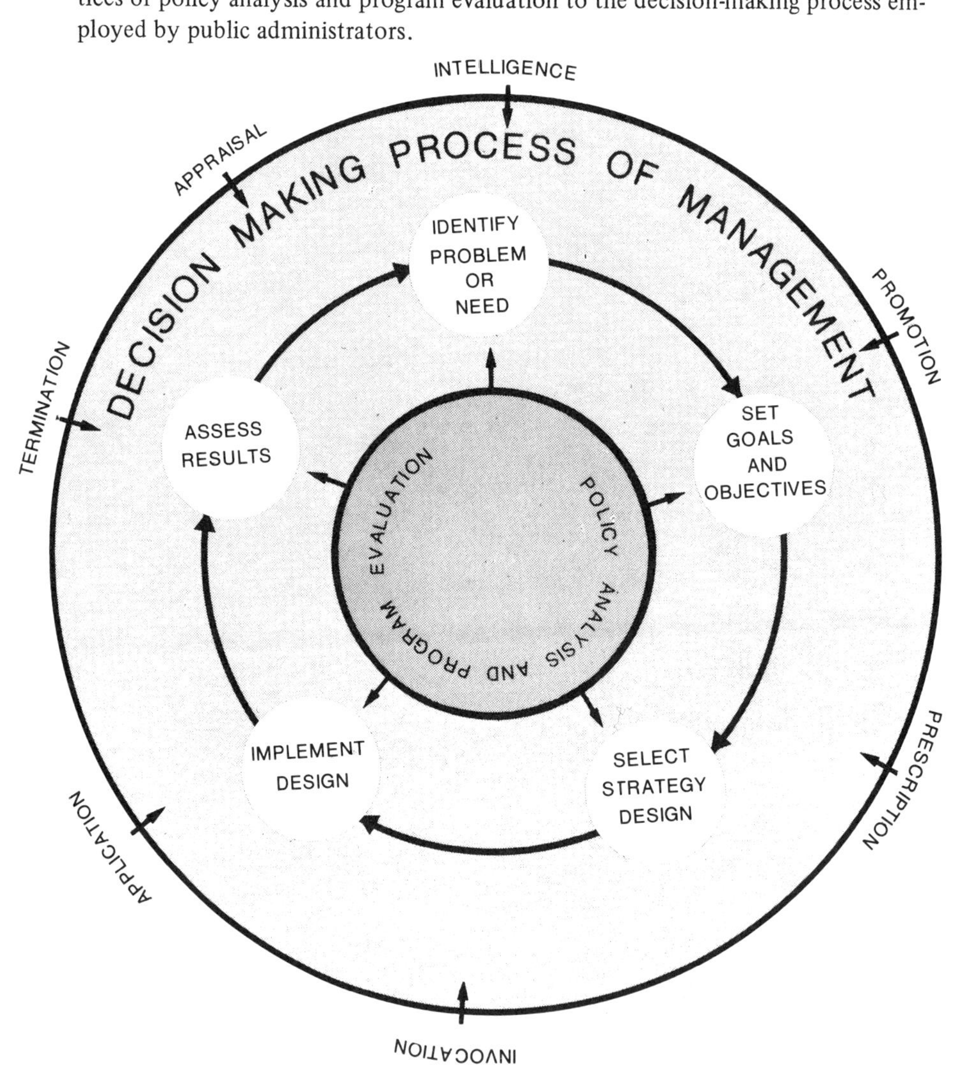

Figure 1 Policy-making processes and approaches for public administrators.

Both policy analysis and program evaluation are approaches used by public administrators to drive key decisions to be made when managing public programs. These approaches include a variety of analytical and evaluative techniques and methods. They include survey research [12], forecasting [13], delphi [14], value tree [15], psychological scaling techniques and methods for problem identification [16], sequential screening and experimentation [17], expected utility measurement [18], *MAUT-Bayes* [19], trade-off methods [20], cost benefit analysis [21], risk benefit analysis [22], simple linear programming [23], goal setting and strategy analysis [24], queing analysis [25], line of balance [26], and discrepancy analysis for program implementation evaluation [27], and non-experimental field research and estimations, quasi experimental and true experimental research [28] for measuring program results.

The decision-making stages of public management operate within a less rational, more incremental, less clearly defined, and more complex policy formulation process than in industry. The environmental process of public policy had led to the domination of interactional models whereas industry is focused through linear sequential causation. However, one needs to view public policy from a transactional perspective, as well, where all variables and factors are viewed relatively. A transactional model would be inherently circular and demand that we understand the relationship of actors and actions and circumstances as ebb, flow, and balance [29]. The extent to which such a model would be useful to policy scholars would depend upon the willingness to redefine, re-relate, and reorganize models and variables alike.

Finally, while policy formulation can be distinguished from program implementation, neither is independent of the other. As Pressman and Wildavsky state: "Means and ends can be brought into somewhat closer correspondence only by making each partially dependent on the other" [30]. Such is the case with policy formulation and implementation in the policy-making process of government. Administrators are challenged to understand more to perform better.

REFERENCES

1. Easton, D. An Approach to the Analysis of Political Systems. *World Politics* 9 (April 1957):383-400; Easton, D. *A Framework for Political Analysis*. Prentice-Hall, Englewood Cliffs, NJ, 1965.
2. Latham, E. *The Group Basis of Politics*. Octagon Books, New York, NY, 1965.
3. Mills, C. W. *The Power Elite*. Oxford University Press, New York, NY, 1956; Mills, C. W. The Structure of Power in American Society. *The British Journal of Sociology* 9 (March 1958):29-41; Dye, T. and Ziegler, L. H. *The Irony of Democracy*. Wadsworth, Belmont, CA, 1970; Dahl, P. A. A Critique of the Ruling Elite, *American Political Science Review* 52 (June 1958): 463-469. 469.
4. Lasswell, H. D. *The Decision Process*. Bureau of Governmental Research, University of Maryland, College Park, MD, 1956.

5. Jones, C. O. *An Introduction to the Study of Public Policy*. Wadsworth, Belmont, CA, 1970.
6. Eulau, H. *Journey in Politics*. Bobbs-Merrill, New York, NY, 1964; Almond, G. Comparative Political Systems. *Journal of Politics* 18 (August 1956): 391-409; Gross, N., Mason, W. S., and McEachern, A. *Explorations in Role Analysis*. John Wiley, New York, NY, 1958.
7. Lindblom, C. L. The Science of Muddling Through. *Public Administration Review* 19 (Spring 1959):79-88; Simon, H. Theories of Decision-Making in Economic and Behavioral Science. *American Economic Review* 49 (June 1959):255-257; Braybrooke, D. and Lindblom, C. L. *A Strategy of Decision*. Free Press, New York, NY, 1963.
8. Steiner, G. A. *Strategic Planning*. Collier Macmillan Publishers, London, England, 1979.
9. Sutherland, J. W. *Administrative Decision-Making*. Van Nostrand Reinhold, New York, NY, 1977, pp. 121-123.
10. Steiner, *Op. Cit.* p. 323.
11. Lasswell, H. R. *A Pre-View of Policy Sciences*. Elsevier, New York, 1971. For other versions of the typology refer to Bauer, R. A. and Gergen, K. J. *The Study of Policy Formation* (eds). Free Press, New York, NY, 1968; Anderson, J. A. *Public Policy-Making*, 2nd. ed. Holt, Rinehart, and Winston, New York, NY, 1979.
12. Babbie, E. R. *Survey Research Methods*. Wadsworth Publishing Co. Inc., Belmont, CA, 1973.
13. Gerstenfeld, A. Technological Forecasting. *Journal of Business* (January 1981):10-18; Chambers, J. C., Mullick, S. K., Smith, and D. C. "How to Choose the Right Forecasting Techniques." *Harvard Business Review* (July-August 1971):45-74.
14. Dalkey, N. *The Delphi Method: An Experimental Study of Group Opinion*. Rand, Santa Monica, CA, 1969.
15. See Keeney, R. and Raiffa, H. *Decision Making with Multiple Objectives: Preference and Value Tradeoffs*. Wiley Interscience, New York, NY, 1976.
16. Coombs, C. H. *A Theory of Psychological Scaling*, 2nd ed. Greenwood, Westport, CT, 1976; Lingoes, J. C. The Multivariate Analysis of Qualitative Data. *Multivariate Behavioral Research* No. 3, (1968):61-94.
17. Wetherill, G. B. *Sequential Methods in Statistics*. John Wiley, New York, NY, 1975. Colton, T. Optimal Drug Screening Plans. *Biometrika* 50 (1963): 31-46; Davies, O. L. The Design of Screening Test. *Technometrics* 5 (1963):483-489.
18. Keeney and Raiffa, *Op. Cit.*, 1976.
19. Edwards, W. A Theory of Decision Making. *Psychological Bulletin* 51 (July 1954):380-417.
20. MacCrimmon, K. R. and Siu, J. K. Making Trade-Offs. *Decision Sciences* 5 (1974):680-704.

21. Mishan, E. J. *Cost Benefit Analysis*, (ed). Praeger, New York, NY, 1972.
22. Green, P. E. *Mathematical Tools for Applied Multivariate Analysis*, (ed). Academic Press, New York, NY, 1976.
23. Dantzig, G. B. *Linear Programming and Extensions*. Princeton University Press, Princeton, NJ, 1963.
24. Battersby, A. *Network Analysis for Planning and Scheduling*. John Wiley and Sons, New York, NY, 1970; Hoare, H. R. *Project Management Using Network Analysis*. McGraw-Hill, Maidenhead, England, 1973.
25. Saatz, T. L. *Elements of Queing Theory with Applications*. McGraw-Hill Book Co., New York, NY, 1961; White, J. A., Schmidt, J. W., and Bennett, G. K. *Analysis of Queing Systems*. Academic Press, New York, NY, 1975.
26. Taylor, W. S. and Watling, T. F. *Practical Project Management*, John Wiley and Sons, New York, NY, 1973.
27. Provus, M. M. *Discrepancy Evaluation: For Educational Program Improvement and Assessment*. McCutchan Publishing Corp., Berkeley, CA, 1971.
28. Campbell, D. T. and Stanley, J. C. *Experimental and Quasi-Experimental Designs for Research*. Rand McNally & Co., Chicago, Il, 1966; Kerlinger, F. N. *Foundations of Behavioral Research*. Holt, Rinehart and Winston, Inc., New York, NY, 1973; Babbie, E. R. *Survey Research Methods: A Cookbook & Other Fables*. Wadsworth Publishing Co., Belmont, CA, 1973.
29. See, for example, Dewey, John and Bentley, Arthur F. *Knowing and the Known*. Beacon Press, Boston, 1949.
30. Pressman, J. and Wildavsky, A. *Implementation*. University of California Press, Berkeley, CA, 1973, p. 143.

Part I
Policy Formulation

The dynamics by which public policy is formed have been widely discussed in the literature. This section extends the literature in several ways.

John J. Kirlin describes policy formation from a broad societal context. This context is marked by distinct and changing paradigms from which policy choices are made. He offers a non-traditional framework for scholars to view policy options and influences. Patrick J. Conklin presents an interview with Elmer Staats, whose accomplishments during his fifteen years as Comptroller General of the U.S. General Accounting Office are unparalleled in public management. During his administration, Mr. Staats participated in the making of policy changes in GAO and observed many unique dynamics that led to changes in national policies. Many insights into the roles that GAO, Mr. Staats, and the legislative, executive and judicial branches of government played in the formation of policy are provided. Extending Patrick J. Conklin's report, Harry S. Havens describes the interaction between evaluation and analysis and how it may influence policy choices in Congress. He provides excellent insight into the role analysis plays in the political world. A. C. Goodman and K. C. Lyall review the influence of five transportation policy options on American urban and regional life. Through analysis they shed light on issues that are associated with an inconsistent and incomplete national transportation policy. Finally, Miriam Ershkowitz reports on an interview which she conducted with Alan K. Campbell. In this interview, she captures the methods, approaches, strategies, tactics and dynamics that were used by Dr. Campbell to lead those in the Federal bureaucracy and Congress toward the enactment and implementation of the Civil Service Reform Act of 1978.

2
Policy Formulation

John J. Kirlin / *School of Public Administration, University of Southern California, Sacramento, California*

Policy formulation can be discussed and studied as a relatively discrete activity in an essentially stable political context. This essay focuses upon policy making in contrary context, as part of widespread change in an unstable political context. At the root of this distinction is the expectation that change in policy, as elsewhere in human society, is not a smoothly linear process, but is, rather, more frequently discontinuous, characterized by periods of marginal adjustment and elaboration of already established practices and periods of more substantial turmoil and change.

A classical formulation characterizes policy making processes as incremental [1] arguing that choice rarely departs far from previous patterns. A second approach to the study of policy formulation places it in a "cycle" of functional phases. Lasswell [2] was among the first to develop this approach, distinguishing seven phases of decision processes (intelligence, promotion, prescription, invention, application, termination, appraisal). Brewer [3] follows in this tradition, dividing policy processes into six phases (initiation and invention, estimation, selection, implementation, evaluation, and termination). May and Wildavsky [4] distinguish among agenda setting, issue analysis, service delivery systems, implementation, evaluation, and termination. The cycle approach encourages those who use it to view policy processes as repetitive and as ideally characterized by rational choice making. Policy choice can be novel, especially in instances where a particular choice is first encountered, but it is more commonly perceived to be a sequence of successive approximations when the policy cycles approach is adopted.

The normative thrust of much of the contemporary effort to develop public policy academic programs and curricula to be to "rational," much in the vein of the synoptic rationality which Lindblom has critiqued as unreasonable. For example, a typical definition of the field of policy analysis gives as its focus ". . . how to make policy decisions rigorously and analytically on the basis of systematic quantitative evidence" [5] (p. 364). This approach is a close relative to the emphasis upon rational analysis central to traditional public administration [6], despite the strenuous efforts of some advocates of public policy as a discipline to distinguish the two [7].

These approaches to the study of policy formulation presume more stability in the political system than I believe is warranted. Stable-state approaches to the study of policy formation do not provide either adequate understanding of the dynamics of periods of major change in public policy making (e.g., the New Deal) nor appreciation of the constraints that these episodic substantial shifts in public policies place upon subsequent choices and action. This essay seeks to develop an understanding of these major shifts first by analyzing three previous such occurances and then by proposing a theoretical framework in which they may be analyzed.

MAJOR SHIFTS IN POLICIES

Three periods of major shifts in policies are examined in this section: The Progressive Era, the New Deal, and the recent period of aggressive pluralism. The first two periods are well-known, while the last, that which I call aggressive pluralism, encompassing the 1965-1980 period, is less commonly perceived to have been a time of extraordinary change in public policies. Lowi [8] has analyzed this period, arguing that it represents the (flawed) flowering of tendencies toward interest group liberalism that had roots in the New Deal period. His analysis emphasizes the surrender of public authority to organized political demands, legitimized by a political philosophy he characterizes as vulgarized pluralism, defining the ".. public interest as a result of the amalgamation of various claims.." by interest groups (p. 51). As will be elaborated shortly, I believe the distinctive feature of the 1965-80 period was not the response to interest groups by the political system, but rather their *creation*. Hence the label aggressive pluralism: the dominant political philosophy sought to create interest groups where none had existed before, or failing to stimulate the organization of the desired interest groups, to provide for publically supported representation of their presumed interests.

Table 1 compares the three periods on four dimensions: contemporary contextual factors, perceived problems requiring public policy responses, policy and institutional innovations, and dominant theories relevant to policy development. Each of the periods is considered in turn. As the Progressive and New Deal periods are more familiar, they are treated at less length than is aggressive pluralism.

Reformers and Progressives (1880's-1920's) were most notable in the sharp break they represented from previously dominant approaches to policy design. Until this period, "government" had been viewed as a modest administrative apparatus carrying out limited functions needed for the common good (e.g. defense). The concern of policy makers was not with the operation of governmental institutions and service delivery but with the capacity of the political system to resolve

Table 1 Three Periods of Major Shifts in Policies

	Context	Perceived Problem	Policy/ Institutional Innovations	Dominant Theories
Progressive Era (1880's-1920's)	Technological & demographic changes, rapid urbanization, growth of middle class, abuses by robber barons and industry.	Graft, corruption, inadequate services, exploitation of labor	Professionalized public service, strong executive, non-partisan local governments, regulation of work place, products and large firms.	Political theory of a public interest, ideology of non-political government emphasizing service delivery, suspicion of private sector.
New Deal (1932-1945)	Economic crisis.	How to solve economic crisis.	Variety of policies and institutions at national level.	Perception that national government has responsibility to solve economic ills, and to help disadvantaged, but no coherent economic or political theory; often partnerships with private sector.
Aggressive Pluralism (1965-1980)	Uneven economic performance, civil rights and environmental protection movements.	How to help poor, to manage the economy, to protect the environment.	Entitlement programs, policies and programs to manage the economy, regulation to protect environment and of a broad range of activities in society, professionalized legislative bodies at national and state levels, public funding for interest group representation, functionally specific governmental entities.	Keynesian economic theory, moral commitment to fight poverty and discrimination, political theory of extreme interest group liberalism, hyper-suspicion of private sector.

conflict among interests and to achieve the desired balance between ability to pursue national objectives and to sustain sub-national political systems. These were the concerns of the framers of the Constitution and they dominated political discourse until the late 19th century. The greatest legacy of the reformers of the late 19th century and the Progressives of the early 20th century was to shift political discourse, and policy choice, from issues of the design of the political system as a device for governance, to issues of service delivery to citizens. Almost equally important was the initiation of suspicion and hostility between the public and private sectors, a legacy originating in very real excesses of individual entrepreneurs and businesses but which ultimately inhibited collaborative activity by the two sectors. While business continued to influence policy making and its practices sometimes served as models for governmental reorganization, the presumption of opposing public and private interests endured in a distinctive fashion when compared to other industrialized democracies [9].

The obvious institutional artifacts of this period are highly visible and greatly impacted subsequent policy making, but the more powerful influences upon subsequent policy choices are the result of these two changes in values or theories. In the absence of equating the political system with service provision by government and development of a bias toward a sharp distinction between public and private sectors, American public administration would not have developed as it did, for example [6]. Moreover, the Progressives presumed that government should be expansive, solving social ills without limit [10], a bias carried forward through the other two periods analyzed. Among the institutional artifacts of this era, civil service systems, strong executives, non partisan local governments and the city manager form of municipal government have proven the most persistent.

The New Deal's major impact was identification of the national government as the institution with responsibility for solving major economic crises. This is, of course, a substantial impact, but it is easy to overlook that this was viewed by many at that time as a role of last resort, supported because neither state and local governments nor the private sector could perform the function of pulling the nation out of the Depression. There was no dominant economic nor political theory which guided policy making nor sustained a large sphere of policy making for the national government after passage of the immediate economic crisis. The lack of theoretical bases helps explain the wide variety of policy initiatives advanced by the Roosevelt administration, the conflict between the President and the Supreme Court, and the reduction in national policy making that occurred after WWII. It was also in this period that the first explicitly redistributive national policies were developed [11], the second major legacy of the New Deal era. During the New Deal and the mobilization for the war effort public policies entailing collaboration between the public and private sectors were more common than in the preceding or following era [12].

In the 1965-1980 period, another major, discontinuous change in policy making occurred. The policy initiatives made during this period are less commonly analyzed as a sharp departure from previous practices of the magnitude of the New Deal or Progressives. But the changes were dramatic. Total government spending as a percentage of GNP increased from 27.7 percent in 1964 (up only slightly from the mid 1950's e.g., 26.5 percent in 1954) to 34.9 percent in 1975 (to decline to 33.1 percent in 1980). Most of the growth in expenditures occurred in federal domestic programs, which grew from 8.5 percent of GNP in 1964 to 15 percent in 1980, while defense expenditures fell from 10.1 percent to 6.5 percent of GNP in the same period and state and local expenditures from own funds increased modestly (9.1 percent to 10.4 percent, also in the same period).

But more than just a growth in expenditures occurred. The national government issued regulations at a volume several times historical levels [13], induced the creation of a plethora of functionally specific sub-state regional agencies to pursue its policies [14], and mandated new organizational forms, management practices and specific activities upon state and local governments [15, 16]. National policy making grew to include almost every conceivable policy problem and the whole of society became significantly more politicized as interests organized to pursue policy objectives or to protect and nurture new policies and programs upon which they were dependent.

Table 1 provides information concerning the context and perceived problems of the period of aggressive pluralism. But the roots of this transformation of policy making are found only incidentally in these factors. Instead, the mainsprings of this period of change are found in the reinforcing confluence of three streams of theory and in the incentive structures faced by elected officials, especially by national and state officials.

The three bodies of theory all have historical antecedents in our political system, but took new forms and added importance in this period. One such "theory" concerns a moral commitment to fight poverty and discrimination, a commitment of substantial strength in this period, based upon long-standing cultural values evoked by the civil rights movement and the discovery of poverty amidst affluence.

The second body of theory was Keynesian economic theory, first consciously adopted in the Kennedy administration and dominant until 1980. This body of theory provided a rationale for the sort of national economic stimulation efforts that had occurred pragmatically in the New Deal, but it did more than provide justification for specific policies. For example, it provided a non-moral explanation of poverty and a general bias in favor of increased public sector expenditures, even giving legitimacy to deficits. Without this justification in economic theory, the growth in public sector expenditures witnessed in this period would have been impossible, no matter how morally or politically attractive, an example of the reinforcing nature of these theoretical developments. As belief in the efficacy of Keynesian theory wanes, its power is more apparent: policy making becomes erratic and interest groups find it difficult to defend access to public expenditures gained under supportive economic theory [17, 18].

The third body of theory concerns the political system, equating democracy with interest group representation [8]. While the framers of the constitution had assumed that factions were inevitable, the Progressives had believed that a general public interest existed and sought to suppress evidence of special interests. During the New Deal era, interest groups were recognized through various consultative/ decision making structures and efforts were made to "balance" representation among diverse interest groups (e.g., business, labor, government). Under aggressive pluralism, policies and institutions were designed not only to accomodate interest groups but to actively create interests. In the early phase of this period, during the years of the Great Society, national policy sought to organize interests believed underrepresented in the political system (e.g., the Community Action Program). By the term of President Carter, the national government had adopted the posture of providing professional representation for interests (e.g. legal services groups and funded intervenors in regulation-writing processes). Moreover, policy often preceded organized interest in this period: for example, the Welfare Rights Organization followed increases in welfare benefits, and local governments and not-for-profit organizations did not seek public service employment programs, but lobbied for their continuation.

While the three theories just discussed (moral commitment to end disadvantage, Keynesian economic theory, and a political philosophy of aggressive pluralism) stimulated considerations of policy choice, formal policies are the products of individuals and institutions, not theories. The final factor contributing to the rise of aggressive pluralism was the change in the incentive structure experienced by elected officials, particularly legislators. During this period, and encouraged by overt policies intended to "reform" electoral practices, the "individualization" of electoral campaigns occurred. Parties had historically (imperfectly) screened individuals interested in running for elected office, provided resources for campaigns and provided identification to voters. The capacity of parties to perform these functions declined during this period [19]. Incumbents, and those seeking office, had to develop alternative strategies for obtaining the resources needed for campaigns. Increasingly, they found those resources, both in the form of campaign financing, and in linkage to potential voters, through special interest groups. In the 1980 elections for the California Legislature, for example, candidates raised three-quarters of their campaign funds from outside of the district in which they were seeking election and approximately 40 percent from state-level political action committees [20]. Success in campaign financing, and, to a lesser extent, at the polls, requires eliciting the support of interest groups. A strong incentive exists to strengthen existing interest groups, to discover latent interests and to create dependence upon future legislative action.

The existence of this incentive structure is a major cause of the dramatic increase in volume of legislation and regulation. Legislative bodies which are more "professionalized," with full-time legislators and extensive staff support, such as the U.S. Congress or the California Legislature, exhibit these patterns most fully.

For example, the California Legislature passes about six times as much legislation annually as the national average for stage legislatures. As further illustration of this dynamic, an analysis of seven policy arenas where the role of the national government expanded substantially in the 1965-1975 decade found that members of Congress were major actors in expanding each, taking more initiative than the President, interest groups, or the affected bureaucracies [13].

Thus, the legacy of the period of aggressive pluralism is a changed political system, just as occurred also as a consequence of the major changes in policy making which occurred during the Progressive Era or in the New Deal. Indeed, I have argued elsewhere that a "second" political system was created, consisting of the set of vertically linked, function-specific systems established during this period [20].

Yet another major shift in policy processes is now underway, largely as the result of the fiscal constraints experienced by all levels of government in this nation beginning in 1976 [20,21]. The causes and shape of this new era are analyzed shortly. Policy shifts unfolding in Washington, D.C. and in state and local governments nation wide will do much to define the new parameters of "ordinary" public policy making for the next few years.

Attention now turns to development of a theoretical framework for analysis of the sort of major, discontinuous shifts in policy that have just been examined. Examples from the Reagan Presidency will be used to see how fully it meets the test of a substantial shift in the parameters of policy making and to seek understanding of the likely trajectory of this new era of fiscal constraint.

A FRAMEWORK

Major shifts in public policy have occurred three times in this century according to the analysis just completed and another such shift is now underway. One inference suggested by this review is that the pace of change in dominant policy paradigms has quickened: the reformers/Progressives wrought their changes a century and more after adoption of the Constitution, the New Deal followed the peak of the Progressive Era by two decades and aggressive pluralism followed the end of World War II by a similar period of time, but was itself challenged by the arrival of fiscal constraints within a decade and the election of President Reagan within fifteen years.

Are major shifts in policy processes the consequence of rational analysis? Of elite domination? Of interest group pressure? None of these possible explanations seems adequate. Instead, it is more useful to approach policy formation as a process of social construction. As social construction, policy processes share much with all human activity. One of the most important features of social construction processes is that they are based in language and theory.

Ostrom would presumably describe policies as he does organizations, as artifacts "... created by human beings with reference to the use of learning and knowledge to serve human purposes" [22] (309). Just as philosophers of science describe theories as social constructions based in language [23], so too are policies. In both, efforts are made to use language with precision. The theorist seeks precision as an aid to understanding and communication. The policy maker adds the need for action and control of the behaviors of others as specific variants of the general role of language in facilitating understanding and communication.

Just as concepts, words representing first-order abstractions, are the building blocks of theory, bridging empirical phenomena and theory [24], so too are they the building blocks of policy. Policy advocates must develop concepts which capture the objectives they pursue. A good example is found in the advocacy of "community-based" mental health care. Cameron [25] analyzed how this policy approach displaced institution-based care in California, characterizing the process as ideological warfare between two competing theories as to the causes of mental illness and efficacious therapies.

To act, policy makers must rely upon language, concepts and theory. To continue the mental health example, new programs and institutions had to be developed and personnel added to achieve a change to the new policy. This is a word-based process: the words of statutes are followed by those of regulations, of program design, of budget categories and control language, or operations manuals and memoranda. The intent is to achieve some desired policy objective by influencing, directing or controlling the behaviors of individuals, both inside and outside government; the tools are words. Throughout, key concepts are invoked (such as "community-based"), words which perform the same function of bridging theory and empirical phenomena as they do in social inquiry.

This discussion suggests that the language used in policy processes is not incidental or peripheral, but of central importance to those processes. Language shapes and constrains perception, choice and actions. It follows, then, that periods of major change in policy choice are times of change in dominant language, and times of stability occur when a widely shared language dominates the policy process. Of course, the term "language" implies similar stability or turmoil in theories and values, as concepts from which policy is shaped only have meaning in relationship to some theory and attendant values.

To be more specific, stability in policy processes requires a dominant political theory and a dominant economic theory. Moreover, the two must be relatively congruent: It is no accident that nations commonly exhibit more or less freedom of individual choice in both economic and political affairs and rarely constraint in one sphere and freedom in the other. Together, the two bodies of theory suggest problems to which public policy should be directed, delineate the division between public and private sectors, and shape prescriptions for public institutions and policy strategies.

Returning to Table 1, this discussion suggests that the direction of "causality," of policy formulation, is from right to left. The context may be considered empirical phenomena, but the other three columns are unabashedly social constructions. One source of pressure for major shifts in policy processes arises as changes in context stress the policies legitimized by the dominant theories. Alternatively, the dynamics of implementing the policies flowing from dominant theories can lead to stress and pressure for change as they (inevitably) fail to achieve desired results. The Progressives may be considered a response to the first type of stimuli for change, the break-down of aggressive pluralism an example of the second type.

Because the disintegration of aggressive pluralism as a dominant policy paradigm illustrates well the importance of language and theory, and is the cause of our current crisis in public policy, it warrants brief analysis. As was suggested previously, the roots of aggressive pluralism were in three convergent theories and the incentive structures faced by legislators. While dominant, this paradigm encouraged an expansive public sector, the politicization of society along interest lines, and attempts to manage the economy through manipulation of demand and interest rates. Once dominant, this paradigm was very powerful, stimulating a great expansion in the public sector, an explosion in policy initiatives from the national government, and a substantial transformation of the nation's political system, all in a decade and a half.

The reasons for the disintegration of aggressive pluralism are found in both economics and politics, and in both real experience and theories. Economic performance stagnated in the mid 1970's. As an example, real disposable income per worker actually declined. At the same time, the dominant Keynesian economic theory was under growing attack [17]. In the political system, citizens became markedly less trusting of government, less stable in attachments to political party, and reduced their political participation in such elemental activities as voting. Much as there was a crisis of economic theory, so too was there of policy and political theory. Evaluation and policy implementation studies, plus journalistic and legislative analyses, revealed that progress toward achieving policy objectives was very uneven, for example. And citizens felt disenfranchised by the shift toward interest group-based politics.

One result, and index, of the disintegration of the domination of policy processes by aggressive pluralism was the movement to fiscal constraint. Beginning in 1976, all levels of government experienced sharp fiscal constraint, sometimes as the result of citizen voting (California's Proposition 13 and Massachussett's Proposition 2½, for example), and sometimes as the result of policy choices by elected officials responding to the pressure for fiscal constraint. Thirty-eight states adopted one or more of the four contemporary types of fiscal limits or substantially reduced taxes in the 1976-1980 period. Expressed as a percentage of GNP, the following measures of fiscal activity declined after 1976: total state and local expenditure, federal grants-in-aid, state and local expenditures from own funds, and state and local debt issuance [20, 21]. Short of expanding fiscal resources, and with its claims to effective economic policy making and political legitimacy under severe challenge, aggressive pluralism lost capacity to dominate policy formulation in this nation.

In this context, the rejection of President Carter's bid for reelection is not that surprising. Whether Ronald Reagan will succeed in establishing a new dominant policy paradigm is not yet evident. His administration is quite self-consciously pursuing relatively coherent political and economic theories. If conservative, self-reliant politics and supply-side economics can achieve dominance over policy making, a new period of stability in policy formulation will result. If, as now seems more likely, these theories do not achieve dominance, but aggressive pluralism remains discredited (which seems very probable), a period of instability in policy formulation will ensue. Previous experience, and the theoretical argument presented here, suggest that the pressure for closure upon some dominant policy paradigm will be great. Still, a decade or more of instability could occur.

POLICY ANALYSIS AND EVALUATION

The implications of this discussion for policy analysis and evaluation are relatively straight forward. Most importantly, the standards for acceptance of the results of analysis and evaluation, of "truthfulness," are not those of logical positivism but rather those of pragmatism. There is no presumption that the world is knowable nor that any science of analysis and evaluation will reveal immutable truth. Instead, the presumption is that understanding is a social construction, unfolding in the interaction of human discourse and empirical phenomena. We prefer to be accurate in our understanding of the world and effective in the choices and actions we base upon those understandings. But understanding remains always *prognoses*, expectations as to what exists and of the consequences of different choices [26].

From this perspective, the links between any understanding resulting from analysis or evaluation and action are always tenuous. Dominant policy paradigms shape perceptions of what is a policy "problem," of possible causal theories, and of possible responsive policies. Dewey [27] presents a classic statement of this position: ". . . knowledge is a function of association and communication; it depends upon tradition, upon tools and methods socially transmitted, developed and sanctioned. . . man acts from crudely intelligized emotion and from habit rather than from rational consideration. . ." (p. 158). Lindblom and Cohen [28] present a more contemporary argument in a similar vein, arguing that "professional social inquiry" is infrequently directly influential in policy making, becoming used only as it permeates "ordinary" knowledge, theories widely held in society. Schon [29] argues similarly, holding that policy making is shaped by "ideas in good currency," the emergence of which is a complex social process. In a more extreme position, Cochran [30] argues that program evaluation is usually inappropriate, missing the emergent properties of society as new relationships are constructed.

Policy analysis and program evaluation are worthwhile activities. But they most frequently are conducted within the constraints of the then dominant policy paradigm. As a consequence, they relate most directly to the problems and policy choices perceived by that paradigm. If they do not fit the theory and language then dominant, they will languish without impact. However, they may be resurrected and employed as the dominant policy paradigm changes. For example, research on housing vouchers conducted, but largely ignored, by policy makers during the epoch of aggressive pluralism, may now influence policy choices. So too may other previously ignored analyses gain visibility. From this perspective society should increase its options for future choice by self-consciously encouraging analysis and evaluation outside of the dominant paradigm. To do so, is, of course, difficult both politically and linguistically; the dominant policy paradigm is dominant precisely because of its hold on the discourse of policy processes. Here, however a nation as complex, diverse and open as ours has a great advantage over more closed societies. Enough lacunae and networks of interaction escape domination by the dominant paradigm that alternative theories and language for policy choice are developed. So too is a federal political system an advantage; variety in policy choices provides greater opportunities for innovation and learning than does the tendency to uniformity of unitary political systems.

REFERENCES

1. Lindblom, C. E. The Science of 'Muddling Through. *Public Administration Review* 19:2 Spring 1959).
2. Lasswell, H. D. *A Pre-View of Policy Sciences*. Elsevier, New York, 1971.
3. Brewer, G. The Scope of the Policy Sciences. Mimeo course syllabus, New Haven, CT, 1978.
4. May, J. and Wildavsky, A. (eds.). *The Policy Cycle*, Vol. 5 in *Sage Yearbooks in Politics and Public Policy*. Sage Publ., Beverly Hills, 1978.
5. Yates, D. T., Jr., The Mission of Public Policy Programs: A Report on Recent Experience. *Policy Sciences* 8:3 (September, 1977): 363-374.
6. Karl, B. D., Public Administration and American History: A Century of Professionalism. *Public Administration Review* 36:5 (September/October 1976): 489-504.
7. Kirlin, J. J., Toward a Political Perspective on (Inter) Governmental Performance in the 1980's. Boston: Paper presented at the Second Annual Research Conference of the Association for Public Policy Analysis and Management, October 25, 1980.
8. Lowi, T. *The End of Liberalism*, 2nd ed. W. W. Norton and Co., New York, 1979.
9. Shonfield, A. *Modern Capitalism: The Changing Balance of Public and Private Power*. Oxford University Press, London, 1965.
10. Waldo, D. *The Administrative State*. The Ronald Press, New York, 1948.
11. O'Lessker, K. Origins of the Redistributive State. *Wall Street Journal*. December 4, 1981:24.
12. McConnell, G. *Private Power and American Democracy*. Vintage Books, New York, 1966. 225-264.

13. Advisory Commission on Intergovernmental Relations. *In Brief: The Federal System: The Dynamics of Growth*. ACIR, Washington, D.C., 1980.
14. Reid, J. N. et al. *Federal Programs Supporting MultiCounty Sub-state Regional Activities: An Analysis*. Economics, Statistics, and Cooperative Service, U.S. Department of Agriculture, Washington, D.C., May, 1980.
15. Lovell, C. et al. *Federal and State Mandating on Local Government: An Exploration of Issues and Impacts*. Graduate School of Administration, University of California, Riverside, Final Report to the National Science Foundation, Riverside, CA, 1979.
16. Office of Management and Budget. *Managing Federal Assistance in the 1980's*. Office of Management and Budget, Washington, D.C., March, 1980.
17. Bosworth, B. P. Economic Policy. In: Joseph A. Pechman (ed.). *Setting National Priorities: Agenda for the 1980's*. The Brookings Institution, Washington, D.C. 1980. 35-70.
18. Bell, D. and Kristol, I. (eds.). *The Crisis in Economic Theory. The Public Interest*. Special Issue, 1980.
19. Ladd, E. C., Jr. *Where Have All the Voters Gone*? W. W. Norton and Co., New York, 1978.
20. Kirlin, J. J. *The Political Economy of Fiscal Limits*. Lexington Books/D.C. Heath, Lexington, MA, 1982.
21. Shannon, J. The Great Slowdown in State and Local Government Spending in the United States: 1976-1984. Advisory Commission on Intergovernmental Relations, Washington, D.C., June, 1981.
22. Ostrom, V., Artisanship and Artifact. *Public Administration Review* 40: 4 (July/August 1980): 309-316.
23. Bronowski, J. *The Common Sense of Science*. Harvard University Press, Cambridge, MA, 1978.
24. Kaplan, A. *The Conduct of Inquiry*. Chandler/Harper and Row, New York, 1963.
25. Cameron, J. M. Ideology and Policy Termination: Restructuring California's Mental Health System. *Public Policy* 26:4 (Fall 1978): 533-570.
26. Rule, J. *Insight and Social Betterment*. Oxford University Press, New York, 1978.
27. Dewey, J. *The Public and Its Problems*. Swallow, Chicago, 1927.
28. Lindblom, C. E. and Cohen, D. K. *Usable Knowledge: Social Science and Social Problem Solving*. Yale University Press, New Haven, CT, 1979.
29. Schon, D. A. *Beyond the Stable State*. Random House, New York, 1971.
30. Cochran, N. Society as Emergent and More than Rational: An Essay on the Inappropriateness of Program Evaluation. *Policy Sciences* 12:2 (August 1980): 113-130.

3
GAO and Evaluation: A Perspective from Elmer Staats

Patrick J. Conklin / *Federal Executive Institute, Charlottesville, Virginia*

Elmer Staats* / *Former Comptroller General of the United States, Washington, D.C.*

INTRODUCTION

As Comptroller General of the U.S. General Accounting Office, Elmer Staats initiated many far reaching institutional changes in that organization which strengthened program evaluation in the legislative branch of government. This interview by Patrick J. Conklin with Elmer Staats reviews his 15 year term of office. Particular emphasis is placed on the perspectives, events, strategies, tactics, and milestones which highlighted his brilliant record in the area of program evaluation.

Conklin:

Elmer, in your opinion, what were the milestones in the development of GAO's concern with "evaluation" during your 15 years of leadership of the GAO?

Staats:

Well, I think to begin with we need to go back and look at the history of the Budget and Accounting Act of 1921. Though GAO was concerned primarily with a very narrow concept of fiscal audit or voucher audit during its early years (that is, up through circa 1950), the framers of the statute—Woodrow Wilson among them—had in mind that GAO should be concerned with more than fiscal affairs.

**Present affiliation*: President, Harry S. Truman Scholarship Foundation; corporate director; consultant, Washington, D.C.

Even though they used the term "accounting" in the title of the GAO, the essence of the legislative debate which took place was that the GAO should be concerned rather with "acountability." It's pretty clear that accounting meant to them more than its narrow sense. They were talking about the GAO as being responsible for advising Congress on whether the intent of the statute was carried out and what the agencies were doing to implement public policy.

Now with respect to "milestones," one would be my own background. When I became Comptroller General, coming from the Bureau of the Budget, my interest was in performance or "program" as much as with the budget process. I remember asking President Johnson when I was appointed what he considered the responsibility of the Comptroller to be. He reflected a minute and said it was my job to tell both of us–the President and the Congress–whether the law was being carried out as intended. In simple terms that is a pretty good definition and that stuck with me.

In 1967-68, roughly two years after I took office, one of the issues that emerged in the Congress was the so-called anti-poverty program–Office of Economic Opportunity and all of the wide range of related programs. In 1967, a partisan question came up in the House in connection with the extension of the statute. The resulting House version contained some amendments with which the Senate disagreed. The compromise in the conference committee was that they would let the bill go forward and be extended pretty much in its original form, but with the proviso that the GAO would undertake an analysis for the Congress of the effectiveness of all the OEO programs. This was to be done within an 18-month time frame. That caused a mild crisis within the GAO because there was a good deal of concern whether the GAO could do that. These were mostly social programs, "soft programs," and there was a question on how we could assess their effectiveness. But we rolled up our sleeves and laid out a work plan; we brought in some consultants; we did a little bit by contract; and the net result was that we did produce an evaluation of these programs and we did it on schedule. What this did in the sense of being a "milestone" was to demonstrate two things: One was that the Congress was interested in this sort of thing, and two, that it could be done.

I wouldn't contend that it was a perfect job because in many cases we just didn't have the data on which to evaluate these programs. There was nothing in the records so a lot of it has to be quasi-subjective. We had to be able to get at it through interviews, observations, and applying new tests on individuals such as Head Start children.

A third milestone would be the Legislative Reorganization Act of 1970. The Legislative Reorganization Act grew out of hearings which had been under way in the Congress long before I had been appointed Comptroller General. The idea was to look at what could and should be done to strengthen the capabilities of Congress. GAO was involved in the deliberations that led to that statute. One of the things that we emphasized was the need to make the GAO charter more explicit. The language of the act provided that GAO would make studies of costs and benefits of the programs either on our own initiative or upon request from committees of the Congress. That was a major milestone. I would be the last to say that this more explicit expression as to what Congress wanted GAO to do was understood by all 535 members, but the key committees, i.e., the Government Operations Committee and the Rules Committee in the House, understood the general thrust, at least.

The fourth milestone would be the Congressional Budget and Impoundment Act of 1974. By this time there was an increasing number of requests from committees of Congress for the program evaluation type of review, and some people on the Hill, particularly staffers, got almost overzealous. They wanted to write into statute that we would have to create an Office of Program Evaluation within the GAO. I argued that that would be wrong on two grounds: I felt that, since I was responsible, I should have freedom to organize internally; more importantly, I felt that *all* of our work would have program evaluation content to it and that to try to separate it out would be a mistake. The Hill went along with that but they did write an even stronger charter in Title Seven of the Congressional Budget Act; this spoke for the first time, not in terms of cost and effectiveness, but of "program evaluation." They went a step further and said that GAO should advise and assist the committees of Congress and *the agencies* in developing ways and means to evaluate program effectiveness, in other words, help set forth the methodology. That clearly gave the GAO the lead role as far as the government was concerned in the field of program evaluation.

Subsequently, (about 1978) we decided in GAO that we should bring together within the GAO a focal point for program evaluation, which could do several things. It could do experimental work, break new ground in areas which posed particularly difficult evaluation problems, especially social programs. The new unit could provide technical assistance with respect to methodology to other divisions of the GAO in any area–energy, health, education, weapons systems, or whatever. We wanted to assemble people who had expertise in things like statistical sampling, questionnaire design, interview techniques, system analysis, the whole range of skills needed in developing information, analyzing it, and presenting it. So we set up an Institute for Program Evaluation, creation of which I consider a fifth milestone.

I might mention just a bit more about the background leading up to this. After we had been involved in program evaluation for quite some time, we decided to set up a peer review panel to look at the product. We asked each of the divisions to pick out, over recent years, three of the most difficult evaluations they had to make. Not the best, not the worst, but the three most difficult. Then we assembled a group from the outside, made up of people who had experience both in academic life and in organizations like RAND, the Urban Institute and others, and had each read three of these reports from the standpoint of what we had done right and what we had done wrong. After they had written up their comments, we brought the group together for a full day, with each of our division directors present, to go over what was right and what was wrong and what could be improved. The Institute's creation emerged, in part, from that kind of a peer review activity.

We also tried to improve the presentation of our reports to make clear what our methodology was—what we had been able to do, and what we had not. We were always under time constraints. Unlike an academic exercise, or a Brookings or an American Enterprise Institute study, we had always to keep in mind that our product was wasted unless it was in the hands of the Congress when they could use it. So we had to "trade off" completeness or thoroughness for timeliness without sacrificing accuracy. There are time-saving short cuts—reducing the size of the sample and things of that type—which do not compromise the findings. This turned out to be a most useful exercise for us.

Conklin:

I'd like to follow up just a bit on that revision of the charter in the Legislative Reorganization Act and the Congressional Budget Reform Act. Where did those ideas get started? What were you thinking about? Who were some of the people involved on the Hill? What were they thinking about? This did represent significant change and development, and I know that the source of ideas tends to get lost very often.

Staats:

It is pretty hard to put your finger on all the key individuals. You recall there was a major growth in the social programs in the '60's. There was a more or less general concern in the Congress, that when the government expanded as rapidly as it did, we might not be getting our money's worth. Were we moving too fast; did we have our priorities right; were the programs being poorly implemented because of their newness or because of the lack of experienced personnel? I think all of these were matters of concern in the Congress and you recall, also, that during that same period there was a lot of interest in the Executive Branch as well in program planning and budgeting systems, and later on in zero-based budgeting and management by objectives.

It is pretty hard to identify specific individuals, but certainly Dick Bolling and Senator Proxmire would have to be on that list, and Congressman, now Governor, Quie, but there were a number of others. It would be hard to give credit to any one individual or even two or three individuals for this development. But within the GAO we wanted to push Congress in this direction, because we felt that that was where the real pay off—and the real need—was.

Another thing you have to keep in mind in this setting is that there had been, beginning in 1950 with the Budgeting and Accounting Procedures Act, an effort to press devolution of the work of GAO into the agencies, especially internal audit. PPBS had as one of its objectives to strengthen program evaluation staffs within the agencies. One of my convictions was that the GAO could never begin to do the whole job and it shouldn't even try. The real progress to be made, I thought, was to strengthen those capabilities in the agencies, with GAO giving oversight, technical assistance, and more or less taking the lead in setting the example of what you can do. When I left the GAO in March of 1981, program evaluation represented roughly 50% of the GAO's work. If you add to that "management effectiveness/performance," then you have something like 90% of GAO's work covering economy, efficiency, and effectiveness. The remaining 10% was in the fiscal area: accounting procedures, auditing procedures, and so forth. The reason that figure is so small is that fiscal audit had been successfully handed off to the agencies (which was clearly the intent of the 1950 legislation).

In the beginning, we had to feel our way in program evaluation by trial and error. And a lot of what we learned was strictly demonstration. A group could say "Here's another GAO report" and they could borrow ideas from it and learn from each other. A lot of what is involved in program evaluation isn't found in textbooks. You find it in experience. Today the GAO is in a position where, because of the diversified backgrounds of its staff, it is able to do more than maybe even we anticipated.

Conklin:

It seems that there is a continuing and legitimate interest in clarifying the roles to be performed by those doing what might be called "internal evaluation" and the roles to be performed by those doing "external evaluation." Could you talk a bit more about some of the kinds of conflicts or misunderstandings you have found that can develop between, say, the central agencies such as GAO and the department or agency taking a look at itself?

Staats:

Well, I guess it's almost a truism that agencies do not appreciate people coming into their organizations uninvited. The natural inclination for a person who has been running a program for 10 years, 15 years, sometimes is "How can these folks from the GAO come over here in a couple of weeks or months and tell me how to do it?" Secondly, if they don't really accept you, there are lots of ways that they can make your job more difficult, such as, for example, holding back on information or making it difficult if you need to interview people. And other kinds of delays can take place. There are lots of ways in which they can show their mistrust or lack of confidence. The agencies don't like to have their problems aired and they often say, "We don't think it's a problem."

Many times, however, they themselves recognize the problems. What we did in many cases, was to take an issue that was already there, that the agencies were already aware of, but one where we could come up with some new focus which had not been considered. Sometimes we would simply take an issue that had been lying around undecided. We developed our data, did our analysis, and came up with our recommendations. The draft report then would go through a review process in the agency, and somebody would say that this is an issue that we had better make a decision on.

Now that isn't to say that GAO and the agencies always agreed, because they didn't. You wouldn't expect them to. The main test here is whether or not the report generated a useful dialogue airing both views.

Conklin:

Can you tell us more about the results of GAO's evaluation efforts?

Staats:

If you look at the annual reports of the GAO you'll see changes that were brought about as a result of GAO recommendations. I think that's the ultimate test. Dollar savings (quantifiable savings that you could measure or audit) coming from GAO reports added up to $20 billion dollars over the past 15 years. Interestingly enough, almost three-fourths of that came in the last 5 years when we began to stress more economy and efficiency type audits, as opposed to fiscal reviews, and started getting into review of "programs."

Eighty percent of those savings were put into effect by the agencies administratively, many times before the reports ever were made public.

Conklin:

Do you encounter resistance to your findings in agencies you evaluate?

Staats:

Yes, a skeptic could say, "There isn't a single generalization you can make about agencies' responses to GAO work." But the main thing again, ultimately, is whether or not the work the GAO does is accurate, is complete, and is objective.

We keep saying credibility is the most important asset that GAO has. Credibility is made up of those things *plus* professional competence. You've got to have people who are regarded as able to make complex analyses. A good operator is not necessarily a good analyst. Fundamentally GAO conducts audits of agency performance. That turns out to be an audit of the competence and the managerial capability, the dedication and the effort to find solutions to problems within agencies.

We became accustomed to certain responses, "Well, we think you've got a point, but we don't agree with your solution;" "We'll set up a committee;" "We'll set up a task force;" "We'll get a contractor to come in;" "We won't buy what you have to sell right now, but we are willing to take a look." You never know whether these are simply to postpone the issue or whether they reflect a serious intent to do something about it. So we say, "OK, we'll put a tickler-file on it; we'll follow it," and within a reasonable time we went back in and took a look and have a second shot at it.

This dialogue that we're talking about between the GAO and the agencies can be kept on an objective level, which is in itself very useful. Many times the GAO's contribution came as a result of discussions that took place as the review took place in the agencies, out in the field, or at the bureau level or even lower. Then when the agency felt that they had a problem which they could do something about, they would go ahead and do it. The GAO's openness with the agency—not only in those exchanges that took place in writing but in letting them take a look at the draft report—helps to build the bridge of confidence, and that can be very constructive.

Conklin:

Let me broaden the scope of this issue of dialogue just a little. You've been on each side of that line between Executive branch and Legislative branch. Let me ask, in your experience, what are some of the real challenges, the real problems in the difference between the way that the legislative side and the executive side of our government look at our world. I think you get into things like the role of interest groups; the sensitivities to what's going on "out there;" the difficulty of the legislative process, at times, in being "precise" in the way the Executive branch administrators may wish the legislators had been "precise." What are some of your thoughts on that issue?

Staats:

Well, of course, I worked in the Executive Office of the President for 26 years in several different administrations before I went to the GAO. But the common denominator of all those different Presidents was that they were anxious to accomplish their objectives by getting Congress to accept their proposals. You go through an elaborate process of developing a legislative program, for example, and in that process you look for a *range* of options; a *range* of ideas. What it comes down to is that when the President puts his name on the message, or he approves the draft bill going forward to Congress, he is trying to sell that particular approach. He knows he may have to compromise somewhere along the line, but he's not about to lay out the pros and cons of all the options he considered. He won't do it that way. He's trying to get a presidential program established. That's the essence of presidential leadership.

But the Congressmen say, "What are the other options?" They are looking for the pros and cons. The member of Congress knows he's not likely to get that information from the agencies unless it's done surreptitiously or he happens to know somebody and takes him to lunch. But such information won't be the "official" position. The official position comes from the White House, and the Office of Management and Budget generally prepares it. The legislative clearance process is in the OMB. When OMB says this program is in accord with the program of the President, this carries a lot of weight on the Hill, particularly when the President's party is in power in Congress. The point I'm making is how do you give Congress the capability to analyze the range of options.

Now, to be sure, as I've already mentioned, some of the committees have very close ties to the agencies that carry out programs for that particular committee. Agriculture would be a very good example. Those agencies aren't always that happy if the President's program is different from what the committee's leanings are, because that puts them in a difficult relationship. They somehow have to carry the President's message, but may convey that they don't have their heart in it. What the GAO can do (and I think you have to mention here also the Congressional Research Service and the Congressional Budget Office) is provide the kind of analytical material needed so that committees can feel more confident that they have information that comes from a source other than the advocate of the presidential program. That's the main point I would make in response to your question.

The GAO is particularly important because it has the largest staff, and has the outreach into the agencies and across the country, and on specific problems can be especially helpful. When you come to things like projecting the impact of different levels of budget on the economy, and of changes in the economy on the budget, I think the Congressional Budget Office is particularly good.

Likewise, the Congressional Research Service has a lot of capability in digging up background information, doing pros and cons analyses on different statutes, i.e., the type of thing which can be done from readily available sources without going back and having to dig out raw data.

We saw in the 1960's and the early '70's rapid expansion in Congressional support. The GAO has grown, CBO was set up in 1974 with the Congressional Budget Act, and the Congressional Research Service was established, really, in 1970 with the Legislation Reorganization Act which converted it from the Legislative Reference Service of the Library of Congress. Now we have the newer Office of Technology Assessment, which functions pretty much like a Joint Committee of the Congress, but it still represents another effort on the part of the Congress to increase its capability. Perhaps even more important has been the growth in the size of the committee staffs, especially since the Legislative Reorganization Act of 1970.

You'll always have something ranging from conversation or dialogue to confrontation between the executive and legislative. One of the things we speculated on was: suppose the Congress and the President were of the same political party, would that mean Congress would turn to the GAO less often? Would Congress be more likely to turn to the agencies? In the event, that did not happen.

I think there is something here more fundamental than the question of the political control of the executive and the political control of the Congress. You've got the issue of the prerogative, as it were, of the Congress to make the final decisions on these programs. I think that's where the interplay takes place. And the GAO has to recognize the realities of that.

Another thing that ought to be mentioned here is that sometimes the committee staffs are not happy with the product that comes out of their own support agency because they may have their own ideas of what they would like to see done. If they happen to agree with the GAO, particularly if the GAO does something at their request, that's one situation. But if GAO studies something on its own initiative, it may pick issues which may create some friction and unhappiness, because they interfere with the predilections and objectives which the staff of the committees have tried to promote within the committee.

Conklin:

I'm sure that fine line that I referred to has sometimes felt like a tightrope. Let me turn to an area in which I know you have long had an interest: The American federal system and the conduct of intergovernmental relations in this country. What are some of the special features and challenges of "evaluation activity" in the intergovernmental arena from your perspective?

Staats:

Let me preface this by saying that one of the phenomena that I don't think we have identified well is the extent to which the federal government, in particular, farms out its programs and objectives to third parties. State and local governments certainly represent one part of that. But you also have international organizations, you have contractors, and you have a number of nonprofit organizations that receive federal money or are chartered to carry out federal programs or objectives. We tried to identify this in a series of lectures prepared in the GAO and published, one in 1971 in connection with the 50th anniversary of GAO, and another in about 1974. (As near as I can tell, that was the first effort to really try to identify quantitatively the extent to which this had taken place.)

Now why were we interested in this? Anybody who receives federal money to some degree has to be accountable. If they're charged with carrying out a federal function, they have to be accountable. How do you hold them accountable if they don't have any organic relationship to the government agency that's involved? That's the issue: How do you audit the World Bank, or the United Nations Food and Agriculture Organization? These are tough issues and there's no good solution, except, perhaps, to try to work with these bodies to be sure they have the kind of information flow which they need for a management information system and to insure that they have good program evaluation staffs, budget staffs, and management analysis capability. You try to help them insure that top management is really on top of the job.

Let me give you an example: In 1967, as I recall, a subcommittee of the House Foreign Affairs Committee took a trip to South America. They were looking at the grants made by the Inter-American Development Bank, among other things. And they were very unhappy when they came back. The projects involved dealt with housing, health, and various other programs sponsored by the IADB. So the chairman proposed an amendment saying that these programs should be audited by the GAO in the same way it audits any agency of the Federal government. That of course stirred a lot of concern in the Inter-American Bank.

I said, "Look, what you are proposing is not practical. This is an international body and if the United States is going to declare unilaterally that it's going to audit these programs, every other country can do the same thing. You have got to find some way to hold the Bank itself responsible for auditing these programs."

So the compromise was that the GAO would set the standards for audit by the Inter-American Bank, and then would work with the Bank to help set up an auditing capability–which they did not then have. Congress further asked us to report to them as to whether we thought the product coming out of that audit was adequate to be sure the Bank was on top of their programs.

Now that was a starter, and from there through changes in the law, the GAO now has similar oversight responsibility for all the international banking institutions. In addition, we went in and did test studies in several of the specialized agencies in the U.N.: The World Health Organization, the FAO, UNICEF, and so on. Some of those bodies were very unhappy with our published reports: "Here's the United States coming in and auditing our organizations."

What we really were after, and what I sense is still very much needed, is to get the United Nations to set up an Auditor General for all the UN agencies. We finally got the State Department to tentatively support that position last year, but, it's still an open issue. The point I'm trying to make here is that you cannot audit or evaluate the third party programs, even though they are spending U.S. money, in the same way the GAO can audit or evaluate a direct line operation of the United States government.

The same thing is true with respect to state and local government. We ran into a situation soon after I became Comptroller General, where some of the states were appealing to the Congress saying that *they* should have the responsibility to audit federally-assisted programs. They didn't like the fact that so many federal agencies had been auditing their programs and, besides, they said, ours was supposed to be a "federal" system. They advocated legislation that provided that, if the GAO certified the adequacy of internal audit in state X, then we, the federal government, would delegate to that state the sole responsibility to audit all its federal assistance programs.

I opposed that legislation. I said that the question of capability in some cases is a very subjective one; and, besides, one auditor may do a very good job but he may be replaced by somebody else who won't do a good job. What would be the practicality of going in and, in effect, decertifying a state after they had had that certification for a long time?

The committee agreed with me on this and I said that I would be glad to commit GAO to work with the state and local governments to try to establish standards for audit and to try to simplify the whole system. In 1972, we issued what we called a "yellow booklet" or a "golden booklet," on auditing standards for public programs. This was a product of four years of work with state and local government organizations and with the American Institute of Certified Public Accountants. (You know they do a lot of auditing for the state and local government.) It was in a sense a cooperative venture to see if we could develop some common standard which we could all accept, in principle at least. We wound up with four different aspects of accountability which they all agreed upon: one was the financial audit, a second was the compliance audit (which had to do with equal opportunity, for example, or safety and health and other standards which are imposed by regulation), a third was what we called the economy and efficiency audit (where the objective is primarily to save money and save personnel, and do the job cheaper), and the fourth was what we called program evaluation (or a program effectiveness or results audit).

The American Institute of CPA's took this standard and put it out in roughly the same form, so their membership would have before them the same set of standards and objectives. I don't know how many copies of that booklet have been distributed–well over 100,000 certainly–and it has been translated into seven different languages. It has widespread acceptability.

I think that what I'm really trying to say is that, when you are dealing with entities that are performing federal functions but are not part of the federal government directly, then you have an added dimension of accountability–more difficult, but nevertheless, just as important.

Revenue sharing was another case in point, but it was even more difficult because the money flowed into the system just like any other source of revenue. The question was "How are you going to sort that out? How can you locate and determine whether that money was well used or not?" I had some real concerns about that. I indicated before the House Ways and Means Committee that I saw appearing some seeds of federal control which would be far worse than the system we had then. Once that money flowed in there, I didn't think there was any way that Congress was just going to lay back and say, "We're not interested in how it is spent." Unfortunately, I turned out to be right, because now you have requirements such as Davis-Bacon and Equal Opportunity which apply to all these programs for police departments and everything else, unless they segregate this money. And if they segregate it, you are back to a categorical grant again.

I have some real worries about revenue sharing, but I think the hope here is that over time—and this isn't solely the province of the GAO—we can develop more capability in state and local government to develop an accountability system and get the kind of people you need to operate it.

Conklin:

Following up on this notion of revenue sharing, what are your hopes and fears, if I could put it that way, with respect to the move towards the bloc grants in the Reagan administration?

Staats:

We were always a strong advocate of the need to bring together into blocs, if you want to call them blocs, some of the categorical grants. We had too many separate grants dealing with the same or related objectives.

The trouble people get into, as I see it, when we talk about bloc grants, is that you have to define what you mean, what kind of a "bloc," and what you put into these blocs.

In principle I think it's a very important objective, but when you come down to the question of what combination of programs you put into a bloc, you pretty much have to deal with it case by case. In effect, what you do is to develop a new and broader "categorical." I think in some ways we would make more progress if we would just call them broader categorical grants. It would help focus attention on the fact that there isn't just one big pool of money out there. What you are trying to do is group common programs into a larger category of grants.

We felt "blocing" would help on auditing; we thought it would cut down on administrative costs; we thought it would solve a lot of problems grant recipients have with the state in getting money when they need it. Another flaw of the categorical approach is that money is often available for one piece of a program but not for the rest of it. We had regulations that were inconsistent with each other just because they came from different agencies or even different parts of an agency. The time for bloc grants is overdue, and I think the experience we've had with the broader categories which have been already put in place would probably demonstrate this.

How far should we go?

Again, I think the only thing to do is to go through the political process and make the best effort you can to make sense out of it. Coupled with this problem, obviously, is that you have strong supporters for particular programs, and you feel that if you have to merge with another program then you're going to lose authority and autonomy which you think would be associated with your particular program.

Conklin:

I'd like to follow through on that line. In your view, interest groups are here, and here to stay. On the whole, do you see them as "problems" or "contaminants" in the system, or as "aids" or "purifiers" or "helpers" in the system, or a little of each?

Staats:

I think some of each. There's no doubt that the interest groups supply lot of information to the Congress and to the executive agencies. It's biased, it's programmatic, it's probably motivated somewhat selfishly. If you are aware of that, however, the information can be very useful. I guess the question is whether or not we have an adequate system for sorting all of this out.

For example, Mr. Stockman in his interview with Mr. Greider in the *Atlantic Monthly* had a lot to say about the various associations and interest groups which are represented here in Washington. There *is* a danger here—I would agree with him that, unless you've got enough discipline in the agencies and in the Congress (and *particularly* in the Congress), it may not be possible to balance these out and not simply react to pressures which come through these organized interest groups. Policymakers have got to be able to look beyond those groups.

These Washington lobbyists are paid, and they feel that their job depends on getting something through the Executive and Legislative branches. That's the test that they apply, and whether or not they are really reflecting the view of their membership or reflecting the constituency of the member of Congress, is a good question. I think the concerns which I have heard a great deal of and which I tend to share, is that Congress may be organized in a way which really does open it up to undue pressure from these groups.

Congress is not the same relatively unified organization that it was in the '30's and the '40's and the '50's. Why this came about is anybody's guess. I suppose that Vietnam undoubtedly had a part to play in it. The attempt to democratize the Congress and give the leadership less authority and responsibility; the growth of the staff of the committees which was always vulnerable to these kinds of groups—all of these played a part.

The real concern that I have, however, is whether or not we've got the discipline and the capability to sort those things out. You can't just say that all these pressures will equalize themselves. That doesn't happen, because there are unequals here.

You will always have the concern about a new weapon system, for example, as to whether it was something which got generated out of the Pentagon or the Joint Chiefs, and whether it meets a real need based on military mission, or was generated because it represented a great block of contracts or employment in States X, Y, or Z. That's the kind of concern that I have.

Conklin:

As just an added thought, what about our friends and colleagues of the fourth estate—what about the role of the press?

Staats:

Very few of them are really interested in the kind of evaluation that we are talking about. There are expectations, to be sure, but the fourth estate is highly competitive and the tendency in the governmental area is to give the leg up to the investigative reporter. That's a good way for someone to get his byline on the front page. You are more likely to do that by finding something that's gone wrong, someone at fault, or by finding fraud, waste, or abuse, than by publicizing someone who has done an exceptionally fine job carrying out programs and rendering a public service. I wish sometimes that we could get all these people to write up stories about the great successes. There *are* tremendous successes. There are also tremendous failures, but why write up just one side of the ledger? That's a disappointing thing, but by and large they are going to write things that will sell newspapers.

Conklin:

Another general kind of question, Elmer, that I'd like to ask is, "Who guards the guardians?" What did you do within GAO in terms of self-evaluation and internal evaluation?

Staats:

Well, I've already referred to the peer review panel that was established. That was one thing we did. We also had outside consultants on many of our problems. We used them on almost all of the major issues we got into. It was our *modus operandi,* in more recent years to get people to come in, either on a paid or an unpaid basis, and look at our methodology: how we were going about things, what the issues were, who the people were that we ought to be talking to, and so on. I think that's invaluable.

Take the questions, for example, of evaluating controls on proliferation of nuclear weapons, and of assigning additional particular responsibilities to GAO by statute. We brought together outstanding people from all over the country for a half of a day, or a day, to debate issues among themselves. The fallout for the GAO was most useful. We were able to pick up a lot of useful material. On one project, for example, we had the advice of two Nobel Prize winners, some of the top people of the country. We repeated that approach on many other issues.

Another thing we did was to create what we call an internal review staff. We didn't call it internal audit; we wanted it to be broader than what was then considered an audit. They had complete freedom and reported to me and to the Deputy Comptroller General. Those reports were not secret but we did not circulate them. Anybody who wanted to see them could come in the office and read them. But we didn't want the staff to be in any sense intimidated by the fact that the information might be out in the newspapers, particularly if the staff was criticizing the auditor of the government itself.

More important, however, is the fact that the GAO is held accountable by virtue of testifying before all the committees of Congress. Its product is out there in the public eye. The testimony load has increased dramatically over the years. When I went to GAO it was very rare that GAO was asked to testify. In 1979 we testified 230 times before the Congress. I was told it ran at least that much in 1981. This, I think, reflects GAO's accountability.

There is also the annual appropriation review. Although this has a lot of defects in it, in the sense of holding GAO to account, it does represent an opportunity for Congress to take a look at GAO. The testimony on the GAO budget is voluminous. Unfortunately, you are often dealing with a mind-set which is more interested in "Did your travel go up?", i.e., the nuts and bolts of the budget. In the end, however, the testimony before an appropriations committee represents an important test of whether GAO is performing as it should.

Finally, there is a responsibility in the Governmental Affairs Committee in the Senate and the Government Operations Committee in the House to oversee the GAO. (They have the same responsibility for the OMB as well.) But if there is a weakness, it is the fact that those two committees tend to perform their function only as it relates to oversight over the executive. They tend to call the GAO in if they are looking at GSA, or at defense contracts, or whatever. What I had hoped to accomplish–and this is one of the things that I did not succeed in–was to use the Annual Report of the GAO in somewhat the same way it is used in the parliamentary system, to give an overview of what GAO is doing. I made this proposal many times, both to the House and to the Senate, and the response generally was, "Well, we think we know how you're doing and we don't really think we need that kind of report."

To me, it isn't the question of whether they *need* it or not, it is a question of whether or not the dialogue which would take place would result in a better understanding of what GAO was trying to do. Maybe they could give GAO some help here and there.

The Congress as a whole was very supportive in terms of GAO's charter. I have already mentioned the growth in GAO's charter. When I went to GAO there were a number of areas which were outside of GAO's jurisdiction. We had never audited the FBI, the IRS claimed that they were not legally under the GAO, the international bodies I've already mentioned were not under GAO's surveillance at all, the banking agencies were clearly not under GAO's jurisdiction. We had a terrible time with the Federal Reserve Board on our audit authority for the banking agencies. Finally the Congress said, "Well, GAO you make an audit at our request; make a review of the issues." They liked the result. It was more difficult after that for Arthur Burns and some others to say "GAO has no competence," "they can't add anything," "we're independent of GAO," "we report to the Congress just like GAO." All these things had been said, and they stimulated all the federal reserve banks to be against GAO review. In the final analysis, Congress gave us the jurisdiction we were looking for. By the time I left, there were no areas where GAO did not have some jurisdiction. I think that says something for the interest of the Congress in improved oversight.

Conklin:

Let me ask a question that gets to the issue of the profession of public administration. As a past president of the American Society for Public Administration, how well do you think public administration generally has dealt with this whole issue of program evaluation/evaluation management?

Staats:

Well, I'm not sure what grade I would give the public administration community. I don't think they have done as well as some of the other disciplines. I think that the business schools, by and large, in their work in systems analysis and in the economics' programs, have developed more of the methodology than has come out of our school of Public Affairs and Public Administration. Even psychology and other behavioral sciences would probably rank ahead. Certainly the public health field would be ahead.

I would like to see more done in the schools of public affairs/public administration. It probably means they're going to have to have more emphasis upon the *tools* that you use: systems analyses, statistics, computer expertise. These are the tools with which you are able to get hold of data, analyze it, and present it. I don't think that it takes anything away from public administration; I think it adds to it.

As you know, I tried to recruit from all these professional schools. GAO today has disciplines in a whole range of subjects: engineering, public health, systems analysis, mathematics, and so on. We have roughly 40% of our staff now, whose basic academic training is in fields other than accounting, and, in addition, many of the accountants have taken additional training and have learned to be very good analysts.

I would like to see more of this in all of the other professional schools. What happens so many times is that you get people brought in from these other disciplines who don't have a good background in government. They don't know about the structure and the operation of government. We talked about intergovernmental relations. Very often people outside of public administration have very little understanding of what the problems are in operating in the intergovernmental system. If you could get more of that in the other schools and could get more quantification and techniques and disciplines in public administration, I think it would be good.

Conklin:

I think many of us have felt that public administration looked upon the evaluation activity as a specialized sub-function and sort of missed, perhaps, the larger point that all managers really have to be program evaluators, all staff people have to be program evaluators. It is part and parcel of their business.

Staats:

I've made speeches and said many times that program evaluation is just as much a responsibility of management as any other aspect of the job. The manager may say that this is for somebody else to do, but that isn't so. He's hired to have that kind of capability somewhere in his organization. Even so, I think we have made progress. I would also like to say here that we ought to be thinking about how you can bring business and public management more closely together. I think the developments in this respect at the Kennedy School at Harvard, at Cornell, MIT, Stanford, UCLA, and so on, are all hopeful. That doesn't mean to say that in all cases you have to redesignate the schools. It't more a matter of working out a common program.

Conklin:

As a final question, Elmer, in the broadest terms that you care to use, what does the evaluation future look like from your perspective, based on your experience in government?

Staats:

I think that whether people want to call it that or not, it's going to have to be increasingly important. The increased focus on the budget is certainly going to have some impact. I just hope that in cutting back the budget we don't cut down the capability of agencies to do more of this sort of thing. It's one way that you can make a better assessment of the priorities, and use a scalpel to cut instead of a meat axe. Whether other people want to recognize it in any formal way or not, I think evaluation has to be part of the process of budgeting, of program formulation, and of handling the legislative agenda. What has to be done, though, is to get better information. We sometimes don't build into programs the data base that we need. Sometimes it isn't at all clear from the legislation what the Congress has in mind. There's a lot of improvement to be made in better definition of legislative objectives, and even setting out milestones, if not in the legislation then in the legislative committee reports. There could be more in the committee reports on setting out the feedback which the legislature wants to get on identified issues. Committees increasingly do that in their requests to GAO, but they could also do that for the agencies. The mistrust of the agencies' evaluation, which I mentioned, will always be there. But I think to some degree it could be overcome if the Congress would say when we renew the legislation, we would like to have, from Agency X, its experience and the pros and cons of doing it this way or that way.

I've given up pretty much on the idea of the so-called "sunset" legislation. I had great hopes at one time that we could come to some agreement on that. I may be wrong, but I don't really see a great likelihood now that we will get anything as formal as people hoped for in the original sunset legislation proposals. If that had gone through, we perhaps would have been in somewhat better shape to say that we're looking systematically at these programs. But again it's no magic formula because you can review a program and you can either do a good job or not do a good job. Going through the process doesn't necessarily guarantee that a serious effort was made to critically and objectively evaluate that program. Even so, I think evaluation is here to stay.

Conklin:

Thank you, Elmer.

4
The Congress and Evaluation

Harry S. Havens / *United States General Accounting Office, Washington, D.C.*

INTRODUCTION

Congress is a collegial, deliberative, decisionmaking body. Evaluation is a function, one of whose principal values lies in its use as an aid to the decisionmaking process. If one accepts both of these statements, it is difficult to escape the notion that Congress ought to be a major user of evaluation. Yet the scholarly literature on the Congress is dominated by carefully documented studies, the conclusions of which all seem to demonstrate that congressmen's votes are determined by factors unrelated to rigorous analysis of costs, benefits or effectiveness.

One school of thought holds that voting behavior is dominated by the ambitions of the incumbent. Legislators vote in line with the interests of the constituency they hope to retain or are seeking to capture [1]. Another theory is that members make their decisions by comparing the policy content of an issue to a set of predetermined policy positions. These policy positions, it is argued, are quite stable over time. As a result, Congress changes policy by changing members, not by members changing their minds [2].

How can it be that a decisionmaking body can ignore what is arguably, at least, a highly potent tool of the decision process? This, too, has been examined on several occasions. One view is that legislators, who represent and are concerned about individual constituencies, simply have little interest in the societal costs and benefits which tend to be the focus of what is often considered to be the mainstream work of program evaluation and policy analysis. Haveman, for example, asserts that "Policy analysis answers questions that legislative policymakers are not interested in either asking or having asked" [3]. Another view is that members do not gather much of their information from written products, which are the predominant communications modes in evaluation. Instead, they collect information, largely orally, from staffs, other members, constituencies, interest groups and the administration [4].

This base of analytical work could lead one to be rather pessimistic about the likely impact of evaluation in a congressional setting. And yet, somehow, the notion persists that Congress, a decisionmaking body, should find some use for a decisionmaking tool. Indeed, that notion persists in the Congress itself. It appears in statutory form in Title VII of the Congressional Budget Act of 1974 [5]. Nor was this a unique event. Over the past decade or so, there have been numerous requirements levied by Congress (some by statute, some by committee report language) for agencies to perform evaluations and report the results to Congress. In another context, the various proposals for "sunset" legislation have usually contained some provision for systematic evaluation of *most* government programs.

It is difficult to dismiss all of these actions as meaningless. No doubt some of them represent rhetorical gestures. But some cases, at least, seem to reflect a serious desire for useful evaluation. And it is possible to reconcile such a desire with existing data on congressional voting behavior.

Not all congressional decisions are of the sort to be governed by the influences of ambition or policy predisposition. And not all evaluation effort is devoted to the major political questions on which these influences are likely to prove most powerful. The term "evaluation", of course, encompasses a wide range of work, from relatively simple assessments of process to very elaborate and complex analyses of program impact. Despite the broad range of possible evaluations, however, most of the work of evaluators deals with the question of how to make a program work better. Such evaluations presume the legitimacy of objectives, rather than challenging them. The recommendations, therefore, focus on improvements at the margin. Only rarely does an evaluation yield evidence which is sufficiently reliable and conclusive to challenge (or validate) the very existence of a program. Most evaluations, therefore, deal with issues which, in principle at least, should not require legislators to rely on political imperatives and ignore the results of the analysis.

In this context, even Haveman's argument that legislative policymakers are not interested in societal costs and benefits loses some of its force. In speaking to marginal improvements rather than global costs and benefits, evaluation is a tool for reducing the cost of a given stream of benefits or for achieving greater benefits at the same cost. Given the present fiscal environment, this is an area in which members are likely to be interested, regardless of their political views of the program as a whole.

Why, then, does the scholarly literature seem to allow so little room for the use of evaluation and analysis by the Congress? And why do evaluators—at least many of them—still bemoan the failure of Congress to make effective use of their work? There are several answers. One is that more use is being made of the work than is commonly recognized among evaluators. Another is that evaluators' goals with respect to the nature and extent of utilization are unrealistic. And still another is that many evaluators have not yet learned how to communicate their work in such a way as to encourage use. Each answer contains an important element of truth. Understanding those answers requires some examination of how Congress actually uses evaluation.

CONGRESS AS CONSUMER

Congress, as an institution, has a unique set of relationships with the process of program evaluation. It is, at one and the same time, a consumer of evaluation, and (often overlooked) a producer of evaluation. It acts in both these roles because it is a collegial, deliberative body whose processes depend on the ability to collect, process and absorb a wide variety of information from a wide variety of sources, to reconcile or compromise diverse points of view, and to reach decisions in the form of enacted statutes.

Congress, however, is not just an institution with institutional behaviors. Congress is also a collection of 535 individual voting members. As discussed above, these members, and their staffs, are guided by a wide variety of motivations, relating to personal values, principles and ambitions.

The literature which seeks to analyze this set of behaviors–and the motivations underlying them–is dominated by the examination of voting records. These are primarily votes cast on the floor although some attention has been given to recorded votes in committee [6]. This is hardly surprising, since voting records represent a readily available body of data which can be subjected to various forms of useful statistical analysis. At the same time, however, this focus tends to ignore some significant activity which may not be reflected in recorded votes. Among these is the frequently informal committee and subcommittee markup process.

Experience in the General Accounting Office has been that direct, instrumental use (the adoption of one's evaluative recommendation) is much more likely to occur in committee deliberations than in the context of a floor debate and vote. Decisions made at the earlier stage, particularly those involving marginal change in the design or operations of a program, may be taken in a consensus fashion, without a formal vote. These decisions, therefore, would not be reflected in the statistical data which is available for analysis. There is some evidence that those who participate actively in committee deliberations occasionally change their views, even on major issues [7]. It is reasonable to expect somewhat greater susceptibility to argument and analysis on issues to which a member attaches only minimal political significance.

The author's experience has been that most legislators distinguish reasonably clearly between decisions which have a conspicuously political content and those which do not. On decisions which are recognized as involving important political considerations, behavior seems quite consistent with the literature. Behavior on other issues is frequently quite different. On these issues, a member is often open to being convinced of the "best" solution on the basis of analysis.

The same distinction may manifest itself in other ways. In developing a new program, for example, the congressman may have relatively unshakable views on the general shape and direction of the program. At the same time, others (the staff, experts, et al.) may be left to fill in the details. Political significance is seen as being attached to the dimensions of the program, not to its details.

Decisions in committee on issues involving details of program design and management are frequently accepted without debate or vote at later stages of the legislative process [8]. The evidence is that other members consciously defer on these details to those who participated in the committee hearings and markup process. Thus, the decision process on the type of issue which is addressed in most evaluations is hidden from the statistical analysis underlying most recent work on congressional decisionmaking.

Given this context, what strategies should the evaluator pursue if utilization is an important objective? At this point it is helpful to distinguish various forms of use [9]. Much of the time, an evaluation is considered to have been used if its recommendations are implemented, representing *instrumental use*. This is certainly one form of use. Often it is the only form which is relevant. But other forms are possible and, for some types of evaluation and in some circumstances these may be more significant. One such form is *persuasive use*, in which recipients use the evaluation as evidence with which to convince others of the correctness of a particular position. Another form is *conceptual use*, in which recipients make the content of the evaluation part of the general intellectual framework with which they approach an issue or set of related issues.

A member's dichotomous decision framework has important implications about expectations for use in a legislative setting. It suggests particularly that these expectations should take into account the political significance of the evaluative conclusions and recommendations. The greater the extent to which the evaluation deals with issues which a member will see as involving political considerations, the less likely it is that the evaluation will be used in an instrumental fashion and the more likely it is that the relevant form of use is persuasive or conceptual. Instrumental use of an evaluation on politically significant issues is certainly possible, but analysis of congressional decision processes suggests that it would be relatively unusual. Evaluators should be realistic in this regard and not be unduly disappointed if it fails to occur. On the contrary, they should anticipate that situation and look for strategies that will facilitate persuasive or conceptual use.

Assuming that the evaluation involves a question on which instrumental use can be reasonably expected, there are strategies which an evaluator can pursue to encourage such use. One such strategy is to choose a topic and a focus which is known to be of interest to one or more influential members. An evaluation of this sort may be initiated by either party, but often culminates in a relatively explicit agreement between the user and the evaluator on the scope of work and timing and form of the resulting product.

Another approach, one which can be combined with the first, is to work closely with committee staff in both the planning and implementation stages to assure that the work will be responsive to their needs and that they understand the content and implications of the evaluation. There are two important reasons for establishing this relationship. On issues which are not politically sensitive, staff frequently have substantial authority to make decisions. In principle, such decisions are no more than tentative, subject to approval by the member. In fact, however, they are often accepted without substantial discussion [10]. Another reason for working through the staff is the relative accessibility of these individuals, as contrasted with the member.

Whether working with staff or with the legislator, instrumental use is much more likely if the evaluator is attentive to key elements in the evaluator-customer relationship. These include reaching agreement on a clearly-defined, relevant, answerable question; maintaining contact with the customer during the study; and searching for the most effective way to communicate the results [11].

Although instrumental use is the goal to which most evaluators aspire, it should not obscure the significance of use in a persuasive or conceptual fashion. Both forms of use exist, although the evidence is both ambiguous and elusive. Persuasive use may actually be difficult to distinguish from instrumental use in a particular case. Suppose, for example, a member cites an evaluation report as the reason for a particular action. That is certainly evidence of use. But it would be misleading to assume that such a statement is strong evidence of instrumental use. The statement may well be an example of persuasive use, citing credible authority in support of a decision the member would have made even in the absence of evaluation.

If one is only searching for evidence that evaluations are used, the form of use may not matter. But if one is seeking to maximize a particular form of use, or to discern the consequences of an evaluation with some precision, the distinctions become significant. From an analytical perspective, the distinctions can probably be made most reliably by reference to the content of the decision. The stability of congressional voting behavior on major political issues becomes an essential assumption in such an analysis. If an evaluation is cited in connection with an issue involving substantial political controversy, it is relatively unlikely that instrumental use is involved. Unless the legislator is voting in a fashion which is a departure from past voting patterns, the citation of an evaluation can be reasonably presumed to represent an example of persuasive use.

It is important not to assume that persuasive use is improper or somehow demonstrates that bias was present in the evaluation. A perfectly sound evaluation may be used in persuasive fashion. If the evaluation is sound and the use does not involve distortion of the results, persuasive use should not reflect adversely on either the evaluator or the user.

Another common example of persuasive use is seen when a report is used by a legislator to help explain an action to others. Kingdon, for example, points out that "Congressmen are constantly called upon to explain to constituents why they voted as they did" [12]. There is the same need to explain or justify actions to other members and to political or administrative officials in the executive branch. In carrying out this function, a legislator might either use an evaluation report as a source of information or simply cite it as support for the action. In this case, the member's views may not have been changed by the evaluation, but the evaluation may have made it easier to act on those views by making it easier to explain or rationalize them.

If an evaluator wishes to facilitate persuasive use, effective communications should be a central element of the strategy. The objective should be to make it as easy as possible for the user to understand and relay the primary message of the report. This means capturing that message accurately in a few words or phrases through the use of descriptive titles and highly condensed digests or executive summaries.

Finally, there is the case of conceptual use. If an evaluation caused a member to see a significant, but previously unrecognized aspect of an issue, it would be a clear case of conceptual use. While probably unusual, such an event would be consistent with the literature on congressional voting behavior. In the policy dimension framework, for example, an evaluation might reveal a policy dimension which was previously hidden. Alternatively, an evaluation might reveal a previously unrecognized effect on the constituency of interest. Admittedly, there is little evidence of such direct conceptual use. In part, of course, the lack of evidence reflects the inherently elusive nature of conceptual use as a target of analysis. The phenomenon of interest occurs in the mind of an individual, where it cannot be directly measured, and reliable surrogates are difficult to identify.

It seems likely, however, that the conceptual use of evaluation commonly occurs in an indirect fashion. The results may become part of the flow of ideas from the academic community, the business community or the media. In these forums, of course, an evaluation competes with other work having similar or conflicting messages and the eventual outcome is likely to represent an amalgam of these ideas.

The indirect nature of much conceptual use suggests strategies for facilitating it. The central objective should be to assure that those with the power to influence thinking are made aware of the work. There is, of course, a wide variety of possible dissemination strategies. The choice of which to pursue should depend on who is to be reached. Each potential audience represents a possible channel back to the Congress. But each audience has its own standards of credibility and preferences on form. Failure to respect such standards and preferences entails the risk (indeed, the likelihood) of failure to reach and convince that audience.

To maximize conceptual use, it may prove necessary to pursue several dissemination strategies simultaneously, each carefully tailored to the needs of one or more target audiences. Some may like frequent (brief) progress reports on work in process, while another group may be satisfied only by a detailed, technically complete final report and a third may not look at anything but a highly condensed executive summary. This sort of communications strategy may seem rather expensive, but the expense may well be unavoidable if major conceptual use is to occur. In addition, of course, the expense of a well-developed dissemination strategy is generally quite small compared to the cost of performing the evaluation itself.

If the general assessment of use set forth above is correct, it suggests (among other things) that the types of evaluations in which Congress is interested may differ significantly from those which the evaluation community as a whole has tended to regard most highly. It helps explain why, with some notable exceptions, Congress has not yet displayed much enthusiasm for sophisticated, methodologically rigorous impact evaluations. On the other hand, the use of evaluation for persuasive or explanatory purposes is consistent with the fact that members display substantial interest in assessments of the extent to which program services are delivered to the intended target groups. Similarly, the absence of overriding political imperatives when considering incremental changes to program design and operations helps explain the continuing interest in process-oriented evaluations designed to yield management improvements and greater administrative efficiency. The strong, continuing interest in evaluations dealing with service delivery and process efficiency is quite evident in GAO's relations with the Congress. Such evaluations are often requested and, when produced (either by request or under GAO's general charter), result in an agreeably high frequency of instrumental or persuasive use.

It is unfortunate that evaluators have paid so little attention to the decision processes of their legislative clients. Indeed, some evaluators would undoubtedly consider serious curiosity on the subject to be inappropriate. One of the results, however, has been that the activities which build stature among evaluators are often not those which are most useful, at least in a congressional environment. Evaluations aimed at improved management efficiency and those which seek to identify the extent of service to target groups do not yet garner a great deal of respect in the evaluation community. Evaluators have been encouraged by some of their peers to look down on anything short of a large scale controlled experiment dealing with program impact. Yet it is precisely this sort of evaluation which is most likely to encounter the political imperatives which militate against the instrumental use of the results. The controlled experiment is powerful as a basis for scientific inquiry; in the congressional arena it seems substantially less powerful.

This is not intended to demean the large-scale controlled experiment, or to suggest that it is irrelevant in the congressional context. The Congress itself has participated actively in decisions to engage in such experiments. The Income Maintenance and Housing Allowance experiments are obvious examples. But one's expectations about the likely impact of such efforts should be realistic. It is not obvious that either of these major experiments has yet had much effect on the nature or design of the programs to which they are relevant. (It is too early to tell if the Administration's housing voucher proposal will lead to substantial changes based on the results of these experiments.)

Some may attribute the relatively modest policy effect of large scale social experiments to inadequacies in their design or execution. Flaws of this sort have certainly been identified, as well as other limitations on the extrapolation of experimental results to the construction of social programs [13]. Experience in recent years seems to suggest that these problems may well be almost inescapable. Acknowledging that we are unlikely to see the "perfect" large scale social experiment lends some credibility to the view that imperfections in the research have caused the loss of policy effect. In the author's view, however, the nature of decisionmaking processes explains the absence of policy effect in a much more direct fashion.

The basic structure of income transfer programs—which was the issue to which these experiments were addressed—is a profoundly (and properly) political issue. In that environment, it would be unreasonable to expect any single analytical effort to have a major effect in the short run. As Schick suggests, "Everything is grist for the congressional mill, and analysis enjoys no preferred position by virtue of its esteem in intellectual circles" [14].

The most that should realistically be expected is that the knowledge gained from these experiments will become part of the intellectual framework of the country over the long run. If this sort of conceptual use occurs, the ultimate effects of the work may well be of great importance. It is unlikely, however, that the cause and effect relationship will ever be more than speculative.

There are other factors, apart from political considerations, which limit the short-run, instrumental use of large-scale impact evaluations. These projects yield complex reports full of ambiguities. Making use of them often requires quite a high level of understanding of the program. Interpreting them properly may well require that the reader also have a rather sophisticated understanding of the research process. This, in turn, requires an investment of time which few legislators can afford. Impact evaluations also tend to take a long time to complete, longer than most congressmen are usually willing to wait for an answer.

There is, and will continue to be some interest in impact evaluation. That interest may well stem, in large part, from the presence of technically trained committee staff, who have the time and interest to follow complex evaluations. There seems to be a trend to increasing the use of such staff. But the constraints on instrumental use are rather severe. As a result, large-scale impact evaluation seems likely to remain less in vogue in a congressional setting than elsewhere in the evaluation community.

Evaluators are correct in observing that much evaluation activity goes unused in the Congress. Many of the reasons lie in the nature of the Congress, which governs what its members perceive as useful. If evaluators wish to see greater use made of their work, they would do well to spend more time studying the way their various clients (legislators, staffers, interest groups, et al.) function and interact, and then produce the sort of evaluation which is appropriate to that context.

Evaluators would also be well advised to think about the appropriate form of communication for the congressional context. That they have not yet done so is most evident in the continuing emphasis on written communications. The evidence in the literature is quite clear that most legislators receive very little of their decision-related information in writing [15]: This view would be confirmed by experienced observers who would point out that this is not necessarily a matter of choice. Most congressmen simply do not have time to read about any subject at length, a characteristic which is equally prevalent, by the way, among decisionmakers in the executive branch.

It is possible, however, to develop somewhat more effective means of communicating. Experience suggests that oral communications, for example, are more effective than written, particularly in a congressional context. Experience also suggests that informal briefings, with opportunity for substantial give-and-take, are more effective than formal hearings. For the evaluator, these techniques may appear less efficient than the written report. An informal briefing can reach only a small number of potential users, while a written report can reach them all. But a report which goes unread has reached no one, while a tailored briefing may reach a few influential members quite effectively, and through them, a much broader group.

In summary, if evaluators give more attention to the nature of the client, they will realize that their work is used more extensively and in a more diverse fashion than they may realize. They will also find ways to increase that use, by doing work of the sort the client is most likely to use and by communicating it in a more effective fashion.

In examining the Congress as a client, however, they will discover something else. Not only does Congress consume evaluation, it produces evaluation. Some of this evaluation activity would hardly be recognized as such by most evaluators.

CONGRESS AS PRODUCER

Serving as one's own evaluator is a characteristic of most (probably all) decisionmakers from time to time. Few have the luxury of being able to refer every issue to an analytical or evaluation staff for full-scale development. In addition, there are some elements of any major issue which are particularly difficult for a separate staff to assess effectively. In a major policy issue, for example, there will be political considerations and value judgments which a separate staff will find it difficult to cover adequately in an analysis. These are matters which are frequently very personal to the decisionmaker and thus best handled personally.

These factors cause any decisionmaker to act as his/her own evaluator some of the time. In the case of the Congress, however, there is the additional factor of collective decisionmaking, without the clearly defined hierarchy of power and authority that characterizes the executive branch (at least in theory). This is combined with a structure of committees, subcommittees, party caucuses, regional groupings, ideological organizations, interest group coalitions and other coalitions of varying degrees of formality and permanence. All these structures serve, among other things, the purpose of collecting, integrating, analyzing and disseminating information believed to be relevant to policy decisions. Each legislator is linked to a number of these entities and is relatively free to choose among them for sources of information. Thus, each of the entities serves as an evaluator, seeking as its client, some significant part of the Congress as a whole.

On the surface, the activities of these groups may not resemble very much the techniques used in the more rigorous parts of the evaluation community. With a little probing, however, some significant similarities begin to appear. In order to recognize these similarities, the observer must move away from the economic efficiency orientation that usually dominates the evaluator's perspective.

All other things being equal, of course, questions of economic efficiency will be of interest to any legislator. But all other things are rarely equal, so other questions will be of interest to members, as well. These other matters are most frequently ones which might carry the label "political efficiency." They are the issues on which the congressman often must serve as his/her own evaluator, and in some cases they are evidently the most significant questions involved in making a decision.

It is useful at this stage again to make the distinction between decisions about details of program design or management and those affecting the very existence or basic focus of a program. As suggested earlier, the former are less likely to carry the label of being a major political issue and thus more likely to be influenced by analysis based on economic efficiency considerations. Once a decision takes on the label of a major political issue, external evaluation is very likely to give way to a personal evaluation based on the calculus of political efficiency. In this calculus, economic efficiency is often a relatively minor consideration.

To the analyst whose basic orientation is dominated by the quest for economic efficiency, the political efficiency calculus leads to decisions which may seem incomprehensible or irrational. In fact, however, the decision behavior of legislators in the political arena is quite rational and usually rather successful. This can be readily demonstrated by the frequency with which incumbent congressmen are reelected. The rationality of the process is very much akin to that of the evaluative process, once one accepts that economic efficiency is not the only standard against which a person may judge the wisdom of an action.

The literature suggests that a member, in facing a politically significant decision, may use any of several standards. The member may:

1. Judge the issue against policy predispositions.
2. Judge the issue in terms of its effects on constituents (or some subset of

of constituents which is considered politically important, or some potential future constituency).
3. Judge the issue in terms of its effects on one's position within the Congress (i.e., relationships with the leadership and with other members).
4. Judge the issue in terms of its effects on relationships with the executive branch (recognizing that the executive branch itself is not monolithic; the President and the various parts of the temporary and permanent bureaucracy may well have divergent views).

Any one of these approaches can involve a very complex evaluative process. Considering the number of politically significant decisions which legislators must make, it is obvious that the depth of the political evaluation is necessarily subject to extreme variation. The evidence suggests that, much of the time, the decision is made on the basis of a rather brief evaluative process. It appears that members often turn to others, either one of the organized groups noted previously or another member—someone whose political judgment the member trusts and whom he/she believes has made the requisite political evaluation—and acts on the advice received from that source or combination of sources.

In any event, the legislator acts on the basis of what is believed to be a competent political evaluation of the issue—whether his own or someone else's. Whoever performs this evaluation, it has a structure and involves a process with distinct similarities to cost-effectiveness analysis. The benefits consist of the relevant people, groups, or organizations who will agree with the vote; the costs consist of the relevant people, groups, or organizations whom the vote will alienate. Given appropriate weights for the relative importance of the various groups, the congressman's decision involves maximizing the former and minimizing the latter.

While the structure and process of political evaluation has distinct similarities to the more familiar types of evaluation, the content is likely to be very different. That content is likely to be dominated by perceptions, and perceptions may have very little to do with what many analysts and evaluators would consider objective reality.

It is this element of the political evaluation which many evaluators and analysts find most difficult to understand and accept. Most evaluators have had the experience of presenting what they consider convincing evidence of a program's failure to achieve its objectives, only to have otherwise intelligent political officials (in the executive branch or the Congress) continue to support the program. There are, of course, a number of possible reasons for this behavior. One is that the politician does not believe the results of the evaluation.

Another explanation, however, is that the political value which the elected official attaches to the program has nothing to do with objectively measurable results. It may well be based, instead, on the label attached to the program and the perceptions created by that label.

There is considerable evidence, for example, that employment and training programs have done little to alleviate structural unemployment. Similarly, community development programs have done little to overcome the physical problems of the inner cities. Indeed, there is some evidence that the complex of policies bearing on these issues may be having significantly perverse effects. Yet political support for these policies has continued relatively unabated on the part of the target constituencies and their elected representatives. (Others, of course, such as the present Administration and a large number of other congressmen, have shown substantially less enthusiasm for these programs.)

It seems likely that this continued support reflects some combination of beliefs, fostered by the label on the program, either that the program is more efficacious than is warranted by the facts or that the program, despite its failings, represents evidence that someone cares. The latter situation, in particular, deserves more attention than evaluators and analysts have given it. In any organized society, it is important that people believe government cares about their problems. Legislators are very attentive to these sorts of perceptions on the part of their constituents, and are likely, at least in some circumstances, to accord them a central place in their political evaluation, even when the perceptions conflict with evidence about objective reality.

It should also be recognized that the evidence on objective reality is not necessarily consistent. There are always ambiguities, even in the best evaluation. In addition, of course, there is the likelihood of competing evidence, adduced by those who look at an issue from a different perspective which portrays a different version of objective reality.

In making a personal political evaluation, a member must integrate this wide variety of types and sources of data, concerning both perceptions and objective reality. This activity is analogous to the data collection phase of a conventional evaluation, even though the data being gathered is quite different.

The most visible part of this activity is the hearings process, but it is frequently not the most important part. Hearings only occasionally elicit data which was not already known to the members of the committee. The views of the witnesses are usually quite well-known ahead of time. Indeed, specific witnesses are often invited precisely because they are known to represent a particular point of view on the issue at hand. This is not to suggest that hearings are a charade. On the contrary, they serve the important purpose of developing a public record about the information which the members used in making their decision. This record (usually published at the conclusion of the hearings) in conjunction with the committee report on the bill or resolution serves the same "document of record" function as the written report of an evaluation.

Apart from the formal hearings process, most of the data collection for the political evaluation takes place in a less structured and visible fashion. The sources are quite diverse, including the media, constituent contacts, other members, the leadership, interest groups, congressional staff, executive branch agencies and congressional support agencies (GAO, CRS, OTA and CBO). They can be tapped in a variety of ways, both formal and informal and, if used, can supply a wide range of data, from "hard" evaluation and analysis to impressions of political reaction. The available time and the importance and sensitivity of the issue will determine how many of them and which ones are used on any particular occasion.

As with any evaluation, not all sources of data are equally reliable or weighty. For example, a member from a relatively remote district may well pay more attention to views expressed in a hometown newspaper than to reports in one of the major national newspapers. Among constituents, the member will give more weight to a leading supporter than to a relatively unknown individual.

Once the data are gathered, the congressman goes through a process of analysis and synthesis. The data are sorted and weighed, usually in a rather informal fashion, and a decision is reached. The process has been, in reality, an evaluation, albeit not one with which most evaluators would identify.

Several cautions need to be recognized in considering this model of evaluation-based congressional decisionmaking. The model, as with any model, is a very simplified version of reality, and this reality is particularly complex. In addition, it is a model which is applicable, at best, in a limited range of situations. Specifically, it may be applicable when a member actually has not made up his mind on an issue, and wants to (and can afford to) spend some time reaching a decision. Much of the time, of course, the decision is largely predetermined, whether on ideological grounds or because of the obvious interests of a large number of constituents, or both. On other occasions, time simply does not permit one to ponder the issue and the member uses one of the numerous shortcuts available for reaching a political decision. In this respect, of course, a legislator is not very different from other decisionmakers. Few can afford the luxury of attempting comprehensively to analyze every issue they face.

If evaluators come to recognize legislators as being quite rational and, indeed, analytical in their approach to political issues, evaluators may also come to a more realistic understanding of the extent to which their work is used, the variety of ways in which it is used and the limits on that use in a political setting. In some situations, and on some issues, our work can be of major instrumental or persuasive use; in others, the work may prove largely irrelevant. We should learn to recognize the different situations, predict them, and be guided accordingly.

REFERENCES

1. Van Der Slik, J. R. and Pernacciaro, S. S. Office Ambitions and Voting Behavior in the U.S. Senate. *American Politics Quarterly*, 7:2 (April 1979): 198-224. See also Schlesinger, J. *Ambition and Politics: Political Careers in the United States*. Rand McNally, Chicago, 1966.
2. Clausen, A. R. *How Congressmen Decide: A Policy Focus*. St, Martin's Press, New York, 1973. The view that the policy orientation is highly stable is

slightly moderated in Clausen, A. R. and Van Horn, C. E. The Congressional Response to a Decade of Change: 1963-1972. *Journal of Politics*, Vol. 39 (August 1977): 624-666.

3. Haveman, R. H. Policy Analysis and the Congress: An Economist's View. *Policy Analysis*, 2:2, (Spring 1976): 235-250.
4. Kingdon, J. W. *Congressmen's Voting Decisions*. Harper and Row, New York, 1973.
5. Public Law 93-344, enacted July 12, 1974. Title VII of the Act carries the label Program Review and Evaluation. (88 STAT. 325).
6. See, for example, Unekis, J. K. From Committee to the Floor: Consistency in Congressional Voting. *Journal of Politics*, Vol. 40 (August 1978): 761-769.
7. See Kingdon, op. cit., especially the discussion on p. 82 of the reasons for reliance on fellow congressmen with expertise.
8. Woodrow Wilson expressed this view particularly strongly when he observed that Congress usually meets "to sanction the conclusions of its committees as rapidly as possible." Wilson, W. *Congressional Government*. Houghton Mifflin Co., New York, 1913, p. 78.
9. This taxonomy of forms of use draws on the existing literature. See, particularly, Leviton, L. C. and Hughes, E. F. X. Research on the Utilization of Evaluations: A Review and Synthesis. *Evaluation Review*, 5:4 (August 1981): 525-548.
10. There is substantial dispute over the importance of staff in the decisionmaking processes of Congress. Kingdon's data suggests a relatively minor role. On the other hand, Malbin, M. J., in *Unelected Representatives*, Basic Books, New York, 1980, indicates a much more influential role on the part of the entrepreneurial, "new style" staff. If Malbin's thesis is correct, it has significant implications for communicating evaluation results usefully. The staff is invariably more accessible than the member.
11. The relationship between evaluator and customer is developed at greater length in Havens, H. S. Program Evaluation and Program Management. *Public Administration Review*, 41:4 (July/August 1981): 480-485.
12. Kingdon, op. cit., p. 46. Later in the same section, he discusses strategies which congressmen use in the process of explaining. One of these strategies involves citing respected authority. While not stated, such authority might include a credible evaluation report.
13. These issues are explicitly addressed in several of the papers published in Boruch, R. F.; Wortman, P. M.; and Cordray, D. S. (eds.). *Reanalyzing Program Evaluations*. Jossey-Bass, San Francisco, 1981.
14. Schick, A. The Supply and Demand for Analysis on Capitol Hill. *Policy Analysis*, 2:2 (Spring 1976): 228.
15. Kingdon, op. cit., Chapter 8. In his interviews, media and other reading rank last among identified sources of influence.

5
Evaluating the Spatial Impacts of National Transportation Policies

A. C. Goodman and K. C. Lyall* / *Center for Metropolitan Planning and Research, The Johns Hopkins University, Baltimore, Maryland*

INTRODUCTION

People vs. Place-Oriented Evaluation

Federal policies directed to the needs of *individuals* or enterprises often have unanticipated and unintended impacts on *places*. The evaluation research literature most often focuses on identifying and tracing the effects of programs on specified target or client groups:

- Are program benefits going to those for whom they were intended?
- Are the benefits having the desired effect on recipients, inducing behavioral changes in the intended direction?
- Are the resulting benefits worth the cost of the program to its various constituencies?

Such evaluation studies lean heavily on randomly assigned samples of recipients and, where feasible, on control groups to detect significant program effects.

The place-oriented or spatial impacts of policies are much less recognized and seldom evaluated, especially in fields thought to be technical or responsive to scientific planning, such as transportation. Studies of transportation needs, modal split choices, travel patterns, and subsidies abound in the literature but little attention has been paid to anticipating the spatial impacts of national transportation policies [1].

The National Urban Policy, enunciated by the Carter Administration in 1978, instituted a procedural requirement that "urban impact analyses" be done as part of the backup documentation submitted by each executive agency with its

---

**Present Affiliation*: University of Wisconsin, Madison, Wisconsin

annual budget request. Such analyses were required for new program initiatives and for proposed changes in programs that would substantially alter their spatial impacts [2]. These analyses were privileged information not available to the public or the Congress except at the discretion of the White House. Urban impact analyses were required to examine the spatial impact of programs/policies with respect to urban versus suburban and rural areas, among cities of different sizes (large cities versus small towns), and across regions of the country (Sunbelt versus Frostbelt). Their purpose was to anticipate potentially adverse spatial impacts of federal policies at an early stage in the policy process when strategic modifications in program design or policy implementation could moderate such adverse urban impacts.

Consider, for example, the Federal Highway Program, instituted in 1945 for the purpose of providing an efficient, high-speed, inter-city transportation network. Heavy federal subsidies for construction encouraged the building of interstate highways that cut through or bypassed existing urban centers and opened up large expanses of undeveloped land in the suburbs. Both housing developers and businesses seeking to expand in the post-war period found suburban development irresistible. The following rapid decentralization of jobs and population out of central cities transformed the face of urban America, established private automobile travel as the main form of commuting, and had an indelible effect on the pattern of new settlements.

Would an urban impact analysis of the proposal for a Federal Highway Program in 1945 have defeated the idea? Probably not; the national goals of mobility, security, and efficiency served by the Program were clear and insistent. It is possible, however, that if the negative urban impacts of the Program had been foreseen, the Federal Highway Program might have been coupled with other policy initiatives in a package designed to increase inter-city accessibility while maintaining cities as desirable residential sites. Such options might have included mortgage financing insurance for older urban homes equivalent to that available through the FHA on new suburban houses, federal assistance for provision of parking facilities in central cities, and greater sensitivity to pleas for the preservation of neighborhoods in the path of interstate highways. The purpose of such spatial evaluations, then, is not to veto policies with potentially adverse urban impacts, but to effect modifications in their designs that can buffer, if not avoid, such impacts.

In the following sections, we analyze the spatial impacts of five current transportation policies, some in effect and some proposed, to illustrate the unintended effects that they may have on the urban form and economy. All five of these policies are likely to be in force by the end of 1982 and all are reversible. There are, in order of completeness of implementation:

1. Deregulation of airline rates and routes
2. Lifting of federal ceilings on gasoline prices
3. Curtailing subsidies to AMtrak

4. Deregulation of interstate trucking
5. Institution of user charges to pay for port dredging and development

We evaluate each of these policies briefly on the following three dimensions:

Spatial patterns—Do they lead to centralized or decentralized locations of residences and business activity?
Economic base—Do they differentially affect the mixes of businesses and work opportunities among cities or between cities and their suburbs?
Equity—How do they redistribute costs and benefits among constituents?

FIVE TRANSPORTATION POLICIES

Airline Deregulation

In 1978, the Civil Aeronautics Board began a rapid deregulation of airline rates and route assignments designed to stimulate competition and variety in services offered by carriers. Deregulation of airline rates and route assignments has produced an interesting set of changes in the levels of service offered to cities and towns of different sizes. Because the pre-existing rate structures subsidized the less heavily traveled routes from "overcharges" to travelers on the more popular routes, deregulation has generally reduced the levels of service to smaller towns and both increased the frequency and decreased the cost of service to larger cities [3]. Some medium-sized cities representing special markets (such as Las Vegas) have also received increases in service. This shift of service from smaller to larger centers has correspondingly increased the use of automobile and truck transportation in smaller markets and, in some places, substantially changed the shipping times for goods produced in these areas. In short, deregulation of airline rates and routes pushes towards greater centralization of some kinds of commercial activity in major urban markets with better air service.

At the same time, deregulation produces greater equity in costs among individual travelers. The new pattern of rates and services after deregulation more nearly matches the prices that travelers are willing to pay with the true costs of providing those services. The cross-subsidies embodied in the regulated rates provided an incentive for travel to smaller centers and over less popular routes at the expense of the travelers to larger, more popular destinations. Now, the latter pay fares that reflect the economies of scale associated with serving major centers.

Decontrol of Gasoline Prices

Many articles in the popular press on urban economic development in the 1980's imply that projected higher energy prices, particularly for gasoline, should lead to more centralized activity, with particularly positive impacts on existing Central

Business Districts (CBDs). Artificially low energy prices after World War II, the argument goes, encouraged decentralization. Since most roads lead downtown, since most office space is downtown, and since most revitalization efforts are directed toward downtown, increased energy prices should lead to a "recentralization" of various forms of economic activity. This recentralization may have substantial impacts on the spatial patterns, economic base, and equity aspects of economic activities.

At the time of this writing, the pump price of gasoline has risen by 300 percent in the past 10 years, a doubling in real price. In March 1981, the Reagan Administration removed all federal price controls on gasoline; and, although the OPEC cartel has periodic disagreements among its members on pricing policies, it is not a prime candidate for collapse. It would, therefore, not be unreasonable to expect an increase in gasoline prices of 50 percent in real terms, in the next 10 years [4]. These higher prices impact significantly on urban structure largely through the location of businesses (with their associated transportation costs), but even more importantly through the commuting behavior of workers.

It is likely that urban structure will become more centralized as real gasoline prices rise. The rate of adjustment, however, will be slow because much of urban structure consists of roads, housing, and plants, three capital goods that are extremely durable. These are not abandoned or left to deteriorate as the result of energy price increases, and even if abandoned or left to deteriorate, do so very slowly. It is more likely that housing and development projects which were planned for the far edges of the metropolitan area will be scuttled, and parcels with good transportation access, in the downtown or near freeways, will become more desirable. Such a "filling in" process will lead to more centralization, but at barely perceptible rates.

It might be argued that gasoline decontrol will induce commuters to use mass transportation, including buses and subway systems, and induce business to locate where the subways are. This may be plausible for cities which have, or are currently building subways; but two points should be noted. First, many subways were designed to bring people from the suburbs to the downtown, but they go both ways. It is not automatic that business seeking to locate on the subway line will choose to locate in the city center. Further, continued extension of subway lines appears to be exceedingly unlikely. Funded largely by the Urban Mass Transit Administration in the 1960's and 1970's, subways appear to be unfeasible under any other arrangement; and, the current political climate is one of opposition to new projects.

The impact of gasoline deregulation on the development of the economic base depends on the suitability and location of the existing infrastructure. Central business areas are often thought to have a comparative advantage based on their existing investment in roads and buildings. This is true only if the existing infrastructure is suitable for business relocation, but recent experience suggests that it is not.

Schmenner [5], in two separate pieces, analyzes businesses' location, relocation, and expansion decisions. He finds, in general, that the most desirable places have good road infrastructure, plenty of land for parking and expansion, and good sewer and power hook-ups. The urban street system, which served central cities well for decades, has not generally kept up; the arterial system directing traffic into the CBD is now badly repaired and congested. Many metropolitan areas have "beltway" systems which have provided excellent locations for businesses that wish to be close to good truck transportation, and in many cases these beltways are entirely outside the central city (Boston and Baltimore are only two examples).

The restricted availability of land is another factor pushing businesses out of the CBD. Firms that originally developed on small parcels with a multi-floor technology, find expansion to be difficult, if not impossible, if they wish to use the more modern land-intensive technologies. The CBD is still a good central location for gathering office workers, yet city after city has seen the exodus of office-related businesses moving closer to their workforces.

In short, the economic development impact of gasoline price deregulation depends largely on the location of the supporting infrastructure. Newer cities with large parcels of developable land and good freeway connections will benefit to some extent from price deregulation. Those without these advantages will see little, if any, benefit.

Many have argued that deregulation will impact most heavily on poor families. Since the poor are located predominately in central city areas, the anticipated impact on urban households is adverse.

Although car-owning poor people will suffer, a very large proportion of the poor and/or elderly do not own cars. To the extent that these people do not travel, or that they use public transportation, the impact will be muted.

Goodman [6] has shown that the burden of a 50-cent gas tax for the Baltimore area as a percentage of income is relatively progressive. Families with incomes of less than $5,000 have a burden on average of 2.75 percent, whereas families with incomes of $15,000 to $21,000 have burdens of 3.96 percent. When examined spatially, however, the analysis shows the suburban impact to be over twice that of the impact in the central city.

In capsule, the impacts of gasoline price deregulation are mixed. Spatial impacts lead to less decentralization, although this does *not* portend any sort of stampede back to the central city. With respect to economic development, the results depend largely on the location of existing infrastructure. The distributional effects are also mixed. The low-income, car-owning central city resident may be badly hurt; but, in general, a disproportionate share of the cost burden will fall on suburban car owners.

Curtail AMtrak Subsidies

The "bottomless pit" of federal subsidies to the national passenger railroad system (AMtrak) has long been a source of public debate. Recent legislative proposals would substantially curtail the federal subsidies going to support rail passenger service to the Northeast corridor of the United States (between Boston and Washington). Existing subsidies to AMtrak's intercity commuter service have been justified as a means of reducing highway congestion in and around major cities and of sustaining more concentrated economic activity in central cities than would otherwise be possible. Reduction in passenger rail service can be expected to accelerate the outmigration of employment opportunities and labor force from cities to suburbs. The necessary increase in the use of automobiles or buses to commute to work will increase congestion on surrounding streets and highways and increase highway maintenance costs to state and local governments.

On a comparative basis, cities with existing train service will be disadvantaged relative to those without such service. Smaller towns may become comparatively more attractive as business and commercial locations. In short, reduction of AMtrak service will produce pressures for further decentralization of population and employment within the Northeast metropolitan corridor.

The equity effects of reduced passenger service work in two different directions. Since many commuters using the AMtrak Northeast corridor intercity are middle-income, compared to those who commute by bus or car, an increase in rail rates will work toward greater interpersonal equity in commuting costs. Middle- and upper-income rail commuters will no longer be as heavily subsidized by lower-income non-rail users. However, there is also likely to be an accessibility effect in which some persons will find the higher rail fares sharply restrict the labor markets in which they can feasibly search for employment. Some effort may also be made to pass higher rail fares on to employers in increased wage demands.

Truck Deregulation

Many urban analysts argue that the motorized truck has done more to accelerate the decentralization of urbanized areas than any other technological development in this century. Standard location analysis views the city as depending on some centrally located transportation depot, around which businesses cluster, and from which goods are sold and delivered. While this may have been true in the nineteenth century when rail transportation was primary, the evolution of the truck has loosened the link between the central business area and the rest of the urban region. No longer must goods be delivered to a central depot and redistributed. Truck delivery combines substantially reduced terminal charges with some line-haul economies of the railroad. Piggy-backing developed over the past quarter century has also extended these capabilities [7].

Until recently, the trucking industry was burdened by several types of regulations. These governed the rates that could be charged, the routes over which goods could be delivered, and the sizes of loads that could be hauled, enforced through state weight regulations. The size regulations have led to higher costs because of the need to break trucks in two at state borders. While there has been some pressure for making these regulations uniform across states, states have rather jealously defended their perogatives to set their own regulations. Local trucking operating within state boundaries is not subject to any federal regulation.

The impacts of federal deregulation upon urban areas do not stem, then, from greater truck competition within the urban areas, but rather from the effects of looser trucking regulations on trucking's competitive position with respect to other modes such as railroads and air freight. To this extent, deregulation must lead to further decentralization of urban spatial structure.

Rate and route regulation have necessarily made trucking more expensive than necessary. Rate regulation prohibits the price competition that can be generated on routes between various cities. Route regulations dictate that some trucks can carry cargoes from one city to another, but not back, leading to the practice of "dead-heading," or the return without any cargo. These increase average costs for the trucking firm which must be passed on to customers.

Removal of these regulations should make interstate trucking, all else equal, more competitive with the alternative transportation modes. To the extent that both railroad and air freight depend on rather expensive terminal facilities and handling costs, these facilities must be centralized. The shift of marginal customers to trucking can weaken the spatial link between transportation users and these terminal facilities and lead to less central locations.

This decentralization is likely to hurt the central city's economic base. Typically, railroad facilities are located in central areas; air terminals may not be quite so centrally located but still elicit considerable surrounding activity. Increasingly competitive trucking makes locations near major thoroughfares more attractive. To the extent that such parcels are more likely to be outside of central cities, the economic base of the cities may be hurt.

Removal of trucking regulations should lead to lower prices for the goods that are being shipped, to the extent that the decreased costs are passed on to the consumers. To the extent that the poor consume larger proportions of their incomes, this should lead to a slight improvement in their well-being relative to the more affluent.

Port User Charges

The federal government has traditionally taken responsibility for maintaining channel depth in the harbors of American ocean ports. Actual port construction and operations have been handled individually following a laissez-faire policy, but most ports with navigable straits have been able to show the favorable cost-benefit calculations necessary to acquire Army Corps of Engineers help in the channel deepening process. Proposed changes in federal policy, however, would make the states responsible for the costs of channel deepening and maintenance. Although the financing mechanism has not been specified, most observers feel that some sort of port user fee will be necessary. To be more economically and politically palatable, such a fee will have to be spread as broadly as possible to all port users.

Clearly, ports that require considerable dredging will be hurt relative to those which do not. Baltimore, for example, is several hundred miles further up the Chesapeake Bay than Hampton Roads and will require more dredging. Moreover, since Hampton Roads is at the opening of the Chesapeake Bay, its dredging decision may directly impact on the possibilities open to Baltimore. Cities such as Seattle or Long Beach which require little channel deepening, will benefit relative to those on the East Coast, such as Baltimore, Philadelphia, or New York, which require large amounts.

Within cities the impact will be selective. If a coal or steel company wishes to have the channel deepened to its particular location, and can pay for it, then this is likely to be done. General channel deepening, for the benefit of many smaller firms, will require government or other coordination, with greater delays. It seems apparent, then, that within urban areas development will be more clustered at points which do have deepened channels. It is not at all clear that all channels in a given port, or all ports, will be deepened and/or will be deepened at the same pace.

The economic base impacts will be most severe upon those cities and states with small financial resources to advance for harbor deepening, and upon those which have customarily had federal government aid in the past, primarily the older ports. To the extent that one port must set user charges higher than another, trade will be diverted from the higher cost port. If, instead, higher property taxes are used to finance channel dredging, then businesses whose livelihood does not directly depend on the port may choose to relocate outside the taxing jurisdiction.

Equity effects of port user fees are troublesome to conceptualize. Since international trade goes through the ports, it can be argued that all residents benefit from their being deepened and that it is appropriate for these costs to be borne federally. On the other hand, it is apparent that most of the spin-off employment and income goes to people in local urban areas. As a result, the cut-back in federal share transfers costs from those outside urban port areas to those in urban port areas.

A further aspect of the equity effect concerns the national defense aspect of port usage. The Navy, in the course of normal operations, is a major user of many ports, most notably Hampton Roads and San Diego, although almost all ports have some military usage. The negotiations of user fees for Naval vessels would be of major concern because it may be argued that the channel depth is at least as important for military reasons as it is for civilian trade. Furthermore, those ports with substantial Navy usage will be able to regain large parts of their federal subsidies in the form of user charges on Naval ships, while those without military traffic will be forced to impose higher fees on ordinary commercial traffic.

CONCLUSIONS

The preceding case studies demonstrate that individual national transportation policies can have important and often overlooked spatial impacts, especially on urban centers. It is also apparent that the package of five national policies taken *together* produce conflicting or countervailing impacts on urban places. Airline deregulation *concentrates* certain economic activities in urban centers while the reduction of AMtrak subsidies *decentralizes* other kinds of activities. The adoption of user fees for maintenance of port facilities strengthens Gulf and West Coast ports while weakening East Coast ports and their dependent economies. Some policies such as airline or truck deregulation produce greater interpersonal equity in the pricing of transportation services while others such as port user charges may reduce interregional equity.

In general, it appears that the five national transportation policies discussed above work to increase interpersonal equity but at the cost of decentralization of economic activity, a weakening of central city economic bases, and increased regional inequities. In short, piecemeal policymaking directed to individuals or firms/enterprises can produce chaotic consequences for places. In evaluating transportation policies then, it is critical to examine both the people- and the place-oriented impacts.

REFERENCES

1. An exception is found in Norman J. Glickman, (ed). *The Urban Impacts of Federal Policies*. The Johns Hopkins University Press, Baltimore, 1980, especially the papers by Stephen H. Putman and David E. Boyce.
2. Executive Order 12074 issued by President Jimmy Carter, August 16, 1978, implemented by Office of Management and Budget Circular A-116.
3. One example of the effects of deregulation is the market for service within California, an unregulated market as considered in Annette M. LaMond, An Evaluation of Intrastate Airline Regulation in California. *Bell Journal of Economics* 7 (1976): 641-657.
4. This is roughly a 3.5 percent increase per year.
5. See Schmenner, R. W. Choosing New Industrial Capacity: On-Site Expansion, Branching and Relocation. *Quarterly Journal of Economics* 94 (1980): 103-119; and, Schmenner, R. W. The Location Decisions of Large Multiplant Companies. Joint Center for Urban Studies (MIT/Harvard, 1980).
6. See Goodman, A. C. Using Microdata to Evaluate the Fifty-Cent Gasoline Tax. manuscript, Johns Hopkins University, Baltimore, MD, (September 1979).
7. Moses, L. and Williamson, H. F., Jr., The Location of Economic Activity in Cities. *American Economic Review* (1967): 211-222, remains one of the best expositions on the relationships between economic activities and urban forces.

6
The Passage of the Civil Service Reform Act of 1978: A Dialogue with Alan K. Campbell

Miriam Ershkowitz* / *Public Management Executive Development Institute, Temple University, Philadelphia, Pennsylvania*

INTRODUCTION

The late Harold D. Lasswell, who with Daniel Lerner developed the concept of policy sciences thirty years ago [1], went on to develop the concept of the policy scientist [2]. This individual plays a key role in public policy-making and implementation at the highest levels of government. Lasswell's model of a policy scientist included an individual trained in political science, public administration or political economy who moves from the ranks of the professorate, to a deanship, and then experiences the

> *move from the care and feeding of a small band of intimate associates to the task of looking after a larger corps of knowledge scientists in relation to a wider social setting. As dean. . . the individual adapts to an environment whose nonscientific and nonscholarly components are especially important. [3]*

From this setting, in which the budding policy scientist plays the role of intermediary between the academic and non-academic environments, he or she goes on to a career in government as a full-time policy adviser which may lead to a post as a policy-maker.

Lasswell notes:

**Present affiliation*: Center for Public Service, Texas Tech University, Lubbock, Texas

> *Policy science careers are not only contextual and problem-oriented; they include a distinctive synthesis of techniques of every kind, whether they involve the gathering or processing of data or the information of theories or solutions. [4]*

Lasswell conceived of the policy scientist as an academically trained expert who uses his or her sophisticated technical knowledge to influence public policy. In achieving this aim, the policy scientist leaves the narrower career track at some point and moves into a broader senior policy making role. Henry Kissinger, Jerome Wiesner, Frank Press and Alan K. Campbell are some contemporary individuals whose career patterns and achievements appear to meet Lasswell's criteria. Although all of these individuals have been interviewed by the press and have written extensively about their own views of public policy-making with respect to specific issues, the public administration literature lacks any in-depth analysis of the important and unique role played by policy scientists. This dialogue with a policy scientist is an attempt to lay the data bases for future research on this important topic [5].

Alan K. Campbell

Alan K. Campbell was a teacher, researcher, dean, consultant, leader of professional organizations, and political activist prior to his selection by President Jimmy Carter to chair the U.S. Civil Service Commission and, following the passage of the Civil Service Reform Act, to direct the newly established Office of Personnel Management. Campbell was the chief architect of the Civil Service Reform Act of 1978, oversaw its passage by Congress and began its implementation during the latter part of Carter's term. Upon leaving Washington, Campbell joined as Executive Vice-President ARA Services, Inc., an international, three billion dollar, 100,000 employee, service firm headquartered in Philadelphia. In early June, 1982, Campbell agreed to tape some responses to questions put to him by this writer. The intent of the dialogue is to place Campbell's view of his experience within the context of the Lasswellian paradigm. This method enables the reader to judge the effectiveness of Lasswell's mode of analysis and lays the basis for data collection from other policy scientists, using a similar methodology.

CAMPBELL INTERVIEW

Ershkowitz:

Thank you for agreeing to be interviewed for *The Annals of Public Administration*. My first question centers on your goals when you came into office. I am particularly interested in your overall purpose with respect to civil service reform.

Campbell:

My major concern was with the lack of understanding and appreciation by the general public of the quality and commitment of career civil servants. I equally felt that in many ways the public servant was his own worst enemy. His resistance to demonstrating the quality of his work; resisting, for example, productivity measures and the like; his fear and opposition to a pay system based on quality of performance. These attitudes combined with the public's desire for a decrease in government's rolé made "bureaucrats" an easy target for politicians and editorial writers. I felt that it was important to try to make changes in the system which, first, would improve the performance in measurable ways of public servants, i.e. changes that would improve productivity and would make it possible for career public servants to rise higher in the ranks by not closing off the political appointed jobs, Assistant Secretary and Under Secretary, to career public servants. Thus, I believed the changes which the legislation would make possible would both improve the performance of government in perceptible ways and simultaneously open up higher level positions for career people.

Ershkowitz:

Did you find the environment in Washington conducive to carrying out such goals?

Campbell:

Not entirely. I found that the environment surrounding new programs is characterized by a rush to judgment and is a critical, rather than a supportive, environment. There is a rush to judgment on anything new that is tried in the public sector. Largely, that is because of the high visibility of government and the fact that those who are self-appointed observers of the situation are basically critics, and they are looking for quick answers. I had phone calls from the press two days after the legislation passed asking, "how's it going" and that makes it very difficult to get the time to make what I would consider fundamental changes. Many social programs have had the same problem. You may remember the early childhood education program, Head Start. All the early judgments indicated that it wasn't working. Five years later, when a more careful evaluation was made, it was found that it had actually done a lot of good for the kids who had been through it. They were doing much better in the 3rd, 4th and 5th grades because they had had the early childhood training. That's one aspect that one has to learn to live with because you're not going to change that. It is particularly difficult for machinery of government issues where there is no supporting constituency. I mean, when the early negative reports on the Head Start program came out, there was at least a small constituency, parents, some educators, arguing that judgments were being made too soon.

Related to this, of course, is the critical environment in which programs are implemented, because all of those who are charged with evaluating programs are primarily interested in finding things that are wrong, whether it is the GAO, the sub-committees on the Hill, or Inspectors General in the department, itself. All of them, in their job descriptions, are supposed to find things wrong. That is how they justify their existence. They, of course, find a ready market in the media for their reports. So the result of that is you have an almost exclusive attention to what is not working. These generalizations apply with particular force to machinery of government issues because you have no counterbalancing support groups, or, at any rate, no groups with any particular clout. In the case of subsidy programs, education or agricultural supports, to name but two, there is a constituency that will rally around machinery of government issues, whether it's personnel management or any other public management program, so machinery of government agencies tend on the whole to be relatively invisible. When they are visible, it's almost always because they are charged with doing something wrong or not doing something it is believed they should be doing.

Ershkowitz:

When you think back about the Congress in the pre-Carter years, the Carter years, and the Reagan years, do you believe that Congress has a commitment to a federal personnel policy as a coherent whole?

Campbell:

I don't think that if you speak of Congress as an institution, that it has a well thought-out policy; obviously, there is a body of statutes which add up to semi-coherent, but often contradictory, policies about personnel. There are some individual members who have a great interest in federal personnel simply because they have as constituents either current federal employees or retirees. Interestingly, from a political point of view, federal retirees are clearly more powerful on the Hill than current federal employees. I don't know why that is the case, but it is. I was talking to Budget Committee Chairman, Jones, just the other day about what might be possible in relation to entitlements for federal retirees, that is, the twice-a-year cost of living increase, and he made the point that he was always amazed at how much political strength federal retirees were able to show in Congress. But even those members that have retirees or current employees in their districts tend not to have any set views about what policy ought to be; instead, they listen to representatives of federal employees.

There are, in a very broad sense, two distinct groups of federal employees: those who are represented by the federal unions, who are primarily rank and file employees; their interests are the same as employees working for anybody, i.e., pay and fringes and, mainly, job security. Then there are the higher level federal managers, some of whom have personal ties to members of Congress based on the substance of their executive agency. These ties to members of Congress based on commonality of interest–agriculture, housing, defense, etc.–provide some protection to these managers. By and large, these managers would prefer that the boat not be "rocked." They obviously want to get pay increases, and they are also interested in job security, although that is seldom threatened, but their greater interest is in maintaining a calm atmosphere in which they can go about their business. They are conservatives. They will tend to oppose public management reforms and can sometimes use their congressional ties to thwart efforts for change.

Ershkowitz:

But are they, in fact, contradicted by the rank-and-file?

Campbell:

The rank-and-file will push harder in relationship to security issues, work rule issues and to some extent even on the pay side than the senior executives do; and, in fact, the kind of protections that the rank-and-file want–job security, automatic pay increases and promotions–are normally seen by the top federal executives as inconsistent with their managerial responsibilities, but that issue doesn't frequently come to a boil.

Ershkowitz:

Do you think it's the same in private corporations, or do you think it's more attenuated. The senior executives in the federal government don't really sit down and bargain the way Chrysler does, or GM does, or your own firm might. Is there a comparison there or not?

Campbell:

The major difference is that to the extent these matters become issues in the government, they are much more visible issues, and that there is no counterpart in private industry to Congress. The effort on the part of some students to use the board of directors as an analogy misses the point completely. Congress does not see its interest in supporting and providing assistance to the executive branch in the same way a board of directors sees its role as essentially being supportive of management. Congress does not see its role that way at all; rather, it sees its role as competitive with the Executive Branch. That creates a whole different environment.

Ershkowitz:

In that connection, are there further changes you would have liked Congress to make had you continued to head the Office of Personnel Management?

Campbell:

First, there was certainly a lot left to be done. The effectiveness of the legislation depends completely on its implementation. I did not, however, intend to stay as Director of OPM whether or not President Carter was reelected. What goodwill I possessed when I came to Washington had been exhausted by the many battles I had had in working for passage of the legislation. I felt it would be better if someone who was committed to what we were trying to accomplish would take over, a person who would not have to carry all the baggage I had collected over four years. I had worn out my welcome with some of the people on the Hill, particularly as a result of the fight over bonuses for senior executives. My relationships with the unions were not easy.

Ershkowitz:

There are so many ongoing evaluations of CSRA, some sponsored by OPM, some by GAO, and some by scholars. There is some criticism, as you well know. Can these evaluators be fair, given what has happened, not so much that Mr. Reagan became President, but that the ideology of the administration changed, and the ideology of the head of OPM changed very drastically from you and your thoughts and the people that you had around you? How do you view the negative evaluations that have been coming out?

Campbell:

Well, the easy thing to say would be that they are the result of the implementation of the CSRA not being done very well rather than being a criticism of the content of the act itself. I think that's too harsh a judgment even if someone committed to the philosophy of the CSRA was running the agency there would be problems because any major change is going to run into resistance, and we were already beginning to feel that resistance before I left office. For example, merit pay; apparently people don't like to be part of a system where they're judged on performance with that judgment affecting their pay. That criticism would be there regardless of who was administering the legislation, and it's going to take a while before performance appraisal systems get good enough and people get confidence in them. There will always be criticism of an incentive pay system because there will always be losers, and the losers are going to be noisier than the winners. The winners will see it as only appropriate that they should be rewarded while the losers are going to blame the system. In your question you mentioned evaluations also being done by academics. When academics analyze or evaluate programs, I think they tend to be looking for what is not working rather than what is working and in that sense have very much the same approach as the journalist or those institutional critics I've already mentioned.

Ershkowitz:

Did you think that before you went to Washington?

Campbell:

No, I did not. I've always known that academics try very hard to differentiate their products from their colleagues, their competitors, and that you can probably do that more dramatically by being negative rather than being positive. The result is that when you take the evaluations that are being done now of the CSRA, it's almost inherent in the very nature of the evaluation itself that the search is for what's not working, rather than what is. In that sense, to the extent that the academic community concerns itself about the viability of public programs, they tend, on the whole, to approach it in a way that will produce negative answers. These academicians take what is in the legislation, especially the preamble to the legislation, which often sets goals that are clearly unreachable (just by the very nature of the political process you have to overclaim, it's one of the most difficult things that I had to learn how to do) and then that becomes the standard against which it is judged in its implementation.

In relation to the work of getting the legislation passed, the academic community did rally around and were a lot of help. Properly mobilized, that community can have a lot of influence. There is just no question that the Senate committee's request to the academic community selecting about 100 top scholars for help in evaluating the legislation had an important impact on the committee's view of the legislation. On the whole, the responses to the committee were overwhelmingly supportive.

Ershkowitz:

Did your previous academic experience help you in coalescing support for the CSRA?

Campbell:

Yes. I think one has to take the public administration groups and the associations of state and local officials as one category, business another category, and labor as a third. In relation to the public interest groups, I had an advantage in that because of my own work in state and local government and the fact that at least three of the public interest groups were headed by Maxwell graduates, (the executive directors were Maxwell graduates), and I had done a lot of work with those organizations. I'd done research for them. I'd been a consultant to them; they were friends. I'd spoken at their conventions, and all the rest. When I went to the academic community, I had a similar head start. Since the public interest groups knew me, they gave me a hearing, were willing to publicly support an issue that wasn't all that important to them after all. Now, and I guess maybe I would separate those public interest groups from the public administration groups, that is, ASPA, NAPA and the Civil Service League. Again, I had an advantage with them in the same way that I had an advantage with the academic community and with the associations of state and local officials. But, again with the public administration groups, I got either wholehearted support as in the case of NAPA, or at least not open opposition as in the case of ASPA. Finally, the business groups, and particularly the Round Table, found supporting this very easy because what we were trying to do is absolutely consistent with what is seen as appropriate personnel management in the private sector. And for the business Round Table, it was a nice issue. It wasn't anything in which any of the members had a direct interest in the sense that they'd get more contracts or that they'd get tax advantages. But I was surprised and tremendously pleased by the amount of effort they were willing to put into it. You know they had people up on the Hill talking to Congressmen about it?

Ershkowitz:

Was that because you had been active in some of the government business associations?

Campbell:

Well, I had some ties, primarily with CED, which helped. But I think, too, that it kind of caught their imagination and was consistent with their view that somehow there was a relationship between this and trying, in general, to improve business and government relationships. You know we're in the middle of this whole controversy about adversary versus cooperative relationships, and this kind of fits in that general debate. The Chamber of Commerce was more difficult, primarily because of the labor relations part of the legislation. Title VII established, by statute, the collective bargaining system before it was based on an Executive Order. But this change was seen at least by the AFL-CIO as a major gain and by the Chamber of Commerce as a step they didn't necessarily want to take. They did send one of "Alerts" out to their members saying that they should oppose the Title VII of the CSRA. Throughout the process I had difficulty keeping the Chamber of Commerce on our side, and the Round Table tried to help in doing that, but the Chamber remained ambivalent through the whole process. By the way, the "Alert" that they sent out warning people about Title VII of the legislation called it "Son of Labor Law Reform."

Ershkowitz:

How cooperative was the Civil Service Commission (CSC) bureaucracy?

Campbell:

The usual demand made by a new group winning power is that they must have people who are responsive to the new administration, who are ideologically and philosophically in tune with the new administration. That's all rhetoric as far as I can see. They usually end up having great difficulty finding people to fill all the jobs they have to fill. In the first wave of enthusiasm after winning power, there is the problem of finding jobs for all of those campaign workers, and there has to be a rationalization for doing it, so you make the responsiveness charge. It's not at all based on reality. Now, the reality is that the career civil servants by and large are perfectly content to deal with policy changes and new directions that relate to basic overall general policies; that really does not bother very many of them. The problem comes in the smaller matters which relate to that general policy. Because of the civil servant's much greater in-depth knowledge of specific fields, he or she will resist what experience has taught him/her will not work.

Ershkowitz:

Would you say that leadership is a kind of a skill, an art?

Campbell:

Yes, I would. We all know that there are some people from outside government who go into government and do much better than others. I think the primary distinction is based on the ability of the outsider to come in and get enthusiastic support from the people who are already there. Those are the ones who make it. The real test is whether the person going in knows what he wants to do and takes the career people into his confidence. The ideology, I mean the professional ideology of the civil servant, is that he or she is there to serve political appointees.

Ershkowitz:

Would you say that was true in the CSC for you personally?

Campbell:

It was really a very difficult environment, but the amazing thing to me was once they became convinced that we were serious about making changes, and once I convinced them that it was in the interest of the career civil servants themselves, they very quickly accepted that I was there with good intentions. They rallied around, some more than others. Over time, I had put together a team made up almost exclusively of career people. It was, I felt, as good a group of people as one could find.

Ershkowitz:

Most of the people were there for a long, long time before you arrived?

Campbell:

That's right.

Ershkowitz:

You had no problem with that?

Campbell:

Took a while.

Ershkowitz:

How long would you say if you had to guess?

Campbell:

Well, if you look at it, there was a period of watchfulness on all sides. But I got there in April (March or April), and we had put together the Task Force to look at this system in June. It worked all summer and produced its reports by September. By December, we had drafted the legislation, except for the labor title. So we did that in nine months from the appointment of the Task Force. And I would say the rallying around of support began in mid-summer. All of them, critics and supporters alike, were convinced that nothing was really going to happen.

Ershkowitz:

That's true, everyone was convinced it would never pass.

Campbell:

That's right.

Ershkowitz:

Why was the task force composed almost solely of career bureaucrats?

Campbell:

That was intentional because they knew more about it than anybody else. There were many people in the career system who were critical of the CSC, including many personnel officers in the agencies. On the other hand, a substantial minority of them wanted to make personnel directors responsible to the CSC, rather than to the head of their own agency. They pushed me really hard about it. I would argue that if you were to have taken the next evolutionary step in public personnel management as it had developed in the public sector, that was a logical step. We fundamentally changed the evolutionary direction that public personnel management had been taking since the 1880's. Now I'm not sure it's going to work because that's running against a lot of time encrusted values and attitudes. I don't think people really understand how different has been the development of public and private sector personnel management. The similarities in things like job descriptions, performance evaluation, job content, and grading are misleading, but once you move beyond technique and examine the purpose of the system, they are really very different and we were, with the new legislation, clearly moving in the direction of the private sector. I did have some problems with some of my academic friends who assumed any private sector model was wrong automatically.

Ershkowitz:

Because they thought it had not worked in the private sector?

Campbell:

No, I think they would argue that the public sector is different, and that is a stronger argument. The fact is it relates to what I said earlier that you can't compare Congress to a board of directors. There are people in the public sector who have interests other than an effective and efficient career service. They believe the system should accomplish purposes other than carrying out in an efficient way the accomplishment of the goals that are assigned to an administrative agency. Protection against patronage, insistence on uniformity, no managerial discretion in personnel decision making were all part of the philosophy which increasingly dominated public personnel management.

Ershkowitz:

On a related issue, do you think decentralization can work?

Campbell:

First, the statute permits the central personnel agency to decentralize the personnel function, but does not require it. Our ideology was to decentralize as much as we could. By the way, there was resistance to the decentralization on the Hill. We had to back off from our original provision which would have required a great deal more decentralization than the legislation which was finally passed does require. In the optional delegation category, where some agencies took it, and others didn't, there turned out to be some problems with it. Whether we, in fact, reduced our cost very much by doing that and then monitoring it is an open question. That's about where we were when the administration changed. There has been a withdrawal of decentralization by the current administration; I'm not sure to what extent. I'm not close to it.

Ershkowitz:

So the bottom line, then, is it has not been given a fair test.

Campbell:

It's not been given a test at all, except for those many things we already did which just became accepted, and they are no longer issues. And that was a lot of "red tape" activities. The flow of paper was reduced. One of our major problems was that we would delegate to an agency, then they wouldn't delegate down any further, and so it would stop at the Secretary level. There wasn't anything we could do about that other than cajole, and we did a lot of cajoling and in some places did get it delegated further down.

Ershkowitz:

The agencies in my experience often had more regulations than the Federal Personnel Manual.

Campbell:

Yes, greater volume and greater detail, though remember those are huge agencies and you've got to have uniformity, they think. People love the protection of uniformity.

Ershkowitz:

I'm interested in the fact that you spent a lot of your personal energy, physical and mental energy, in terms of getting support for the bill. Is it your sense that a person can do that once in a life time? To put it another way, do you think that's something that a person can do repeatedly, or is it unique? If you were to go back—let's say Mr. Kennedy were to become President—and you were to go back as head of another agency, could you do it again for another piece of legislation?

Campbell:

Yes, I think you need some time to catch your breath, but I don't think that it necessarily is once in a lifetime. It depends on how old you are when you first do it, and the amount of physical energy one puts into it. I think it is not so much a product of the objective situation as it is of early toilet training. It really has to do with personality make-up. I think that you need people with that kind of personality make-up in order to get things done in the public sector. And I think that at least in my case one has to have a real commitment that what you're doing is important and will make a difference.

Ershkowitz:

Could you have done it without physically traveling so much? I don't know how many miles you logged.

Campbell:

I don't think that it would have been possible to have done it without getting out and talking directly to the people who are going to have an impact on whether it passed or not and talking with federal employees where the need was as much to be reassuring as it was to build enthusiastic support. There was a great deal of fear out there, and one needed to try to offset that. Now, simultaneously, I was out there building support; I must have met with 25 or 30 editorial boards across the country, and that was a very different sell than the sell I was making to the federal employees. I mean, as I would go from meeting to meeting the nature of what I emphasized would be quite different. And I talked to civic groups. It was difficult maintaining public visibility about what we were trying to do, and I was convinced that if we did not get it passed on that first wave of support and enthusiasm, we would fail. Editorial writers would quit writing editorials about it after awhile, how long can you remain excited about Civil Service issues? The same thing is true of our interest groups. How long could we have held the attention of the public interest groups and so forth? If we were not successful in getting it passed in the first wave, I was convinced that the critics would take over and we'd lose.

Ershkowitz:

On this issue of your personal reassurance to employees, that's interesting because that's a little bit like becoming a political figure. That kind of personal reassurance is what Murray Edelman says renders the masses quiescent [6]. In a sense, when people went out and saw that you were a reasonable human being, that helped your campaign to win support for CSRA. In this connection, do you think that only you could do this personally as opposed to sending a staff member?

Campbell:

Yes, I think that helped. I had to do a certain amount of it; obviously, we had to also send surrogates in many cases. I think it was important in part because a lot of what the rank and file employees were reading was negative. People tend to forget that when they see we had the *New York Times*' support, we had the *Chicago Tribune*, we had the *St. Louis Post Dispatch*. That might not have been nearly as important as the fact that the *Federal Times* was against us, that most of the newsletters of the unions were against us and they had to be answered. A lot of people didn't understand that the employees were being told a lot of negative and critical things that the general public didn't know anything about.

Ershkowitz:

Were there some Congressional personalities that were really either blocking you or extremely helpful to you?

Campbell:

It was a great advantage to us that during the hearings and the floor debate Mo Udall was acting chairman of the Post Office and Civil Service Committee. Mo had a deep interest in the legislation, and he had credibility with federal employees because he had developed and gotten passage of the pay comparability legislation in the 1960's. One of the interesting things many people don't know, even though I keep telling the story, is that I had not been in my new job as Chairman of the Commission for two weeks when I got a long letter from Mo saying how we'd gone much too far in protecting civil servants and that we had to get some flexibility in the system, and he sent me a set of articles from the *New Republic* and other journals making that point. I immediately answered saying, "You're absolutely right, and we are writing legislation to do something about it."

Ershkowitz:

So he helped, obviously; in a sense he was a positive force. That was a little bit of luck, right?

Campbell:

Yes, and you see the interesting thing about it is that Mo, who is in the liberal wing of the Democratic Party tied to labor, gave us support exactly where we needed it. Ed Derwinski, the minority leader on the Committee, supported the legislation, and he was then able to get John Rhodes, the House minority leader, not to oppose it. That wasn't easy, since Rhodes' natural inclination was to oppose it simply because it was "Carter Legislation." Rhodes at first saw no reason to help Carter achieve a legislative victory. The first time I met with him, he said, "Scotty, you still haven't convinced me that there's any reason why we should help this administration get a bill passed here." Derwinski was persistent, and after several meetings Rhodes agreed not to oppose. So, you know that the Derwinski and Udall combination was the key to our victory, and I take absolutely no credit for it; it sort of fell into our lap.

Ershkowitz:

It was serendipitous?

Campbell:

Yes.

Ershkowitz:

Why don't you talk about your working with the President?

Campbell:

Well, again, it's almost the same thing as with Udall. If the President had not made a decision to give a lot of time and effort to is, we would not have passed it that first year it was on the Hill, which was the summer of '78. I have a feeling that it would never have passed. The President met with literally dozens of members of Congress individually and in groups. He met with both House and Senate Committee members, sometimes with both Democratic and Republican members together, sometimes separately. I always had difficulty with the Democratic side because Derwinski kept calling it "his" legislation. The President's commitment was never better illustrated than in his preparation for the televised town meeting devoted to the reform which was needed in Washington. We prepared a rather large set of background papers for him. We sent him too much, but he took it all to Camp David for a weekend. The following Monday morning when I went to see him to discuss the legislation, he was in the little room off the oval office, and I was sitting in the oval office. He walked in with a smile, carrying all this stuff we had given him under his arm and said, "You know, Scotty, this stuff's really boring." I said, "You're absolutely right, Mr. President."

Ershkowitz:

Did you have a task force to help the legislation pass when it was on the floor?

Campbell:

Yes, we did; we met every night from seven to nine o'clock and went over what happened that day and over plans for the next. We would send the President a memo about what had happened. We would also request that he call particular Congressmen indicating the problem and suggest what he might say. And those memos went almost daily to the President throughout the summer of '78, until House passage in September.

Ershkowitz:

And did he make the calls?

Campbell:

Yes, no question about it. He also devoted a cabinet meeting to the legislation and directed the members of the Cabinet to call members on their committees. For example, one of the Congressmen, I forget who it was now, said he was never so surprised in his life to have gotten a call from Secretary Vance on behalf of CSR. You don't normally think of your Secretary of State doing that.

Ershkowitz:

Let me ask you just one last question. Why did you so strongly favor a single-headed agency versus a multi-headed agency, and do you think that OPM could ever achieve the status of OMB?

Campbell:

The last part of the question explains why I felt so strongly about having a single-headed agency. The central thrust of the legislation was to make the personnel function a management tool for the President in running the executive branch. Not only did the Commission stand in the way of that, the fact that it was a Commission was symbolic of its role as a protective screen from the President. The interest of the White House was seen as being political rather than management oriented. But it is my firm belief that as long as you had the Commission there, even with a management-oriented President, there would be an inherent reluctance on his part to use the personnel management tool. To the degree he wanted to use that tool, he turned not to the CSC but to OMB, and it was OMB which set employment ceilings, administered freezes, set pay increases and other crucial personnel functions. I would argue that more often than not, OMB gave the President wrong advice. Being the budget agency, it thought almost entirely in dollars rather than management terms. And the result was not only did the President turn to the wrong agency for advice, he got the wrong advice. And I wanted to change that, to get the President to see the Director of OPM as the management leader of his administration. Incidentally, that has not been accomplished.

ACKNOWLEDGMENTS

Temple University, Department of Political Science, underwrote the cost of transcription of the interview. Gisela Webbi was very helpful in the editing of the manuscript.

REFERENCES

1. Lasswell, H. D. *Pre-View of Policy Sciences*. American Elsevier Publishing Co., New York, 1981, p. XI.
2. *Pre-View* is the most succinct exposition of this concept.
3. *Pre-View*, p. 5.
4. *Pre-View*, p. 9.
5. Nothing in this article other than Dr. Campbell's direct quotations should be construed as representing his views. He neither agrees nor disagrees with the Lasswellian interpretation of his role in developing and working for passage of civil service reform.
6. Edelman, M. *The Symbolic Use of Politics*. University of Illinois Press, Urbana, IL, 1964.

Part II
Policy Analysis

Within specified policy frameworks, public managers set goals and objectives, develop and analyze program alternatives and select those alternatives that have greatest promise for the accomplishment of their goals. This area of management is termed "policy analysis."

Stuart S. Nagel describes policy analysis as a discipline and area of research. His article is a rather comprehensive definitive work. Morton A. Myers, of the U.S. General Accounting Office, reviews the manner by which analysis is conducted there and how it is intended to aid Congress. Sidney Katz and Joseph Papsidero discuss the role that policy analysis can play in improving long term health care; Ronald F. Kirby provides an analysis of government policies in urban transportation.

His article is followed by an examination of innovative personnel management practices at the Naval Weapons Center, China Lake by Lloyd C. Nigro and Ross Clayton. Lastly, E. J. Soderstrom and B. H. Bronfman explore recent contributions of policy analysis and evaluation as they pertain to energy and environmental policy.

When combined, these articles provide insight into the use of analysis in policy management.

7
Policy Analysis

Stuart S. Nagel / *Political Science Department, University of Illinois, Urbana, Illinois*

POLICY ANALYSIS

Policy analysis research can be defined as research that deals with choosing among alternative public policies those that will maximize or achieve a given set of goals under various constraints and conditions. That kind of research and training has increased substantially over the past ten years in social science programs and in government agencies. Indicators of that growth include new organizations, schools, journals, curricula, government job openings, academic job openings, book series, conferences, books, articles, scholarly papers, reports, courses, legislative provisions, and evaluative government agencies.[1]

GENERAL MATTERS

The general growth which began about 1971 had been stimulated by three sets of factors that might be referred to as pushing, enabling, and pulling factors. The pushing factors or social forces include the intense concern as of 1970 for policy problems relating to civil rights, poverty, Vietnam, women's liberation, and environmental protection. In the later 1970's the issues shifted to an increased concern for inflation, energy, productivity, and the Middle East, but still with considerable intensity. In order to be able to convert those pushing factors into meaningful policy analysis products, the social sciences had to develop better methods, interdisciplinary relations, data banks, and data processing equipment, which has occurred over the last 20 years. They constitute the enabling factors. Policy analysis

1. On the general nature of policy analysis research, see [1], [2], [3], [4], and [5].

has also been stimulated by the increased attractiveness or pull of government as a source of research funding and job opportunities, as well as the government's increased concern for getting more output out of reduced tax dollars.

Since the new development of a more systematic concern for policy analysis research in the early 1970's , a number of trends have occurred in that research. Policy analysis has four key elements to it, all of which have been undergoing change over the past 10 years. The elements are (1) the goals with which policy analysis is concerned, (2) the means for achieving those goals, (3) the methods for determining the effects of alternative means on goal-achievement, and (4) the policy-analysis profession which is applying those methods in relating means to goals. On the goals element, there is a trend toward taking goals as givens and attempting to determine what policies will maximize them, as contrasted to taking policies as givens and attempting to determine their effects. There is also an increase in concern for questioning the goals themselves. On the means element, there is an increasing concern for means that are politically and administratively feasible. There is also an increasing concern for drawing upon a greater variety of disciplines for suggesting alternative means or policies. On the methods element, changes have particularly occurred. They include building on business analysis, but increasingly recognizing the public sector differences. They also include an increased concern for valid methods, but ones that are simpler to apply and communicate. Methods changes also include an increased emphasis on pre-adoption modeling, rather than just post-adoption analysis. Finally, on the matter of the development of a public policy profession, there are numerous new institutions that relate to training, research, funding, publishing, associations, and placement opportunities. There is also increased utilization of the general methods and substance which the policy analysis profession has been developing.

It is the purpose of this paper to discuss those four sets of nine trends in policy analysis research. Those trends were selected because they are changes which have occurred over the last ten years with regard to policy analysis research that are especially important in actually or potentially affecting a great variety of policy analysis projects. Illustrative examples in this article will often be taken from the policy fields of crime, poverty, and the environment, but one can easily reason by analogy to other substantive policy problems. No quantitative data, such as a time series analysis, is presented in order to demonstrate these trends. They are based on an impressionalistic analysis of the contents of policy-relevant journals, books, conference papers, and other manifestations or policy-analysis research over the last ten years, as well as the specific examples cited under each trend.

In the context of this chapter, goals refer to the benefits that one is seeking to achieve and the costs that one is seeking to avoid in arriving at public policy decisions. Policies refer to the alternative government decisions that are available for possibly achieving given goals under various constraints and conditions. Methods refer to the procedures whereby one can determine the relations between alternative policies and given goals. Methods also refer to the procedures whereby one can conclude from given goals, available policies, and established or assumed relations what policy or combination of policies ought to be adopted.

Policy analysis differs from program evaluation mainly in its emphasis on:

1. Taking goals as givens and discussing how they can be best achieved, rather than taking policies as givens and discussing their effects.
2. Evaluating decisions before, rather than after they are reached.
3. Evaluating decisions across places and times, rather than as of a given place and time.

Evaluating a halfway house for released convicts in Champaign, Illinois, as of January, 1984 would be an example of a program evaluation. Evaluating halfway houses in general as a means of reducing crime among ex-convicts, as compared to release on parole or unconditional release, would be an example of policy analysis.

Policy analysis differs from policy formulation mainly in its emphasis on evaluating alternative policies, rather than describing how policies are formulated. Policy formulation is, however, quite relevant to policy analysis, since good policy analysis requires an awareness of how policies get adopted. Otherwise there is a tendency for policy analysts to recommend policies that have little political feasibility with regard to getting adopted. Likewise, program evaluation is also quite relevant to policy analysis, since evaluating individual programs often provides hypotheses, data, and explanations concerning the relations between policies and goals.

TRENDS THAT RELATE TO GOALS OR VALUES

Maximizing Given Goals

Policy analysts have traditionally taken policies as givens, and they then attempt to determine their effects, especially their effects on the intended goals. There is, however, a trend toward more taking of goals as givens and then attempting to determine what policies will maximize or optimize them. The effects or impact approach is more associated with program evaluation in psychology and sociology. The optimizing approach is more associated with economics and operations research. The crime reduction field provides a good example of both approaches. Impact research on crime reduction includes studies of the effects of the use of (1) halfway houses for released convicts, (2) diversion from traditional criminal procedure, in prosecuting arrested persons, and (3) women police in making arrests. Those research projects and others may produce interesting and possibly useful results. They do, however, tend to be rather piecemeal approaches to the problem of crime reduction.

On the other hand, if one begins with the goal of crime reduction, one may be stimulated to think of policies that might otherwise be missed, since they have not been adopted or tested for impact. Starting with the goal of crime reduction causes one to think in terms of decreasing the benefits of crime, increasing the costs of crime, and increasing the probability that those costs will be imposed. With that three-part breakdown, one can then proceed to more specific potential policies. Decreasing the benefits of crime may lead one to innovative ideas that relate to hardening the targets of criminal behavior, such as making business firms less vulnerable to robbery and embezzlement, and making individuals less vulnerable to assault. Decreasing the benefits of crime may also lead one to recognizing that the benefits of theft and assault may include peer group recognition from fellow gang members, which may stimulate ideas with regard to how peer group recognition might be changed. Changes could include working with gangs to channel their aggressive behavior in the direction of community improvement, as was done with some Chicago street gangs that were co-opted into the civil rights movement and the war on poverty in the 1960's.

Increasing the costs of crime tends to lead to two general types of suggestions. One type involves increasing the severity of the penalties for those who are convicted. Increased severity may have some deterrent effect on the general public, but it does not seem to be very effective on the criminals themselves. The second type of cost relates to opportunity costs with regard to available career opportunities that are lost as a result of being arrested or convicted for criminal behavior. Increasing those costs, however, may mean substantial social change so as to provide meaningful career opportunities to the poor and relatively uneducated people who are most likely to be involved in criminal behavior. Middle class people do not engage in mugging, largely because they have too much going for them that they would risk losing. Those who are muggers, however, may engage in such behavior because it is more profitable than the alternatives available, taking into consideration the benefits to be received from a successful crime, the costs that would be incurred from an unsuccessful crime, and the probability of success.

With regard to increasing the probability that the cost will be imposed, we are referring to increasing the probability of a criminal wrongdoer being arrested, convicted, and negatively sanctioned. To increase that probability, one could decrease the due process requirements under which police and prosecutors are supposed to operate. Doing so would allow for easier arrest on mere suspicion and easier conviction on the basis of hearsay or illegally obtained evidence. To increase that probability one could also seek to improve the professionalism of police and prosecutors, so they can operate more efficiently within the rules that are designed to protect the innocent from harrassment or conviction. This matter illustrates that policies come from a variety of sources including constitutional, legislative, administrative, partisan, popular, and philosophical sources.

Many policy problems involve the government seeking to encourage socially desired behavior. If one begins with the question of how can such a goal be maximized, then one tends to be channeled into discussing ways of decreasing the benefits and increasing the costs of undesirable behavior, with those benefits and the costs discounted by the probabilities of their occurring. That kind of approach of emphasizing broad incentives is increasingly occurring in policy analysis. It is part of the general trend toward thinking in terms of maximizing goals, rather than the more piecemeal approach of thinking in terms of the effects of one or more narrowly focused policies.[2]

Sensitivity to Social Values

Policy analysts are becoming more sensitive to social values, with more questioning of goals when evaluating alternative policies. There are now a number of research and training programs across the country that emphasize the analysis of goals, rather than or in addition to the achievement of goals, such as the programs at Notre Dame, Maryland, Georgetown, Duke, and the Hastings Institute. Goals can be analyzed through survey research to see to what extent they are supported, through relational analysis to determine how achieving them would affect higher values, or through philosophical analysis to determine how they fit into more general philosophical systems.

An example of the questioning of traditional policy analysis goals might be the recent symposium on "Social Values and Public Policy" developed by William Dunn of the University of Pittsburgh. At least one article in that symposium argues that the previous emphasis on economics-oriented goals of effectiveness, efficiency, and equity needs to be supplemented by the political science goals of public participation, predictability, and procedural due process. A concrete example might be the goals or criteria for judging the OEO Legal Services Program or its parts. In that context, effectiveness can be measured in terms of the number of units of successful service provided. Those units may be cases opened, cases won, or clients serviced in various fields of law at various levels of the judicial system. Efficiency can be measured in terms of the costs per unit of service. That kind of measure might be the total number of cases for the whole program divided by the total budget in a given year, or a similar measure for each office or individual legal services agency. Equity refers to how equally those units of service are distributed across the 50 states, between urban and rural areas, among poor people of different racial or ethnic groups, or among other classifications of potential recipients of the legal services. One could also measure how much equity the program produces by seeing the extent to which the program reduces the inequality of access to the legal system between poor people in general and people who are not poor.

In the Legal Services context and in a more general way, it may not be enough for the program to be effective, efficient, and equitable. One may be willing

---

2. On optimizing analysis, as contrasted to impact analysis, see [6] and [7]. Optimizing analysis tends to be associated with operations research and economics, as in [8], [9], and [10]. Impact analysis tends to be associated with political science and social psychology, as in [11], [12], and [13].

to sacrifice some achievement on those three goals in order to have a more desirable delivery process. In other words, how the legal services are provided may in itself be important, and not important just because one delivery system is more effective, efficient, or equitable than another. When one refers to a desirable administrative process, they tend to mean one or more of three things, namely (1) participation in the decision-making by the target group, the general public, relevant interest groups, or certain types of decision-makers whose involvement appeals to desires to use democratic procedures for achieving given goals, (2) a predictability in the decision-making by way of following objective criteria in making decisions, and (3) a procedural fairness in the decision-making that enables those who feel they have been unfairly treated to have (a) notice of rejection or wrongdoing, (b) a right to present evidence, (c) a right to confront one's accusers, (d) a decision-maker who is not also an accuser, and (e) an opportunity for at least one appeal.

In the context of the OEO Legal Services Program, the extent to which these three process-type goals are being achieved can be roughly measured by: (1) the extent to which representatives of the poor, the bar, and the general community participate in the general decision-making of each legal services agency and also the extent to which each agency establishes a client advisory group; (2) having objective family income criteria for determining who is eligible for free legal services, such that different decision-makers are less likely to arrive at different conclusions on eligibility or how the cases should be processed; and (3) having a procedure whereby people who are denied free legal services can object in at least an informal proceeding with a right to appeal to someone at a higher level in the program.[3]

TRENDS THAT RELATE TO POLICIES OR GOAL-ACHIEVING MEANS

Means That Are Politically and Administratively Feasible

Policy analysis is showing increasing sophistication with regard to considering political and administrative feasibility. In the past, policy analysis has often resulted in recommendations that did not adequately consider the likelihood of the recommendations being adopted by the political decision-makers, or what might happen when it came to implementing or administering the policy recommendations. The concern for political and administrative feasibility reflects the increasing role of political science and public administration in policy analysis.

The environmental policy field provides a good example of the need for considering political feasibility. Economists often recommend some form of pollution tax, discharge fee, or effluent charge in order to minimize pollution. Such a tax in

3. On social values in policy analysis, see [14], [15], [16], and [17].

the water pollution field might involve requiring all firms on a given river segment to be taxed in accordance with the amount of pollution generated by each firm. Before levying the tax, engineers could determine the total cost of keeping the river segment at a given quality level by building a downstream filtration plant. If that total cost is $10,000,000 a year and firm X contributes 5 percent of the pollution in the river segment, then it should pay 5 percent of the $10,000,000. Under such a system, each firm would have an incentive to reduce its pollution in order to reduce its assessment. If reducing its pollution is more expensive than the assessment, the firm can pay the assessment which will then be used to clean up the river segment before the pollutants damage downstream communities.

The main advantage of such a system is that it internalizes the cost of the external damage that business firms are doing by polluting rivers or other water systems. In the absence of such a system, the costs are absorbed by the general public in the form of waterborne diseases and general taxes, thereby losing the potential deterrent effect of a pollution tax. That economic advantage, however, is the main political disadvantage of such a system. By making the business firms so explicitly bear the costs of their expensive pollution, they would thereby be aroused to exert great efforts to prevent such legislation from being adopted. If the sky over Washington was supposedly dark with Lear jets when the Carter administration considered deregulating natural gas, one can imagine how black the sky would be if there were a serious proposal for a pollution tax which would affect virtually all industries, not just the natural gas industry. The political unfeasibility of such a solution to the pollution problem under present circumstances is illustrated by the fact that when Congress established the National Water Quality Commission, the Commission was prohibited from even investigating the pollution tax as an alternative to the regulatory anti-pollution system which is part of the 1972 water pollution legislation and the 1970 air pollution legislation.

What may therefore be needed as a politically feasible anti-pollution policy are more indirect and selective approaches. These include federal government subsidies to municipalities and tax rewards to business firms. In other words, legislation that subsidizes is generally more politically feasible than legislation that taxes, especially legislation that taxes business firms. Politically feasible anti-pollution policies also include ones that emphasize case-by-case litigation through the courts, rather than an expensive blanket requirement for a given industry. Thus, business interests do not seem to be as opposed to allowing rare or occasional damage suits, injunctions, or even fines as contrasted to prohibiting automobiles or cigarettes that exceed strict pollution thresholds. An optimum anti-pollution policy could therefore be defined as one that minimizes pollution within the political constraints of present adoptability.

The housing policy field provides a good example of the need for considering administrative feasibility. Economists in the late 1960's often recommended government programs designed to convert poor people from tenants into homeowners. In theory, the idea sounds fine. By becoming homeowners, poor people would have a greater stake in their dwelling units, and thereby take better care of them. They would be especially unlikely to burn them down as they were sometimes doing during the 1960's. By becoming homeowners, poor people might acquire a more positive self-image and a more favorable attitude toward society, thereby becoming better citizens in ways other than just taking better care of their homes.

Partly in reliance on that kind of economic analysis, the Nixon administration pushed a homeownership program for the poor that involved government-guaranteed mortgages with low payments per month comparable to what the Federal Housing Authority had for years been providing for middle class people. The program turned out to be a rather dismal failure. Homes were sold to poor people at inflated assessments, often as a result of sellers bribing government assessors to exaggerate the value of the homes in order to increase the government guarantee. Homes were also sold to poor people without adequately informing them of the expensive maintenance costs and defects in the plumbing, heating, or electrical systems. As a result, maintenance and repair costs were often too high for poor people to handle, and they used the mortgage payments for repairs, thereby incurring foreclosures. Some of these foreclosed houses exchanged hands more times than a repossessed used car, since houses are normally more durable than cars. The program was wracked with the same kind of supplier fraud as the medicaid and medicare programs with doctors, dentists, pharmacists, optometrists, nursing home owners, and others overcharging for services rendered and not rendered.

What may have been needed in designing the program is more concern for the effects of alternative administrative systems. Perhaps a big mistake of the Nixon homeownership program was that it involved government funding through the private-sector real-estate system. An alternative way of administering or delivering the program would be for salaried government employees to sell homes to the poor that the government would have previously obtained by tax foreclosures, government purchases, or government construction. Salaried government employees selling government-owned housing to poor people would have no incentive to inflate the assessed valuation of the property, or to withhold information on likely maintenance or repair costs. There is a possibility of government employees being bribed to sell defective housing to the poor in anticipation that it will be foreclosed at a profitable foreclosure, but that behavior is less likely to occur among salaried employees than among those who are lawfully receiving a commission for every house they sell or re-sell. An analogous government program is the Legal Services Corporation which consists of salaried government attorneys providing legal services to the poor. No attorney from the Legal Services Corporation nor its predecessor, the OEO Legal Services Agency, has been involved in any scandal related to overcharging the poor for actual or fictitious services. Such a system would be administratively feasible for selling houses or supplying medical services to the poor. The system might, however, not be politically feasible for medical services, given the fear of the American Medical Association that such a system would lead to socialized government medicine for the total population. There is no likelihood that the government is going to go into the real estate business for the total population, and thus having salaried government home finders for the poor might be politically feasible.[4]

Means Suggested by a Variety of Disciplines

Policy analysis is becoming increasingly interdisciplinary in its methods. All the social sciences have now developed courses, textbooks, journals, and other disciplinary communication media, which emphasize policy analysis methods from both a disciplinary and an interdisciplinary perspective. There is an increasing synthesis of statistical methodology and deductive mathematical models.

A good example of the need for a more interdisciplinary perspective on policy problems might be the negative income tax experiments conducted about 1970 in New Jersey and other states. The key policy variable was how much money should be given to welfare recipients. The policy was generally expressed in terms of percentage of needs. Welfare recipients were randomly assigned to categories whereby some received welfare payments at 50 percent of needs, others at 75 percent, and still others at 100 percent or 125 percent. The key goal variable or dependent variable was ambition to get a better job. Each group was given a pretest and a posttest with regard to both attitudes and behavior on the ambition variable. The general theory or hypothesis was that recipients receiving only a low percent of needs would have a low ambition level because of a low self-image and lack of adequate nutrition. Recipients receiving a high percent of needs would also have a low ambition level because they would have less incentive to get a better job since their needs are already being satisfied. The recipients in the middle theoretically would have a relatively high ambition level.

The experiment involved economists who were concerned with the monetary aspects of the study, and psychologists who were concerned with measuring ambition and the experimental methodology. That methodology was excellent in terms of randomization, experimental controls, and pretest-posttest measurement. The results, however, were generally disappointing in that virtually no differences were found in ambition levels regardless of the amount of welfare payments received within the range tried.

Perhaps, however, the right hypotheses or policy variables were not being tested. If political scientists and public administrators had been more involved, they might have pressed for testing the effects of alternative delivery systems. The main alternatives are the compulsory caseworker versus a check in the mail with

---

4. On political and administrative feasibility, see [18], [19], [20], [21], and [22]. On the administrative failure of the HUD program designed to provide home ownership for the poor, see [23].

no caseworker monitoring how the money is spent. One could argue that a caseworker stimulates ambition to get a better job by providing welfare recipients with useful job information and by harrassing them into wanting to get off welfare by obtaining a better job. On the other hand, one could argue that not having a caseworker stimulates ambition to get a better job because caseworkers may create a state of dependency and a lowered self-image that interferes with being ambitious. One could also talk about degree of monitoring control and argue that at low levels, ambition is down because there is no monitoring push; and at high levels, ambition is down because the monitoring becomes oppressive. Ambition would thus be at a peak between no monitoring and oppressive monitoring. The important thing is that none of this reasoning was tested because there was inadequate concern for the political science/public administration aspects of the problem of how to set up a welfare system. With a broader combination of disciplines, the $15,000,000 spent on the negative income tax experiments might have been more meaningfully spent.[5]

TRENDS THAT RELATE TO METHODS

Building on Business Analysis

Policy analysis research has been building on business analysis, but it is developing its own methodology. Policy analysis builds on the basic business principle of maximizing income minus expenses, although in public sector analysis, the words get converted to benefits minus costs. As with business analysis, policy analysis is often concerned with the ratio between benefits and costs, especially where the benefits and costs cannot be measured so as to be able to subtract the costs from the benefits as a criterion for judging alternative policies. Public sector agencies may, however, be more concerned with achieving a minimum benefits level than private firms are, and less concerned with exceeding a maximum costs level. Both policy and business analysis often rely on a concern for the extent to which the marginal or incremental costs can be justified by the incremental benefits of making changes in policies.

Possibly more important than the similarities between policy and business analysis are the differences which are being increasingly recognized. One difference is the greater difficulty in measuring costs and especially benefits in evaluating alternative public programs. For example, how well a private law firm is operating as compared to another can be somewhat easily determined by examining their respective profit-and-loss statements. The firm that has the bigger profit or dollar-income minus dollar-expenses is generally considered as doing better, especially if both firms are the same with regard to the number of people among whom the profits are to be divided. Evaluating local offices of the Legal Services Corporation

---

5. On interdisciplinary relations in policy analysis, see [17], [24], [25], and [26].

may, however, be quite different. Instead of dollar income, the benefits might be conceptualized in terms of the satisfaction scores of evaluation teams consisting of lawyers and representatives of the poor. That was done in 1970 as part of the Nixon administration's attempt to downgrade the more aggressive legal services offices. The evaluation teams, however, scored the more aggressive programs higher, because they exhibited more technical legal competence, and the evaluation teams were dominated by prominent lawyers who respected legal competence. If the teams had been dominated by representatives of the poor, the offices that were providing more routine case handling and less abstract appellate work might have been scored higher. This example indicates the ambiguity of measuring benefits in public sector programs, as contrasted to those in the private sector.

Another difference is the greater concern for equity considerations in public sector evaluations. That can be illustrated by many federal programs that involve giving grants to the states such as the anti-crime grants of the LEAA program. If each state were considered to be like a local branch office of a national business firm, the firm would feel little reluctance to close one or more of those local offices if they were not operating well, as judged by the firm's standards. Federal allocations, however, generally have to provide minimum amounts to each state regardless how inefficiently they might be or how efficient it might be to transfer those funds to other states. Those minimum allocations represent equity, rather than efficiency, considerations which business firms do not have to be as sensitive to.

Another difference is that alternative public policies are often judged not by how well they score on positive benefits analogous to income but rather how well they score on negative detriments like crime, pollution, disease, inflation, unemployment, and other negative social indicators. Dealing with criteria like those can create peculiar methodological problems. For example, which is more efficient, a city with 100 crimes and $50 in anti-crime expenditures, or a city with 200 crimes and $25 in anti-crime expenditures? One cannot compare the ratios of 100/$50 and 200/$25 the way one can compare benefit/cost ratios. Dividing 100 crimes by $50 to arrive at a 2 crimes/$1 ratio is meaningless. It implies that if we were to reduce our expenditures from $50 to $1, we would reduce crime from 100 crimes to only 2 crimes. How to answer the question meaningfully as to which city is more efficient may require a sophisticated time-series analysis to determine the marginal rate of return for an incremental dollar in each city. That kind of analysis may, however, be virtually impossible because there are so many uncontrollable variables that influence crime and anti-crime expenditures, and because crime may have more of an influence on expenditures than vice versa.

Still another difference between policy and business analysis is the more labor-intensive nature of public programs. That generates more complicated administrative psychology problems than one finds in the business world. For example, a typical business allocation problem may involve allocating between alternative raw materials or manufacturing processes, such as oil versus coal as an energy source. Such decisions can be based solely on the marginal rates of return of the alternative materials or processes. A typical public-sector allocation problem might involve allocating between two agencies, where one agency scores high on marginal rate of return because it has shown substantial improvement in recent years as a result of small increments in its budget. The second agency may be getting the same budget increments, but showing little improvement because it is already operating at a high level of efficiency. Rewarding the inefficient but improving agency may have a demoralizing effect on the efficient but non-improving agency. That does not occur when allocating between barrels of oil and tons of coal. The administrative psychology problem is even more illustrated by the common situation of cutting an agency's budget because it has been able to achieve a high desired level of output with less money than another less efficient agency. That kind of situation either encourages inefficiency in achieving output, or encourages wasteful spending at the end of budget periods.[6]

Using Valid But Simpler Methods

Policy analysis is developing increased precision in its methods, but at the same time is increasingly recognizing that simple methods may be all that is necessary for many policy problems. This is especially so since the typical policy problem asks which policy is best, not how much better it is than the second best policy, and not how all the policies compare with each other on an interval scale or even a rank-order scale.

The policy problem of how to provide counsel to the poor in civil cases might be a good example to illustrate how insights can be obtained even when relations are only expressed in terms of direction rather than magnitude or shape. Three competing alternatives for providing counsel to the poor in civil cases are (1) attorneys who volunteer to be on a list of free attorneys available when poor people have legal problems, (2) attorneys who are salaried by a government agency like the Legal Services Corporation for representing poor people, generally on a full-time basis, and (3) attorneys who represent poor people and are reimbursed for doing so by the government as part of a judicare system analogous to medicare. Four basic goals might be considered in comparing those three policy alternatives, namely being (a) inexpensive, (b) visible and accessible, (c) politically feasible, and providing (d) specialized competence plus reasonably aggressive representation.

For each goal, we can indicate the policy alternative that is relatively more positive meaning the alternative that most achieves the goal. On being inexpensive, the volunteer system gets a plus, with the salaried attorney and especially the judicare system getting relative minuses. On being visible and accessible, the salaried

6. On relations between business analysis and public policy analysis, see [27], [28], [29], and [30].

attorney gets a relative plus, with judicare and especially the volunteer attorney system getting relative minuses. On being politically feasible, both the volunteer and judicare systems create no substantial political problems, especially the volunteer system, and might thus be scored pluses, but the salaried attorney system has had political problems, which gives it a minus. The salaried attorney system, though, tends to result in specialized competence and more aggressive representation which gives it a plus, with minuses to the volunteer and judicare systems on that goal.

With that information, one can say that the volunteer and salaried systems seem to be tied with two pluses apiece. The volunteer system scores well on being inexpensive and politically feasible, whereas the salaried system scores well on being visible/accessible and being specialized/aggressive. To resolve that tie, those goals need relative weights. A conservative evaluator or policy-maker would probably place relatively more weight on being inexpensive and politically feasible, and would thus tend to favor a volunteer system. A liberal evaluator would place more weight on being visible/accessible and specialized/aggressive, and would thus tend to favor the government salaried system. Like most policy analysis, no conclusions can be reached without specifying the relative weights of the goals, even if there is agreement on what the goals are. The policy analyst, however, can clarify what policy is best in light of given goals and value weights. The important thing in this context is that insights can sometimes be obtained concerning what policy is best by working with relations between policies and goals that are just expressed in terms of relative direction without specifying the exact magnitude of the relations.

In measuring policies and goals, simple dichotomies or trichotomies can also often be meaningful and provide insights in choosing among alternative policies for achieving given goals. In deciding among alternative policies, the relative value of the goals to be achieved generally needs to be determined, but not their absolute value. This means that if three goals are being simultaneously considered, one does need to know how many times more valuable each goal is relative to the least valuable one, but seldom anything more complicated than that. Policy analysis can often work with small non-random samples because (1) the solutions are not so sensitive to sampling differences; (2) the sensitivity can be determined by partitioning the sample; (3) the samples are often purposively representative or cover a universe of legal jurisdictions; (4) the lack of place units can be partly offset by having many time points, as in a quasi-experimental policy-interrupted time-series; and (5) the lack of sample cases can be offset by in-depth analysis of the places studied.

Information on relations between policies and goals can sometimes be obtained easier and more meaningfully by surveying knowledgable people, deducing from known relations, or by making assumptions, rather than by using a complicated statistical regression analysis. Policy analysis generally does not need complete causal models, but only portions that deal with the causal relations between the goals sought and the policies available. The causal relations among other related variables are generally irrelevant for making policy decisions, although possibly relevant for a complete understanding of what accounts for variation on a dependent variable. Policy analysts in this context are like psychiatrists prescribing an anti-depressant drug to ward off suicide while the patient undergoes a spontaneous recovery. It is not necessary to know exactly why the anti-depressant drug has that effect, although it might be helpful to know. It is generally enough to know the extent to which it works, although pure physiological science is concerned with the effects of drugs on the body even if they have no practical significance. Likewise a policy analyst can recommend certain police procedures for reducing crime without knowing exactly why they work, and especially without knowing the relations between crime and everything else that relates to crime.

When determining an optimum policy level where doing too much or too little is undesirable, one can try many alternative numerical values for the policy until one arrives at the value that produces the lowest total costs, the highest total benefits, or the highest benefits minus costs depending on how the goal to be maximized is phrased. When determining an optimum mix in allocating scarce resources across activities or places, one can allocate the total budget in proportion to the non-linear regression coefficients, or in proportion to overall scores that have been assigned each place or activity with regard to their relative efficiency on various dimensions. Those general ideas for dealing with optimum level and mix problems enable one to arrive at the same solutions that might otherwise needlessly involve complicated calculus.[7]

Pre-Adoption Modeling

Policy analysis is pro-active or pre-adoption, rather than reactive or post-adoption. Too often the effects of an adopted policy cannot be meaningfully determined because of the lack of availability of a meaningful control group or experimental group or the lack of availability of before-data or after-data. Waiting for policies to be adopted before they are evaluated may also lead to harm being done before the unsatisfactory policies can be changed, and it can lead to inertia and vested interests which resist needed changes. As a result, there is an increasing trend toward using pre-adoption projections or deductive modeling, rather than just post-adoption before-and-after evaluation.

A good illustration of predictive modeling involves attempting to determine the effects on conviction rates of changing from 12-person juries to 6-person juries. At first glance, one might think an appropriate way to determine that relation would be simply to compare the conviction rates in a state that uses 12-person juries with those of a state that already uses 6-person juries. That approach is likely to be meaningless, however, because any difference we find in the convic-

---

7. On the simplicity of meaningful rational policy analysis, see [31], [32], and [33].

tion rates may be determined by other differences, such as the characteristics of the law, the people, or the cases in the two states or two sets of states, rather than by differences in their jury sizes.

As an alternative, one might suggest making before-and-after comparisons in a single state or set of states in order to control for the kinds of characteristics which do not generally change so much over short periods of time. If the conviction rate before was 64 percent with 12-person juries, the conviction rate afterwards with 6-person juries might be substantially lower rather than higher, although most criminal attorneys would predict a higher conviction rate with 6-person juries. The conviction rate might, however, fall by virtue of the fact that if defense attorneys predict that 6-person juries are more likely to convict, then they will be more likely to plea bargain their clients and to bring only their especially pro-defendant cases before the 6-person juries. Thus, the nature of the new cases, not the change in jury size, would cause at least a temporary drop in the conviction rate, and there would be no way to hold constant the type of cases heard by the new 6-person juries.

As an alternative that does not require that 6-person juries be adopted, one might suggest working with experimental juries, all of whom would hear exactly the same case. Half the juries would be 6-person juries, and half would be 12-person juries. This experimental analysis, however, has the big defect that it involves a sample of only one case, no matter how many juries are used. Whatever differences or nondifferences are found may be peculiar to that one case, such as being pro-prosecution, pro-defense, highly divisive, or simply unrealistic, and the results may thus not be generalizable. What is needed is about 100 different trial cases on audio or video tapes selected in such a way that 64 percent of them have resulted in unanimous convictions before 12-person juries and 36 percent in acquittals or hung juries, as tends to occur in real jury trials. It would, however, be too expensive a research design to obtain and play so many trials before both a large set of 12-person juries and a large set of 6-person juries, especially if the experiment lacks representative realism.

As an alternative to the cross-sectional, the before-and-after, and the simulation approaches, a deductive approach might be especially appropriate for trying to determine the impact of jury size on the probability of conviction. Such an approach involves deducing from what we know about 12-person juries to the behavior of 6-person juries. We know that 12-person juries convict at a .64 rate, and we know that individual jurors on 12-person juries vote to convict at a .677 rate. If jury decision-making conformed to an independent-probability model like coin-flipping with 12 coins, then jurors should vote to convict at a .964 rate, since .964 is the 12th root of .64. If jury decision-making conformed to a co-effects and reciprocal causation model like bowling with 12 pins, then jurors should vote to convict at a .640 rate, since jury decision-making would be averaging the individual juror propensities. Knowing that jurors actually vote to convict at a .677 rate tells us they are closer to the bowling model than the coin-flipping model. We can thus weigh the two models accordingly, and then consider what would happen if we only needed to take the 6th root of .64 rather than the 12th. Through that kind of deductive reasoning, one can conclude that going from a 12-person jury to a 6-person jury would result in going from a conviction rate of .64 to one of .66, assuming other variables remain constant. That kind of deductive reasoning was favorably referred to by the U.S. Supreme Court in recently deciding on the constitutionality of changing jury sizes from 12 to either 6 or 5.[8]

TRENDS THAT RELATE TO PUBLIC POLICY PROFESSION

New Professional Institutions

There is substantial growth occurring in policy analysis training programs, research centers, funding sources, publishing outlets, scholarly associations, government agencies, and other public affairs institutions.

Training programs associated with policy studies can be classified in various opposing categories, but it is quite possible to have programs that are in both categories. The categories include whether the program is emphasizing (1) graduate or undergraduate work, (2) training for government or teaching, (3) multiple disciplines or one discipline, (4) methodology or substance, (5) classroom or field experience, (6) university budget money or grants and contracts, (7) policy processes or evaluation of policy alternatives, (8) federal or state and local, (9) cross-national or national, and (10) questioning general societal goals or accepting them. Perhaps the most distinguishing characteristic of various programs relevant to the interests of political scientists is whether they emphasize a political science approach as in the Berkeley Graduate School of Public Affairs, an economics approach as in the Harvard Kennedy School, or a social-psychological approach as in Northwestern's Evaluation Research Program. Those diverse orientations are increasingly coming together in recognition that each has a unique and valuable emphasis to contribute. Political science emphasizes process and feasibility; economics emphasizes deduction and optimizing; and social psychology emphasizes experimentation and attitudes.

Non-governmental research centers in the policy studies field can be divided into those that are at universities (such as the Yale Institution for Social and Policy Studies or the UCLA Institute for Social Science Research) or those that are not at universities (such as Brookings, Abt Associates, Urban Institute, Mitre, and the American Enterprise Institute). Like training programs, research centers can also be classified in terms of quality, but that is much more difficult to do. There are some research findings that university research centers are good on general principles and creativity, but non-university centers are generally better on

---

8. On pre-adoption predictive models, see [34], [35], [36], and [37].

following detailed specifications and meeting time-constraints. What may be needed are more research centers that can draw upon academic creativity, while still being effective in responding to government requests for proposals.

Funding sources in the policy studies field include both government agencies and private funding sources. Leading government sources with a broad orientation include the National Science Foundation (especially units formerly associated with the Division of Applied Research and the Division of Policy Analysis) and the National Institute of Mental Health. Virtually every government agency has the authority to issue a purchase order to buy research products relevant to the interests of the agency, including Defense, Energy, HUD, HHS, Justice, USDA, Transportation, Commerce, Labor, Education, etc. Leading private sources with a broad orientation include the Ford Foundation (especially the National Affairs Division and the Committee on Public Policy), Rockefeller, and Russell Sage. Numerous private foundations have specialized interests in various policy problems, as indicated by the *Foundation Directory*.

On the matter of publishing outlets, there are a number of new journals in the field including *Policy Sciences, Public Interest, Policy Studies Journal, Policy Studies Review,* and *Public Policy Analysis and Management*. Disciplinary social science journals like the *American Political Science Review* are publishing more articles with a policy orientation than 10 years ago. A number of scholarly publishers have established a book series or a set of books that deals with policy studies. These include Lexington, Sage, Ballinger, Duxbury, Elsevier, Goodyear, Marcel Dekker, Pergamon, Praeger, St. Martin's, and Academic Press. Some of the better known series include the Sage Yearbooks in Politics and Public Policy, the Sage Policy Studies Review Annual, the Lexington-PSO series, and the Elsevier Policy Sciences Book Series.

There are now a number of new associations in the policy studies field. Like training programs and journals, they can be partly classified in terms of whether they are associated with political science, economics, or sociology-psychology. The Policy Studies Organization (founded in 1972) is especially associated with political science. The Association for Policy Analysis and Management (founded in 1979) is especially associated with economics, although so is the more mathematical Public Choice Society. The Evaluation Research Society (founded in 1977) especially represents psychology and sociology, and it is in the process of merging with the Evaluation Network and the Council for Applied Social Research. Psychologists and sociologists are also represented by units within the APA and ASA, namely the Society for the Psychological Study of Social Issues and the Society for the Study of Social Problems. There may be a need for more interaction and coordination across these associations in order to promote more interdisciplinary projects such as joint symposia, publications, research, convention panels, legislative testimony, and other activities.

As for placement opportunities, they include the training programs and research centers previously mentioned. For many academic fields, placement opportunities include private business. The counterpart in policy studies is mainly government agencies. They represent the heart of policy studies since there would be no government policies without government agencies. In other words, they not only represent an outlet for placing students and placing ideas, but also a reciprocal source of ideas relevant to improving the work of the training programs and research centers. Some government agencies, however, are now more actively involved in planning and analyzing alternative policies than are other agencies. Federal agencies are especially active, but state and local agencies are becoming more so with the passage of legislation requiring more systematic analysis and the need to stretch tighter budgets. Among federal agencies, the planning, analysis, and evaluation units at HUD, HHS, Labor, and Defense are generally well-regarded, along with executive office agencies like OMB and Domestic Council. In doing policy analysis, Congress has the help of the General Accounting Office, Congressional Budget Office, Office of Technology Assessment, and the Congressional Research Service.[9]

Increased Utilization

Systematic policy analysis is becoming increasingly used in government at the federal, state, and local levels and in the executive, legislative, and judicial branches. That utilization reflects an increased sensitivity among policy analysts to dealing with actual data, not just abstractions. At the same time, policy analysis is developing broad principles that cut across specific subject matters.

There are three general ways in which political and social science gets used in government. Those ways relate to general orientation, policy decisions, and administrative decisions. On the matter of general orientation, people in government are probably substantially influenced by the training they have received concerning governmental and social science matters in graduate school, college, high school, and elementary school. That kind of general background is to some extent shaped by academic political and social scientists who write textbooks for use in courses at all four of those levels, especially American government textbooks and to a lesser extent high school civics textbooks. The high school materials are generally written by people with backgrounds in schools of education rather than social science departments, but they often collaborate with social scientists and even more often draw upon the literature of political and social scientists.

When it comes to adopting general policies, research of a policy studies nature may be referred to, although not necessarily general social science research. For example, when Congress is contemplating the adoption of a new criminal sentencing system, the hearings do refer to research that has been done on discretionary sentencing versus non-discretionary sentencing, imprisonment versus community-based corrections, imprisonment versus capital punishment, or other such issues.

---

9. On the professional institutions of policy analysis research, see [38], [39], [40], and [41].

One can, however, argue that just because hearings or Justice Department reports refer to such research, does not mean the research changes the minds of policy-makers. That would be a rare occurrence. What the research probably tends to do is clarify and reinforce preconceived perceptions, values, and recommendations. For example, sentencing with less discretion for parole boards and judges is now widely accepted by policy-makers. Lessened discretion was previously being advocated in criminology research to provide greater deterrence and to reduce disparities. Conservative policy-makers tend to like the deterrence justification and liberal policy-makers tend to like the disparities-reduction justification. Thus if policy research can reinforce preconceived values, then it can serve a useful purpose in accelerating the adoption and respectability of new public policies. Policy research that cuts across places and time points can also have important theoretical significance in understanding the causal relations between policies and goals.

When it comes to making specific administrative decisions, neither policy studies nor social science is likely to be consulted. The relevant knowledge in those situations is factual knowledge specific to the situation and the job. If any kind of material is likely to be consulted, it would probably be some kind of in-house report. That report, however, may be prepared by a person with a graduate or undergraduate background in political science, public administration, or a related social science.

In order to facilitate communicating policy research to policy practitioners, the following devices might be helpful:

1. More research projects that involve academic-practitioner collaboration.
2. More journals that can communicate technical findings in nontechnical language to a wider audience.
3. More requirements in legislation that proposed programs be accompanied by environmental impact statements, technological assessment, and social assessment, and that ongoing programs be periodically evaluated.
4. More staff personnel associated with legislatures, administrative agencies, and courts whose function is to distill and translate scholarly research to make it more useable to busy policy-makers, and to inform the research community more clearly as to what is needed.
5. Interaction by way of relevant convention panels, conferences, think tanks, visiting appointments of academics to government agencies, visiting appointments of practitioners to academic programs, and inviting practitioners to participate in academic symposia.
6. Rewarding practitioners for presenting papers and publishing articles, and rewarding academics for doing consulting and other work with government agencies. Those reward systems are changing, although slowly.[10]

10. On research utilization, see [42], [43], [44], [45], and [46]. On differences between university research centers and non-university ones, see [47].

SOME CONCLUSIONS

One can conclude that there has been considerable growth in policy analysis research during the 1970's, particularly with regard to considerations that relate to optimizing methods, social values, political/administrative feasibility, interdisciplinary relations, business analysis, methodological simplicity, deductive modeling, professional institutions, and research utilization. What does the future seem to hold for policy analysis research?

The direction is likely to be toward more growth, or a stabilizing at a high level of academic and governmental activity. The growth is likely to continue since the causal forces responsible are still continuing. Those causal forces include (1) the public concern for public policy problems, (2) the improved ability of social science to deal with policy problems, and (3) the increased attractiveness of government as a social science employer and research sponsor including the increased government concern for trying to stretch its scarce resources. With regard to the more specific trends, they also seem to be still increasing, or stabilizing at a high level.

Those trends do seem to be desirable in enabling policy analysis to be more effective in arriving at policies that will maximize societal benefits minus societal costs. If that is an appropriate criterion for judging alternative policies, then it likewise seems to be an appropriate criterion for judging changes in policy analysis.

In general, policy analysis research seems to be thriving as a subdiscipline of various social sciences, as a discipline in itself, and as an interdiscipline drawing upon people, courses, and ideas from other disciplines. This is indeed an exciting time to be in the field of policy analysis in view of its growth and vitality.

REFERENCES

1. Dunn, W. *Public Policy Analysis: An Introduction*. Prentice-Hall, Englewood Cliffs, NJ, 1981.
2. MacRae, D., and Wilde, J. *Policy Analysis for Public Decisions*. Duxbury, Belmont, CA, 1979.
3. Nagel, S. *Policy Evaluation: Making Optimum Decisions*. Praeger, New York, 1981.
4. Stokey, E., and Zeckhauser, R. *A Primer for Policy Analysis*. Norton, New York, 1978.
5. White, M., Clayton, R., Myrtle, R., Siegel, G., and Rose, A. *Managing Public Systems: Analytic Techniques for Public Administration*. Duxbury, North Scituate, MA, 1980.
6. Nagel, S., and Neef, M. *Policy Analysis: In Social Science Research*. Sage, Beverly Hills, CA, 1980.
7. Palumbo, D., Fawcett, S., and Wright, P., (eds.). *Evaluating and Optimizing Public Policy*. Lexington-Heath, Lexington, MA, 1981.

8. Beltrami, E. *Models for Public Systems Analysis*. Academic, New York, 1977.
9. Gohagan, J. *Quantitative Analysis for Public Policy*. McGraw-Hill, New York, 1980.
10. Zeckhauser, R., and Schaefer, E. Public Policy and Normative Economic Theory. In Bauer, R., and Gergen, K. (eds.). *The Study of Policy Formation*. Free Press, New York, 1968.
11. Finsterbusch, K. *Understanding Social Impacts: Assessing the Effects of Public Projects*. Sage, Beverly Hills, CA, 1980.
12. Grumm, J., and Wasby, S. (eds.). *The Analysis of Policy Impact*. Lexington-Heath, Lexington, MA, 1981.
13. Langbein, L. *Discovering Whether Programs Work: A Guide to Statistical Methods for Program Evaluation*. Goodyear, Chicago, IL, 1980.
14. Dunn, W. (ed.). *Social Values and Public Policy in Theory*. Duke University Press, Durham, NC, 1982.
15. Fleishman, J., and Payne, B. *Ethical Dilemmas and the Education of Policymakers*. Hastings Center, Hastings, NY, 1981.
16. Gregg, P. (ed.). *Problems of Theory in Policy Analysis*. Lexington-Heath, Lexington, MA, 1976.
17. MacRae, D. Jr. *The Social Function of Social Science*. Yale University Press, New Haven, CT, 1976.
18. Huitt, R. Political Feasibility. In Ranney, A. (ed.). *Political Science and Public Policy*. Markham, Chicago, IL, 1968.
19. Majone, G. On the Notion of Political Feasibility. *European Journal of Political Research* 3 (1975):259-274.
20. Mazmanian, D., and Sabatier, P. (eds.). *Effective Policy Implementation*. Lexington-Heath, Lexington, MA, 1981.
21. Meltsner, A. Political Feasibility and Policy Analysis. *Public Administration Review* (1972):859-866.
22. Nagel, S. Political Science and Public Administration as Key Elements in Policy Analysis. In Nagel, S. (ed.). *Improving Policy Analysis*. Sage, Beverly Hills, CA, 1980.
23. McFarland, C. *Federal Government and Urban Problems: HUD Successes, Failures, and the Fate of Our Cities*. Westview, Denver, CO, 1978, 125-152.
24. Charlesworth, J. *Integration of the Social Sciences Through Policy Analysis*. American Academy of Political and Social Science, Philadelphia, PA, 1972.
25. Nagel, S. (ed.). *Policy Studies and the Social Sciences*. Lexington-Heath, Lexington, MA, 1975.
26. Webber, G., and McCall, G. *Social Scientists as Advocates: Views from the Applied Disciplines*. Sage, Beverly Hills, California, 1978.
27. Lewin, A., and Shakun, M. *Policy Sciences: Methodologies and Cases*. Pergamon, New York, 1976.
28. McKenna, C. *Quantitative Methods for Public Decision Making*. McGraw-Hill, New York, 1980.

29. Nagel, S. What is Efficiency in Policy Evaluation? in Palumbo, Dennis, (ed.). *Evaluating and Optimizing Public Policy*. Lexington-Heath, Lexington, MA, 1981.
30. Thompson, M. *Benefit-Cost Analysis for Program Evaluation*. Sage, Beverly Hills, CA, 1980.
31. Carley, M. *Rational Techniques in Policy Analysis*. Heinemann, London, England, 1980.
32. Hesse, R., and Woolsey, G. *Applied Management Science: A Quick and Dirty Approach*. Science Research Associates, Chicago, IL, 1980.
33. Nagel, S. "Simplifying Basic Methods." In Nagel, S. *Public Policy: Goals, Means, and Methods*. St. Martin's Press, New York, 1983.
34. Gass, S., and Sisson, R. *A Guide to Models in Governmental Planning and Operations*. Sauger, Bethesda, MD, 1974.
35. Greenberger, M. *Models in the Policy Process*. Russell Sage Foundation, New York, 1976.
36. Nagel, S. and Neef, M. Determining the Impact of Legal Policy Changes Before the Changes Occur. In Gardiner, J. (ed.). *Public Law and Public Policy*. Praeger, New York, 1977.
37. Wheelwright, S., and Makridakis, S. *Forecasting Methods for Management*. Wiley, New York, 1973.
38. Dror, Y. *Design for Policy Sciences*. American Elsevier, New York, 1971.
39. Horowitz, I., and Katz, J. *Social Science and Public Policy in the United States*. Praeger, New York, 1975.
40. Meltsner, A. Creating a Policy Analysis Profession." In Nagel, S. (ed.). *Improving Policy Analysis*. Sage, Beverly Hills, CA, 1980, 235-249.
41. Nagel, S. *The Policy Studies Handbook*. Lexington-Heath, Lexington, MA, 1980.
42. Horowitz, I. (ed.). *The Use and Abuse of Social Science*. Transaction, New Brunswick, NJ, 1971.
43. Lazarsfeld, P. (ed.). *The Uses of Sociology*. Basic Books, New York, 1967.
44. National Science Foundation. *Knowledge into Action: Improving the Nation's Use of the Social Sciences*. Government Printing Office, Washington, D.C., 1969.
45. Weiss, C. (ed.). *Using Social Research in Public Policy Making*. Lexington-Heath, Lexington, MA, 1977.
46. White, M. (ed.). *Management and Policy Science in American Government: Problems and Prospects*. Lexington-Heath, Lexington, MA, 1975.
47. Bernstein, I., and Freeman, H. *Academic and Entrepreneurial Research: The Consequences of Diversity in Federal Evaluation Studies*. Russell Sage Foundation, New York, 1975.

APPENDIX: SOME ASPECTS OF POLICY ANALYSIS RESEARCH DURING THE REAGAN ADMINISTRATION

The Reagan Administration took office as of January, 1981. This Appendix is being written as of February, 1982. We have thus had an opportunity to observe the Reagan Administration for one year. The following tentative conclusions might be drawn concerning the state of policy-analysis research as a result of that year:

1. More people are being fired from government jobs than are being hired. The general impression of people at the Office of Personnel Management, however, is that among those being hired, a preference has developed for hiring people with analytic skills. The primary criterion is substantive expertise relevant to the job opening. For example, when there is an opening in a given department (like Energy, Labor, HUD, etc.) at the management level, a general prerequisite is a knowledge of the subject matter. Between two people who are about equal in substantive knowledge, a preference will generally be given to the one who has analytic skills from a disciplinary or interdisciplinary program in policy analysis, program evaluation, or related methods.

2. Research money for social science has been greatly reduced, but the percentage available for policy-relevant projects may have increased. For example, the Program in Political Science within the National Science Foundation has been renamed the Program in Political and Policy Science, reflecting an increased concern for policy research relative to more abstract political science. Likewise the Division of Social Science has been renamed the Division of Social and Economic Science. The NSF Division of Policy Research and Analysis has had a budget increase, although it is primarily concerned with natural-science policy like energy, technology, environment, and biomedical, rather than social-science policy like poverty, crime, education, and economic regulation.

3. The academic marketplace is in bad shape but the Personnel Newsletter of the American Political Science Association shows plenty of jobs in the fields of policy studies and public administration. In the October, 1981, newsletter, 33 of the 124 listed schools advertised for positions which used public policy and/or public administration in their descriptions. The percentage of policy-relevant positions advertised in the personnel newsletters of sociology, economics, and the other social sciences also seems to be high and not decreasing.

4. The Reagan Administration is interested in showing that many government programs produce greater costs than benefits. In order to demonstrate that for numerous agencies, it is helpful for many federal employees to have an awareness of how one performs a cost/benefit analysis. As a result, there has been an increased demand for providing such training on the part of the OPM Management

Sciences Training Center. Cost/benefit analysis may become for the Reagan Administration what zero-based budgeting, management by objective, and planning-programming-budgeting was to previous administrations. Cost/benefit analysis is quite close to policy analysis. Thus increasing that kind of training among present and future federal employees will further add to the growth of policy analysis.

5. Specialized evaluation units within HHS, HUD, and other agencies have been greatly cut back since 1980. One should, however, take as a baseline the year 1970 when there were virtually no such agencies or a policy analysis field. One should also have a longer-term future horizon that thinks in terms of 1990, rather than just 1982. If one thinks in terms of 1970 to 1990, then government work is becoming more technical with an increasing demand for skills that relate to policy analysis.

6. There may be substantial increases in opportunities for policy analysts at the state and local levels. Those levels of government are taking on new responsibilities, and they are improving their technical competence.

7. The Reagan Administration has been accused of deciding policies on the basis of ideological criteria, rather than on the basis of systematic predictions of the consequences of alternative policies. There may, however, have been as much ideological decision-making in previous Democratic administrations, but with a different ideology.

8. There is nothing to indicate any lessening of the trends of policy analysis research with regard to maximizing given goals, sensitivity to social values, a concern for political and administrative feasibility, interdisciplinary relations, building on business analysis, methodological simplicity, pre-adoption predictive models, professional institutions, and research utilization. These developments, though, will have to taper off eventually as they become more established, although probably at a high level of activity.

8
Policy Analysis in Support of Congressional Oversight

Morton A. Myers / *United States General Accounting Office, Boston, Massachusetts*

To the ordinary citizen, the size and complexity of today's government is beyond comprehension, and as public awareness of "relative resource scarcity" deepens, public dissatisfaction with government operations grows. The issues that are being raised now within the context of public policymaking reflect a broad and deep concern with how government works. The public is asking government to:

- understand and reconcile the responsibilities, capabilities, limitations, and interrelationships of the different levels of government;
- understand and manage the network of interrelationships among the three branches of the Federal Government;
- assure that the electorate and its political leaders can guide, influence, control, and hold accountable–indeed, govern–the administrative structure and process of our government; and
- find appropriate means for assuring, on a continuing basis, that the administrative structure of government performs its assigned duties with maximum efficiency.

Issues such as these also suggest a strong desire for government to explain why we face a condition of "resource scarcity" when technological plentitude surrounds us. The nation has begun to appreciate that our national economy is not

An agency reorganization in 1983 significantly altered GAO's organizational structure. Its 11 operating divisions were consolidated into 4 operating and 3 functional divisions. An Office of Chief Economist was created and the responsibilities of PAD were assigned to various of the new entities.

now growing at past rates and that government does not have nearly unlimited resources with which to perform its functions. Having perceived the boundaries of effective national involvement, the public is questioning existing programs, curtailing the creation of new ones, and adjusting our living habits and our expectations of the future.

To a large extent, the nation's condition of constrained resources is blamed on public policy decisions made in the 1960s and 1970s. Yet accusations of government ineptitude are made without recognition that what government does is decided within the give and take of democratic policymaking. All of us, through our elected representatives, agreed that fundamental social, political, and environmental goals could be achieved by implementing broadly formulated legislation. But no one foresaw adequately the full implications of our costly involvement in Vietnam, or the subsequent problems of economic stagnation, energy shortages, rising unemployment, and the sad debacle of Watergate.

We can make some gains while having to adjust to fewer resources. We can conserve what we have on hand. And what better way to conserve our available resources than to improve Congress' ability to oversee government so that policies not only embody what is fair but also do not stray too far from what is practicable?

Underlying the political rhetoric we demand from the President and Congress—especially when the economy is not working well—is a real concern and a genuine quest for improved decisionmaking. For the present, that concern may mean fewer government activities and a smaller national budget, but eventually it also may mean programs that are more cogently chosen, more effectively designed, and more equitably applied.

The quest for improvement is diligently pursued by Congress, a point often overlooked by the analytic community. Too often, Congress' oversight functions are ignored by those seeking improvement. Perhaps this is because Congress is regarded as largely a critic and reviser of policies initiated by the executive, with no systematic way of overseeing how policies are carried out. One of the challenges for the policy analyst is not to be aloof of Congress' desire and need for analytic support.

Policy Analysis and Congressional Oversight

A brief review of the way policy analysis relates to the oversight function of Congress seems appropriate. Some see policy analysis as a method of identifying preferred policy alternatives, whose ". . .main concern is with the understanding and improvement of macro-control systems, especially public policy-making systems" [1]. This broad definition of policy analysis is a meaningful one as long as it acknowledges that making policy choices is an almost daily event in Congress. It is Congress' policymaking activity and its reliance on analytic support for that activity that provide analysts with the unique opportunity to add to the improvement and understanding of public policymaking.

Congress raises and deliberates many policy questions as it works to fulfill its oversight responsibilities. In essence, oversight pertains to Congress' efforts to learn about the past, present, and future. Thus, oversight encompasses all the techniques Congress uses to inform itself about the implementation, results, effectiveness, and adequacy of its legislative work and the nature and direction of pending and future initiatives. The information that is the product of oversight is vital to Congress in two respects: (1) it helps members reconcile the sometimes lofty goals expressed in legislation with the reality of government operations and actual results, and (2) it supplies Congress with the analyses it needs to identify the policy implications of new proposals and to weigh the strengths and weaknesses of those implications once they are revealed by the analytic process. It is this latter point that expresses this author's view of policy analysis as it applies to congressional oversight. In this environment, analysis supports the complete range of Congress' oversight activities: from the deliberation of various policy alternatives before making a decision to the assessment of results of programs that are already in place and operating [2].

The foregoing suggests two important points for the analyst concerned with congressional oversight to take into account. One, much of what is debated in the public policy arena is not decided on the basis of analytic studies. Many, probably most, of the issues Congress faces evoke strong likes and dislikes; hence, an individual congressman's values are likely to be a key factor in deciding policy. The analyst may not be able to model personal values, but neither should he or she ignore them—and above all, the analyst should be aware that, although analysis helps separate the wheat from the chaff, in public policymaking the aim of policy analysis is not to replace judgment, but to enhance it.

Two, choosing the best policy from those available suggests the little leeway analysts have for making uninformed policy decisions. Scarcity dictates that policies be chosen with care, lest they fall too short of satisfying the criteria of efficiency, effectiveness, and equity. In a very real sense, analysts cannot afford to do otherwise, for they haven't the luxury of submitting policy alternatives to national tests of trial and error.

Care and conservation also demand that analytic information be organized in ways that will facilitate congressional decisionmaking. The analyst does this by activating the analytic process—identifying objectives and criteria, examining past experience, developing alternatives, devising ways of estimating and consequences of choosing particular alternatives, and comparing the benefits and costs associated with each alternative. This is the more technical aspect of policy analysis, and it is a crucial one because Congress is inundated with competing demands for its time and attention. When the analytic process is combined with an appreciation of the role of political judgment and with an awareness that resource constraints necessitate improved oversight, then analysis becomes a valuable tool for making informed policy decisions.

Congress' Demand for Policy Analysis

Congress' contemporary reliance on policy analysis springs from its responsibility to oversee the myriad administrative agencies that implement the legislation (one form of policy instrument) Congress enacts. Both theory and practice emphasize the role of Congress in holding public officials accountable for their procedural and policy decisions. In theory, it is quite clear that national policy goals are set by statutes. Even as administrators of the executive branch exercise quasi-legislative and quasi-judicial powers, public policy goals are to be served by the boundaries Congress places on those powers as set forth in legislation. In practice, the problem of accountability remains.

Since the beginning of our federalist government, Congress has asserted its right to ensure that its policies are carried out in accordance with its wishes. In 1792, it conducted its first investigation, a power later upheld by the Supreme Court as an appropriate auxiliary to legislative oversight. Congress' investigations encompass inquiries concerning the implementation of existing laws as well as proposals for new ones.

The most obvious techniques of congressional oversight of policies already in effect are the authorization and appropriations processes. These permit Congress to determine the goals government pursues, how government is organized, the amount of money agencies may spend, and the specific purposes for which the money is spent. When an agency's requests for new authority or funds come before Congress, the various authorization and appropriations subcommittees in each House use the occasion to review agencies' past behavior and future plans, and to offer whatever criticisms the committee members think appropriate. One embodiment of the congressional effort to maintain oversight of financial matters was its passage of the 1921 Budget and Accounting Act. The Act created the General Accounting Office, a legislative support agency "independent of the executive departments to review, control, and audit Government accounts, and report on operations throughout the Federal Government." As Congress' oversight responsibilities have increased in size and complexity, GAO's audit and accounting functions have also grown to include program evaluation and policy analyses for congressional use.

Besides the foregoing, Congress can, and does, oversee policy in various other ways: through its right to confirm and impeach and by exercising its representative function. From the latter it receives feedback from constituents on the results and effectiveness of government. Most of these techniques, however, are applied after-the-fact, and are viewed as monitoring activities. This is called the "post facto and discrete" model of oversight: "Those. . . who have a post facto view of oversight see it (1) as a review or investigation of past actions; and (2) as focused upon rather discrete acts or specific instances of wrongdoing, inefficiency, or failure to act as Congress mandated" [3].

But increasingly, Congress has had to think about oversight as something greater in scope than merely requiring administrators to explain their actions. Given our resource limitations, a reactive approach to policymaking is not sufficient. In recent years, Congress has sought to improve its ability to oversee by expanding and increasing the sophistication of its analytic support base. Some see these efforts as Congress' attempt to make sure that policymaking is not the exclusive prerogative of the President and the executive branch. It is suggested that competition with the executive is not a "wrong" motive, but rather a natural, and probably inescapable, outcome of our system of checks and balances. Sometimes policy analysts may become impatient with Congress' decentralized and essentially parochial character, finding its committee system vexingly fragmented, with no promise of reward for those who undertake analytic studies for Congress' edification. Instead of being stymied by Congress' political nature, analysts should consider that body a real-life laboratory for applying everything they know.

During the 1970s, Congress strengthened its role in the federal budgetmaking process, increased the number of its professional staff, equipped itself with two new analytic support agencies—the Office of Technology Assessment and the Congressional Budget Office—and directed its committees to engage in or make use of analytic work. Other changes were brought about by the passage of the Legislative Reorganization Act of 1970, the Congressional Budget and Impoundment Control Act of 1974, and changes to the rules of each House [4].

These two Acts went far in supplying Congress with the analytic assistance it needed to conduct effective oversight. The 1970 legislation authorized GAO to review and analyze the results of government programs, including the making of cost-benefit studies, on its own initiative or at the behest of either House or a congressional committee. The 1974 Congressional Budget Act went further. By amending the earlier legislation, it enlarged GAO's program evaluation responsibilities and directed it to identify committees' needs for fiscal, budgetary, and program-related information.

GAO's Response to Congressional Demands for Analytic Support

GAO organized the Program Analysis Division as its lead division for carrying out the directives of the 1974 Act. PAD is one of GAO's 11 operating divisions, each of which is responsible for auditing the operation and results of a specific number of federal agencies and programs. PAD's mission, however, differs from the others; it is defined primarily by the professional skills to be employed and the nature of the analysis, rather than the issues and programs to be reviewed. Specifically, PAD's mission is to:

- Prepare analyses having a broad perspective, particularly where economic factors are important and major program implications are involved.
- Provide leadership and assistance in focusing GAO's analytical resources to support congressional decisionmaking processes for such major program issues.
- Improve the usefulness of and access to federal fiscal, budgetary, and program-related information for Congress.
- Provide specific leadership, direction, and management of GAO work in science and technology, program and budget information for congressional use, and economic analysis of alternative program approaches.

To fulfill this mission, PAD has assembled a staff with a wide range of disciplines (mathematics, economics, sociology, political science, philosophy, public and business administration. and accounting, to name a few), whose sphere of interest and activity extends beyond evaluating the accomplishments of ongoing or completed federal programs. A short discussion of some of GAO's work illustrates how it helps Congress to perceive oversight as "...preventive as well as corrective" [5].

PAD is investigating alternative ways government can accomplish economic policy. Virtually any type of policy analysis entails comparing alternatives. Decisionmakers must know the trade-offs among competing alternatives in order to decide the most appropriate mix of policy instruments. PAD has been particularly interested in the merits and shortcomings of three economic policy instruments—user charges, credit assistance, and direct subsidies [6].

Another subject of study GAO pursues is tax policy. Lately, novel demands have been placed on the federal tax system. Policy-makers now turn to taxes not only to raise revenues for public purposes—their historic role—but also to serve nonrevenue objectives. A sizable fraction of federal spending is carried out today by means of tax expenditures, selective tax reductions for special groups and for people engaged in special activities (e.g., the tax deductions for medical expenses). Using taxes to achieve regulatory objectives has also been discussed by Congress, though few such "tax penalties" have been enacted. In 1978, President Carter proposed an anti-inflation policy that would use the tax system to encourage employees to moderate their wage demands.

The task that falls on those who design federal tax policy is to reconcile and, if possible, harmonize the conflicting demands that are made on our tax system. Doing so requires careful analysis of the effects of various policy instruments and forecasts of how those effects would change if the instruments were changed. The studies PAD is planning, or has underway, are directed at making the federal tax system fairer and more efficient [7]. GAO's objective is that PAD's tax policy analyses will contribute to the quality of congressional oversight.

PAD is also GAO's responsible unit for studies of science and technology. Since virtually all national policy instruments contain science and technology components, Congress has strong requirements for analytic support in this area. PAD's analysis of future trends is that two broad sets of conflicting pressures will increasingly influence the outlook for U.S. science and technology. The first is the pressure for more and better science and technology, driven by the international economic situation, the condition of our domestic economy, and the need to resolve major technology-based social problems (energy and materials shortages and environmental pollution, for example). International competition is likely to grow in the next decade and the lead in science and technology enjoyed by the United States during most of the post-war period will almost certainly continue to erode. As other countries achieve a rough parity with the United States in economic and scientific performance, the pressure will grow to improve U.S. performance An important part of improving that performance will be increasing the contribution science and technology can make to the economy.

Second is the growing pressure for public accountability for science and technology. This demand takes the form of financial accountability–making sure public funds are spent prudently and in accordance with public priorities–and a broader, more social form–making sure that the consequences of technology, regardless of who pays for it, serves the public interest.

PAD concentrates on the need for Congress to recognize that science and technology are issues that cut across nearly all federal programs. To focus awareness on this point, PAD's studies address: (1) the organization and process of science and technology policymaking, (2) the development and maintenance of the U.S. science and technology resource base, (3) the federal role in fostering effective working relationships within the science and technology system, and (4) the application and diffusion of science and technology [8].

As mentioned earlier, the budget process is one of the key methods of congressional oversight and, ultimately, policymaking. Under Title VIII of the 1974 Congressional Budget Act, GAO is directed to improve the fiscal, budgetary, and program-related information available to Congress. PAD is closely involved in carrying out these directives. Before the Act's passage, the House and Senate had operated with a decentralized appropriations process that gave no overall control of government funding to any single legislative unit and provided no effective vehicle for debating and deciding on overall fiscal policy. Unlike the executive branch, where the Office of Management and Budget had final overall control of federal spending, Congress dispersed the federal budget proposals to a variety of committees and subcommittees–each power centers unto themselves.

The 1974 Act was Congress' attempt at creating a system of establishing budget ceilings and spending priorities, and to relate both to government revenues. Congress must now treat spending and tax measures both collectively and individually. In doing so, it confronts such fiscal policy issues as the effect of the budget on inflation, unemployment, and economic growth.

The Budget Act also requires members for the first time to make choices and thereby set priorities. For example, for health programs, the choices are to increase revenues through higher taxes, accept a larger deficit, or balance the addition by cutting other programs. Much of the work of PAD's budget group is to keep Congress supplied with certain of the analyses it needs to operate the congressional budget process specified in the Act and to recommend ways the process can be improved over time [9].

Assuring the Use of Policy Analysis as a Tool for Congressional Oversight

A chief problem facing the analytic community is to assure that its efforts are effective–that they are used to formulate new or "good" policies or to improve existing ones. Undoubtedly, most analysts hope for more than just an ivory tower exercise. Like other analytic organizations, GAO faces the fact that policy implementation does not automatically follow once a policy alternative has been suggested—or even accepted by Congress. (Analysts also know that their work is rarely the last word on the subject.)

It pays us, as GAO analysts, to monitor the results of our work. Having some idea of our effectiveness helps us convince Congress to rely on analysis to perform its oversight function. Moreover, GAO is interested in internal accountability for the same reasons that any public agency is interested in it. GAO spends tax dollars to do its work. But in its case, of course, accountability is even more important: GAO is responsible for helping Congress hold other federal agencies accountable for *their* work.

GAO has paid a lot of attention to assuring the utility of its work. Admittedly, the system is the product of trial and error. It has evolved, and is still evolving, as GAO has responded to Congress' changing and growing demands for analytic work. However, to a large extent, we practice what we preach. We have had to put into place many of the elements of long-range planning, management accountability, and relating programs to explicit objectives that we recommend to agencies of the executive branch. The result is that GAO's analyses are subject to many internal tests of effectiveness before they are delivered to Capitol Hill.

Most of GAO's work is planned and organized along functional lines, or issue areas. PAD, for example, is the lead division for science and technology, congressional budget and program information, and economic analysis of alternative approaches. GAO's rationale for planning by issue area is twofold. First, it allows jobs to address an immediate subject as well as make a contribution to broad issues of importance to Congress and to the country. Second, it is a practical framework for GAO managers to judge the worth and relevance of new jobs and to allocate staff efficiently. New problems or subject areas needing analytic attention are developed as lines-of-effort within each issue area. The lines-of-effort coalesce around topics of concern to Congress and subject-matter experts within and outside government, past neglect of the subject or an absence of cohesive studies devoted to it, and special GAO expertise that indicates we could make a significant contribution.

The focus of the issue-area approach is our program plan, a comprehensive guide that maps the substantive problems the issue area proposes to study and the specific lines-of-effort needed to conduct the studies. The plan is an evolving document; each revision describes the accomplishments and resource use of previous lines-of-effort. An essential ingredient is congressional input.

Part of each program plan is an "accountability model," a statement of the progress achieved against each goal of the prior plan. It describes how current assignments conform to the lines-of-effort, the type of product intended (such as a report, staff study, letter, or briefing), the concrete results expected, and the work remaining to be done. Since a single job may touch on more than one division's issue area, the model also lists projects requiring interdivisional collaboration.

Preparing the program plan is a serious endeavor, as it constitutes one of GAO's basic methods for holding its staff accountable. Once every 18 months, each division meets with the GAO Program Planning Committee (PPC), a top management group that reviews the plans to ensure that proposed work is consistent with overall GAO policy and strategy. The PPC assesses the plans from the point of view of whether there has been a change in the context of the issue area, whether events indicate new or additional congressional needs, and whether or not GAO resources should be reallocated.

At the division level, individual assignments flowing from the lines-of-effort are controlled and monitored through GAO's project planning and management approach (PPMA). This system requires work to pass through five consecutive phases: proposal, scoping, planning, implementation, and evaluation. The document that facilitates PPMA is the assignment plan. As formulated by the end of the planning phase, it breaks down major assignment issues into discrete segments, analyzes each segment in terms of the tasks necessary to develop it, and identifies the number and disciplines of staff needed to carry out the assignment. The assignment plan serves as our tool for job control and revision and it provides the standards against which job results and staff performance are measured.

Congress' growing need for analytic studies and comments on proposed legislation has also put pressure on GAO to increase the sophistication of its methodological and research capabilities. PAD's approach to assessing the use of appropriate methodologies is to substantiate the assumptions underlying its assignments and to delineate the alternatives it considered when selecting the strategy to accomplish the assignment's objectives. PAD's requirement for methodological soundness is not easy to avoid. Published GAO reports contain a "scope, objectives, and methodology" section that explains precisely what was done, why it was done, and why the data presented constitute a valid basis for conclusions and recommendations.

In addition to a rigorous in-house review, PAD also takes great care in making sure its studies receive a thorough external review before it deems them ready for Congress' consideration. For many projects, PAD engages expert consultants to evaluate its work, especially when the project presents a new approach to solving a problem or if it addresses a sensitive issue that might generate heated debate. Typically, PAD also submits draft reports to executive agencies for comment—both for their substantive review and as an opportunity for them to refute or concur with GAO's findings, should those findings affect agency operations in some way. GAO seeks the opinions of outside reviewers, thereby securing invaluable "tests" of its work, which enhances the credibility of the recommendations GAO makes to Congress.

For the Future: A Broader View

These, then, are the major systems GAO has put into place to assure that its analytic capability is effective and useful to Congress. However, the congressional decisionmaking world is not, as much as GAO would like it to be, a place of well-defined problems, discernible goals, and clear measures of outputs. Applying analysis as an aid for oversight in such circumstances is tricky; devising valid and clear methods of tracing the effectiveness of analytic studies is even trickier. It is a rare decisionmaker—especially one subject to the vagaries of politics—who can define precisely the role of any one factor in his decision process. Indeed, where analytic assistance plays a key role, the decisionmaker often is not overtly aware of it, because the results of the study may be filtered and fed to the decisionmaker through a variety of sources such as staff, other members of Congress, lobbyists, the media, and constituents. In addition, of course, analysis is only one of the factors affecting decisionmaking. It competes with a host of far less rigorously defined factors that compose the drama of national policy information.

Thus, one can never have precise measures of the weight Congress attaches to GAO's work as a resource for informed oversight. Given what little analysts know about the process of public policymaking, GAO analysts are not alone in this uncertainty. It should be noted, however, that Congress asked PAD to testify 17 times during fiscal year 1980. PAD's testimonies ranged from such specifics as the states' ability to regulate the insurance business and the need for government to achieve greater equities in Federal land payment programs to broader issues, such as comments on proposals for congressional oversight reform and long-term planning for national science policy.

The growth of Congress' oversight function and its reliance on analysis has been a political reaction to many stimuli, not the least of which is the public's demand for more accountability in government (or more bluntly, *proof* that government programs accomplish something). A logical next step, and what is seen as the future challenge for analysts, is to foster a prescriptive and proactive approach to congressional oversight. Such an orientation demands an understanding and an appreciation of the political environment and the necessity of applying analytic techniques to the study of the public policymaking process itself. Extending our analytic perspective in this way will help Congress use scarce resources more effectively and enhance the quality of its decisionmaking.

The policy analysis community needs to narrow the gap between government's ability to construct public policy instruments and the paucity of knowledge about how to design and operate systems that permit the rational use of such instruments [10]. A natural outgrowth of assisting Congress with its oversight responsibilities is to move in this direction.

In the late 1970s, members of both the House and the Senate sponsored sunrise and sunset legislation as a means of strengthening congressional oversight [11]. GAO supported these reforms, believing they would help Congress acquire knowledge about program operations and results, and interpret such knowledge so it could judge the effectiveness of existing and proposed laws. Although Congress has not taken final action on these proposals, GAO continues to advise on the subject of oversight reform, which it views as a vehicle for promoting the understanding and improvement of public policymaking. In a recent report to Congress, GAO said:

Success will depend upon the commitment of the leaders and participants to the goals of the reform. New laws can only create mechanisms and procedures which will permit this commitment to be effectively translated into action. The Congress, the Executive, and ultimately the nation must:

1. *think, debate, and act with a long-range perspective because the full implication of policies often is not felt for several years or decades;*
2. *focus more of their analyses, debates, and actions on broad policies and groups of interrelated programs;*
3. *try harder to analyze the probable effects of policy changes before they are implemented;*
4. *be more specific and realistic when setting goals and expectations for policies, programs, and administrative reforms;*
5. *grant administrators the authority and resources needed to render congressional goals and expectations plausible, or to revise them to fit available resources;*
6. *establish evaluating and reporting procedures that compel administrators to produce clear statements about the performance of the programs and activities for which they are accountable; and*
7. *act promptly to make changes when needed [12].*

There have been few times as opportune as the present for taking stock of the limits and capabilities of our public policymaking process. Analysts can do much to make the administration of government more adaptable, responsive, and accountable. Changes in spending priorities and in the tax structure can be made through the existing budget process, as seems to be happening. But these are only the first steps of what is needed if a rebuilding of public confidence in government's capacity to govern is seen. We need to look deeper than this at the processes by which we decide what objectives to pursue and how to pursue them. We need to look, not just at failures of programs, but at the weaknesses in the design of the programs which caused the failures. Helping to eliminate or prevent those design weaknesses should be, and increasingly is, the fundamental objective of policy analysis in the congressional oversight process.

REFERENCES

1. Dror, Y. *Ventures in Policy Sciences*. Elsevier, New York, 1971, p. 14.
2. See U.S. General Accounting Office, *Finding Out How Programs Are Working: Suggestions for Congressional Oversight*, (PAD-78-3), Nov. 1977. In this report, the Program Analysis Division outlines the process for congressional committees to use in reviewing the implementation and results of legislation.

3. Hammond, S. W., Fox, H. A., Jr., Moraski, R., and Nicholson, J. B. Senate Oversight Activities. *Techniques and Procedures for Analysis and Evaluation: A Compilation of Papers Prepared for the Commission on the Operation of the Senate*. Committee Print, 94th Cong., 2d Sess., U.S. Government Printing Office, Washington, D.C. 1977, p. 72. Hammond, et al, interviewed Senators and senatorial staff. "Sixty-eight Senators singled out oversight—specifically 'improving access to and the usability of information available to the Senate in its oversight of the executive branch'—as the second highest priority item on a list of nine problem areas." (p. 70).
4. For example, Committee Reform Amendments of 1974, passed as H. Res. 988 (93rd Cong., 2d Sess.), require each standing committee of the House (except Appropriations and Budget) to either establish an oversight subcommittee or to order each of its subcommittees to carry out oversight functions.
5. Hammond et al., *op. cit*. p. 72.
6. See, for example, two reports to Congress: *Analysis of the Allocation Formula for Federal Mass Transit Subsidies*, (PAD-79-47), Oct. 1979 and *Federal Charges for Irrigation Projects Reviewed Do Not Cover Costs*, (PAD-81-07), Mar. 1981.
7. See, for example, *Tax Expenditures: A Primer*, (PAD-80-26), Nov. 1979, and two reports to Congress: *The Value Added Tax—What Else Should We Know About It?*, (PAD-81-60), Mar. 1981, and *Life Insurance Company Income Tax Act of 1959: An Analysis and Specific Recommendations for Change*, (PAD-81-1), in process.
8. See, for example, three reports to Congress: *The Office of Science and Technology Policy: Adaptation to a President's Style May Conflict with Congressionally Mandated Assignments*, (PAD-80-79), Sept. 1980, *Science Indicators: Improvements Needed in Design, Construction, and Interpretation*, (PAD-79-35), Sept. 1979, and *The Congress Should Use Consistent Criteria to Assess Small Business Innovation Initiatives*, (PAD-81-15), in process.
9. See, for example, two reports to Congress: *A Mission Budget Structure for the Department of Agriculture—A Feasibility Study*, (PAD-80-08), Nov. 1979, and *Funding Gaps Jeopardize Federal Government Operations*, (PAD-81-35), Mar. 1981.
10. See Dror, Y. *Ventures in Policy Sciences*. Elsevier, New York, 1971.
11. Sunset requirements provide that programs must be reauthorized periodically if they are to continue. If programs are not, the "sun will set" for them. Sunrise provisions would require that legislation authorizing new programs contain statements of objectives sufficiently detailed to permit effective evaluation. These statements would be used as standards for planning and managing programs and for determining program effectiveness when programs are reviewed by Congress.
12. See U.S. General Accounting Office, *Observations on Oversight Reform*, (PAD-81-17), 1981, pp. 1-2.

9
Policy Analysis in Long-Term Care

Sidney Katz / *Department of Community Health, Brown University, Providence, Rhode Island*

Joseph Papsidero / *Department of Community Health Science, Michigan State University, East Lansing, Michigan*

INTRODUCTION

Highlighting the concerns and directions for long-term care in the United States, we observe that about three to four percent of the civilian, noninstitutionalized population are hampered from moving about by one or more chronic conditions. Between one-fourth and one-third of those with limited mobility are confined to the house, and one-fourth of these are confined to bed. Another large proportion need help in getting around, either from another person or by special aids. The remaining persons have trouble getting around freely but do not require the help of another person or a special aid [1]. In addition, most of over one million persons in nursing homes have some type of mobility limitation; and an increasingly large number have the chronic diseases which lead to limitations in mobility [2].

According to estimates from the Congressional Budget Office (CBO), 11.8 to 16.8% of the people 65 years old and older are functionally disabled [3]. In contrast, among those 18 to 64 years of age, the estimate is between 1.2 and 3.9 percent. The CBO projects an increased demand for long-term care from an estimated 5.5 to 9.9 million persons in 1975 to between 7.4 and 12.5 million in 1985. Expenditures by all levels of government for long-term health and social services were about $5.7 to $5.8 billion dollars in 1975, while private expenditures totalled between $5.9 and $7.7 billion. As a result of population aging, increased use of services, inflation, insufficient competition, and predicted increases in comprehensive health insurance coverage, the CBO projects a potential demand of between $60 and $87 billion dollars in the late 1980's. Clearly, the expected demand and cost requires rational social approaches to long-term care.

Since the 1940's, social forces called for public action with regard to long-term care. Beginning with Medicare in 1965, a series of programs were instituted to accept this responsibility. Often, such efforts lacked the adequate information base that would make the planning and programs sufficiently rational. As a result, serious and costly mistakes continue to be made that delay aid for those who need it. Among the lessons learned over the past 20 years is the recognition that Medicare and Medicaid were not designed to deal with long-term care [4, 5]. The nation was not prepared for the increased administrative burdens and costs that accompanied Medicare [6]. The public learned that more services do not necessarily lead to more care, and more money does not automatically lead to better care [7, 8]. In fact, some services are not beneficial.

Medicare was designed to finance limited medical coverage for the aged, while the intent of Medicaid was to provide broad health care financing for those on public assistance [9, 10]. In defining the limits of payment, the Medicare and Medicaid approach does not address appropriately the individual's entry into long-term care and the discontinuance of care. Decisions about entry into care and about the services needed are made by physicians and nurses, generally in institutions. Regulations concerning eligibility are interpreted flexibly, generally in order to obtain government reimbursement for services. Since professionals define entry into care and allocate services, inappropriate use of services can result. Better specification of the entry, and exit would improve the cost-effective use of Medicare and Medicaid financing. For example, entry and exit criteria that reflect available information about the expected impact of long-term care should be incorporated into the decision-making process for payment.

Through the Social Security Amendments of 1972, Congress provided for the establishment of the Professional Standards Review Organizations (PSRO) Program to assure that needed services are of good quality and are performed as economically as possible [11]. To date, effective quality assurance mechanisms have not been implemented to meet the needs for multidisciplinary and comprehensive long-term care. In the currently fragmented system of health services, quality assurance for long-term care is left to each separate individual or organization that delivers services. Thus, the assurance of quality can only be fragmented and uncertain, conceptually and in practice.

In a subsequent action, Health Maintenance Organization (HMO) legislation required the provision of long-term care services as part of the services package, including services in intermediary and long-term care facilities, rehabilitative services, and home health services [12]. Also required were preventive long-term services. Such requirements have important implications for the organization of the program, for the delivery system, and for information and evaluation systems.

The National Planning and Resources Development Act of 1973 sought to integrate and improve our planning and regulatory efforts [13]. Under this Act, planning agencies are expected to have strong technical assistance and clear roles in the regulatory decision-making process. Although planning and regulatory needs for long-term care are addressed by agencies, our experience base permits only a very uncertain estimate of demand, supply requirements, and supply response [3]. As a result, planning guidelines for long-term care are insufficient everywhere.

The recent restricted national economic environment has restricted the prospect of National Health Insurance as a financing vehicle, as has the trend to increase State and local government involvement in financing and delivery of health services. In relation to long-term care, we continue to experience the rising costs of care to older Americans, the paucity of effective quality control, the lack of adequate training for long-term care, and the need for home health services [1].

We do not have a rational policy for long-term care. Without such a policy, costly legislative changes and administrative reorganizations are unavoidable. Indecision and controversy over current and future programs will continue. At the same time, the aged population will increase, as will its use of services. New technologies, inflation, and expanded demand will greatly increase expenditures for services [1]. With regard to the absence of a rational policy for long-term care, a problem to be resolved is the failure to conduct policy analysis in the context of a suitably encompassing framework of information, especially one that includes information about the needs of people with chronic conditions and about the impacts that can be expected as a result of long-term care [14]. Another problem concerns the availability of information about needs and impacts. In this paper, these problems are addressed by, first, presenting a framework for evaluations of system performance. Then, the aims of evaluation are described, and the information that is needed and available is also described. Finally, we draw on our experiences with a long-term care archive to illustrate a proposed direction for improved policy analysis.

Since different disciplines have different legitimate views on how to approach health policy analysis, we wish to reemphasize the boundaries of this paper. The intent is to focus on information about: (1) the long-term care needs of the population in terms of functional health, (2) changes in functional health, and (3) impacts of services on functional health. The focus on such information derives from two observations. One has been expressed by the Institute of Medicine (National Academy of Sciences) in a report on the 1976 Anglo-American Conference on Care of the Elderly, which stated that "maintenance of functional independence is an important goal for public policies affecting the elderly" [15]. Associated recommendations strongly reflected this priority. The second observation is that information on needs and outcomes, in terms of function, is an essential component in analyses of cost-effectiveness and is not yet recognized sufficiently in policy-related analyses and decisions. It is beyond the scope of this paper to produce the total strategy for the rational long-term care policy that is needed. We shall not, for example, deal comprehensively with competing uses of public funds, demography-based issues of supply and demand, possible monopolies in the organization and delivery of care, and multiple values and intents. This paper *will* describe the current availability and use of the required information about function in the context of a meta-framework for policy analysis that is concerned with cost-effectiveness. As such, it aims to contribute an important ingredient to long-term care policy analysis.

FRAMEWORK FOR POLICY ANALYSIS

Policy analysis is enhanced when a framework is available that identifies both the kinds of information used to define policy and the analytic processes [16]. As a refinement of a previous formulation, Figure 1 describes basic elements of a framework for the systematic analysis of information about long-term and its use in a policy-related context [17]. Basic to the analytic framework is a process wherein information for policy analysis is derived from appraisals of systems performance in terms of interactions among: (1) inputs that indicate needs and demands; (2) processes related to the provision of long-term care services; (3) outputs

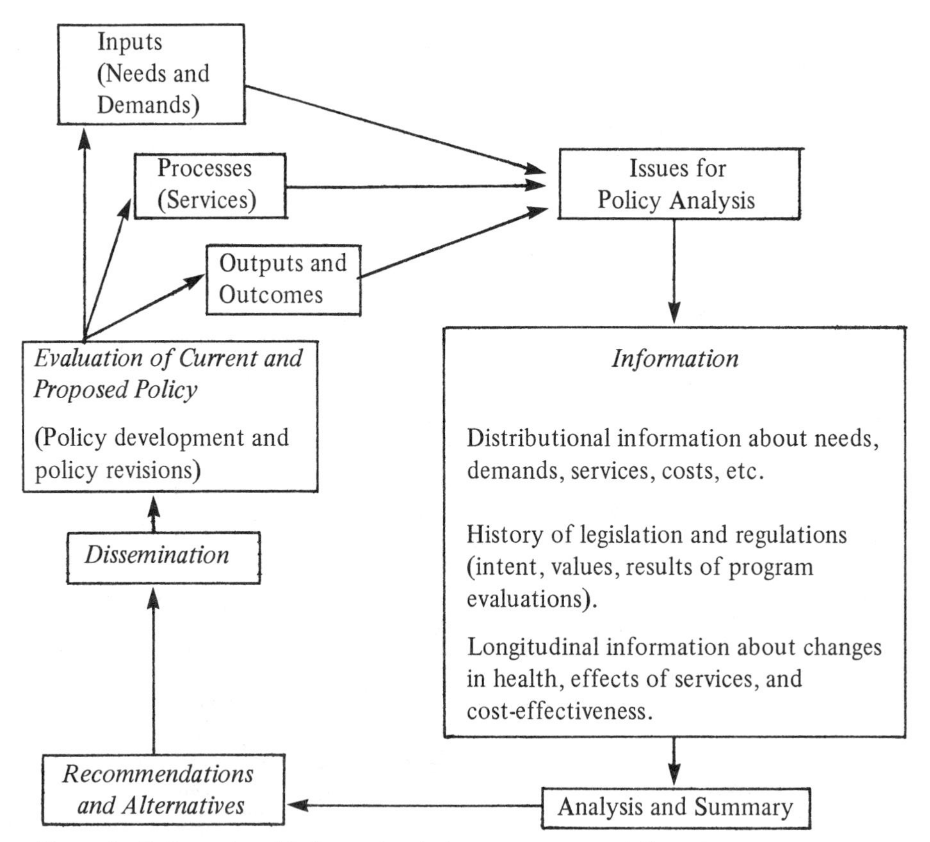

Figure 1 Policy-related information in long-term care: A flow-diagram

in terms of the use of services and costs of care; and (4) outcomes that identify the end results of certain courses of action. Based on system or program appraisals using the foregoing elements, issues are identified for goals such as improved access, quality maintenance, and cost-containment. Once issues are identified, information is analyzed as it pertains to detailed questions asked about health, illness, and the quality of life in physical, psychological, social, and environmental terms. In this way, problems related to needs and demands are defined with regard to health and illness as well as other co-existing social problems and needs such as housing, justice, and welfare. The types and magnitudes of such problems are described, as well as their origins and determinants, and the projected courses of events. In addition to needs and demands, the interventions, services, and resources are defined, including their effects on whom and at what cost. The basis for such information —whether scientific evidence, professional experience, or no evidence—is clarified. The intent and values reflected in current and proposed legislation and regulations are also summarized in terms such as eligibility criteria, criteria for discontinuing services, scope and amount of services, financing, organization, and program evaluation. In the light of current knowledge about long-term care, alternate views of policy consistent with such knowledge are synthesized, providing for modifications where gaps in knowledge pose uncertainties.

The information flow and components referred to above and in Figure 1 are further described in Table 1. The kinds of information identified in Table 1 are for illustrative purposes and are not intended to be all-inclusive. Further, the information flow indicated in Figure 1 is not a closed system. Other conditions will exert their influence such as political priorities, change in social policies, general economics, and political structures.

Needs or demands in Table 1 are broadly defined inputs that encompass health, illness, and the quality of life, expressed in physical, psychological, social, and environmental terms. Needs are the conditions that warrant assistance or action. They may or may not be perceived or expressed by the person in need. Needs are among the most important predictors of utilization and are generally described in terms of diagnosis, functional limitation, perceived illness, symptoms, or poor self-rated health status [18]. In contrast, demands are expressed desires in terms of services sought, whether needed or not. Other inputs are the resources allocated and available to respond to needs and demands. Included are resources such as manpower, facilities, equipment, regulations, and performance standards.

The process component of the information is concerned with long-term care services which are organized and delivered to meet the needs or demands of clients and professionals. These are described in terms such as their kinds, amounts, coordination, organization, financing, delivery, and controls of cost and quality. Services also include activities and supports such as income support, consumer education, homemaking, nutritional support, medical services, and legal aid. The outputs of service-related programs are described in terms of the utilization of services and the characteristics of the participants who use the services. They are described in terms of costs to the individual, family, and community, as well as the appro-

Table 1 Information Components for Policy Analysis in Long-Term Care[1]

Inputs Indicating Needs and Demands[2]	Processes Relating to Services	Outputs of Programs	Outcomes
Vital statistics and demographics, including levels of health and disease, functioning, and well-being	Services offered	Participation, including numbers served and types of services received	Levels of health
	Coordination of services		Levels of well-being
	Quality control	Use of services	Levels of functioning
Consumer demands and patterns of use of services	Consumer education	Costs of care	Consumer satisfaction
	Professional development	Appropriateness and quality of care	Professional satisfaction
Professional perceptions and expectations	Organization, management and financing	New knowledge	
Resources	Cost control		

[1] Items selected for illustrative purposes.
[2] Not included are other important and competing social conditions and needs that must be considered when analyzing health policy in relation to other domains of public policy.

priateness and quality of care. Outcomes are the responses to services described in terms of health status, well-being, and satisfaction.

The foregoing information and analytic approach reflect a concern for services—their planning, financing, organization, staffing, management, delivery, utilization, and cost—as their services affect needs and demands in achieving certain outcomes. The goal is to make practical decisions that will improve the effectiveness of national and community approaches to health maintenance, illness prevention, and the quality of life. The concern is also to clarify socially responsible approaches, namely, to promote improved availability, accessibility, and efficiency. To these ends, the framework facilitates program evaluation that can lead to rational decisions about services, derived in large part from available qualitative and quantitative knowledge. From the viewpoint of the consumer, the evaluation system should, for example, require and enable different services decisions for the for the disoriented 90-year-old person who suffers a fractured hip than for the coherent 70-year-old person with a fractured hip who has no complications [19,20].

UNIQUENESS OF LONG-TERM CARE

For the foregoing framework and aims, policy analysis in long-term care requires an information base that recognizes the unique features of aging and long-term care—especially with regard to needs, care, and the goals of care. Foremost among the unique features is the significance of function to the aged and to those with chronic conditions. Chronic conditions usually cause or hold the potential for causing a substantial and cumulative degree of disability. Those who develop disabilities have need for help with such daily functions as bathing, dressing, and walking. This increased need for help often occurs at a time when there is a loss of able friends and family. Concurrently, health care is required on a continual basis. As socioeconomic productivity decreases, financial resources become depleted with serious consequences for the person, family, and community.

Long-term care differs from acute care in the sociodemographic characteristics of the clients or patients and the nature of their illnesses and problems. Functional status defines the need for long-term care and is the socially-relevant focus of care. Although chronic conditions and disability affect all people, the magnitude of such problems increases with age and peaks among the aged. Those who require long-term care are likely to have two or more illnesses that draw on multiple services. They are also likely to experience repeated hospitalizations, short lengths of home health services, and many transfers from one level of care to another. The cost of care is a significant burden.

The goals of long-term care differ from those of acute care. The organization of services differs, as does the mix of providers. Success in curing chronic conditions has not kept pace with success in curing acute conditions. As a result, goals of long-term care are thought of as restoration and maintenance of function at the maximum level possible, as opposed to cure [21]. Required are adequately prepared professionals and allied manpower. Required also are an interdisciplinary orientation and coordinated resources. Since homemaking, medical, and income services are likely to be needed for long periods of time, long-term care is both a treatment situation and a living situation. It encompasses income maintenance and organized services that enable persons to remain at home with informal, supportive aid from relatives or friends. For the very disabled, quality of care equals the quality of life.

With regard to the mix of providers, it is currently considered necessary to bring together professionals with skills in medical, psychosocial, and vocational services since the variety and complexity of needs cannot be met by any one of the helping professions working alone. The need to integrate their skills has led to development of the concept of team care. The tasks of multidisciplinary teams "involve the assessment of the complex set of problems of the long-term patient, definition of patient goals and specific service needs in terms of the whole person and his setting, and follow through and surveillance to insure continuity of care responsive to changes in the patient" [21].

MEASUREMENT OF HEALTH STATUS

Functional assessment of problems, measured in physical, psychological, and socioeconomic terms, reflects the needs and demands of chronically ill and disabled people. These measures describe individuals or groups under care, objectively and in commonly understood language. The measures provide a conceptual basis for defining homogeneous groupings in populations. Objective, well-studied, valid, and reliable measures contribute to the explanation of the origins of the problems. They provide predictive information about the use of services and the outcomes of care. Such measures are available and have been used. In this regard, we review, next, important aspects of the historical background of health status measurement in individuals and populations, emphasizing the evolution of measures of function and related classification systems.

In the late 1800's and the early 1900's, in Europe and in the United States, information about functional status was obtained in health interview surveys [22]. This information represented the beginnings of contemporary concepts of disability or dysfunction in the measurement of health status. The content of information systems broadened, and methods of measurement became more refined. For example, periodic interviewing at two-week intervals, was introduced as a strategy to solve problems of recall [23]. Diary-keeping in the Eastern Health District Study served the same purpose [24]. This study also used hierarchically-ordered classification of dysfunction and intensity of services as a means of evaluating severity of illness.

As the importance of chronic disease and long-term care become apparent, the Commission on Chronic Illness was established in 1949. The Commission improved methodology in health status measurement with regard to classifying severity of illness, multi-phasic screening, and follow-up techniques [25]. The National Center for Health Statistics was established in 1956 and made significant contributions to defining and measuring chronic conditions, restricted activities, mobility, impairments, and home care [26]. The Health Survey of Finland in the 1960's introduced measurement of perceived morbidity as another basis for assessing need [27].

The Commission on Chronic Illness demonstrated the usefulness of combining more than one attribute into a multidimensional profile. Specifically, the Commission combined criteria of disease and physical dysfunction, dividing people into three groups; (1) those with maximum disability regardless of disease, (2) those with less disability and a major chronic disease, and (3) those with less disability and minor or no disease. Thus, two dimensions, disability and diagnosis, were used concurrently to classify people. Relatedly, profiled measures of activities of daily living have been used in surveys and experiments to provide information about health needs, severity of illness, and care outcome [19, 28, 29].

In the 1960's, national interest in assessment was reflected in activities designed to establish a uniform system of patient assessment [30]. For example, collaborative research produced the *Patient Classification for Long-Term Care: User's Manual* [31]. The manual contains a set of descriptive terms which are patient-oriented, multidimensional, objective, relevant to the goals of long-term care, and can be used to describe different levels of patient needs. Subsequently, a multidisciplinary group developed the *Long-Term Health Care Minimum Data Set*, sponsored by the National Center for Health Statistics [32]. Some of the same researchers worked on both the *User's Manual* and *Minimum Data Set*. Examples of related, currently available information systems include the Functional Life Scale, the Long Range Evaluation Summary (LRES), the Burke Stroke Time-Oriented Profile, and the Long-Term Care Information System [33, 34, 35, 36]. Related assessment systems have also been used in health studies and social surveys of noninstitutionalized populations in cross-national studies of elderly populations [27, 28, 37, 38].

AVAILABLE INFORMATION

Information on needs for long-term care have been collected in national, regional, state, and local populations. Increasingly, the information describes the functional status of people in common language, especially in terms of activities of daily living (ADL) where most ADL measures contain several elements in common [14, 27, 37, 39, 40, 41, 42, 43, 44]. Available, also, are national estimates of disability in terms of activity limitations and estimates of handicaps and impairments [45, 46, 47, 48]. Since common measures are not widely accepted for psychological and socioeconomic functioning, comparisons in these terms are generally not reliable.

Much information is available about people in long-term care programs and about the programs themselves. Such programs can be divided into three groups: (1) technology-rich institutions such as chronic disease and rehabilitation hospitals, (2) basic living institutions such as nursing homes, and (3) noninstitutional care in the home or other community settings. Facility surveys, most commonly of nursing homes, have described the residents or patients, staffing, services, utilization of services, and costs [3, 43, 44, 49, 50, 51]. Similar information is readily available for home care [52, 53, 54, 55].

There is an important lack of information about the units of individual items of care used by people with varying needs for long-term care, and even a greater lack of information about the "packages" of services related to various levels of need. Relatedly, the absence of uniform cost-accounting across the nation is a major problem to policy analysis in long-term care. Although information is available on insurance coverage and expenditures, systematically-collected comparable information on financing is not available [56, 57, 58].

Importantly, functional assessment has provided information about the effectiveness of long-term care. A review of studies of impact demonstrates that experiments on the impact of care have been reported in geographically-dispersed segments of populations and in selected local groups [19, 29, 59, 60, 61, 62, 63, 64]. Branch reported changes in health for a cohort, based on sampling the population of Massachusetts [39]. Other outcome information has come from nonexperimental longitudinal and follow-up studies [20, 34, 65, 66, 67, 68, 69, 70, 71, 72, 73, 74, 75, 76, 77]. Information about outcomes in large segments of the population is limited. In all the studies, measurements of functional status were important indicators of change or impact. As in the case of studies of need, tested and established measures of activities of daily living (ADL) were employed frequently, and the ADL measures had several elements in common. Measures of psychological and social functions were less uniform among the various studies.

Illustrative of studies of impact on function, Lehmann and associates reported on the results of individualized rehabilitation programs for patients with stroke [71]. A profile of activities of daily living was used to assess progress between admission and discharge. Comparing the observed changes in function with natural history of stroke, the authors proposed that the gains could not be attributed solely to spontaneous recovery and that the rehabilitation team had an important impact.

In a controlled experiment, comprehensive clinic care of patients with rheumatoid arthritis was coordinated with care at home [78]. Coordinated treatment, when compared to the usual form of care, was beneficial by functional and clinical measures. The same investigators then carried out two major experiments, namely, the Continued Care Study and the Chronic Disease Module Study [19, 29].

In the Continued Care Study, patients 50 years and older discharged home from a chronic disease rehabilitation hospital were randomly assigned to a treatment or to a control group. Treatment consisted of regular visits to the patient's home by a public health nurse, working with the patient's physician and with community resources. It was found that younger, less disabled, and less severely ill persons were more likely to benefit from home care in physical and mental function after receiving long-term visiting nurse services than were similar people in a control group. Admissions to nursing homes were delayed among those who received visiting nurse services. The presence of visiting nurse services was associated with increased use of hospitals and other services among the oldest, very disabled, and severely ill people when compared to controls. Despite the increased use of services, this high risk group did not benefit in physical and mental function in the presence of home care. This study plus the following studies illustrate the information that is available to help develop socially responsible goals for cost-effective long-term care programs. These types of information also constitute experimental evidence to be referred to in policy-oriented program evaluations.

The Chronic Disease Module Study, an experimental study, tested a less costly form of care: continuing home visits by health assistants who worked with a small team consisting of a physician and a nurse or social worker. Patients in ambulatory care facilities or about to be discharged from acute care hospitals in five Michigan communities were randomly assigned to treatment or control groups.

Younger, less disabled, and less severely ill persons experienced higher levels of satisfaction and morale after receiving services by a health assistant than did similar people in the control group. Avoidance of functional deterioration was not demonstrated as an effect.

The National Center for Health Services Research carried out an experiment to evaluate the effectiveness of geriatric day care and homemaker services as alternatives in long-term care [79]. Adult day care or homemaker services were delivered to an experimental group of Medicare-eligible people in each of six sites for one year. A control group continued to be eligible for services covered by Medicare, but did not receive project services. Maintenance of functional capacities as well as improvement were viewed as beneficial outcomes. The experimental groups had more beneficial outcomes than the control groups. Statistically significant differences were found in physical functioning levels for the day care sample and in contentment levels for the homemaker sample.

DIRECTIONS FOR DOCUMENTATION

In order to validate the continuing changes in technologic interventions, McDermott stated that the challenge of the future is to store information so that it can be retrieved to evaluate performance of technology over time [80]. He indicated that "because of ethical constraints, comparison with past experience will probably be the only method we will have" for such validation, especially for long-lasting conditions. He concluded that a computer-stored data bank is the approach of choice. With regard to long-term care technologies, he stated that the "differing outcomes of an almost infinite variety of manifestations" of long-lasting conditions are "eminently suited to the methods of computer technology;" and he urged immediate implementation.

In previous sections, we presented the case for information about functional needs and impact as unique and crucial in the evaluation of performance of long-term care technologies. As Cluff said, "It is time to recognize that the primary objective of medical care is to improve patient function and to reduce the degree of illness" [81]. If our efforts fail to recognize this principle "much rhetoric will flow about the costs of medical care, the inadequacies of doctors and the unrealistic demands of patients," but "little will be accomplished." Cluff concluded that predictive information about the outcomes of chronic conditions was "necessary to reduce empiricism and increase discrimination in medical care" as "the only sure way to improve the quality of care and reduce health care costs."

Believing that the views of McDermott and Cluff are correct, we have been developing and using an archive of specialized information in policy analysis of long-term care. A unique feature of the archive is the inclusion of data sets that describe (a) needs of the population in terms of functional health status, (b) amounts of changes in such health status during given periods of time, and (c) impacts of long-term care services. Continuing collection of such data provides an increasing capacity to make available specialized and integrated information for policy and planning. Acquired data sets are incorporated into the archive in conjunction with a documentation process that critically examines the characteristics and quality of data. Overviews are developed that describe each study in a standard format. The overviews introduce the available data to potential users of the archive. In addition, a codebook is developed that uses a standard format and allows investigators to communicate effectively with computer programmers.

More than 60 studies have been examined as possible candidates for the archive, and others continue to be identified. Currently, eight data sets have been fully incorporated into the archive and are available for secondary analysis. These data sets were the results of the following studies: (1) Continued Care Study [19]; (2) Chronic Disease Module Study [29]; (3) Highland View Hospital Study [70]; (4) Bryn Mawr Study [82]; (5) 222 Homemaker-Day Care Experiment [79]; (6) Long-Term Care Information System [36]; (7) Health and Social Needs of the Elderly in Massachusetts [39]; and (8) Einstein Day Hospital Experiment [83]. The data sets are currently being used in secondary analyses that focus on improved information for quality assurance in long-term care, planning and organization of long-term care services, and the application of multidimensional information about function to predict need, use of services, and outcomes of long-term care.

The foregoing example of a specialized data archive on long-term care serves to implement the framework for policy analysis outlined earlier in this paper. It responds to the unique aspects of long-term care, particularly with regard to information about needs and outcomes of care in terms of function. Such information is thereby, added to the base of available knowledge where it can contribute to the development of rational public policy and to the attempt to meet the long-term care needs of the growing population of disabled people among us.

ACKNOWLEDGMENT

This project was supported in part by Grant Number HS 03760 from the National Center for Health Services Research, OASH and by the Administration on Aging (older Americans Act, Title IV-E, 90 AT-2164).

REFERENCES

1. U.S. Department of Health, Education and Welfare. *Forward Plan FY 1977-81*. DHEW Publication No. (OS) 76-50024, Washington, D.C., 6, 122-124, 137-140.
2. Bright, M. Demographic Background for Programming for Chronic Diseases in the United States. In Lillienfield, A. M. and Gifford, A. J. (eds.). *Chronic Diseases and Public Health*. The Johns Hopkins Press, Baltimore, Maryland, 1966, 13-21.

3. Congressional Budget Office. *Long-Term Care for the Elderly and Disabled*, U.S. Government Printing Office, Washington, D.C., 1977.
4. U.S. Department of Health, Education, and Welfare. *Report of the Task Force on Medicaid and Related Programs*, U.S. Government Printing Office, Washington, D.C., June 1970.
5. Margolis, E. Changing Values-Problems of Geriatric Care in the U.S.A.: An Outsider's View. *Medical Care* 12 (November 1979): 1122.
6. Feldstein, P. and Waldman, S. Financial Position of Hospitals in Early Medicare Period. *Social Security* 31 (1968): 18-23.
7. Teeling-Smith, G. More Money into the Medical Sector: Is This the Answer? *International Journal of Health Services* 3 (1973): 493-500.
8. Ginzberg, E. *Health Manpower and Health Policy*. Allanheld, Osmun and Co. Publishers, Montclair, New Jersey, 1978.
9. U.S. Congress. *Public Law 89-97, Medicare, Title 18 of the Social Security Amendments Act of 1965*, Washington, D.C., 1965.
10. U.S. Congress. *Public Law 89-97, Medicaid, Title 19 of the Social Security Amendments Act of 1965*, Washington, D.C., 1965.
11. U.S. Congress. *Public Law 92-602, Social Security Amendments of 1972*, Washington, D.C., 1972.
12. U.S. Congress. *Public Law 93-222, Health Maintenance Organization Act, Part 110*, Washington, D.C., 1973.
13. U.S. Congress. *Public Law 93-641, National Health Planning and Resources Development Act*, Washington, D.C., 1974.
14. Katz, S., Hedrick, S. C., and Henderson, N. S. The Measurement of Long-Term Care Needs and Impact. *Health and Medical Care Services Review* 2 (Spring 1979): 1-21.
15. Committee on Care of the Elderly, Institute of Medicine. *A Policy Statement: The Elderly and Functional Dependency*, National Academy of Sciences, Washington, D.C., June 1977, 8, 11-35.
16. Burt, M. R. *Policy Analysis: Introduction and Applications to Health Programs*. Information Resources Press, Washington, D.C., 1974.
17. Katz, S. and Papsidero, J. A. Information, Evaluation, and Policy for Long-Term Care. In Emlet, H. E., Young, J. P., Shuman, L., Baum, M. and Williams, S. (eds.) *Operations Research and National Health Policy Issues*. Operations Research Society of America and the National Center for Health Services Research, 1977. Available from Analytic Services, 400 Army-Navy Drive, Arlington, Virginia 22202.
18. Staff of the Subcommittee on Health and the Environment. *A Discursive Dictionary of Health Care*, U.S. Government Printing Office, Washington, D.C., February 1976, 108.
19. Katz, S., Ford, A. B., Downs, T. D., Adams, M., and Rusby, D. I. *Effects of Continued Care: A Study of Chronic Illness in the Home*. DHEW Publication No. (HSM) 73-3010, Washington, D.C., 1972, 59-67, 71-75.

20. Katz, S., Heiple, K. G., Downs, T. D., Ford, A. B., and Scott, C. P. Long-Term Course of 147 Patients with Fracture of the Hip. *Surgery, Gynecology and Obstetrics* 124 (June 1967): 1219-1230.
21. Katz, S., Halstead, L., and Wierenga, M. A Medical Perspective of Team Care in Sherwood, S. (Ed.) *Long-Term Care: A Handbook for Researchers, Planners, and Providers*. Spectrum Publications, Inc., New York, 1976.
22. Collins, S. D. Sickness Surveys in Emerson, H. (ed.). *Administrative Medicine*, Nelson, New York, 1951, 511.
23. Downes, J. Causes of Illness Among Males and Females. *Milbank Memorial Fund Quarterly* 28 (October 1950): 407.
24. Downes, J. and Collins, S. D. A Study of Illness Among Families in the Eastern Health District of Baltimore. *Milbank Memorial Fund Quarterly* 18 (January 1940): 5.
25. Commission on Chronic Illness. *Chronic Illness in the United States, Vol. IV, Chronic Illness in a Large City*. Harvard University Press, Cambridge, MA, 1957.
26. National Center for Health Statistics. Health Survey Procedure: Concepts, Questionnaire Development, and Definitions in the Health Interview Survey." PHS Publication No. 1000. *Vital and Health Statistics Series 1, No. 2,* Rockville, MD, 1964.
27. Kalimo, E. and Sievers, K. The Need for Medical Care: Estimation on the Basis of Interview Data. *Medical Care* 6 (January-February 1968): 1-17.
28. Branch, L. G. Functional Abilities of the Elderly: An Update on the Massachusetts Health Care Panel Study. In Haynes, S. G. and Feinleib, M. (eds.). *Second Conference on the Epidemiology of Aging*. U.S. Department of Health and Human Services, NIH Publication No. 80-969, July, 1980.
29. Papsidero, J. A., Katz, S., Kroger, S. M. H., and Akpom, C. A. *Chance for Change*. Michigan State University Press, East Lansing, MI, 1979.
30. Ryder, C. F., Elkin, W. F., and Doten, D. Patient Assessment, An Essential Tool in Placement and Planning of Care. *HSMA Health Reports* 86 (1971): 923-932.
31. Jones, E. *Patient Classification for Long-Term Care: User's Manual*, DHEW Publication No. (HRA) 74-3107, Washington, D.C., 1973.
32. Technical Consultant Panel, National Committee on Vital and Health Statistics. *Long-Term Health Care Minimum Data Set*, U.S. Dept. HEW, Public Health Service, Hyattsville, MD, 1979.
33. Sarno, J. E., Sarno, M. T., and Levita, E. The Functional Life Scale. *Archives of Physical Medicine and Rehabilitation* 54 (May 1973): 214-220.
34. Granger, C. V., Sherwood, C. C., and Greer, D. S. Functional Status Measures in a Comprehensive Stroke Care Program. *Archives of Physical Medicine and Rehabilitation* 48 (December 1977): 55-561.
35. Feigenson, J. S., Polkow, L., Meikle, R., and Ferguson, W. Stroke Time-Oriented Profile (BUSTOP): An Overview of Patient Function. *Archives of Physical Medicine and Rehabilitation* 60 (November 1979): 508-511.

36. Katz, S. and Falcone, A. R. Use of Assessment of Data for Long-Term Care Planning, Program Decisions, and Statistical Accounting. *New Challenges for Vital and Health Records*, National Center for Health Statistics, DHH Publication No. (PHS) 81-1214, Washington, D.C., 1980, 39-44.
37. Shanas, E., Townsend, P., Wedderburn, D., Friis, H., Milhoj, P., and Stehouwer, J. *Old People in Three Industrial Societies*, Atherton Press, New York, 1968.
38. Shanas, E. *National Survey of the Aged: Final Report*, Project No. HEW (OHD) 90-A-369, Administration on Aging, Washington, D.C., 1977.
39. Branch, L. G. *Understanding the Health and Social Service Needs of People Over Age 65*, Center for Survey Research, University of Massachusetts and the Joint Center for Urban Studies of M.I.T. and Harvard University, 1977.
40. Newman, S. J., Morgan, J., Marans, R., and Pastalan, L. *Housing Adjustments of Older People: A Report of Findings from the Second Phase*. Unpublished manuscript. Institute for Social Research, University of Michigan, Ann Arbor, MI, 1976.
41. Office of Nursing Home Affairs. *Long-Term Care Facility Improvement Study. Introductory Report*. DHEW Publication No. (OS) 76-50021, U.S. Government Printing Office, Washington, D.C., July, 1975.
42. Trussel, R. D. and Elinson, J. Chronic Illness in a Rural Area. *Chronic Illness in the United States (Vol. III)*, Harvard University Press, Cambridge, Massachusetts, 1959.
43. U.S. Department of Health, Education, and Welfare. *The National Nursing Home Survey: 1977 Summary for the United States*, DHEW Publication No. (PHS) 79-1794, Washington, D.C., July, 1979.
44. Department of Health and Human Services. *Utilization Patterns and Financial Characteristics of Nursing Homes in the United States: 1977 National Nursing Home Survey*, DHHS Publication No. (PHS) 81-1714, August, 1981.
45. Colvez, A. and Blanchet, M. Disability Trends in the United States Population 1966-76: Analysis of Reported Causes. *American Journal of Public Health* 71 (May 1981): 464-471.
46. Klebe, E. R. *Key Facts of the Handicapped*. Congressional Library of Congress Research Service, Washington, D.C., April 1, 1975.
47. National Center for Health Statistics. Current Estimates from the U.S. Health Interview Survey. *Vital and Health Statistics*, Series No. 10, Rockville, Maryland, 1977.
48. U.S. Department of Health and Human Services. *Prevalence of Selected Impairments. United States - 1977*. DHHS Publication No. (PHS) 81-1562, Washington, D.C., February 1981.
49. Blue Cross Association. The Availability of Financing of Nursing Home Care. *Blue Cross Reports* II (April-June 1964): 1-16.
50. Mitchell, J. B. and Sumner, M. *Methodology for Finding, Classifying and Comparing Costs for Services in Long-Term Care Settings*, Project No. SRS 500-76-002, Abt Associates, Cambridge, Massachusetts, 1976.

51. Mullner, R., Killingsworth, C., Matthews, D., and Byre, C. S. Inpatient Medical Rehabilitation: 1979 Survey of Hospitals and Units. *Archives of Physical Medicine and Rehabilitation* 61 (August 1980): 341-345.
52. Ricker-Smith, K. and Trager, B. In-Home Health Services in California. *Medical Care* 16 (March 1978): 173-190.
53. U.S. Department of Health, Education, and Welfare. *Persons Receiving Care at Home*, PHS Publication No. 584-B28, National Center for Health Statistics, October 1961.
54. U.S. Department of Health, Education, and Welfare. *Home Care for Persons 55 Years and Over. United States - July 1966-June 1968*. DHEW Publication No. (HMS) 72-1062, July 1972.
55. U.S. Department of Health, Education, and Welfare. Medicare Utilization of Home Health Services, 1974. *Health Insurance Statistics*, H1-79, November 1972.
56. U.S. Department of Health, Education, and Welfare. Health Care Coverage: United States, 1976. Advanced Data, 44, September 20, 1979.
57. U.S. Department of Health and Human Services. Who are the Uninsured? *National Health Care Expenditures Study Data Preview 1*, National Center for Health Services Research 1980.
58. U.S. Department of Health and Human Services. Employer and Employee Expenditures for Private Health Insurance. *National Health Care Expenditures Study Data Preview 7*, National Center for Health Services Research, 1980.
59. Blenkner, M., Bloom, M., Wasser, E., and Nielson, M. Protective Services for Older People. *Social Casework* 52 (October 1971): 483-522.
60. Christensen, K. and Lingle, J. A. Evaluation of Effectiveness of Team and Non-Team Public Health Nurses in Health Outcomes of Patients with Strokes or Fractures. *American Journal of Public Health* 62 (April 1972): 483-490.
61. Medicus Systems Corporation. *Protocol Reference Manual. Section 222, Demonstration and Evaluation of Long-Term Care Alternatives*. Unpublished manuscript, Chicago, Illinois. Developed for National Center for Health Services Research, 1975.
62. Nielson, M., Blenkner, M., Bloom, M., Downs, T., and Beggs, H. Older Persons after Hospitalizations: A Controlled Study of Home Aide Services. *American Journal of Public Health* 62 (August 1972): 1094-1101.
63. Posman, H., Kagan, L. S., LeMat, A. F., and Dahlin, B. *Continuity in Care for Impaired Older Persons. Public Health Nursing in a Geriatric Rehabilitation Maintenance Program*. Unpublished manuscript. Department of Public Affairs, Community Service Society of New York, 105 East 22nd Street, New York, New York 10010.
64. Skellie, F. A. and Coan, R. E. Community-Based Long-Term Care and

Mortality: Preliminary Findings of Georgia's Alternative Health Services Project. *The Gerontologist* 20 (June 1980): 372-379.
65. Katz, S., Ford, A. B., Chinn, A. B., and Newill, V. A. Prognosis After Strokes, Part II. Long-Term Course of 159 Patients. *Medicine* 45 (1966): 236-246.
66. Adler, M., Hamaty, D., Brown, C. C., and Potts, H. Medical Audit of Stroke Rehabilitation: A Critique of Medical Care Review. *Journal of Chronic Disease* 30 (1977): 461-471.
67. Anderson, E., Anderson, T. P., and Kottke, F. J. Stroke Rehabilitation: Maintenance of Achieved Gains. *Archives of Physical Medicine and Rehabilitation* 58 (August 1977): 345-352.
68. Comptroller on Chronic Illness. *The Well-Being of Older People in Cleveland, Ohio.* Unpublished manuscript. U.S. General Accounting Office, Washington, D.C., 1977.
69. Hurtado, A. V. *Final Project Report. Integration of Home Health and Extended Care Facility Services into a Prepaid Comprehensive Group Practice Plan*. Unpublished manuscript. Kaiser Foundation Research Institute, Portland, Oregon, 1969.
70. Katz, S., Ford, A. B., Moskowitz, R. W., Jackson, B. A., and Jaffe, M. W. Studies of Illness in the Aged: The Index of ADL: A Standardized Measure of Biological and Psychosocial Function. Journal of *American Medical Association* 185 (September 1963): 914-919.
71. Lehmann, J. F., DeLateur, B. J., Fowler, Jr., R. S., Warren, C. G., Arnhold, R., Schertzer, G., Hurka, R., Whitmore, J. J., Masock, A. J., and Chambers, K. H. Stroke: Does Rehabilitation Affect Outcome? *Archives of Physical Medicine and Rehabilitation* 56 (September 1975): 375-382.
72. McCaffree, K. F. and Harkins, E. G. *Executive Summary of Evaluation of the Outcomes of Nursing Home Care*. Unpublished manuscript available from Health Care Study Center, Battelle Human Affairs Research Center, 400 N.E. 41st Street, Seattle, Washington 98105, October, 1976.
73. Miglietta, O., Chung, T., and Rajeswaramma, V. Fate of Stroke Patients Transferred to a Long-Term Rehabilitation Hospital. *Stroke* 7 (January-February 1976): 76-77.
74. Mitchell, J. B. Patient Outcomes in Alternative Long-Term Care Settings. *Medical Care* 16 (June 1978): 439-452.
75. Moskowitz, E., Lightbody, F. E. H., and Freitag, N. S. Long-Term Follow-Up of the Poststroke Patient. *Archives of Physical Medicine and Rehabilitation* 53 (April 1972): 167-72.
76. Newman, M. The Process of Recovery after Hemiplegia. *Stroke* 3 November-December 1972): 702-710.
77. Spasoff, R. A., Kraus, S., Beattie, E. G., Holden, D. E. W., Lawson, J. S., Rodenburg, M., and Woodcock, G. M. A Longitudinal Study of Elderly

Residents in Long-Stay Institutions. *The Gerontologist* 18 (June 1978): 281-292.

78. Katz, S., Vignos, Jr., P. J., Moskowitz, R. W., Thompson, H. M., and Svec, K. H. Comprehensive Outpatient Care in Rheumatoid Arthritis: A Controlled Study. *Journal of American Medical Association* 206 (November 1968): 1249-1254.
79. Wan. T. H., Weissert, W., and Livieratos, B. Geriatric Day Care and Homemaker Services: An Experimental Study. *Journal of Gerontology* 35 (March 1980): 256-274.
80. McDermott, W. Evaluating the Physician and His Technology. *Daedalus: Doing Better and Feeling Worse: Health in the United States*, Winter, 1977.
81. Cluff, L. E. Chronic Disease, Function and the Quality of Care. *Journal of Chronic Disease* 34 (1981): 299-304.
82. Stroud, M. W., Katz, S., Hedrick, S., and Guenon, J. *A Summary Report Concerning Patients at Bryn Mawr Hospital Rehabilitation Center*. Unpublished manuscript. Office of Health Services, Education, and Research, Michigan State University, East Lansing, Michigan, 1978.
83. Cummings, V., Kerner, J. F., Arones, S., and Steinbock, C. *An Evaluation of a Day Hospital Service in Rehabilitation Medicine. Final Report*. U.S. Public Health Service, Office of Research, Statistics and Technology, National Center for Health Services Research, August 1980.

10
Analysis of Government Policies in Urban Transportation

Ronald F. Kirby / *Productivity and Economic Development Center, The Urban Institute, Washington, D.C.*

INTRODUCTION

Government involvement in the planning, construction, regulation, and operation of urban transportation systems has increased dramatically over the last three decades. Following post-war federal housing policies which encouraged suburban development, state and federal highway programs were expanded in the late 1950s to accommodate and reinforce the rapidly increasing demand for automobile travel. These programs were followed in the 1960s by efforts to re-capitalize failing mass transit systems and to increase safety and emission controls on the private automobile. The 1970s saw a major escalation in government programs to reduce the air pollution and energy consumption attributable to private automobiles, along with rapidly growing government financial involvement in the planning and operation of mass transit systems.

The 1980s began with a new concern at the top of the urban transportation agenda: fiscal stringency at all levels of government stimulated a search for new financing techniques and improved management measures for urban transportation. Many road improvements and transit plans were postponed or curtailed due to tight public budgets. In addition, serious financial problems in the automobile industry led to new pressures for relaxation of the ambitious automobile design standards enacted in the 1970s. These problems created a political consensus for rethinking the entire range of governmental activity in urban transportation.

The continually shifting emphasis in urban transportation policies over the last thirty years has provided a number of important lessons on what can be achieved, at what price, and with what levels of public support. These lessons now must be applied in the formulation of urban transportation policies and programs for the 1980s and beyond. The following sections review the recent history of urban transportation, summarize the conclusions which have been drawn from evaluating this experience, and propose some new policy considerations for the future.

A HISTORY OF CHANGE

The concern that led to the first major governmental involvement in urban transportation around the turn of the century was for the *connectivity* of the road and public transit systems [1]. Taxes were raised to provide funding for state and local public works departments to construct a hierarchy of state and local roads. The Federal Highway Act of 1921 called for the designation of the Federal-aid highway system, a limited system of interstate and intercounty highways. During the same period separately built streetcar lines within urban areas were consolidated into unified systems with common fares and service levels.

Federal highway legislation in 1934 and 1944 strengthened the federal role in financing highways, and earmarked a portion of the federal assistance for research and planning. In the late 1940s and early 1950s most of the states earmarked highway user tax revenues for highway projects, and in 1956 the U.S. Congress enacted the interstate highway program. The result was a substantial increase in the combined federal and state expenditures for urban highway construction; from $718 million in 1955 to $2.07 billion in 1962 [2].

The growing recognition that new road segments had to be planned as components of urban transportation *systems* led to a series of comprehensive urban transportation studies over the period from 1944 through the late 1950s. The Federal Highway Act of 1962 made such planning efforts requirements of federal assistance, and set a deadline of July 1, 1965 for the completion of comprehensive transportation plans in all metropolitan areas with central cities having populations over 50,000 [1].

The primary motivation for this rapid growth in highway expenditures has been attributed to the concern of the automobile, oil, steel, rubber, and trucking industries that the postwar expansion in automobile ownership and use not be constrained by road capacity limitations [2]. The highway lobby clearly was successful during this period in convincing the Congress and the American public of the desirability of rapid road expansion between and within urban areas. The major concern of comprehensive transportation plans during this period was facilitating traffic movement.

In their preoccupation with road expansion during the 1950s government agencies paid little or no attention to the growing problems of public transit systems. With few exceptions, U.S. cities insisted that despite rapidly declining ridership, transit systems should maintain extensive services and cover their costs from farebox revenues. As revenues began to fall short of the full costs of service provision in the late 1950s, transit operators postponed replacement of capital equipment and encountered increasing difficulty in maintaining adequate services.

The early 1960s brought public acceptance of the view that governmental assistance to transit was warranted for capital replacement and expansion, though operating costs still were firmly believed to be recoverable from the farebox. With the enactment of a program of federal capital assistance in the Urban Mass Transportation Act of 1964 there began an era of extensive transit capital replacement and expansion. A locally-funded rail system was initiated in San Francisco, and in other cities new public transit authorities were formed to purchase the assets of private bus companies, all with the understanding that public financial assistance would be limited to capital purchases.

Public capital assistance permitted the transit industry to rejuvenate its plant and to improve services throughout the late 1960s. Eventually, however, the forces of declining ridership, increasing costs, and public insistence on extensive low-fare service combined to create operating deficits which grew from a national total of $11 million in 1965 to $288 million in 1970 and $1.7 billion in 1975 [2]. In 1974 the U.S. Congress enacted a new section of the Urban Mass Transportation Act to fund up to 50 percent of transit operating deficits, subject to a formula limit for each urbanized area based on population and population density. State and local governments provided funds to match the federal program, and by the late 1970s over 50 percent of transit operating expenses were covered by public subsidies.

Transit enjoyed a period of great political support throughout the sixties and seventies. In addition to securing major programs of capital and operating assistance, transit advocates obtained a provision in the Federal Aid Highway Act of 1973 which permitted cities to exchange interstate highway funds for equivalent levels of transit funding. The remarkable legislative success of transit advocates during this period has been attributed to the broad idealogical appeal of transit:

> *Whether one's concern was the economic vitality of cities, protecting the environment, stopping highways, energy conservation, assisting the elderly and handicapped and poor, or simply getting other people off the road so as to be able to drive faster, transit was a policy that could be embraced. This is not to say that transit was an effective way of serving all these objectives, simply that it was widely believed to be so. [2].*

The growth in legislative support for transit in the sixties and seventies was accompanied by several legislative actions aimed directly at reducing the undesirable side effects of automobile use. The 1950s focus on relieving traffic congestion gradually was replaced by concerns over vehicle safety, air pollution, and energy consumption. Stimulated by Ralph Nader's highly publicized attack on the safety of the Chevrolet Corvair in 1966, the U.S. Congress enacted the National Traffic and Motor Vehicle Safety Act which established the National Highway Traffic Safety Administration (NHTSA).

Since its inception, NHTSA has promulgated a number of vehicle safety standards requiring changes in automobile design. Many of these standards have been highly controversial. While certain actions have become accepted practice (such as requiring installation of seat belts and recalling vehicles with manufacturing defects), other measures have not been accepted by the general public (such as requiring ignition interlock systems and passive restraint equipment). Controversy also continues over the cost-effectiveness and political acceptability of various vehicle design measures to improve safety.

Federal involvement in controlling motor vehicle emissions began with the Motor Vehicle Air Pollution Control Act in 1965, which empowered the Secretary of Health, Education and Welfare to impose emission standards on new vehicles for any emissions considered dangerous to human health. Over the next five years the secretary promulgated standards closely following those developed by the State of California. The Clean Air Act Amendments of 1970 set a number of ambitious criteria and deadlines for reduction of vehicle emissions, pertaining both to vehicle design and to the level of vehicle use in urban areas with air quality problems.

As it became clear that the criteria were too ambitious, the deadlines were repeatedly postponed by administrative action permitted under the original legislation. (Congress itself ruled out some of the measures proposed to reduce vehicle use.) In 1977 the Congress enacted new amendments to the Clean Air Act which extended the final deadline for achieving air quality standards by ten years. Although substantial progress has been made in reducing vehicle emissions through vehicle technology improvements, Congress has authorized delays in the achievement of these standards as well.

The Arab oil embargo of 1973-1974 brought energy consumption to the top of the urban transportation agenda, and concern over the energy consumed in urban travel continued throughout the remainder of the 1970s. In addition to reinforcing earlier support for public transit, the energy problem generated great interest in car pooling, van pooling, and specialized bus services. It also focused additional attention on the design of the automobile, this time with respect to fuel economy.

In 1975 the Congress enacted the Energy Policy and Conservation Act. This legislation directed automobile manufacturers to increase fleet average fuel economy from 14 mpg in 1974 to 18 mpg in 1978, 19 mpg in 1979, 20 mpg in 1980, and 27.5 mpg in 1985. Penalty payments were provided for manufacturers failing to achieve the prescribed levels. In 1978 Congress enacted further conservation measures including a gas guzzler tax. Plans also were developed at this time for emergency gasoline rationing. Continuing gasoline price increases in the late 1970s resulting from OPEC price increases maintained the pressures for energy conservation, and shifted consumer demand toward more fuel-efficient automobiles.

The national elections in November of 1980 produced a major shift in federal policies. In 1981 the Congress enacted cutbacks in almost all domestic programs and increases in defense spending. In addition, the Reagan administration initiated a major effort to relax what it considered to be overly burdensome federal regulations, preferring to rely as much as possible on market forces and voluntary activities to achieve desires social objectives. Proposals also were made to devolve as much regulatory and funding responsibility as possible to the state and local levels of government.

The initiatives of the Reagan policymakers were aimed at correcting what they viewed as the unsatisfactory performance of previous urban transportation policies and programs. These initiatives were aimed primarily at cutting back programs considered to be ineffective rather than at introducing new kinds of government involvement. While not all the evaluators of these programs agreed with the Reagan administration perspective, a number of common themes had emerged in their assessments, and a degree of consensus had begun to develop on many of the important issues.

EVALUATION TO DATE

The massive highway investments of the 1950s and 1960s initially were undertaken with considerable public support and enthusiasm. The rapid growth in car ownership after World War II had created a large constituency for road expansion, and few people at the time foresaw the deleterious side effects of unrestrained accommodation of the automobile. There were *some* vocal critics, however: Lewis Mumford [3], in particular, argued strongly that the highway program was a great mistake:

> *When the American people, through their Congress, voted a little while ago for a twenty-six billion-dollar highway program, the most charitable thing to assume about this action is that they hadn't the faintest notion of what they were doing. Within the next fifteen years they will doubtless find out; but by that time it will be too late to correct all the damage to our cities and our countryside, not least to the efficient organization of industry and transportation, that this ill-conceived and preposterously unbalanced program will have wrought.*

The first signs of a broadening disenchantment with the highway program emerged as the interstate system began to penetrate the developed portions of urban areas. Residents affected by highway construction began to organize into citizens' groups to oppose the completion of certain highway segments. Some highway alignments through inner-city neighborhoods raised racial issues by in effect disrupting black neighborhoods for the convenience of white suburban commuters.

A growing awareness of the negative side effects of urban highway expansion gradually led to more stringent transportation planning requirements. The Federal-Aid Highway Act of 1962 required that highway plans and programs be "formulated with due consideration to their probable effect on the future development of urban areas", and that projects be "based on a continuing, comprehensive transportation planning process carried out cooperatively by states and local communities." In late 1969 these planning guidelines were amended to require that citizen groups be allowed to participate actively in all phases of transportation planning, from goal setting through the selection of projects. The result was increasing opposition and delay for urban segments of the interstate system, and the eventual abandonment of several of them.

The urban interstate program did not live up to its expectations. Key segments were never completed because of the unexpected and undesirable side effects of massive highway construction in developed areas. And those portions that were completed did not seem to the general public to effect significant reductions in traffic congestion. Though peak congestion periods were shortened in most metropolitan areas, and nonrush hour speeds increased dramatically, rush hour commuting speeds were increased by relatively small amounts and congestion persisted [4]. The disruptive effects of highway construction perceived by urban residents were much greater than had been expected, as were the levels of economic activity lured from central areas to the suburbs [5]. In addition, air pollution and gasoline consumption in the nation's cities were undoubtedly greater than they would have been under a less ambitious urban highway program.

The history of the urban highway program suggests that had its long-run implications been fully appreciated at the outset, a rather different set of decisions would have been made. In this respect, Lewis Mumford's assessment shortly after the enactment of the program was prophetic. Mumford's assessment was prophetic in another respect as well: it is now too late to "correct" many of the undesirable impacts of urban highways. For better or worse, the structure of urban areas in the U.S. has been permanently affected by the highway program. Though many undoubtedly wish otherwise, policymakers now must accept that urban societies are and will continue to be heavily automobile oriented.

By comparison with the highway program, government involvement in financing mass transit is a relatively recent activity. Though local governments have regulated transit services and fares since the turn of the century, in most cities transit systems were financially self-supporting until the mid-1960s or even later.

As rapid increases in postwar automobile ownership and use gradually eroded the transit market, transit operators were forced to ask local regulators for authority to implement fare increases and service cutbacks. When they were unable to obtain the fare and service changes they needed to maintain profitability, the operators began to seek financial assistance from government bodies at the local, state, and federal levels. Government assistance eventually was provided, but not before the financial condition of the transit industry had deteriorated to the point of crisis in several cities.

Mass transit has been considered primarily a local responsibility, with few areas of direct interest for the state and federal governments. Consequently, the higher levels of government have been reluctant to become too heavily involved in financing mass transit. In its initial mass transit assistance program in 1964, the federal government decided that its funds should be used only for capital expenditures, and that operating expenses should continue to be covered out of the farebox or from other non-federal revenue sources. The rationale for this policy stemmed from a concern that use of federal funds for operating expenses would encourage inefficient operations. Since the federal government could have little or no influence over the expenditure of operating funds, it was reasoned, federal funds should not be used for that purpose.

In 1964 the U.S. Congress was persuaded that a federal program of capital assistance would provide the basis for viable mass transit systems in the nation's cities. Unfortunately, the reality was completely different. Many cities used federal funds to purchase and upgrade the assets of their private transit companies, only to find a few years later that they had incurred new financial obligations resulting from growing operating deficits. In some cities, major new rail transit investments were made in the naive belief that fare revenues would cover operating expenses. Substantial operating deficits were the result of these undertakings as well.

The federal capital assistance program certainly did not achieve its objectives of providing a long-term cure for the ills of mass transit. Moreover, the restriction of federal funds to capital expenses had some perverse impacts on transit efficiency. Transit operators retired many of their vehicles prematurely because federal assistance made new vehicles relatively inexpensive. And a few cities chose to develop capital-intensive rail systems rather than less capital-intensive buses, when buses would have been less costly overall [4].

When growing political support for transit finally led in 1974 to the provision of federal funds for operating assistance, the new program was separated legislatively and administratively from the earlier capital assistance program. As part of its effort to reduce the growth of federal domestic programs, the Reagan administration proposed in 1981 to eliminate the operating assistance program and to return to capital assistance as the only form of federal financial involvement in mass transit. Evaluation data drawn from six years of federal experience were used to argue that operating assistance had encouraged excessive cost inflation in transit operations. These impacts, together with the wasteful capital expenditures attributed to the capital assistance program, suggest that the structure of federal mass transit assistance has had the undesirable side effect of undermining transit efficiency.

A further shortcoming of federal transit assistance has been its neglect of the less conventional paratransit modes of public transportation [6]. Car pools, van pools, subscription buses, shared taxis, and jitneys can all contribute to the objectives of the federal mass transit program if they are encouraged to play appropriate roles. By directing virtually all of its attention and assistance to conventional mass transit, the federal government has overlooked the potential of less expensive paratransit alternatives. Though the gasoline shortages of the 1970s created new interest in high occupancy modes like car pools and van pools, other paratransit operations like shared taxis and jitneys still receive little attention. Interest in these options has increased somewhat at state and local government levels, however, despite the absence of strong federal encouragement.

Governmental influence in highways and transit derived primarily from government financing activities. By comparison, government efforts to mitigate the undesirable aspects of automobile use have relied almost entirely on *regulation*. Three major goals have been pursued: improved safety, reduced air pollution, and reduced energy consumption.

The primary evaluation criterion for regulatory strategies has been cost-effectiveness, and much of the policy debate has been concerned with the validity of the cost-effectiveness estimates associated with different strategies. Another topic of debate has been the degree to which the government is being unnecessarily paternalistic in dictating government levels of safety or air quality to individual drivers and communities. More recently, the financial difficulties of the automobile industry have raised additional concerns that government regulations on automobile design may be placing undue financial burdens on the manufacturers of automobiles.

Evaluations of alternative strategies for improving safety and reducing pollution and fuel consumption generally have concluded that major improvements can be achieved only by improving the performance of the automobile [4]. While other measures such as driver training and expanded transit services can make significant contributions, the levels of improvement sought by government legislators cannot be achieved without major changes in the design of the automobile itself. Consequently, the controversial evaluation issues have been concerned primarily with the nature and timing of the changes proposed in automobile design rather than with the general strategy of modifying the automobile through regulation.

In the safety area, most of the controversy has focused on the procedure generally considered one of the most cost-effective ways of reducing traffic fatalities: the installation of passive restraint systems such as airbags or automatic seat belts. The major concerns about requiring the installation of passive restraints are the overall capital costs involved, the possibility that even automatic seat belts will be deliberately defeated by users, and that mandating such installations displays governmental paternalism. The importance of the last point is reinforced by the unwillingness of government policymakers to require the use of existing seat belts, a strategy which has effected substantial reductions in fatalities in other countries. Other proposed design regulations such as bumper standards and removal of interior obstructions to driver vision also have been controversial because of cost and paternalism implications.

The great interest during the 1960s in reducing various forms of environmental pollution was translated into a number of legislative standards and administrative regulations. In the case of motor vehicle emissions, the criteria and deadlines established by the Clean Air Act Amendments of 1970 were extremely ambitious, and they have since gradually been weakened or postponed. The desire for cleaner air has not necessarily decreased, however. Evaluation of the various standards and regulations imposed on automobile emissions and urban air quality simply has concluded that the original proposals were rather coarse instruments which require modification and fine-tuning.

A number of specific modifications to air quality regulations are receiving consideration. Some relaxation of emission standards by geographic area might greatly reduce the costs of emission controls [4]. The introduction of fleet emission standards rather than individual vehicle standards also might reduce costs without major sacrifices in benefits. Any major changes will require amendments to the Clean Air Act, however, and may well be opposed vigorously by environmental groups. Since very specific standards have been incorporated into legislation, changes probably will be politically difficult to accomplish, no matter how much they may contribute to the overall cost-effectiveness of the air quality program.

Fuel economy standards for automobiles were a product of the rather traumatic fuel shortages experienced in the mid-1970s. As such, they were part of a broad range of governmental initiatives responding to a sudden energy crisis. Though the standards were unpopular with the automobile manufacturers at the time, they are proving to be highly effective in reducing gasoline consumption. The standards may also have helped the financial condition of the U.S. automobile manufacturers by forcing the industry to shift to smaller cars in time to respond to the changing consumer demand. Of course, a substantial tax on imported petroleum might have had an even more beneficial impact had it been a politically feasible option. Perhaps some combination of petroleum taxes and fuel economy standards will emerge as an acceptable strategy in the future.

Several major difficulties continue to challenge the regulation of automobile performance. First, the public policy objectives involved are somewhat contradictory. Small cars use less fuel and emit less pollution than large cars, for example, but they are also less safe. And while diesel-powered vehicles use less fuel than gasoline-powered vehicles, they have substantially greater levels of particulate emissions. Second, advances in vehicle technology are gradually changing the costs of achieving certain levels of safety, emission control, and fuel consumption. And finally, public perceptions of the relative importance of regulatory policy objectives appear to be changing over time. Considerable flexibility will be required to respond to these changing conditions and values, a characteristic which hitherto has been sadly lacking in governmental initiatives.

LESSONS FOR THE FUTURE

The evaluation of urban transportation programs to date provides important lessons for the development of policies and programs for the future. If the past is a reliable guide, community values will continue to change to some degree over time. In addition, the political process will tend to favor simplistic strategies over more complex but more effective ones, and well-intentioned programs often will produce disappointing and even undesirable results.

The likelihood of changes in community values suggests that programs should be designed with enough flexibility to detect the need for modifications and to permit them to be made. Earmarking a fixed tax per gallon of gasoline for highway construction was successful in funding a massive highway program, for example, but has proved highly inflexible in the face of a shift in community priorities towards mass transit and highway maintenance. In order to detect and respond to these shifts in priorities and values, programs must include a continuing evaluation component and a means for incorporating evaluation results into the program.

The occasional failure of programs to produce the expected results further emphasizes the need for continuing evaluation and for the flexibility to make program changes suggested by evaluation results. The capital grant program for urban mass transportation achieved its original objective of recapitalizing the transit industry, but went on in later years to encourage premature capital replacement and excessive reliance on capital-intensive solutions to mass transportation problems. Although close study and evaluation of the program have confirmed these impacts, changes cannot be made to it without major new legislative initiatives. Once established, programs of this kind have tended to remain essentially unchanged largely because of legislative inertia.

To date, the political process which shapes governmental involvement in urban transportation has been driven more by crisis pressures and by the lure of dramatic, visible programs than by careful assessments of costs and impacts. As a result, government programs often have been once and for all initiatives, amenable to revision only under new crisis pressures. The highway, mass transportation, and automobile regulation programs all fit this description to some degree.

Coupled with the resistance of elected officials to measures which are unpopular with well-organized constituency groups, these characteristics of the political process pose special problems for program planners. In addition to the technical merits of the programs, planners must consider the potential for initial political acceptance and for later modification as the need arises. In particular, they must be alert to the dangers that programs conceived under crisis pressures will eventually become "blunt instruments" inappropriate to emerging needs, and that wishful thinking will be allowed to justify overly simplistic programs when more complex responses are needed.

Past experience suggests that the greatest difficulties confronting the evaluators of transportation policies lie not so much in the framing of the initial criteria as in modifying the criteria to reflect changing priorities, and not so much in predicting initial consequences as in dealing with uncertainty over time. Evaluation criteria developed during initial policy implementation frequently have required modification to reflect changing values and unexpected outcomes. And while the short-run consequences of new policies usually have conformed to expectations, long-run consequences frequently have not. The evaluation challenge, therefore, is less a matter of improved data and methodology than a need for more rapid incorporation of evaluation results into the policy-making process. There is little in past experience to suggest that improved data and methodology could substitute for more frequent evaluation and revision of policies and programs.

The pressures of tight budgets at all levels of government in the early 1980s has created opportunities as well as problems for urban transportation. Strong incentives now exist for political leaders to revise programs which have not been generating the desired types or levels of benefits. Strong incentives also exist for managers of transportation facilities and services to increase efficiency and productivity. These conditions combine an urgent need for improved policies and strategies with a political climate favorable to change. A new opportunity now exists to incorporate the evaluation lessons from past policies and programs into improved strategies for the future.

REFERENCES

1. Creighton, R. L. *Urban Transportation Planning*. University of Illinois Press, Chicago, IL, 1970.
2. Altshuler, A. A., with Womack, J. P., and Pucher, J. R. *The Urban Transportation System: Politics and Policy Innovation*. The MIT Press, Cambridge, MA, 1979.
3. Mumford, L. *The Highway and the City*. Harcourt, Brace and World, New York, 1963.
4. Meyer, J. R., and Gomez-Ibanez, J. A. *Autos, Transit, and Cities*. Harvard University Press, Cambridge, MA, 1981.
5. Muller, T., Neels, K., Tilney, J., and Dawson, G. The Economic Impact of I-295 on the Richmond Central Business District . Contract Report No. 5068-01, The Urban Institute, Washington, D.C., 1977.
6. Kirby, R. F., Bhatt, K. U., Kemp, M. A., McGillivray, R. G., and Wohl, M. *Paratransit: Neglected Options for Urban Mobility*. The Urban Institute, Washington, D.C., 1975.

11
An Experiment in Federal Personnel Management: The Naval Laboratories Demonstration Project

Lloyd G. Nigro / *Department of Political Science, Georgia State University, Atlanta, Georgia*

Ross Clayton / *School of Public Administration, University of Southern California, Los Angeles, California*

INTRODUCTION

The latest effort to improve the performance of the federal personnel system is the 1978 U.S. Civil Service Reform Act. In this case study, we will examine a novel, agency-developed, effort at personnel management innovation made possible under provisions of Title VI of the CSRA. Two Navy research and development centers in California, the Naval Ocean Systems Center (NOSC) in San Diego and the Naval Weapons Center (NWC) at China Lake, are currently undergoing the first demonstration project to be approved by the U.S. Office of Personnel Management. Since this demonstration involves important changes in traditional approaches to position classification, pay administration, and performance evaluation, its outcome could have major implications for personnel administration throughout the federal system and, indeed in many state and local governments. Therefore, we believe it important that students of public personnel administration and practitioners be aware of what is going on at these laboratories. The case study is organized into five sections as follows:

1. Background on the CSRA in general, Title VI, and the programs they are designed to address;
2. The specific reasons why the demonstration project was conceived and proposed by the Navy Centers;
3. The principal features of the demonstration;

4. A review of the process used to produce the final evaluation design: and
5. A brief description of the reasons why this "bottom up" effort at personnel management innovation gained government approval.

THE CSRA: MANAGEMENT-ORIENTED FEDERAL PERSONNEL ADMINISTRATION

Passage of the CSRA in 1978 represented a significant victory for those who for decades had been arguing that the federal personnel system required strong executive leadership. Reforms designed to strengthen executive control, streamline personnel practices, and increase managerial flexibility have been the themes of a series of reports and recommendations going back some forty years. Particularly in regard to the structural reorganization of federal personnel administration and the establishment of the Senior Executive Service, the CSRA incorporates major elements of recommendations made by the Brownlow Committee (1936-37) and the First and Second Hoover Commissions (1949 and 1955). In other words, the CSRA's emphasis on management-oriented personnel administration is not new. What is new, of course, is that the CSRA is the first comprehensive reorganization and re-orientation of the federal personnel system to win Congressional approval since the Pendleton Act.

The key elements of the CSRA are by now well known. Briefly, those of special relevance here are the following.

1. A sweeping reorganization of the administrative structure for personnel management. The Civil Service Commission is abolished, and its functions have been divided among several agencies. The Office of Personnel Management (OPM) is now the President's "arm" for personnel management and labor relations. The Merit Systems Protection Board (MSPB) is an independent agency charged with responsibility for assuring that OPM and the administrative agencies covered by the Act conform to merit principles. The Federal Labor Relations Authority (FLRA) is responsible for administration of the federal labor relations program, as enacted in Title VII of the CSRA. Under specified conditions, the Equal Employment Opportunity Commission (EEOC) shares jurisdiction over complaints of discrimination with MSPB.
2. The pre-CSRA government-wide performance appraisal system was repealed, and the Act requires federal agencies to establish new systems which: (a) provide for regular appraisals of job performance, (b) encourage employee participation in the setting of performance standards, (c) use appraisals as a basis for personnel actions, (d) produce accurate evaluations of performance based on objective job-related criteria, and (e) provide for rewarding superior or outstanding performance while allowing the opportunity to assist those whose performance is sub-standard.

3. For managers and supervisors in grades GS-13 through GS-15, a merit pay plan is established. For this group, within-grade step increases are eliminated, and they can be paid any rate between the minimum and maximum for their grade. Funding for the merit pay pool is drawn from money that would have been spent on step increases and comparability funds remaining after OPM has made its initial allocation (at least 50 percent of the comparability pay raise must be given automatically, but OPM may grant more). Merit pay decisions must be based on the individual's performance as determined by the agency's appraisal system.
4. Under Title VI of the CSRA, OPM is authorized to conduct and support public management research and to implement demonstration projects intended to test innovative methods. No more than ten such demonstrations may be active at any given time. Each demonstration is limited to a maximum of 5,000 covered employees, and a demonstration must be completed within five years. OPM is authorized to waive existing personnel laws and regulations (with the exception of those covering political activities, EEO, and leave, insurance, and annuity provisions). Waivers cannot violate merit principles or permit otherwise prohibited personnel practices. OPM is required to develop, publish, and hold public hearings on demonstration plans, and it must notify affected employees and the Congress of the proposed demonstration at least six months in advance of implementation. Three months prior to implementation, OPM must again report to the Congress. The CSRA requires OPM and agency management to consult or negotiate with unions where negotiated agreements that would be affected exist. If the employees involved are not covered by a negotiated agreement, management must consult with them in a good faith effort to obtain suggestions and to deal with real as well as perceived problems.

The structural reorganization of the federal personnel system has been accomplished, but significant issues concerning the actual powers and responsibilities of the various units remain to be resolved. Prior to the election of President Reagan and the appointment of Donald Devine as its director, OPM had chosen to interpret liberally the CSRA's provisions for decentralizing and the delegation of authority in such areas as hiring. The present administration adheres to a far more restrictive interpretation insofar as OPM-agency relations are concerned. With regard to interpretation of Title VI, the demonstration project described here was conceived, designed, and approved in an atmosphere that was very supportive of agency-level initiatives. Under former OPM Director Alan K. Campbell, OPM encouraged federal agencies to propose demonstrations, assumed a consultative and supportive role, and defined its responsibilities largely in terms of *evaluation* of demonstration outcomes. We do not know how the Reagan administration interprets Title VI. Director Devine has stated on several occasions that the Naval

Laboratories Demonstration Project will likely be the *only* project conducted during the Reagan administration.

Although the Reagan administration has expressed support for the merit pay concept, implementation has not gone smoothly. Performance appraisal systems conforming to CSRA standards and merit pay were to be fully operational on the agency level by September, 1981. Many agencies did have performance appraisal systems in place by that date, but the first scheduled pay-out under merit pay was delayed for most agencies after the GAO disagreed with the methods used by OPM to calculate how much money would be needed. In retrospect, the technical and "political" problems associated with implementation were predictable. The CSRA's goals are ambitious, and the changes required are extensive. Even after the formal procedures for implementation are in place, it will be some time before we know if the merit pay concept will achieve its objectives relating to employee performance and organizational effectiveness.

Performance Appraisals and Pay Administration: Performance Gaps in the Pre- CSRA System

In mandating the development of discriminating and organizationally relevant performance evaluation in conjunction with merit pay, the CSRA addresses what were seen to be serious problems afflicting federal personnel administration. Existing evaluation methods and practices were not considered to be managerially functional. Many federal employees saw little connection between performance ratings and pay and other personnel actions. Several surveys of employee attitudes made during the 1970's had revealed that only about 50 percent saw a positive connection between performance and pay [1]. In 1979, OPM conducted a survey of some 14,500 federal workers. Although the respondents were somewhat more positive about the relationship between performance and pay, the findings summarized in Table 1 reveal considerable dissatisfaction with the pre-CSRA performance evaluation system. [2]

OPM conducted a follow-up survey of GS-13 and above personnel in 1980. The findings suggest that the situation regarding performance appraisals and pay had not improved very much in the opinion of those queried. Forty-three percent of the respondents believed that ratings are assigned regardless of performance. In 1979, 62 percent of GS-13+ personnel reported that they believed performance appraisals do influence personnel actions. In 1980, however, only 48 percent expressed this belief. Finally, 51 percent did not think that the appraisal system would discriminate among levels of performance [3]. Excluding SES personnel, almost all of whom had gone through one cycle of appraisals in 1980, most merit pay employees were undergoing their first experience with the CSRA-based systems in 1981. Therefore, as of this writing, it is clearly too early to say if these data suggest serious problems are emerging.

Data obtained from the laboratories undergoing the demonstration may provide useful advance indications of how performance appraisal and merit pay will

Table 1 Opinions of Federal Workers Concerning Pre-CSRA Appraisals and Pay-Performance Linkages (1979)

	D	DK	A
Performance Appraisals Do Influence Personnel Actions Taken In This Organization	22	17	62
This Organization Considers Performance Appraisal To Be An Important Part Of A Supervisor's Duties	18	21	61
My Performance Ratings Presents A Fair And Accuract Picture Of My Actual Job Performance	26	23	51
	NH	SH	H
Did Your Last Performance Appraisal Help You To:			
(A) Assess Your Strengths And Weaknesses?	44	33	23
(B) Determine Your Contribution To The Organization?	42	30	27
(C) Improve Your Performance?	46	31	23
	NI	SI	I
How Important Is The Quality Of Your Performance In Determining Your Pay?*	15	23	62

*GS-13+ only
Key: D=Disagree; DK=Don't Know; A=Agree; NH=Not Helpful; SH=Somewhat Helpful; H=Helpful; NI=Not Important; SI=Somewhat Important; I=Important
Due to rounding error, row percentages may not add up to 100%.

fare throughout the federal system. Laboratory personnel are now well into their second cycle, and attitudinal as well as objective measures of the demonstration's impact should begin to reveal trends by late 1982.

Personnel Administration as Management: Supervisory Authority and Discretion Under CSRA

A major complaint against the pre-CSRA system was that it did not allow supervisors to use personnel policies as positive management tools. Under CSRA, OPM and the federal agencies are encouraged to develop policies and procedures which enhance supervisory discretion and promote management-oriented personnel practices. As Table 2 reveals, federal supervisors could be expected to welcome this change.

OPM's preliminary report on its 1980 findings does not include any data on perceptions of supervisory authority. However, 1981 data on attitudes at the demonstration laboratories shows movement toward feelings of enhanced authority and discretion. It is not possible to extrapolate this trend to the entire federal service because supervisors at two control laboratories actually report *less* authority and discretion. Whether or not this indicates that the mainline CSRA program is in trouble remains to be seen, but, at this juncture, it appears that the demonstration laboratories are doing better at the task of increasing supervisory control over personnel management [4].

The Naval Laboratories Demonstration Project and the CSRA

It is against the background described above that the experiments at NWC and NOSC are taking place. In certain very important respects the changes being tested at the laboratories go beyond the limits placed on other agencies which must work

Table 2 Perceptions Of Supervisory Authority In Personnel Management (1979)

Item	D	DK	A
I Do Not Have Enough Authority To Remove People From Their Jobs If They Perform Poorly	36	9	55
I Do Not Have Enough Authority To Hire Competent People When I Need Them	33	6	60
I Do Not Have Enough Authority To Promote People	38	6	54
I Do Not Have Enough Authority to Determine My Employees Pay	20	9	71

*GS-13 (Data from NOSC and NWC in 1979 do not differ significantly)
Key: D=Disagree; DK=Don't know; A=Agree
Due to rounding error, row percentages may not add up to 100%.

within laws, regulations, and policies not waived under provisions of Title VI. In areas such as employee coverage by grade, classification structures and procedures, and merit pay formulae, the demonstration laboratories are exploring alternatives not now open to the rest of the federal establishment. This does not mean, however, that the demonstration project deviates from the concept of management-oriented personnel administration that is central to the CSRA. It is a logical extension of the assumptions and purposes driving the CSRA. As such, its results will likely provide a preview of the CSRA's future.

REASONS FOR THE DEMONSTRATION

In general terms, the purpose of the experiment at NOSC and NWC is to determine (under controlled conditions) what happens when line managers are given more authority over and responsibility for personnel actions. As will become clear in our description of the process used to arrive at an evaluation design, OPM approached the demonstration as a "micro" level test of the assumptions underpinning the CSRA's "macro" emphasis on management-oriented personnel practices. The Navy's approach on the other hand, was somewhat more direct. Its overall objective is summarized in the project proposal.

> *The purpose of this project is to demonstrate that the effectiveness of federal laboratories can be enhanced by allowing greater managerial control over personnel functions. [5]*

From the Navy's standpoint, the demonstration is an exercise in problem solving. More specifically, managers at the two laboratories were convinced that the pre-CSRA personnel system severely restricted their capacity to manage human resources effectively. Therefore, they saw the provisions of Title VI as an unusual opportunity to make changes which, they hoped, would greatly improve their capabilities in this area. Accordingly, the dominant features of the demonstration were expressly designed to solve five organizational "problems."

First, the existing position classification system and its associated procedures was judged to be overly complex and confusing to line managers. Managers were dependent on the expertise of personnel analysts who, through their control over classification decisions, effectively limited supervisory control over pay and performance standards. Classification rules were inflexible, and the process itself was cumbersome. Recruitment was frequently slowed and the laboratories were often not able to make competitive salary offers to high qualified candidates. Internal transfers and movement from one functional area to another were often difficult at best. The grade structure, in combination with policies related to average grade level and high grade level ceilings, limited management's ability to move employees up or down in the system. Finally, classification-related actions were time consuming and, therefore, laboratory personnel specialists were not able to concentrate fully on providing timely support services to line management.

Second, the pre-CSRA performance appraisal and pay practices used at the laboratories were seen to be largely ineffective as positive management tools. Like their counterparts throughout the federal government, laboratory supervisors found it difficult, if not impossible, to connect performance with pay. In other words, laboratory management believed that it did not have an organizationally functional or controllable incentives system to work with.

Third, pay rigidities caused by the classification system and the lack of any demonstrably strong relationship between pay and performance were thought to be crippling the laboratories' recruitment programs. It also led to retention problems for high performing GS-12's and GS-13's. Management believed that being able to offer competitive beginning salaries in conjunction with the assurance that pay would keep pace with performance would significantly improve the laboratories' success in recruiting and retaining highly qualified and motivated personnel.

Fourth, reduction-in-force procedures did not, in management's estimation, adequately reward employee performance or reflect value to the organization. The established criteria included performance but, in effect, did not give it more importance than such variables as veteran's status, service computation date, etc. The system also allowed competition for retention to cross career fields and levels of difficulty (grades) without regard for the skills requirements and task priorities of the organization. Consequently, there was concern about the human resources management problems that would result if the existing RIF policies were ever implemented on a significant scale.

Fifth, supervisors were dissatisfied with the adverse action procedures required to handle cases where otherwise productive employees faced problems involving alcohol, drugs, or conflicts of interest. For supervisors, adverse action procedures were complex, time consuming, and involved penalties which did little of a positive nature to remedy individual or organizational problems. Consequently, supervisors often did not take prompt action when these kinds of situations came to their attention.

Using this inventory of problems or "performance gaps" as its starting point, the Navy approached the task of designing the demonstration with a set of specific objectives in mind. These objectives may be divided into two categories: implementation objectives and outcome objectives. The basic implementation objectives were the following.

1. Re-structure the classification system in order to streamline its administration and to increase line management's influence on classification actions.

2. Develop and put into operation a performance appraisal system with high organizational utility and broadly based support among laboratory personnel.
3. Establish policies and procedures that directly link performance appraisal outcomes with pay actions.
4. Increase the weight given to performance in development of RIF retention registers and restructure the retention competition system in order to prevent human resources management problems if RIF's do become necessary.
5. Make available "suspended" adverse action penalties for appropriate cases of alcohol-substance abuse and conflicts of interest.

The outcome objectives may be summarized in the following terms.

1. Stimulate higher levels of performance on the individual, work-unit, and organizational levels.
2. Significantly improve the laboratories' success in the competition for high quality new employees.
3. Meaningfully reduce the turnover of high performing employees.
4. Focus the professional activities of Center personnel department staff on support services to line management.
5. Improve the probability that high performers will be retained under RIF conditions.
6. Increase the likelihood that supervisors will recognize alcohol-substance abuse and conflict of interest problems and respond positively to them through referrals to counseling programs and other appropriate mechanisms.

These objectives were the foundations upon which representatives of NOSC and NWC constructed the major elements of the demonstration project. In the next section, we turn to a description of the major changes proposed by the Navy and approved by OPM.

PRINCIPAL ELEMENTS OF THE DEMONSTRATION PROJECT

We will limit our discussion here to a description of how the laboratories went about the task of achieving their implementation objectives. Outcome objectives will be discussed in the context of the evaluation design.

A New Classification System

Perhaps the most radical feature of the demonstration is a complete re-structuring of the old classification system. In order to simplify the classification process, to minimize the number of actions required, and to greatly broaden the pay ranges available to employees, the GS-5 through GS-18 structure was replaced by five "levels" for professional/scientific, engineering and administrative employees. Each level groups positions by occupational category and responsibilities but, in contrast to the previous system, broadly defined standards and benchmarks are used to determine assignments to levels. After a direct transition using pre-demonstration pay as the basis for initial placements within levels, management now has considerable leeway to control what employees get paid within the limits set by the minimums and maximums for each level. Thus the new arrangement stresses supervisory discretion within guidelines set by the general standards used to identify the level to which a new or changed position should be assigned. Table 3 summarizes the new classification structure.

From the laboratories' standpoint, the new classification structure has some important benefits. It clears the way to making more competitive offers to highly qualified or scarce skills candidates for jobs because managers have greater pay ranges to work with. It reduces the number of classification actions, thereby reducing the work loads of line management and personnel specialists. Highly promotable employees can advance rapidly since they are required to spend only one year in-level although the average time is longer. The pay range available to reward high performing employees is greatly extended. The system is flexible enough to allow dual career ladders where scientific and technical personnel may continue working in their disciplines rather than having to move into "management" jobs in order to increase their pay. Finally, in many cases, classification-related barriers to internal mobility are eliminated.

An Extended Merit Pay System

In order to directly connect performance and pay, the laboratories have installed a modified version of the CSRA merit pay plan for all GS-13 through GS-15 personnel. The most significant deviation from the CSRA model is the inclusion of all scientists and engineers (GS-5 and above) and all non-scientific or engineering personnel GS-13 and above. The changed performance appraisal system applies broad performance standards to levels and functional categories and requires the development of more specialized standards for specific positions. In addition,

Table 3 Demonstration Classification Structure

I - New Professional	GS- 5 (Step 1) to GS- 8 (Step 10)
II - Associate Professional	GS- 9 (Step 1) to GS-11 (Step 10)
III - Professional	GS-12 (Step 1) to GS-13 (Step 10)
IV - Senior Professional	GS-14 (Step 1) to GS-15 (Step 10)
V - Professional Exceptional	GS-16 (Step 1) to GS-18 (Step 10)

individualized performance objectives must be established through a joint goal-setting process involving employees and their direct supervisors. Supervisors are expected to use all three sources of criteria to evaluate performance and to assign ratings.

The pay system ties compensation directly to performance ratings. Under the demonstration, high performers are very highly rewarded in comparison to their low-performing counterparts. In fact, the demonstration goes a step farther than the CSRA by creating conditions under which some employees may receive *no* pay increase (i.e., not even part of a comparability increase). Although the methods used to calculate pay-outs during the first year of the demonstration were somewhat different, Table 4 provides a good general summary of how the demonstration links pay and performance for both laboratories.

The incentive pay pool from which these increases are to be drawn is composed of funds made available for within grade increases, quality step increases, sustained superior performance awards, and promotions no longer necessary under the new classification system.

A Performance-Oriented Retention Policy

As we have already noted, under RIF conditions, federal personnel policy emphasizes seniority and veteran's status as factors which must be considered in the construction of retention lists. In contrast, the demonstration approach stresses performance. The first factor to be considered during a RIF is the performance

Table 4 The Demonstration Merit Pay Plan*

Performance Rating		Pay Increase**
Outstanding	(O)	Comparability + 2X
Exceeded Objectives	(E)	Comparability + X
Met Objectives	(M)***	Comparability
Below Objectives	(B)	50% of Comparability
Needs Improvement	(N)	No Increase

* System used at NOSC.
**The dollar value of X is set after the distribution of ratings is determined. A points method is used, and a dollar value for each point is calculated using a pay algorithm.
***M rated employees in Levels III and IV who are below the midpoint for their level receive an added amount to accelerate their reaching the midpoint.

rating each employee has received. Personnel are initially ranked within each competitive grouping, career fields and levels on the basis of performance. Tenure, veteran's preference, and length of service are then used to rank within performance categories.

Suspended Adverse Action Penalties

A suspended penalty option has been made available to laboratory management. Penalties may be suspended for six months if it is believed that the employee concerned will sincerely try to solve his or her problem. After six months, if the problem has been resolved to management's satisfaction, the penalty may be cancelled.

OPM Approval

OPM approved the demonstration project in April of 1980. In so doing, it authorized the laboratories to implement all of the changes described above. By the end of 1980, NOSC and NWC were operating under the demonstration system. In large measure, OPM's final approval was based on its acceptance of an evaluation design and methodology keyed to the demonstration's *outcome objectives*. The evaluation design itself was the product of over two years of coordinated efforts by laboratory personnel, OPM staff, and faculty from the University of Southern California. [6] In August, 1981, after a delay caused by the transition from the Carter to the Reagan Administration, OPM contracted with a private consulting firm to do the evaluation. Under terms of the contract, a series of annual reports was to be produced and a final, comprehensive, report submitted to OPM after the fifth and final year of the demonstration. However, in 1982, OPM decided to conduct the evaluation on an "in-house" basis.

EVALUATING THE DEMONSTRATION

Predictably, the task of developing an evaluation design satisfactory to the concerned parties was not easily accomplished. The scope of the demonstration, the number of major interventions, and the ambitiousness of the objectives generated complex logistical and measurement problems. These technical issues were complicated by the need to integrate the perspectives of Navy-laboratory representatives, OPM staff, and those in the USC group. Fortunately, the process of designing the evaluation began as soon as the laboratories expressed serious interest in putting together the demonstration package. All concerned were directly involved in the critical phases of what turned out to be a two-year process. The product was an evaluation strategy that: (1) was logistically as well as technically feasible, and (2) applied standards and criteria acceptable to both OPM and the Navy, and (3) assured an objective external evaluation.

The Perspectives and Roles of the Participants

The final evaluation plan integrated and, in several key areas, compromised the interests and viewpoints of the Navy, OPM, and the USC group. A preliminary evaluation scheme, published in the *Federal Register*, served as a starting point.

Navy representatives were consistently supportive of methods that could be used to produce objective longitudinal tests of the predicted causal relationships between interventions and expected outcomes. Both laboratories agreed to the extensive use of interviews, case studies, and survey questionnaires. They were also willing to provide internal records and documents. Understandably, the laboratories did not want to create conditions under which the evaluation would become overly obtrusive and, in response to this concern, a number of methodologically desirable but potentially disruptive procedures were dropped in favor of less direct methods. Most directly affected were measures of work unit and laboratory performance-effectiveness.

OPM personnel, although sympathetic to the Navy's concerns, pressed for approaches that would satisfy their needs in two areas. First, they wanted to obtain data which could be used to evaluate the extent to which the demonstration interventions might be applicable throughout the federal bureaucracy. More specifically, findings of direct relevance to personnel policies and procedures were imperative. Recognizing that statistically strong relationships between the demonstration interventions and laboratory effectiveness were unlikely, OPM concentrated on obtaining information that could be used to directly evaluate the extent to which the demonstration improved the functioning of the laboratories' personnel systems. Second, since it is the primary sponsor and consumer of the evaluation, OPM continually stressed the need to develop and conduct a methodologically sound and externally credible evaluation. Accordingly, its staff insisted on a highly detailed and carefully justified design.

At times, it was evident that the laboratories and OPM were engaged in a "struggle" over the latter's interest in "mining" the demonstration for multiple purposes and the former's concern that the evaluation concentrate on Center impacts. Therefore, in addition to its role as a technical consultant, the USC group spent a great deal of time working to interpret the ongoing dialogue between OPM and the Navy and to formulate alternatives which, if not perfect, were acceptable to both. In a number of instances, the group was able to suggest unobtrusive methods and limited sampling techniques which made possible the collection of information that OPM wanted. As each aspect of the evaluation was agreed to, the USC group proceeded to collect and analyze the required "baseline" or pre-implementation data.

The Evaluation Design

Given the space available here, it is impossible to provide a detailed description of the evaluation design approved by OPM. The interested reader should consult

OPM's request for proposals [7]. What follows is a very general summary of the design, data sources, and analytic methods. Figure 1 provides an overview of the evaluation model.

As Table 5 indicates, the evaluarion will focus on three categories of variables and measures: (1) implementation objectives; (2) impacts on social-psychological factors and personnel system functions; and (3) long-term outcomes related to individual, unit, and laboratory performance. The design specifies predicted relationships among these variables and sets forth the methods to be used to test derived hypotheses. In order to collect the data necessary to operationalize the design, a large array of field methods and instruments will be used.

Among the more important instruments and data sources are the following.

1. *Employee Attitude Survey (A Survey)*. The A Survey is a modified version of the Federal Employee Attitude Survey (FEAS). It was administered to a 25 percent sample of Demonstration and Control lab personnel between November 1979 and February 1980 to obtain baseline data. It was developed from the FEAS, emphasizing measures specifically relevant to the demonstration interventions and their anticipated effects.

Table 5 The General Evaluation Model

Implementation Measures	Intervening Impacts	Performance Outcomes
1. Classification system 2. Performance appraisal system 3. Merit pay system	1. Motivation 2. Perceived equity 3. Job satisfaction	1. Individual performance
4. Performance-based retention system 5. Suspended penalty option policy	4. Mobility 5. Recruitment success	2. Unit performance
	6. Managerial discretion 7. Differential turnover 8. Personnel department resources allocations and performance	3. Laboratory performance

The survey will be administered annually for the five year life of the evaluation. It will provide perceptual data regarding implementation status and proximate impacts.

2. *Workforce Data Base*. A data file generated from a variety of information on work unit personnel will be made available by each of the participating laboratories. It will include information such as performance ratings and pay of lab personnel that will be used to assess implementation and its impacts. The data will be collected on an annual basis. After the initial data file is constructed, updating the file will consist primarily of inputting data that are routinely available through the automated personnel files at the laboratories.
3. *Personnel Department Records*. Personnel department records will be used to provide data on a variety of variables. These measures will use the personnel data in their existing forms or be generated from simple ratios or averages of the data. They will be provided by the personnel departments on an annual basis.
4. *Interviews/Questionnaires*. The external evaluators will conduct structured interviews with supervisors from a 10 percent random sample of laboratory work units to obtain information regarding implementation of the classification system. In addition, data about the performance appraisal system will be obtained through questionnaires administered to these unit supervisors, their subordinates, and department heads. Department heads will also assess unit performance through annual questionnaires.
5. *Case Studies*. Intensive multidimensional case studies of unit performance will be conducted by the external evaluators in a maximum of ten units at each demonstration site. To minimize disruptions, case study data will be collected at three different intervals. The external evaluators will annually examine records at case study sites and conduct interviews with unit and department heads and laboratory directors.
6. *Multi-Attribute Utility Analysis*. A panel of approximately 100 experts knowledgeable about Navy labs and their products and services will assess each laboratory's performance on a variety of dimensions. These data will be obtained through questionnaires distributed to the experts and to laboratory Commanding Officers and Technical Directors by the external evaluators on an annual basis. In addition, these experts will provide subjective assessments of a variety of external constraints imposed upon the laboratories, such as budgetary constraints and difficulty of laboratory goals.
7. *Personnel Department Productivity Measurement System*. The Office of Personnel Management will install and administer a work productivity measurement system to assess changes in the pattern of personnel department activities and unit costs. The data will be collected semi-annually

or quarterly and will focus on changes in staff time devoted to numerous personnel transactions.

8. *Budget Records.* The laboratories will provide a variety of budgetary data on an annual basis. The data will be provided in a form currently available or easily derived from existing records. The external evaluators will provide information regarding the Federal budget, which is being to measure environmental constraints.
9. *RIF Simulation.* Since a significant reduction in force is unlikely during the demonstration period, a simulation will be conducted to provide comparative retention registers under the old and new retention systems. The laboratories will run the simulation in November 1983.
10. *Federal EEO Records.* The laboratories will provide EEO statistics currently maintained for preparing standard annual EEO reports. The Office of Personnel Management will provide EEO data for other federal agencies so that EEO trends can be evaluated for the demonstration.

In addition, there will be several sources of data available from the Internal Navy Evaluation of the demonstration project. These will include a "mini" version of the "A" survey, unobtrusive measures that are being obtained, and annual summaries of the Internal Evaluation. The Western Region of OPM is also conducting on-site visits, and data from these visits will be available to the contractor.

Although compromises were necessary, the evaluation design is a strong one, and it does not impose unrealistic demands on the laboratories. If the design is carefully executed, it should produce findings directly relevant to federal personnel policies and practices. More generally, the five-year evaluation results should be of great interest to those working in the fields of performance appraisal, organizational incentives, and the social psychology of employee motivation and job satisfaction.

GAINING APPROVAL OF THE DEMONSTRATION PROJECT

Why was the Navy Laboratories' proposal for a demonstration project approved as the first, and so far only, major experiment in personnel management under Title VI? In this final section, we provide an analysis of how this project emerged and gained approval. A number of interrelated factors affected the project at various stages in its evolution. We will focus upon structural factors and processes which were central and may have relevance to future efforts to undertake demonstration projects.

In our discussion, no effort will be made to single out particular individuals, although there were a number of able and dedicated public servants who played key roles at various stages.

Initiation Stage: Organizational Interest and Top-Level Support

Both of the Navy laboratories involved in this demonstration project had a history of concern over the impact of Federal personnel policies on their abilities to perform their assigned missions. The NWC had long sought increased flexibility and discretion in the personnel area. When John Macy was Chairman of the Civil Service Commission in the sixties, he personally visited China Lake to discuss these matters. NOSC had been one of the DOD laboratories which participated in Project REFLEX, a previous DOD experiment with personnel management. In short, both organizations were prepared to take the initiative when the opportunity presented by Title VI became apparent.

Shortly after passage of the CSRA, Director Campbell visited the University of Southern California to explain provisions of the Act, including Title VI. Coincidentally, that same week an employee of NWC was on campus, and the potential of Title VI was communicated to the laboratories. Meetings between NWC and NOSC began shortly thereafter, and a fast start was made in developing a proposal.

The fact that the impetus for proposing this demonstration project came from the field should not go unnoticed. The proposal was very much a "bottom up" effort which originated where problems were being immediately experienced and commitment to performance objectives was very high.

Design Stage: Inter-Organizational Cooperation

Personnel of the two laboratories collaborated effectively from the outset. The top management of both laboratories were used to working with one another and had a reservoir of mutual trust and respect. Many of the employees who took central roles at NOSC had previously worked at NWC and had ongoing work relationships that supported a cooperative orientation.

Management at the two laboratories assigned both technical and administrative employees to work on the design of the demonstration project. Key roles were played by employees of the personnel departments who understood current personnel policies and practices and where they were constraining line managers. what feasible solutions might be proposed.

Faculty of the University of Southern California were invited to participate as the proposal was being developed. Initially they served as a sounding board for proposals by laboratory personnel. Subsequently, U.S.C. faculty assumed responsibility for developing a design to evaluate the demonstration project if it were approved.

A number of factors seemed critical to this stage. The personnel specialists involved in the design were committed to a norm of enabling the line manager to manage, a point of view supported by laboratory management. A second factor was the willingness of those involved in designing the proposal to hold it "tentative" and open to input and modification as the process unfolded. This flexible approach, when coupled with a collaborative spirit and avoidance of "pride of authorship" problems, promoted a broad base of support in the laboratories.

The availability of talented individuals and financial resources required to develop the proposal also was a factor. A substantial amount of time was expended in the design stage. In addition, the willingness of the Navy laboratories to pay a portion of the costs for developing and implementing a design for OPM's external evaluation of the project was a positive consideration.

The ease with which a sound working relationship developed between the University of Southern California team and laboratory personnel merits mention. The bases for this relationship were many. There have been close, personal and professional relationships between the involved organizations for two decades. Many of the Navy personnel who worked on the design of the project hold graduate degrees from USC. Many of the USC faculty who were involved had taught or served as consultants at the laboratories.

Selling Stage: An Effective Coalition

Gaining approval of the demonstration project proposal and its associated evaluation design was facilitated by a number of factors. OPM's desire to fully implement the CSRA, including Title VI, assured a careful review of the proposal. The absence of strong vested interests opposed to the proposal also helped. Only token resistance came from veteran's groups, and no strong union interest arose, probably because blue collar workers were not included in the proposed experiment. The paucity of quality rival proposals from other federal agencies also led to OPM giving prompt and full attention to the Navy submission.

The two Navy Centers had a number of strengths going for them in terms of their ability to sell the proposal within the Navy and DOD, and subsequently to OPM. First, their organizational existence depends in part on their abilities to sell projects to their R & D clientele. Both Centers have considerable expertise in developing proposals and marketing them in Washington, D.C. This expertise was readily transferable to the demonstration project.

Center personnel have well honed sensitivities to the politics of the Navy Department and of DOD. From the very outset of the proposal they were alerting relevant individuals in their chains of command and in the civilian personnel community, including the San Francisco Regional Office of OPM which provided strong support and able advice. By the time a draft proposal was available, much of the necessary "base touching" had been done, and potential problems and obstacles had been addressed.

As the selling phase progressed, many presentations to Navy and DOD officials were made and briefings were held for members of Congress and their staff.

Concerns of OPM regarding both the proposal and evaluation design led to appropriate modifications to the draft. The willingness of the Centers to bargain and negotiate and to compromise if required helped considerably in gaining OPM's approval. In retrospect, the original proposal was not changed substantially by this process. The evaluation design, however, became much more sophisticated and its projected costs rose commensurately. [8]

Pre-Implementation Stage: Staying on Track

At the close of 1979 OPM notified the Congress of the proposed demonstration project, and a six month long pre-implementation stage began. During this period the Congress could, if they wished, hold hearings, and, if so inclined, prevent the demonstration project from being implemented.

During this stage the laboratories continued their highly participative processes of refining the proposal. Supervisory and employee training programs were undertaken and pre-implementation data were collected. OPM held hearings at China Lake, San Diego and Washington, D.C. Some objections were raised during the hearings, but they did not delay implementation. Concerned Congressional staff visited the Centers to be briefed on site. An "eleventh hour" Congressional staff request for a delay in project implementation until hearings could be held by a Congressional Committee was politely but firmly denied by OPM on the basis that it came too late. The demonstration project was begun on July 13, 1980.

The Future

Over the next few years, we hope to continue reporting on the unfolding experience and outcomes of this demonstration project. Although the two Navy Centers and their personnel may be atypical in some respects, we believe that significant insights into personnel management will be obtained from this experiment that should have considerable relevance for other federal, state and local government organizations [9].

REFERENCES

1. See Federal Personnel Management Project, *Option Paper Number Six*: *Job Evaluation, Pay, and Benefits Systems*, U.S. Government Printing Office, Washington, D.C. October 14, 1977, p. 58.
2. The OPM survey was administered to a stratified random sample of 20,000 federal employees. The response rate was about 73 percent. Data reported here are unweighted. Navy responses to the survey were very similar to those of other civilian workers. For detailed analyses of the OPM findings, see U.S. Office of Personnel Management, *Federal Employee Attitudes*; *Phase 1*:

Baseline Survey, 1979, and Federal Employees Attitudes; Baseline Survey, 1979 (U.S. Department of the Navy) , OPM Office of Planning and Evaluation, 1980, (unpublished document).

3. See U.S. Office of Personnel Management, Federal Employee Attitudes; Phase 2: Follow-Up Survey, Preliminary Report , OPM, 1980 (unpublished document).
4. These data were obtained through a 1981 Survey of personnel at NOSC and NWC, and two control laboratories. The instrument used was a modified version of the OPM questionnaire.
5. See *Federal Register*, Part IV, Vol. 44, No. 234, December 4, 1979, p. 69883.
6. These activities were funded by the Navy through a contract with USC.
7. OPM-RFP-46-81.
8. USC projected annual costs of about $125,000. OPM funded the contract for the first year at $100,000.
9. OPM's decision to conduct the "external" evaluation raises serious questions concerning the evaluation's credibility. Hopefully, OPM will provide convincing documentation, whatever its conclusions.

12
Contributions of Evaluation Research and Analysis to Energy and Environmental Policy

E. J. Soderstrom / *Oak Ridge National Laboratory, Oak Ridge, Tennessee*

B. H. Bronfman* / *Bronfman Associates, Oak Ridge, Tennessee*

INTRODUCTION

Energy and environmental[1] (E/E) issues are major social concerns which will likely intensify in the future [1]. Interest in the social aspects of E/E issues is made manifest in the thousands of studies generated by academic and government-supported researchers. The voluminous bibliographies compiled by Morrison, et al. [2, 3] and the Technical Information Center of the U.S. Department of Energy [4] testify to the breadth of this research.

In spite of all the social science research which has been conducted on E/E issues, Schnaiberg [1] and others (e.g., Wilbanks [5]) would argue that much of the work has been excessively myopic and abstract. Few social scientists have dealt directly with such questions as:

- How can the public sector address the problems arising from the use of energy and other natural resources?
- What programs have been initiated to address these problems?
- Have these programs been effective and efficient in resolving the problems?
- Is there a better, alternative approach for addressing the problems?

Attempts to answer these questions provide the information needed to improve the formulation and implementation of E/E policy.

**Present affiliation*: Portland Operations, Evaluation Research Corporation, Portland, Oregon.
[1]By energy/environment issues, we limit our discussion to energy programs and the effects of those programs on the social environment

Addressing the policy-oriented type of questions suggested above provides needed information for judging whether the implemented policy has been misguided or ineffective. In providing such information, social science research has the potential for enlightening a decision making process on a topic which directly affects all of society.

Among social scientists, a group which should be particularly inclined to participate in research to understand the impacts of public policy on social issues are evaluation researchers. Evaluation research has been defined as the creative application of social science research methods to policy-oriented issues [6, 7]. Evaluation research, however, is more than the mere application of methods. By its very nature, evaluation research is intimately related to the policy process [8, 9]. It is this intimate relationship with the policy process which sets evaluation research apart from other applied social science research (ASSR). Whereas much of ASSR is primarily concerned with studying the phenomenon or problem, evaluation research, as a subset of ASSR, focuses on the policy or program instituted to deal with the phenomenon or problem [10]. In ASSR the problem is the independent variable, in evaluation research it is the dependent variable. This is not to say that ASSR has no interest in, or influence on, policy issues. It does; but this is not necessarily the primary purpose. An essential feature of evaluation research, on the other hand, is determining what, if anything, a policy or program is accomplishing in view of original intentions for rectifying the problem. Although a good deal of ASSR on E/E issues has been conducted, little has been directly related to policy issues. Lacking this relationship, such ASSR can not properly be considered evaluation research. Where the connection to policy has been more explicit, the research has, typically, been prospective in nature and inadequately validated.

The purpose of this article is to explore the contributions of evaluation research to public policy issues in the areas of energy and the environment. For reasons that are explored in this paper, evaluation research has not played a significant role in E/E policy issues. The potential, however, is great when developments in related areas of social science research are considered. After examining the evaluation research which has been conducted, we review other relevant trends, and conclude by suggesting an integrative framework for prospective analysis and evaluation research which draws from contributions of these related developments.

EVALUATION RESEARCH IN ENERGY AND ENVIRONMENT

If one were to use some common measures (e.g., conference papers and publications in professional journals) for determining professional or disciplinary interest, it would appear that E/E programs have not been the focus of much evaluation research. For example, at the 1981 joint meeting of the Evaluation Research Society and Evaluation Network, only two panels and symposia out of more than 100 and about four papers out of more than 300 delivered dealt either directly or indirectly with energy or environmental issues. The bulk of the three-day meeting dealt with more typical social programs such as health, education and human services. *Evaluation Review* and *Evaluation and Program Planning*, two of the mainstream professional journals, have published only a few articles in the E/E area during their relatively brief histories.

Creating a Need for Evaluation

Regulatory programs are relatively inexpensive for the government to implement when compared to the income redistribution policies characterizing service delivery programs. Whereas service programs develop costly infrastructures to insure that monies are translated into services, the major public sector expense incurred in regulatory programs is in the formulation and enforcement of the standards. Moreover, regulatory programs are expected to have direct beneficial impacts on the majority of society, while the direct benefits of most service programs accrue only to certain special, typically under-privileged, populations. The presumed large societal return for such small investments of public dollars thus, until recently, insulated regulatory programs from the movement toward tighter fiscal and managerial accountability (a movement to which evaluation research can trace its roots).

Regulation versus Service Delivery Programs

Although the demand for evaluation is not new, the tremendous growth in the number of evaluative studies in the past decade can be traced to the interest in critical examinations of the social service programs of the "war on poverty" era of the early 1960s through the late 1970s. Many of the programs initiated during this era of social welfare experimentation, however, are distinctly different from most E/E programs. Rather than focusing on providing a service to improve human conditions—policies of resource distribution and redistribution [11]—E/E programs have been oriented toward regulation or research and development (R&D). Most major E/E legislation, such as the National Environmental Policy Act (NEPA) and the Clean Air Act, do not call for the delivery of any new services. They require, instead, the promulgation of standards which must be met to protect the public and the environment from unnecessary problems and degradation. In the environmental area, regulations may take such forms as establishing levels of allowable toxic emissions from smokestacks or rules for the disposal of hazardous waste. Energy regulations have included oil and natural gas price controls, pro-rationing rules (e.g., well spacing requirements and depth-acreage allowable schedules), and import quotas, to cite a few. The differences between service delivery and regulatory programs interfered with both establishing a perceived need for evaluative information and conducting evaluation studies. This situation is examined below.

Social service delivery programs have been the focus of the overwhelming majority of evaluations. Between 1975 and 1977, for example, three-fourths of all federal program evaluation dollars were spent evaluating services provided by the Departments of Health, Education and Welfare, Housing and Urban Development, and Justice [8].

When federal energy policy began to shift toward an emphasis on energy conservation after the Arab oil embargo of 1973, many of the programs initiated sought to provide services directly to energy consumers (see Table 1). These services were as diverse as weatherizing low-income family homes through the Weatherization Assistance Program to establishing a telephone energy-information hotline through the Energy Extension Service to provide residential energy-use audits through the Residential Conservation Service. Yet, in their provision of educational and assistance services, they are similar in thrust to other federal social programs.

As might have been expected, the shift in energy policy toward providing services brought with it as an increased interest in evaluation. In light of growing public interest in energy conservation, such services generated expectations for immediate and dramatic reductions in energy consumption. Rapidly expanding budget requirements for these programs quickly brought conservation programs into conflict with supply enhancement R&D programs for limited federal resources. Adequate information was not available on factors affecting energy use and performance of DOE projects to decide how much emphasis to place on conservation programs relative to supply programs, or which particular conservation programs deserved strongest support [12]. Given these competing demands for resources and information deficiencies, it is not unusual that a number of reviews of energy conservation programs emphasized the need for program evaluation [12, 13, 14].

A number of evaluations were recently undertaken of these service programs. At the federal level, evaluations were conducted on the EES program of providing

Table 1 Major Energy Conservation Legislation

Year	Act	Program Established
1975	Energy Policy and Conservation Act (P.L. 93-163)	State Energy Conservation Program (SECP)
1976	Energy Conservation and Production Act (P.L. 94-385)	Weatherization Assistance Program (WAP)
1977	Energy Extension Service Act (P.L. 95-39)	Energy Extension Service (EES)
1977	Department of Energy Organization Act (P.L. 95-91)	Office of Conservation
1978	National Energy Conservation Policy Act (P.L. 95-619).	Residential Conservation Service (RCS)

outreach information and technical assistance to small energy users [15], the Low Cost/No Cost program designed to inform New England homeowners of 11 inexpensive actions that could be taken to save up to 25% on residential energy bills [16], and the Twin Rivers Project which examined the role of residential behavior in identical energy-efficient homes to determine requirements for an effective retrofit strategy [17]. At the state level, evaluations were completed on telephone energy conservation hotlines [18] and weatherization of low-income homes [19].

Most conservation program evaluation efforts have taken place at the local level. Often these evaluations were sponsored by utilities promoting conservation efforts to reduce demand as substitutes for investment in new generating capacity. Utilities evaluated such programs as "time-of-day-pricing" where the cost of electricity is higher during periods of highest demand (reviewed in [20]), providing residential energy-use analyses with recommendations for cost-effective energy conservation measures (reviewed in [21]), various procedures to provide feedback to homeowners about their rate of energy use (reviewed in [22]), and the impact on energy consumption of using average monthly payment plans versus conventional "pay as you go" billing [23].

Other institutions have also sponsored efforts to reduce energy consumption. Some of these efforts, such as that by the University of Colorado to reduce consumption in university buildings, were evaluated [24]. However, because only limited financial resources are available for such localized studies, such systematic evaluations are relatively rare.

Service delivery-type programs, however, constitute only a relatively minor portion of federal energy policy. Judging from budget requests for FY 82 and FY 83, the role of such programs is likely to diminish further under the present Administration. Given the loss of fiscal impetus from the federal level, it is likely that many state and local programs will contract accordingly. Thus, as has historically been the case, federal E/E policy is returning to a primary concentration on R&D and regulation; albeit at substantially reduced levels under the Reagan Administration.

These policies have remained, for the most part, excepted from the critical scrutiny provided by evaluation research. While these policies are developed with the best of intentions, such intentions should not be confused with informed public policy. It is only recently that consideration of the private costs of complying with regulations, coupled with the increasing expense of enforcing regulations against non-compliance, have created demands for more accountability in regulatory programs. Generic evaluations of energy and environmental regulatory policies have been undertaken. Kneese and Schultze [25], for example, examined the impact of pollution control rules and regulations, and Mead [26] studied the performance of energy regulations. In spite of these general efforts, few evaluations have been undertaken of specific regulations. In part, this results from logistical problems in conducting an evaluation.

Problems in Conducting Regulatory Evaluations

Because regulatory programs are not concerned with delivering services, they typically have few tangible manifestations which might be readily measured and assessed when implemented. The situation is further complicated by the fact that impacts associated with the implementation of these policies or programs often do not appear immediately but rather are delayed. The delays have less to do with policy implementation than with the fact that the solutions to the problems these policies address are long term in nature. For example, the impact of water quality regulations on reducing the level of water pollution may not be noticeable for a long period. This is because the regulations focus on controlling the levels of present and future emissions in an effort to slow the rate at which the water is being fouled. But these rules can do nothing about the past levels of pollution and irreversible damages. Cleaning the water is, in most cases, a natural process which occurs over a period of time.

As a result, the evaluation of policy impacts may take a considerable number of years. This, in turn, may mean the information will not be available when it is time for a decision on whether to abolish, extend or modify the rule. Furthermore, the delayed appearance of policy impacts may confound any analysis due to the introduction of a number of factors, such as the initiation of other similar programs and technological innovations which may also be in some way responsible for the observed effect.

Some evaluations of non energy-related environmental programs were able to circumvent these problems. Friesema et al. [27] and Wright et al. [28] used existing, archival data sources to perform retrospective, longitudinal studies of the long-range consequences of natural disasters. These studies were both directed at assessing whether the Title V provisions of the Disaster Relief Act Amendments of 1975, for federal assistance in the long-term economic recovery of disaster-stricken areas, should be implemented. Maki et al. [29] and Berk et al. [30] also collected archival data sources to perform time series analyses to determine the impacts of local regulations aimed at reducing water consumption in a number of California communities during the droughts of 1976-1977. The Committee on Community Reactions to the Concorde [31] capitalized on the staged nature of the introduction of Concorde aircraft operations in the United States to evaluate the impact of noise associated with those operations. This circumstance allowed information to be obtained during the evaluation of the early landings at Kennedy Airport in New York City and Dulles Airport outside Washington, D.C. used to make recommendations for regulating the initiation of operations at later sites [32].

Retrospective versus Prospective Analyses

The above examples appear to be isolated. There has been little interest in, or support for, conducting retrospective analyses of regulatory programs. This is not to say there is no interest in analyzing the impact of regulations. The interest, however, is typically in prospective analyses conducted prior to implementation. The laudable intention has been to provide an analysis of potential impacts prior to introduction of any regulation, rather than to rely on such mechanisms as evaluated trials during staged implementation of a regulation. Although there has been little legislative or institutional impetus for retrospective evaluations, prospective analyses have been continually mandated for proposed regulatory programs. NEPA, for example, requires an assessment of the potential impacts of any major federal action, such as construction of a nuclear power plant, to be used in the planning and decision making concerning the proposal. The need for prospective analysis for making decisions was recently re-emphasized. In an effort to curb excessive federal regulation, President Reagan issued Executive Order (EO) 12291 on February 17, 1981. In mandating a Regulatory Impact Analysis for all proposed regulations, the EO states:

> *Administrative decisions shall be based on adequate information concerning the need for and consequences of proposed governmental action. . .*

In the E/E area, two types of prospective analysis have been developed: impact analysis (IA) and technology assessment (TA). In general, both approaches seek to determine the potential impacts on the biophysical and social environments of change due to any major federal action in IAs or due to technology in TAs.

PROSPECTIVE ANALYSIS IN ENERGY/ENVIRONMENT

The impetus to conduct such policy analyses as IAs and TAs grows out of an increasing awareness that the social environment and biophysical environments are complexly interrelated and inseparable [1, 33, 34]. This view means that any change imposed on the environment by society, through the introduction of a technology to produce energy for example, was, in turn, causing change in society. Thus, just as with the provision of services, regulatory and R&D policies have impacts. These impacts are especially apparent as these policies are made manifest by technological changes. The growing realization is that every improvement made in the name of social progress contains costs for some person or group. Further, sometimes these costs equal or outweigh the benefits accrued. Often the public is unwilling to bear the costs of unintended consequences of technological expansion, or accept the assertion that direct benefits outstrip indirect costs.

In a society long dependent upon technological change and consumption of natural resources, an increased understanding of technological change was necessary to ensure the maximum benefits of stable growth and development over succeeding generations. As a result of these concerns, legislation was enacted to institutionalize new methods and organizations intended to expand technological planning.

Impact Analysis (IA)

IAs predict and assess the environmental consequences, both physical and social, of policies, programs, or projects while still in the planning stages [35]. The beginning of IA can be attributed directly to the enactment of the NEPA in 1969. Section 102(c) of NEPA requires systematic, interdisciplinary assessment of impacts of all proposed major federal actions deemed to significantly affect the quality of the human environment. Of particular importance to social scientists, the *Calvert Cliffs* decision of 1972 established the precedent for social impact analysis (SIA) as a legitimate area of inquiry in such assessments. This precedent has been further institutionalized through policies set by such agencies as the Council on Environmental Quality (CEQ), the Army Corps of Engineers, the U.S. Nuclear Regulatory Commission (NRC), the Environmental Protection Agency (EPA) and the DOE by their support and review of mandated environmental impact statements (EIS). Thousands of impact statements have been completed on a variety of large-scale federal projects ranging from construction of highways to synthetic fuels facilities [36].

IAs, as may be noted from the above definition, are conducted before projects or programs have been implemented. IA's have typically been conducted without the benefit of valid empirical evidence concerning actual impacts. In attempts to add order and discipline to a new and evolving process, Fitzsimmons et al. [37], Finsterbusch and Wolf [38], McEvoy and Dietz [39] and Rau and Wooten [40] have developed "handbooks" or "guidelines" for preparing environmental impact statements. The state of knowledge has been further codified through the production of a number of bibliographies cataloguing impact analyses in various areas [41, 42, 43, 44]. While such bibliographies and handbooks are helpful in systematizing and adding rigor to the IA process, the process remains prospective in focus.

Social scientists working in the area of SIA, however, have recognized the importance of doing rigorous retrospective research in the EIS process. Shields [45] for example, has called for the development of "grounded theory" in the context of SIA, and Soderstrom [34] has detailed a framework in which the empirical evidence for such a theory might be obtained.

Yet, as Meidinger and Schnaiberg [46] point out, SIA has had little of the verification commonly thought to be a distinguishing feature of scientific inquiry. Few sponsored attempts have been made to validate SIA projections. Some research was sponsored by the NRC in a series of "post-licensing" studies, in which retrospective examinations of communities with operating nuclear power plants were undertaken [47, 48]. Additionally, a comparative case study of 14 operating nuclear power plants, also sponsored by the NRC, took a more comprehensive, retrospective look at operating nuclear power plants [49]. The Electric Power Research Institute (EPRI) sponsored a socioeconomic analysis of electricity generating facilities, both nuclear and fossil-fueled, again in a retrospective framework [50]. Currently a project is being sponsored by the Bureau of Land Management (BLM) under the title of the "Social Effects Project" [44]. This project is designed to address the social effects of energy development in the West. The scope of this effort is wider than previous SIA research, and a theoretical framework is being developed and tested. It is, furthermore, a retrospective study that relies on primary data collection in impacted communities and secondary data on a regional scale.

While enlightening and necessary for providing empirical data, this retrospective research was designed primarily for hypothesis development and descriptive analysis, rather than to verify the prospective analyses. For the most part, sponsors have been unable, or unwilling, to commit resources to such verification or evaluation, and thereby assure the validity and reliability of the projections.

Technology Assessment (TA)

TA is described as a class of policy studies examining a wide range of societal consequences resulting from the introduction of a new technology or the use, or extension, of existing technologies in new or innovative ways [51]. The role of TA is the anticipation or projection of impacts and the recommendation of policies to assist in the efficient deployment of technologies.

As might be noted from the definitions, TAs are very similar to impact analyses. While the differences between the two types of policy studies are seldom clear cut, TAs tend to be broader in focus than impact analyses. TAs typically assess a technology in general, whereas impact analyses usually are limited to assessing a particular project's embodiment of a technology. Thus, a TA may be performed on the generation of electricity using nuclear power, while an impact analysis would discuss the consequences of a specific nuclear power plant at a particular location.

TA was promoted as a means of informing policymakers on the technical and socioeconomic merits or consequences of a technological program [52]. Interest in TA was made manifest through the passage of the Technology Assessment Act of 1972 and subsequent establishment of the Congressional Office of Technology Assessment (OTA). TA was further institutionalized by TA programs begun in such executive branch agencies as EPA, DOE, and the President's Office of Science and Technology Policy.

TAs were conducted in such areas as solar and renewable energy, conservation, hazardous waste policy, and nuclear fission and fusion energy. In the case of solar energy development, for example, both OTA and DOE sponsored TAs [53,

54, 55]. These studies, as with most TAs, explored the future impacts of technology deployment and suggested ways of alleviating projected barriers to the introduction of these technologies.

Shortcomings of IAs and TAs

Technology assessments and impact analyses, then, are future-directed exercises which attempt to project potential consequences of change, often induced by technology. Ideally, they are used to inform policymakers in the formulation or reformulation of energy or environmental policy.

Arnstein and Christakis [56] suggest a range of possible outcomes of such analyses:

- Modification of the project
- Specification of a program of environmental or social monitoring
- Stimulation of R&D to deal with adverse consequences of the project
- Stimulation of research to specify or define risks
- Development of latent benefits
- Identification of regulatory and legal changes to promote or control the technology or project
- Definition of institutional arrangements appropriate to the project
- Definition of intervention experiments to reduce negative or enhance positive consequences
- Delay the project or technology until some of the preceding steps are completed
- Stop the project or technology
- Provide a reliable base of information to parties at interest.

Often, however, these analytic efforts are restricted to "modeling" efforts, and just as often they are used to justify, rather than contribute to, policy development [46, 51]. In large part this situation may be due to the perceived lack of credibility and value-ladenness inherent in such analyses when confronted with inadequate data bases and analytic techniques [34, 57].

It would be naive to suggest that facts give answers. But it is not naive, as Riecken and Boruch [58] point out, to suggest that a body of established findings will at least provide a firmer common ground on which to conduct interpretive debates. Historically, however, once a TA or impact analysis is undertaken at the beginning of a program or project, it is seldom revisited in a policy context. While several proposals have been made to validate results of the "front-end" TAs or IAs [59, 60, 61] such efforts have not been undertaken. Yet, such prospective assessments require a capacity for rational forethought that, to no small extent, depends on an understanding of the processes from which the future is generated. Because few retrospective evaluations have been undertaken, however, little valid information is available from which to gain such an understanding.

In view of the potentially important role that such prospective analyses can play in the formation of E/E policy in terms of shaping the development of a technology and rules pertaining to its implementation, it seems reasonable to expect that TAs and IAs be based on such valid information. Through investigation and validation of the prospective analyses, evaluation research can fulfill the role of providing factual information about the actual impacts of E/E regulatory and R&D policies.

INTEGRATION OF RETROSPECTIVE AND PROSPECTIVE ANALYSES

In order for E/E policymaking to be conducted in a truly enlightened manner, the two policy research traditions of retrospective and prospective analyses must be fully integrated. At present, the efforts are disjointed. Evaluations have been conducted on service delivery programs, but the programs were typically not preceded by a thorough impact analysis. TAs on most major R&D programs, and impact analyses on specific implementations of technologies and regulations, have been conducted; few, however, have been followed up and evaluated.

Both analytical elements, retrospective and prospective, are necessary for a comprehensive evaluation. Rossi et al. [14] suggest that a comprehensive evaluation cover four types of activities which roughly mirror the life-cycle of a program: problem analysis, program design, program implementation, program impact evaluation. Soderstrom et al. [62] have depicted the process as in Figure 1.

Although depicted as discrete phases, each element should be understood as part of an iterative cycle. Each element requires a different type of analytic activity,

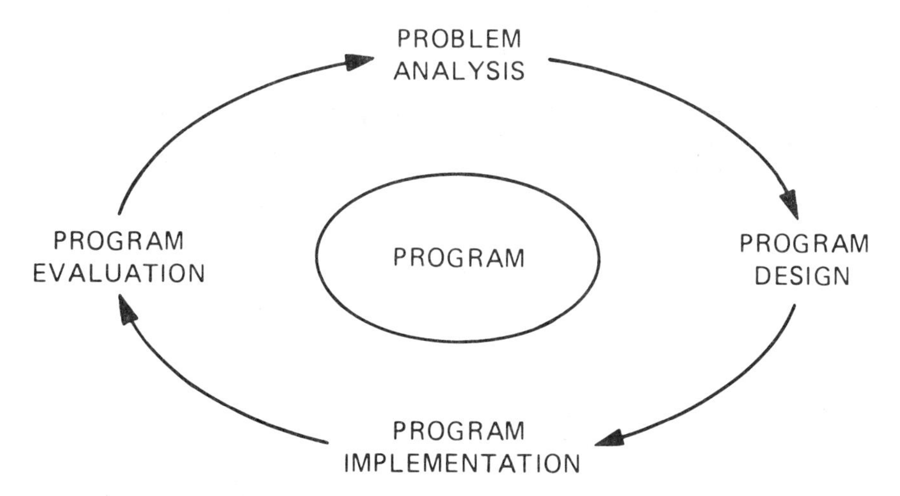

Figure 1 Life-cycle evaluation process.

with all the elements combining to form a comprehensive analysis. The cycle typically begins with the identification and analysis of a problem and proposed solution. Based on information gathered from other sources, such as evaluations of other, similar programs, the proposal is assessed to determine the potential consequences. Taking this analysis into account, an acceptable program is designed and implemented. Once implemented, the program is monitored to ensure that it is operating properly and to accumulate information on the appearance of impacts. As operations stabilize, and time is allowed for impacts to appear, an evaluation is undertaken to determine what impact the program is actually having on the problem. This information becomes an integral component for the design of future program directions. Such information and analysis, in turn, become inputs into the complex process which ultimately results in policy decisions and resource allocations.

While such a process has been used to some extent in evaluating service-delivery programs [62], the same process is necessary for energy and environmental regulatory and R&D programs. What is necessary is a shift away from sole reliance on speculative prospective assessment, toward a process of evaluation research to gain an understanding of the resultant impacts. The addition of monitoring and evaluation would not supplant initial prospective analyses; these are necessary, yet missing, adjuncts to the current assessment process. A detailed framework for establishing such an evaluation process for energy and environmental programs has been discussed elsewhere [34].

Combining retrospective and prospective analyses for energy and environmental programs allows for the input of evaluation information throughout the life-cycle of the program. The addition of a follow-up component to the initial projections provides not only for the validation of the projection, but also allows programs to be implemented as experiments. The effects of the program can be carefully studied while in operation, and the desirability of further such projects can be meaningfully considered in light of these findings. For those programs or projects for which major change is not feasible (e.g., siting of large-scale technological developments such as nuclear power plants), the monitoring and evaluation components can provide information necessary to improve prospective analyses used as a basis for decisions regarding the next implementation of a similar project or program as well as suggest strategies to mitigate the adverse consequences of the extant project. Viewing evaluation research as an on-going process combining prospective and retrospective analyses makes evaluation of E/E regulatory and R&D programs feasible; the potential benefits of ongoing evaluation research (i.e., program modification and/or mitigation) makes its use desirable.

ACKNOWLEDGMENTS

Research sponsored by the Office of Conservation and Renewable Energy, U.S. Department of Energy, under contract no. W-7405-eng-26 with the Union Carbide

Corporation. The authors wish to thank Bob Braid, Sam Carnes, John Sorensen and especially John Reed for their helpful comments on earlier versions of this paper.

REFERENCES

1. Schnaiberg, A. *The Environment: From Surplus to Scarcity*. Oxford University Press, New York, 1980.
2. Morrison, D. E., Hornback, K. E., and Warner, W. K. *Energy - A Bibliography of Social Science and Related Literature*. Garland, New York, 1975.
3. Morrison, D. E., Hornback, K. E., and Warner, W. K. *Energy II - A Bibliography of 1975-1976 Social Science and Related Literature*. Garland, New York, 1977.
4. U.S. Department of Energy. *Energy: Social and Economic Aspects - A Bibliography*. (DOE/TIC-3383) Technical Information Center, Oak Ridge, TN, 1980.
5. Wilbanks, T. J. Potential Contributions by Behavior Analysts to Meeting U.S. Energy Needs. Paper presented at the *Symposium on Behavior Analysis and Public Policy*, Milwaukee, May, 1981.
6. Suchman, E. A. *Evaluative Research: Principles and Practices in Public Service and Social Action Programs*. Russell Sage, New York, 1967.
7. Weiss, C. H. *Evaluation Research*. Prentice-Hall, Englewood Cliffs, NJ, 1972.
8. Cronbach, L. J., Ambron, S. R., Dornbusch, S. M., Hess, R. D., Hornik, R. C., Phillips, D. C., Walker, D. F., and Weiner, S. S. *Toward Reform of Program Evaluation*. Jossey-Bass Publishers, San Francisco, CA, 1980.
9. Rossi, P. H., Freeman, H. E., and Wright, S. R. *Evaluation: A Systematic Approach*. Sage Publications, Beverly Hills, CA, 1979.
10. Rossi, P. H., Wright, J. D. and Wright, S. R. The Theory and Practice of Applied Social Research. *Evaluation Quarterly*. 2 (May 1978): 171-191.
11. Lowi, T. J. American Business, Public Policy, Case Studies, and Political Theory. *World Politics* 16 (1964): 677-715.
12. U.S. Environmental Protection Agency. *Review of the Department of Energy's Conservation and Solar Energy Programs*. (EPA-006/7-B1-001) Washington, D.C., 1981.
13. Office of Technology Assessment. *Conservation and Solar Energy Programs of the Department of Energy: A Critique*. (OTA-E-120) Washington, D.C., 1980.
14. U.S. General Accounting Office. *Energy Conservation: An Expanding Program Needing More Direction*. (EMD-80-82) Washington, D.C., 1980.
15. U.S. Department of Energy. *Evaluation of the Energy Extension Service Pilot Program: Report to Congress*. (DOE/CS-0074) Washington, D.C., 1979a.

16. U.S. Department of Energy. *The Low Cost/No Cost Energy Conservation Program in New England: An Evaluation*. Washington, D.C., 1980.
17. Socolow, R. H. and Sonderegger, R. C. *The Twin Rivers Program on Energy Conservation in Housing: Four-Year Summary Report*. (Report No. 32) Center for Energy and Environmental Studies, Princeton University, Princeton, NJ, 1976.
18. Hirst, E. Combining Archival Search with Telephone Surveys: Evaluating Energy Information Centers. In Connor, R. (ed.). *Methodological Advances* in Evaluation Research. Sage Publications, Beverly Hills, CA, 1981.
19. Hirst, E. and Talwar, R. Reducing Energy Consumption in Low-Income Homes: Evaluation of the Weatherization Program in Minnesota. *Evaluation Review* 5 (October 1981): 671-685.
20. Lawrence, A. (ed.). *Forecasting and Modeling Time-of-Day and Seasonal Electricity Demands*. Electric Power Research Institute, Palo Alto, CA, 1977.
21. Berry, L., Soderstrom, J., Hirst, E., Newman, B., and Weaver, R. *Review of Evaluations of Utility Home Energy Audit Programs*. (ORNL/CON-58) Oak Ridge National Laboratory, Oak Ridge, TN, 1981.
22. Seligman, C., Becker, L. J., and Darley, J. M. Encouraging Residential Energy Conservation Through Feedback. in Baum, A and Singer, J. E. (eds.) *Advances in Environmental Psychology, Vol. 3*. Lawrence Erlbaum Associates, Inc., Hillsdale, NJ, 1981.
23. Becker, L. J., Rabinowtiz, V. C., and Seligman, C. Evaluating the Impact of Utility Company Billing Plans on Residential Energy Consumption. *Evaluation and Program Planning* 3 (1980): 159-164.
24. McClelland, L. and Cook, S. W. Energy Conservation in University Buildings: Encouraging and Evaluating Reductions in Occupants' Electricity Use. *Evaluation Review* 4 (February 1980): 119-134.
25. Kneese, A. V. and Schultze, C. L. *Pollution, Price and Public Policy*. Brookings Institute, Washington, D.C., 1975.
26. Mead, W. J. The Performance of Government in Energy Regulations. *American Economic Review* 69 (May 1979): 352-356.
27. Friesema, H. P., Caporaso, J., Goldstein, G. Lineberry, R., and McCleary, R. *Aftermath: Communities after Natural Disasters*. Sage Publications, Beverly Hills, CA, 1979.
28. Wright, J. D., Rossi, P. H. Wright, S. E., and Weber-Burdin, E. *After the Clean-up: Long Range Effects of Natural Disasters*. Sage Publications, Beverly Hills, CA, 1979.
29. Maki, J. E., Hoffman, D. M., and Berk, R. A. A Time Series Analysis of the Impact of a Water Conservation Campaign. *Evaluation Quarterly* 2 (February 1978): 107-118.
30. Berk, R. A., Cooley, T. F., LaCivita, C. J., Parker, S., Sredl, K., and Brewer,

M. Reducing Consumption in Periods of Acute Scarcity: The Case of Water *Social Science Research* 9 (June 1980): 99-120.

31. Committee on Community Reactions to the Concorde. *Community Reactions to the Concorde: An Assessment of the Trial Period at Dulles Airport.* Assembly of Behavioral and Social Sciences, National Research Council, National Academy of Sciences, Washington, D.C., 1977.
32. Dintzer, L. W., and Soderstrom, E. J. Making a Case for an Interface Between Quasi-Experimental Designs and Social Impact Analyses. *Evaluation and Program Planning* 1 (1978): 309-318.
33. Porter, A. L., Rossini, F. A., Carpenter, S. R., Roper, A. T., Larson, R. W., and Tiller, J. S. *A Guidebook for Technology Assessment and Impact Analysis.* North Holland, New York, 1980.
34. Soderstrom, E. J. *Social Impact Assessment: Experimental Methods and Approaches.* Praeger Press, New York, 1981.
35. Wolf, C. P. Getting Social Impact Assessment into the Policy Arena. *Environmental Impact Assessment Review.* 1 (March 1980): 27-36.
36. Council of Environmental Quality, *Environmental Quality.* Washington, D.C., 1980.
37. Fitzsimmons, S. J., Stuart, L. T. and Wolf, P. C. *Social Assessment Manual.* Abt Associates, Cambridge, MA, 1975.
38. Finsterbusch, K. and Wolf, C.P. (eds.) *Methodology of Social Impact* Assessment. Dowden, Hutchinson and Ross, Inc., Stroudsburg, PA, 1977.
39. McEvoy, J. and Dietz, T. (eds.) *Handbook for Environmental Planning: The Social Consequences of Environmental Change.* John Wiley & Sons, New York City, 1977.
40. Rau, J. G. and Wooten, D. C. *Environmental Impact Analysis Handbook.* McGraw-Hill, New York, 1979.
41. Shields, M. A. *Social Impact Assessment: An Analytic Bibliography.* U.S. Army Corps of Engineer Institute for Water Resources, Fort Belvoir, VA, 1975.
42. Cortese, C. F. and Jones, B. The Sociological Analysis of Boom Towns. *Western Sociological Review.* 8 (January 1977): 76-90.
43. Freudenberg, W. R. The Social Impact of Energy Boom Development on Rural Communities: A Review of Literatures and Some Predictions. Paper presented at the *Annual Meeting of the American Sociological Associations*, New York City, 1976.
44. Branch, K. Bureau of Land Management's Social Effects Project. *Environmental Impact Assessment Review.* 2 (1981): 104-107.
45. Shields, M. A. Grounded Theory Construction in Social Impact Assessment. In Finsterbusch, K. and Wolf, C. P. (eds.). *Methodology of Social Impact Assessment.* Dowden, Hutchinson & Ross, Inc., Stroudsberg, PA, 1977.

46. Meidinger, E. and Schnaiberg, A. Social Impact Assessment as Evaluation Research. *Evaluation Review* 4 (August 1980): 507-535.
47. Purdy, B. J., Peelle, E., Bronfman, B. H., Bjornstad, D. J., DeVault, R. C., Mattingly, Jr., T. J., and Soderstrom, E. J. *A Post Licensing Study of Community Effects at Two Operating Nuclear Power Plants*. (ORNL/NUREG/TM-22) Oak Ridge National Laboratory, Oak Ridge, TN, 1977.
48. Shields, M. A., Cowan, J. T. and Bjornstad, D. J. *Socioeconomic Impacts of Nuclear Power Plants: A Paired Comparison of Operating Facilities*. (ORNL/NUREG/TM-272) Oak Ridge National Laboratory, Oak Ridge, TN, 1979.
49. Branch, K., Chalmers, J. and Pijawka, D. Toward an Integrated Approach to Socioeconomic Assessment of Energy Resource Development. In Frazier, J. W. and Epstein, B. J. (eds.) *Proceedings of Applied Geography Conferences*. Vol. 4, 1981.
50. Denver Research Institute. The Impacts of Power Plant Construction: A Retroprospective Analysis. *Environmental Impact Assessment Review*. 1 (1980): 417-421.
51. Coates, J. F. Technology Assessment - A Tool Kit. *Chemtech* (June 1976): 372-383.
52. Daddario, E. Qu. Technology Assessment: Statement of Chairman, Subcommittee on Science, Research, and Development. 90th Congress, 1st Session, Washington, D.C., 1967.
53. Office of Technology Assessment. *Application of Solar Technologies to Today's Energy Needs*. (OTA-E-66/V.1) Washington, D.C., 1978.
54. U.S. Department of Energy. *Distributed Energy Systems: A Review of Related Technologies*. (USDOE/PE-03871-01) Washington, D.C., 1979b.
55. U.S. Department of Energy. *A Technology Assessment of Solar Energy Systems: Three Solar Urban Futures*. (USDOE/EV-0052/1) Washington, D.C., 1979b.
56. Arnstein, S. R. and Christakis, A. *Perspectives on Technology Assessment*. Science and Technology Publishers, Jerusalem, 1975.
57. Hoos, I. R. Some Fallacies in Futures Research. *Technological Forecasting and Social Change*. 11 (1978): 335-344.
58. Riecken, H. W. and Boruch, R. F. Social Experiments. *Annual Review of Sociology*, 4 (1978): 511-532.
59. Porter, A. L. and Rossini, F. A. Evaluation Designs for Technology Assessments and Forecasts. *Technology Forecasting and Social Change* 10 (1977): 369-380.
60. White, I. L., Ballard, S. C. and Hall, T. A. Technology Assessment as an Energy Planning Tool. In Lawrence, P. *New Dimensions to Energy Policy*. Lexington Books, Lexington, MA, 1979.
61. Connolly, T. Porter, A. L. and Rossini, F. A. On the Evaluation of Assess-

ment and Assessments. *Technological Forecasting and Social Change*. 12 (1979): 73-76.

62. Soderstrom, E. J., Berry, L. G., Hirst, E., and Bronfman, B. H. *Evaluation of Conservation Programs: A Primer*. (ORNL/CON-76) Oak Ridge National Laboratory, Oak Ridge, TN, 1981.

Part III Evaluation

Evaluation is an assessment of a program's worth. It is retrospective in nature and is accomplished by comparing program performance and/or results with a given set of standards—often the program objectives or other criteria that the evaluators use. The evidence used to determine a program's worth can be as soft as judgment data and as hard as cause effect estimates using highly complex, randomized true experimental research designs.

In this section, Thomas D. Cook presents a comprehensive description of the function and purpose of evaluation from an applied social research perspective. He proposes seven questions about evaluation, that, if addressed by evaluation managers, can help to assure a greater utility and impact of their evaluation products. As a complementary piece to Professor Cook's article, Albert C. Hyde reviews the historical development of the field of evaluation in its formative stage. His is a unique review of the literature up through 1975. He addresses the early development of principles and practical methologies that preceded the actual development of a professional evaluation focus. He labels Edward A. Suchman's book, *Evaluative Research*, (which was written in 1967) as a seminal work in the field and then goes on to identify key works that contributed to the synthesis of the field up through 1975. Dr. Hyde's article is a scholarly interpretation that will be of interest to scholars of this subject area.

Four articles are included that describe evaluation activities in specific national program areas. Lois-ellin Datta provides a comprehensive review of national educational evaluations. Her work is complemented by Beryl A. Radin's review of two Congressionally mandated education evaluations. Combined, these two articles shed considerable light on the practice and politics of educational evaluation. William J. Page, Jr. reviews evaluation as it is practiced in human services. He addresses the application, utility and prospects of evaluation in this area. Grover Starling reviews evaluation as it relates to national defense programs and strategies. His analysis challenges many of the current practices of audit and evaluation within the defense establishment.

As the target group of social services generally consist of high numbers of members of minority groups and women, David Lopez-Lee, Inc. identifies methodological issues that need to be taken into consideration by evaluators in order to further assure validity and reliability in their measures. Enid F. Beaumont analyzes the current state of the art of evaluation in a growing field within human resources management—training and development. She builds the case for increasing the use of training evaluation in spite of the serious methodological and political constraints which currently prevail in this special area.

Finally, and as a capstone to this section, Joseph S. Wholey reviews policy options incentives, and other strategies to improve the management of evaluation in large public agencies. His article will be especially of interest to those individuals who are interested in policy management using systematically designed feedback and control mechanisms.

These articles provide a unique definition of program evaluation as a tool used to aid in the management of public policy.

13
Evaluation: Whose Questions Should Be Answered

Thomas D. Cook / *Department of Psychology, Northwestern University, Evanston, Illinois*

WHAT IS EVALUATION?

The Historical Background

It is well known that the public sector lacks a compelling standard of value such as "profit" provides to the private sector. It is also known that the public sector considerably expanded in the 1960's and 1970's as social programs were begun in the hope of ameliorating a host of social ills. The absence of a convenient and legitimate standard like profit, and the rapidity with which social programs grew, led to the development of systematic evaluation. Rapid growth meant that most of the new programs were planned and implemented in haste and that their efficacy could not be taken for granted. The absence of a standard meant that when programs were begun, they could not be linked to data collection mechanisms that routinely provided the simple type of feedback that accountants provide for senior managers and boards of directors.

Although evaluation became socially legitimized in the 1960's, it clearly existed before then: From the earliest days of the republic, individuals and political parties have commented upon the geographical distribution of government-provided benefits; informed individuals in government and the media have used their sources to discover which programs seemed to be "working" or "not working"; and as long as 200 years ago, studies were conducted to assess the relative efficacy of different attempts to combat scurvy in order to improve the performance of the merchant marine.

However, the evaluation spawned in the 1960's was more "systematic" than had been the case in the past. By this I mean that it was sometimes politically legitimized through legislatively mandated requirements to evaluate; that it was administratively supported through funds specifically earmarked for evaluation and through the creation of federal, state, and local offices that had evaluation in their title; and that it was academically supported through the growth of new evaluation theories and methods, the creation of societies of professional evaluators, and the founding of some training and degree programs in evaluation. This is not to suggest that evaluation is securely institutionalized in its present form and scope. Some of us are, after all, old enough to have seen a number of managerial fads come and go. The comments above are only intended to suggest that a basis for institutionalization was created after 1960 that did not exist earlier.

One of the most striking ways in which modern evaluation seems systematic is in the use of traditional social science methods to describe program operations and their consequences. Before 1960, most evaluation had relied on scuttlebutt, ad hoc reports and statistics, and occasional site visits; and the gathering and synthesizing of such information was rarely called "evaluation." After 1960, an attempt was made to base evaluation on widely-acknowledged principles of survey research, experimentation, econometric analysis and cost-effectiveness research. Qualitative techniques were also espoused, including such methods as participant observation, the conduct and synthesis of case studies, and in-depth interviews. This advocacy of social science methods was made in the hope of increasing the validity of evaluation results by making them dependent on the supposedly critical methods of the more formal sciences. We can discern in this the perennial desire for more "objective" knowledge and the hope that such knowledge will be used more often, and more efficaciously, to guide policy actions than is the case with feedback based on less formal methods.

The Multiple Objects of Evaluation

At its most global, evaluation is concerned with "assigning value." But to what? In the world of commerce and consumer protection, it is products that are usually evaluated. Typically, such evaluations serve to identify products that might be unsafe or to raise consumers' consciousness about the attributes and qualities of different types of automobiles or dishwashers. Evaluation can also be of people, as with personnel selection and the awarding of merit increases. Though the evaluation of both products and people is relevant to the field of public administration, I shall not consider them henceforth since they are not as crucial as the evaluation of policies, social programs, projects, and project elements.

Congress and the executive branch establish *policies* as national goals (e.g., the alleviation of poverty, the promotion of positive pregnancy outcomes, etc.). Such policies are given form as one or more *social programs*. In this sense, both the Maternal and Child Health (MCH) program of the Department of Health and Human Services, and the Women, Infants, and Children (WIC) program of the Department of Agriculture embody a national policy to improve maternal and child health. Although some exceptions exist (e.g., the Social Security Program), most social programs consist of a heterogeneous array of locally implemented *projects*.

Thus, MCH funds are used at the local level to fund clinics, to pay health service providers, and to fund health education projects. Finally, each local project can consist of many *elements* or activities, each with a different, perhaps overlapping, purpose. An MCH clinic, for example, may include such diverse elements as prenatal maternal care, screening tests for cervical cancer, and child dental care.

Distinctions are not often made between the evaluation of policies, programs, projects, and project elements. Indeed, all are commonly lumped together as part of "program evaluation." Yet different evaluation approaches are required when one rather than the other entity is the primary focus of evaluation. Moreover, we shall shortly see that different groups with a stake in policy and evaluation prefer feedback about different entities. A lack of clarity about the particular object being evaluated can easily lead to misunderstanding between the evaluator, the persons commissioning an evaluation, and the persons being evaluated.

These points can perhaps be exemplified rhetorically. If you wanted to evaluate how well policies aimed at alleviating poverty had worked, would you use the same methods when you tried to evaluate CETA in general, when you tried to evaluate a local CETA project in Toledo, or when you evaluated the outreach efforts of CETA officials in Toledo? Would political appointees in the executive branch be equally interested in evaluations of (1) outreach efforts in Toledo, (2) project effects in Toledo, (3) global effects of CETA, or (4) effects of all the poverty programs combined? Would the CETA director in Toledo or the Toledo official in charge of outreach be equally interested in questions about national policies, national programs, local projects or local project elements? The answer to all of these questions is probably "No." An important implication of this answer is that, in designing or interpreting evaluations, high priority has to be assigned to determining the object most worth evaluating, the object actually being evaluated, and the objects in which particular stakeholder groups are most interested.

Evaluation Questions

When contemplating his or her task, the evaluator can ask an almost limitless number of questions about a policy, program, project or project element. Moreover, conducting the evaluation is likely to make more questions emerge, some of which could not have been reasonably conceived earlier. But despite the wealth of possible evaluation questions, I believe that most can be usefully grouped under seven headings.

Client Questions. This type of question is characterized by an emphasis on who a policy, program, project, or element is designed to reach and who it actually reaches. The product of such research is a profile of service providers and recipients, often with a particular emphasis on estimates of the size and characteristics of the recipients, hopefully relating such estimates to evidence about the clients' need for the services in question and to guesses about the extent of unmet demand and the unused capacity to provide services. Thus, evaluating a program aimed at pregnant women "at risk" would require conceptualizing and measuring the degree of risk, counting the number of women served, assessing the percentage of those served who are at risk, assessing which types of women at risk are more likely to be served, and estimating what the supply and demand for services would be if the program were made more widely available. Distributional issues are also subsumed under this heading, as when the target group is subdivided by race, ethnicity, age, etc., to probe whether some groups are receiving services more often than others.

Surveys and checks of program records are most often used for answering questions about the number and type of clients. The importance of such questions depends on many factors including: (1) *program maturity*–If a program is new, little formal or informal knowledge will exist about its popularity and availability to target groups; (2) *program costs*–if a program is potentially available to many persons, its costs might escalate dramatically if it were widely taken up; (3) *existing theory about outreach*–if some economically disadvantaged groups are to be reached, for example, some evidence indicates that it will often be more difficult to reach them than to reach less disadvantaged groups; (4) *program publicity*–if few funds are available for publicizing a program (as with educational television), the need to examine the number and type of clients reached increases since the fear is that the program may not be very successful on this count.

Implementation. To plan a program or project, and to disburse funds for the planned activities, does not guarantee that the activities will take place. None may; some may; or a subset may occur at some sites and a different subset at others. Although some activities may occur that are part of the plan, others will be local adaptations of the plan, or local substitutions designed to serve the same ends as the plan. Some may even be totally unrelated to activities allowed by regulations, as happened as with some local uses of community development bloc grant funds. Since plans and regulations are such imperfect guides to activities that actually occur, one important set of evaluation questions concern what was implemented and how well this relates to program plans.

Implementation is a multi-dimensional concept. For any one service, my preferred explication distinguishes between (1) the quantity of it provided, (2) the quality of implementation, and (3) the appropriateness of the service to the presumed need that justified the initial funding of a program or project. Any explication has also to consider that clients often receive a mix of services rather than a single one, as in the previous example of maternal child care programs that provide food, education, clothing, and cash. The above dimensions are interconnected in practice. One can readily conceive of services that are infrequently provided but with high quality and relevance when they are (e.g., 30 minutes per week of some thoughtful educational curriculum that is well presented and meets a demonstrable need). One can also imaging frequently implemented and relevant services provided poorly (e.g., several hours of instruction per week that are delivered in an incomprehensible fashion). And one can have frequently and skillfully implemented services that are not appropriate (e.g., several hours per week of a structured curriculum taught well but inculcating skills that are beyond the students' ability to comprehend). Most descriptions of implementation deal more with the quantity and mix of services than with their quality and relevance. The techniques used to describe implementation are manifold, including site-intensive partipant observation, observation on a time-sampling basis, questionnaires administered to service providers and recipients, and reviews of project-level archival data.

Implementation data are used as indicators of whether services are being delivered particularly poorly or well, so that steps can be made to make improvements where this seems called for. They are also used in conjunction with outcome measures to assess whether individuals who receive different mixes of services are influenced differently by them. They are sometimes also used for billing purposes. When this occurs, the risk is high that the recorded data will be biased, making them potentially problematic as measures of usage.

Evaluations are most likely to stress questions of implementation when the policy, program, project, or project element under review is relatively immature, and uncertainty exists about whether services can or will be provided in anything like the fashion planned. Implementation is also more likely to be emphasized with programs that provide funds but do not closely specify which objectives they are to be spent for. Revenue sharing, community development bloc grants, and many crime grants are of this type. Implementation measures also loom important in studies of causal influence when it is suspected that: (1) there will be considerable heterogeneity in exposure to a program among those who are eligible; or (2) there will be some exposure to program-like activities by the presumed "no-treatment" controls. Finally, implementation and its improvement is more of a concern to some stakeholder groups that others—typically being of greatest relevance to the professions providing services and to administrators at the local level. While such persons usually assume that their services are effective, most of them also believe that they can be improved upon by making low-cost modifications to how services are provided. Any feedback about elements of practice that can be readily changed is potentially useful to them.

Effectiveness Questions. Perhaps the most unique feature of modern evaluation is its stress on issues of effectiveness—on what a program is doing to those who receive its services. Effectiveness relates to the direct causal consequences of a program or project on those who receive or deliver service.

Since knowledge of effectiveness depends on inferences about causal connections between a program and observed outcomes, it is not surprising that the major methods used in evaluations of effectiveness involve either experimental designs or econometric analyses of one type or another. In recent years, the case has increasingly been argued that qualitative methods are also appropriate for causal analysis. This is because they sometimes allow the ruling out of most plausible alternative interpretations of any links that are observed between participating in a program and a changed pattern of outcomes [1, 2]. Cause-probing methods are most likely to be used when evaluating small-scale pilot projects that are being considered as future policy options—this is the rationale for "social experiments" [3]; when evaluating mature programs where little doubt exists that the intended clients are being reached with services that are implemented well; when project elements are being analyzed and it is logistically feasible to assign different elements to different persons; and when the demand for services outstrips the supply available. Effectiveness questions are, in general, of more interest to federal officials and other guardians of the "public interest," including representatives of target client groups, than they are to local practitioners or administrators.

The analysis of effectiveness is complicated by a number of factors. Most programs, projects, and project elements have poorly explicated objectives, or even objectives that are in obvious conflict with each other. This makes it difficult to determine how objectives are to be measured. It also renders more difficult the process of prioritizing objectives so that, assuming finite evaluation resources, one can concentrate on the objectives of greatest importance. For instance, the objectives of the national school lunch program are, on the one hand, to consume surplus commodities so as to maintain the income of farmers and, on the other hand, to provide lunches for children that meet at least one-third of minimal daily nutrition requirements. An evaluation that placed most stress on the maintenance of farm incomes would be quite different in form from an evaluation designed to assess what children are served during school lunch and what they actually eat. Yet, in the best of possible worlds, both objectives would be studied together since maintaining farm incomes may hinder nutritional goals—e.g., if children find some of the government-supplied foodstuffs unappetizing and refuse to eat them, even though they would have eaten equally nutritious alternatives that are not being supplied free and so schools cannot afford to serve them.

Scriven [4] has elegantly argued that evaluations should be "goal-free." Some evaluations attempt to assess the extent to which a program has reached its intended goals. Scriven claims that this approach to evaluation is insensitive to unanticipated effects, to intended effects that, politically, could not be listed as program goals, and to questions about the relevance of program goals to client needs. It is by now axiomatic that evaluators should expect positive and negative effects that were not specified in the goals of a program or project. In some cases, the unanticipated effect comes to outweigh the anticipated in importance, as with the drug Thalidomide. The same may also be true of policies that stimulated motoring but, in so doing, weakened railroads, hastened the decay of inner cities and increased concentration in the nation's global economy. It may also be true of a project like "Sesame Street" that has probably widened achievement gaps between advantaged and disadvantaged preschoolers, making the latter at an even greater disadvantage on entering school. It may also be true of programs to provide dried milk and formula for infant feeding in lesser developed countries—an event that has probably hurt the nutritional status of some children compared to when they were breast-fed. The implication is that evaluators should be sensitive to effects of all types and not just to those that follow from an analysis of overt program goals.

A final difficulty in the conceptualization of effects concerns the degree to which they are proximal or distal. Proximal effects are those that are supposed to follow directly upon exposure to a program, project or project element. Many of these immediate changes are believed to be necessary if later—and thus more distal—effects are to occur. Much public health research is overtly predicated on theories of causal flow. For instance, a media-based prevention campaign may be designed, and evaluated, in terms of a causal flow model postulating that exposure to the prevention material causes (1) learning of them, (2) a change in belief, (3) a change in attitude, (4) an attempt to abstain (from, say, smoking or drinking alcohol), (5) social support for the decision, (6) maintenance of the change, (7) related changes in lifestyle, (8) better health and (9) a longer life. Should the theory be wrong, the postulated effects may not come about; should the causal links be weak (i.e., low probability events), the flow of causal influence may not reach the end of the chain; should an exogeneous influence be manifest during the evaluation a distal effect may not occur that would normally have occurred.

The dilemmas that causal chains pose for the evaluator include: (1) which dependent variables should be measured, for while the earlier ones have a greater likelihood of showing effects, they are less impactful in their social consequences; and (2) if the theory is true, when will transitions occur from one state to another, for should the evaluator be wrong in his or her specification of causal lags he or she may miss some true effects that have already occurred or that may not occur until later.

The reality of time-bound causal chains highlights the evaluator's dependence on the substantive theory that buttresses each program or project—a theory that is sometimes more incomplete than complete, more covert than overt, or more desired than available. Yet it is vital to explicate the theory behind the program, whatever its warts. As Wholey [5] and Chen and Rossi [6] have maintained, this explication may itself suggest (1) the inadvisability of going beyond evaluation planning, especially in cases where crucial theoretical links are known to be wrong; or (2) the utility of focusing empirical efforts on crucial links that are untested as opposed to links that are less crucial or have been repeatedly tested and found to be empirically robust over a wide range of settings and persons.

Impact. As I use the term, impact involves a subclass of possible effects—*viz* those that influence systems of which program recipients are a part or with which they interact. Thus, if one examined the effects of a job training program by examining local unemployment figures, this would be an impact assessment. Although individuals who had been in the program would be part of the population on whom the rate was based, others who had not been exposed to training would also be included. Impact would also be involved if one examined how the training influenced local aggregate indicators of family life, marriage stability, or local sales tax receipts. Unlike with effects, impact analyses are not restricted to influences on the clients themselves, as would be the case if an evaluation were restricted to the job search behavior, earnings, or expenditure patterns of graduates of the local project.

Impacts are generally more difficult to bring about than effects, especially proximal effects. Indeed, many effects are presumed to be necessary for impacts to occur. Thus, for a local job training project to reduce the local unemployment rate, more of its graduates would have to get jobs than would have been the case were the project not there. The difficulty of bringing about impacts makes the advocates of particular programs and projects apprehensive if funding agencies favor impact criteria in evaluation plans. Such a preference is not infrequent, for the funders of programs and projects want to see an improvement in the indicators that initially justified the program. These are typically aggregate-level indicators—e.g., in the drug abuse area, funders would be delighted to see a local project impact on indicators of the local crime rate, of drug-related accidents, and of labor force participation. Yet the managers and practitioners in the project would resent being held accountable by these criteria, for (1) each of them is multiply caused and many of the causes are beyond the project's control, (2) each is computed for a catchment area where only a minority of the population ever comes to the center, and (3) only a minority of this minority comes often enough that their visits can be presumed to have any effect on their behavior.

Impact measures are preferred when programs and projects are meant to be diffused over a wide area. A case in point would be a media campaign that is transmitted to a whole city and is designed to promote healthy eating and life styles. Although some of the city dwellers may never hear the persuasive messages or meet any of the treatment implementers, they are still typically counted as part of the study population and dependent variables are calculated as rates or percentages of the total population. To differentiate between citizens with and without exposure to the campaign materials would provide a more sensitive test of whether a prevention campaign worked when the message gets across. But for individuals and agencies interested in community-level impacts, whether the message gets across or not is part of the problem to be tackled. And so their preference is for measures of success that are based on the total population and not just on those persons who have had exposure to the campaign materials.

Cost Analysis. Programs, projects, and project elements incur dollar costs. Often, descriptions of these costs are all that is required, as when the total cost of the program, project, or project element is calculated over a given time period, or when specific cost estimates are attributed to different elements within the program or project. The latter is particularly useful, for one learns how much of the costs of a school meal are attributable to, say, labor, capital expenditures, interest payments, the purchase of different types of agricultural commodities (separating out commodities that schools purchase with their own funds as opposed to those offset by government "bonuses" designed to stabilize farm prices). Because of the many ways cost categories can be defined and the multiple ways expenditures can be classified even after the categories are established, it is not easy to break expenditures down into their cost components. Yet the exercise can cast an edifying light on what is spent for various tasks and can suggest where changes need to be made. Also, analyses of component costs are crucial in studies where these costs are expected to shift. Thus, if one evaluated a demonstration in which school districts were supplied for school lunches with the cash equivalent of donated commodities, it would be vital to examine whether more ground beef was bought. Donated commodities are worth just under one billion dollars per year. If purchases shift just one-tenth of 1 percent from dairy products to ground beef this means that, nationally, about one million dollars more might be spent on beef and that much less on dairy products.

Cost analyses are not restricted to accounting functions. They are also used in cost-effectiveness analyses where the goal is to compare the dollar costs required to cause a unit change in particular outcome measures. Such computations allow one to compare relative effectiveness, as when one examines whether cash is more effective than donated foods in improving the nutritional status of school children, or when one assesses whether police patrols on foot are more effective in reducing crime than patrols by car. Cost-effectiveness analyses are appealing because of the focused choice they are thought to promote between different ways of reaching a desired end. Their problems stem from the dependence on quantifying impacts in dollar terms, on tapping the universe of inputs for each alternative, and on measuring less visible costs, especially opportunity costs and any future costs that might result from changes that a program or project has caused.

Some evaluators want to go a step further and conduct cost-benefit analyses. These require assigning dollar values to effects and impacts as well as to inputs. The difficulties of assigning dollars to impacts are legion: How does one do this for satisfaction or happiness? How far into the future should effects and their benefits be imputed? How does one deal with the consequences of opportunities foregone? How does one differentially weigh—if one does at all—the consequences one is sure about and those that are more in doubt? How does one deal with the accumulation of imprecise estimates of central tendency when multiple outcomes are being synthesized into one benefit figure? The number of assumptions that cost-benefit analysis demands makes some commentators dubious about its validity. Of its theoretical utility there can be little doubt, since valid cost-benefit analyses would permit one to evaluate the pros and cons of any program or project without the explicit need for comparison with other programs or projects. Dollars are an easily understood metric, and they command considerable political attention.

Consequently, cost-benefit ratios provide global summaries about a program in a form whose simplicity and memorability make them difficult to ignore, whatever their validity.

The Analysis of Causal Processes. To establish a robust relationship between participating in a project and benefitting from it will rarely explain why the project is effective. Knowing about such causal processes can considerably help in redesigning parts of the project so as to improve its overall efficacy. If one found, for example, that a job training project increased the employment rate of its graduates, one could then ask whether the effect is attributable to the job skills learned, to increased awareness of specific job opportunities, to learning techniques of self-presentation at job interviews, etc. Once we learned what the effective elements were, it might then be possible to highlight these features and to downplay any less effective ones.

The utility of probes of causal process is even more evident with programs, projects, and project elements that do not appear to be effective. By itself, evidence of ineffectiveness is ambiguous. Is the concept behind the program at fault? Is the concept effective, but it happens to be poorly implemented in this particular case? Is the concept often effective but dependent on certain necessary conditions that were not present in the particular evaluation? Is the concept effective, but the evaluation so poorly implemented that it could not have detected a true effect? Without a probe of *why* the program appeared to be unsuccessful, little is learned from an evaluation that produces no effects.

The utility of evaluation does not absolutely depend on the elucidation of causal processes. We still do not know, for example, why aspirin or antihistamines work as they do, nor why some persons benefit from psychotherapy while others do not. Yet few of us would deny the utility of aspirin or antihistamines, and many persons do not want to give up psychotherapy. Although the major purpose of evaluation is to discover better ways of ameliorating social ills, this does not require knowledge of causal laws. But such knowledge helps considerably.

Assigning "Meaning" and "Value" to Obtained Results. The results of an evaluation have to be given meaning and value. I mean many things by this, including that they are translated into the frame of reference of readers, that their robustness and comprehensiveness is estimated, that their implications for action are assessed, that counterevidence is elicited and weighed, that the results and assumptions of the evaluation are subjected to critical appraisal, and that their implications for important social values are forced out. Without such an analysis of "meaning" we have evaluation findings that imply the assignment of value to a program but do not make explicit the valuing. We have findings that need transferring into an evaluation.

Not everyone concerned with evaluation is keen to see evaluators assign meaning. Some persons are concerned lest the assignment of meaning and value obscures the difference between facts and interpretations. This distinction is difficult to maintain if one believes, as I do, that all observations are impregnated with the implicit (or explicit) theories of observers. A belief in the theory-ladenness of observations forces one to the conclusion that all facts include interpretation. Yet we also know that some observations are repeatedly made across a heterogenous set of observers who bring different theories to bear, among which are all those that have been currently identified as implying a unique direction of bias. Observations of this kind are presumably less biased in the sense of being impregnated with a single theory. While their existence is not sufficient to promote an absolutely watertight distinction between fact and interpretation, they at least suggest that some observations are more likely than others to contain a high degree of interpretation. Would not a discussion of the policy implications of an evaluation of the Women, Infant and Children (WIC) nutrition program imply more interpretation than an analysis of attendance records at a randomly selected set of WIC centers, especially if the records were directly collected either by observers with no obvious axe to grind or by observers with diametrically opposed axes? A sophisticated argument in favor of the separation of facts and interpretations would require that we *provisionally* treat as "facts" only those findings that have been critically assessed from a variety of perspectives and for which no currently plausible alternative exists.

It is not difficult to see why many evaluation contractors are loath to include in the evaluations they conduct the task of assigning meaning. The task seems "subjective," and it is likely to alienate agencies on whom the next contract depends. It is also not difficult to see why funding agencies usually do not relish grantees and contractors assigning meaning, other than that involved in a discussion of the methodological assumptions and limitations of the work. Funders do not want to have to defend or attack conclusions of obvious policy relevance that they have not drawn themselves; they understandably prefer to preserve maximal flexibility for the future. Yet we shall see later that the assignment of meaning has a closer correspondence with how evaluation results are typically used than is the case with any of the six other question types. When properly conducted, using the methods of debate, judicial argumentation, policy analysis, or philosophy of ethics, an analysis of the implications of findings can "enlighten" readers and give them the benefit of multiple perspectives on a program's conceptualization, accomplishments, improvement, and relationship to fundamental social values.

The Methods of Evaluation

Evaluation is not associated with any particular methods. Rather, it is characterized by a catholicity and eclecticism derived from the great variety of questions it discovers and poses. Issues concerning the clients and providers of services are often answered using surveys or analyses of records; issues of implementation are often broached using on-site observational techniques, management audits, archival research, or the use of questionnaires; effectiveness is often probed using experiments (or quasi-experiments), econometric techniques such as structural equation modeling, or the ad hoc ruling out of recognized alternative interpretations; impact analysis often proceeds by means of time series studies using archived data or multi-wave surveys harnessed to a quasi-experimental design framework; cost analyses use the methods of accounting or economics; the probing of micromediation tends to use on-site observation or structural equation modeling; while analyses of the meaning of results can involve Socratic discussions between representatives of a variety of conflicting perspectives or a regular policy analysis of alternative courses of action.

There is here an obvious link between methods and social science disciplines. The survey techniques used to describe clients are most often used by quantitative sociologists and political scientists; the observational techniques often used in implementation studies are most often associated with anthropologists and more qualitative sociologists and political scientists; experimental methods are preferred for causal analysis in education, psychology and statistics while econometric methods are preferred in economics and most of quantitative sociology and political science; the time series analysis of communities is most associated perhaps with public health and macro-economics; cost methods have been developed by accountants and economists; methods for probing causal processes come from all disciplines (since this task is more closely related than all the others to the theory development mandate of most basic sciences); while the assignment of meaning uses methods taken from ethics, policy analysis, the law, and rhetoric.

It is unrealistic to expect any single evaluator to have up-to-date knowledge on all these fronts. This is why many large evaluations involve a team of researchers with different disciplinary backgrounds. The relevance of multiple methods and disciplines may also be one of the sources of pressure to restrict the range of questions posed in evaluations. Comprehensive evaluations dealing with all of the seven types of questions previously analyzed are rare. There are, of course, reasons for the non-comprehensive character of most evaluations over and above those attributable to the predilections for questions and methods associated with particular disciplines. Foremost among these are: the persons commissioning the evaluation want only selected questions answered; funds and time do not permit answering more than a few questions well; and some of the questions require that other questions have already been answered. For instance, in many contexts it does not make sense to ask what effect a program or project is having until one is sure that the program is reaching the clients and is being implemented in something like its promised form. It does not make much sense to probe causal mediating processes prior to assessing causal effects and impacts. Because of these links between question types, my prior discussion of them was, I believe, ordered in the sequence of question-asking that makes most sense for most programs.

The most serious challenge posed by the catholicity of evaluation questions and methods concerns priorization: When should particular questions be stressed most heavily? This issue would not be so pressing were it not for the fact that prioritizing on one type of question will generally lower the quality of answers to other questions. For instance, most surveys that are carefully designed to assess who a program is reaching will be cross sectional, and resources will be spent on the sampling frame and the measurement of attendance. This hardly provides an optimal design structure for causal inference and does not bode well for the quality with which effects are measured. *The task, then, is to develop a theory that helps prioritize among research questions and, thereby, also among research methods.*

Such a theory depends, I believe, on two factors over and above what is already known with "reasonable certainty" about a policy, program, project or project element: (1) Who are—or should be—the major audiences for the evaluation, and (2) How are evaluation results most often used in the policy domain? Clearly, if different audiences tend to have different information needs and some audiences have a better claim than others on evaluators' attention, then this should help prioritize among question types. Similarly, if some questions tend to lead to answers about which little is done subsequently, such questions should have a lower priority than questions that lead to action.

THE AUDIENCES FOR EVALUATORS

Who Pays the Piper?

Most evaluations are paid for from public funds administered by government agencies. Such agencies have a major stake in specifying evaluation questions. Sometimes, their stake is largely instrumental as when Congress mandates an evaluation. In rare cases, the mandate may be so explicit as to prioritize the research questions, and specify the sample size, leaving relatively little discretion to the agency and the evaluation contractors. More often, when Congress specifies the questions, they are very general, and it is the responsibility of agencies and contractors to rephrase questions to make them operational.

Although the situation is changing, it still seems to me that few evaluations involve specific questions that were Congressionally mandated. There more often seems to be a mandate that evaluation should take place, but little elaboration of what the specific research questions of that evaluation should be. Consequently, members of the executive branch have considerable latitude in formulating questions, if they so desire. The executive branch is heterogeneous in its interests. My own experience suggests that a distinction needs to be made between two types of interest. On the one hand are senior executives, both political appointees and civil service, who are (1) more interested in current policies and programs than in current projects or project elements; and are more interested (2) in costs, the numbers of clients reached, and the effects and impacts of services than they are in the quality of implementation of services or in the causal mediation of effects. At a lower level are Federal executives whose mandate is to oversee specific programs or projects, including some that they have helped nurse into action and some that have a high profile within the agency. The interest of such officials is often less in policy or in program and project-level impacts. Rather, they want to take program or project effectiveness for granted, and see evaluation as a tool for improving the delivery of services. If such persons consider effects at all, they often prefer to analyze what the program or project is accomplishing at its best (i.e., where implementation is exemplary and measurement is proximal and valid) rather than at its most average.

Since the senior-level bureaucrats are always present in the consciousness of their lower-level employees, it is inevitable that the major pressure at the government level is to use evaluations to provide a retrospective summary of accomplishments. Usually this will be of ongoing programs, but it can also be the summary of a demonstration of some novel idea whose policy relevance is being partially assessed through the evaluation. When ongoing programs are at issue, the tendency is usually to evaluate them according to some or all of their objectives. Such an approach has serious drawbacks when the objectives are unclear or contradictory, or when it reduces the evaluator's sensitivity to side effects and to analyses of whether the program or project addresses real needs.

Other Stakeholders. It is obvious that parties other than government employees and elected officials have a stake in policies, programs and projects and in evaluations of these entities. For instance, evaluations of bilingual education and school bussing are discussed by academic experts, school boards and organizations representing school boards, teachers and organizations representing teachers, parents and organizations representing parents, superintendents and organizations representing them, etc. Evaluations of a negative income tax experiment are monitored and interpreted by academic experts, social workers and organizations representing them, as well as by organizations representing the less economically advantaged. Evaluations of the effects of psychotherapy are scrutinized by associations of psychiatrists, psychologists, social workers, and hospital administrators, as well as by public interest groups and the various arms of Congress and the Executive Branch. Evaluations of cash as an alternative to the distribution of free food commodities in the school lunch program are followed by the dairy and meat lobbies, the representatives of processed food manufacturers, of farmers, of school boards and citizen groups.

Which questions do these different stakeholder groups want to see answered? This varies by the group under discussion. But for the most part these groups do not share the perspective on "accountability" that runs through most executive and legislative concerns. To them, the perspective seems too historical, too summative, and too program centered, based more on identifying what has been accomplished than on identifying simple changes that could be made to improve functioning at the local level. For the most part, the other stakeholders we have identified accept programs and projects as being permanent, however provisional they may be labelled, and seek to make them better in ways that will improve their own welfare. Rarely is the rationale for the program or project questioned as it is in the accountability-centered agenda of public servants.

This difference means that most of the other stakeholder groups want to know, not so much who they are reaching, but how they can improve their outreach; not so much how well services are being implemented, but how implementation can be improved; not so much what effects the program or project is having, but how it can be made more effective; not so much how impactful it is, but how it can be made more so; not so much how costly it is, but how its cost-efficiency can be improved; not so much why effects are occurring, but how the subset of manipulable causes can be extended; not so much what has been accomplished, but why it is worth accomplishing. The future orientation of many of these groups clashes starkly with the past orientation of many senior federal officials.

Of course, not all federal officials can be so characterized; and many would protest that the past orientation does provide some clues about changes for the future. All this is true; but the possibility still exists that a past orientation may reduce the yield from evaluations compared to what it might have been had the future orientation been initially salient so that it guided the choice of sampling, measurement, design, and analysis plans. It is also true that some of the other stakeholder groups are *on occasion* interested in summaries of past accomplishments at the program level. But this does not negate the possibility that the purpose of evaluation is often different for senior federal and legislative officials when compared to practitioner groups, bureaucrats at the local level, client groups and academics.

These last groups are not, of course, homogeneous in what they want from evaluation: Practitioner groups tend to stress issues related to the availability of clients, the implementation of services, and the processes that bring about effects; bureaucrats at the local level tend, in my experience, to stress outreach, costs and fiscal accountability; public interest groups emphasize the availability of services and drawbacks to better implementation; while academics tend to stress the casual mediation of effects or the reasons for low impacts. Consequently, letting any one of these groups decide on the major evaluation questions would result in a different study and different interests being served by the evaluation.

The Normative Issue

Whose interest, and thus whose questions, should be paramount in evaluation? To those trained in public administration the answer may be simple: The interests of the senior manager and those to whom he or she is most directly accountable—i.e., to Congress, the representative of the voting public. Seen from this perspective, the senior manager's job is easiest when an evaluation is Congressionally mandated. Then, the manager and his/her colleagues will have a clearer understanding of the will of Congress, certainly more so than when a study is not specifically mandated. But in all cases, senior managers still have to decide on the final form of the guiding evaluation questions. This being so, questions are likely to be summative, retrospective, and effect/impact centered, since the purpose of public policy is to bring about changes that improve the state of the nation, and evaluation is a tool with which to hold accountable the persons who use public funds to try to bring about such changes.

In cases where evaluations center around questions about the effects and impacts of social programs, one problem with the normative model is its blindness to the reality that few programs die. Moreover, those that die rarely do so because of feedback from evaluations. Programs do, however, contract and expand; and even when a program's funding is constant in real dollar terms, there is often local turnover in the counties, cities and neighborhoods that receive program funds and services. Some drop out; and others come in. In light of this, the argument goes, would it not be better to orient evaluations towards discovering ways to improve how a program functions in the future rather than towards ascertaining how effective it was in the past. At the very least, the argument continues, one should not invariably assume that program-level issues are the only ones worth raising, for local projects do turn over and regulations can be written based on evaluation results which specify which types of local project will be funded and which will not.

More than anyone else in public administration, Wholey [5] has been responsible for raising consciousness about the problematic nature of question-formulation in evaluations designed to meet the needs of senior managers. His technique of evaluability assessment is, in essence, a device for forcing managers to phrase, and defend, the form of evaluation questions in order to arrive at a series of questions with presumed maximal utility. Our guess is that, when pressed, senior managers do indeed often come to see the advisability of using evaluations to make modifications in current functioning rather than to place a verdict on past performance.

A second objection to the normative orientation of evaluation towards the accountability criteria of senior managers is that such managers imperfectly represent the "public interest" that is embodied in Congress. Most evaluations are not specifically mandated, and managers have considerable latitude for determining what is to be done. Since Congress is so heterogeneous, any manager's own values and interests will intrude on judgments of what is worth knowing. Why not, the argument goes, frankly recognize the pluralistic foundations of American democracy and try to design evaluations so that, to the extent possible, they directly take account of the unique and common information needs of different stakeholder groups. In mental health, such groups include: Federal agencies, professional groups of psychiatrists, psychologists, social workers, hospital administrators and nursing home owners, groups representing former and current patients, and groups purporting to represent the public interest. In education, the stakeholder groups include school superintendents, teachers, parents, schoolboards, purveyors of school materials, defenders of the public interest, and academics. In community development, the stakeholders are federal and state officials, city managers and elected officials, local banks, local chambers of commerce, local unions, etc.

The pluralist perspective on question-formulation makes the evaluator less an interpreter and prober of the needs of senior managers and more a juggler of the information needs of multiple stakeholder groups that differ in political power and the ability to articulate their needs. Thus, the evaluator has to "somehow" elicit the needs of all groups at a high level of consciousness. He or she also has to "somehow" prioritize and reconcile them so that an evaluation takes place which, in fully recognizing the constraints of budget, time and professional skill mix of the evaluators, probes only a subset of all the issues one would like to have probed. But how does one arrive at the subset?

My own experience as an outside evaluator collaborating in evaluations based on a pluralist model is that the interests of formal decision-makers usually carry greater weight because they are footing the bill. But some of the issues raised by other groups can also be built into the evaluation, even if fewer evaluation resources are devoted to probing them. Designing evaluations in this way is often seen by senior managers as a boon, for it can increase the commitment of the other groups to the evaluation and (presumably) to the use of its results. Also, the administrators, practitioners and clients to whom social programs are targetted are part of the larger political constituency of senior managers. Meeting some of their information needs through evaluation may well make the senior manager seem sympathetic and responsive to the persons and organizations delivering and receiving services.

My own suspicion is that evaluation should be for all the relevant stakeholder groups and not just for central decision-makers. The reasons for this are partly normative, in that the direct representation of plural, sometimes unique, interests is a closer approximation to the affected public interest than is the interpretation by senior managers of an often vague or absent Congressional intent. The reasons are also partly behavioral, in that cooperation with the evaluation and eventual use of its results may be more likely when the different stakeholder groups have participated in it from its inception and have tailored some issues to their needs.

At this point, we have to be careful to note that the dichotomy between a centralist and pluralist model is not always clear. A case in point is the Congressionally mandated demonstration and evaluation to test what happens when districts in the school lunch program are supplied with cash or letters of credit instead of bonus agricultural commodities. While this phrasing of the issue was mandated by Congress—together with a specific experimental design, including sample sizes (sic!)—the phrasing was arrived at after consultation with representatives of of industries seeking to supply more processed and frozen foods to schools, with representatives of school boards who want more control over what is bought, and with representatives of the beef industry who anticipate increased sales if school districts can purchase what they want with the cash value of the commodities that are not donated. Moreover, we can assume that Congress was not ignorant of the possibility that more parents, children and school officials might support the school lunch program if the lunches more faithfully reflect what children prefer to eat.

Thus, the Congressional initiative was not taken in a vacuum; it reflected the real and anticipated interests of several stakeholder groups. It did not, of course, reflect all the interests; as can be imagined, the dairy and farming lobbies were not strongly in favor of it. But the initiative was partly pluralistic in its origins, even though in a formal sense it emanated only from the central government. The distinction between a centralized and pluralist model is relative in practice, and not absolute. But it is useful, for it highlights the roles that the evaluators can adopt: that of the interpretor of questions received from above, or that of the juggler who explicitly seeks to identify interested stakeholder groups, to elicit the issues they want broached, to prioritize among the issues, and to incorporate as many issues as possible into a feasible evaluation plan that respects time lines, budget ceilings, and staff skills.

HOW ARE EVALUATION RESULTS USED?

Definitions of Usage Based on the Program or Project Being Evaluated

It used to be commonplace in evaluation to bemoan the low frequency with which evaluation reports were read and their results used. Implicit in such wailings was a definition of utilization that stressed results *determining* policy decisions–a definition based on uncovering clear causal connections from the results being delivered to a decision being made. That such a definition is naive needs no elaboration given the role of politics and values in decision-making, the rapid turnover of Federal and Congressional officials, the way some issues "spontaneously" wax and wane so that, by the time results are in, the issue to which the evaluation was addressed is irrelevant.

A more refined version of the same definition has results playing a major, but not decisive, role in decision-making along with such factors as: (1) the values of decision-makers; (2) the extent to which interest groups exert articulated pressure; (3) the profile of the issue in the national media; and (4) the overlap between those who are supposed to make decisions when the evaluation begins and those who are supposed to make them when the results are available. The few isolated examples of this kind of usage suggest some conditions under which it may occur. One of the most noteworthy examples concerns Hill [7] who spent considerable time with Congressional staffs eliciting their questions about compensatory education, then conducted an evaluation geared to these questions, while all the time keeping the staff briefed. The results were cited and used when new regulations were written. Not all the results were used; and not all new regulations were based on evaluation results. But, under the conditions outlined, the data did play a major, but not sole-determining, role in deliberations. Patton [2], Scanlon and Walker [8], and Scanlon and Wholey [9] have also repeatedly stressed the crucial role that close collaboration between the evaluators and the decision makers can play in increasing utilization.

For some scholars it is unrealistic to define utilization by referring to the degree to which evaluations constitute decisions. It is enough that the evaluations are cited in any formal or informal deliberations surrounding policy change even if the evaluations are only briefly mentioned and are assigned trivial weight when compared to the weight assigned to values and interests. Behind this definition is the premise that in a democracy we should not want the implications of data to supercede the values and interests that represent, however imperfectly, the "will of the people." In this conception, evaluations should constitute inputs into debates, and that is all. However, once they are entered into debates the evaluation results, if clear, should be an input that lends some weight to certain parties. But results are not always clear in their action implications. Rather than making issues simpler, some studies make them more complicated by redefining the issue or casting a new light on its utility. Lindblom and Cohen [10] argued that evaluation results are often of this kind. If so, they fit more naturally into contexts of discussion than decision.

Ample evidence suggests that evaluations are often used in debates. Some tentative generalizations are even beginning to emerge about the conditions under which such debate-centered usage occurs, whether at the highest levels of Congress or at more mundane levels in an operating agency. Media coverage is important for such usage (sometimes prompted by vigorous debates at academic conventions and in major journals). It also seems to be important whether an evaluation is Congressionally mandated as opposed to being part of an omnibus regulation to evaluate; whether the substantive issue has a high profile when the evaluation results are completed; whether the evaluators brief federal officials face-to-face about the results; whether the evaluators' reputations are stellar; and whether the results support actions that are anyway preferred on other (usually more political) grounds. This last factor worries some commentators who see evaluations playing no unique role in determining decisions. But the results still aid some points of view more than others, making it easier to gain support for initiatives that would probably have been taken anyway, and making it more difficult to gain support for preferred initiatives that should perhaps not be taken.

The list of factors promoting debate-centered usage has not thus far included characteristics of the evaluation itself. We do not yet know to what extent methodological characteristics of studies facilitate usage. However, it seems reasonable to assume that the nature of the evaluation questions asked influences usage in the short term. Cronbach and his associates [11] have emphasized that most social programs at the state or national level have constituencies supporting them; and if they don't, they quickly develop them. The politically impacted nature of programs makes it unlikely that they will be significantly reduced or expanded because of feedback about the effectiveness or impact of a program. However, it is reasonable to assume that program operations could be modified if more was known about implementation of the processes facilitating or inhibiting effectiveness. The implication of Cronbach's analysis is that evaluation questions should be oriented towards where there is leverage in the system; and for most social programs leverage is not provided by retrospective results about outcomes but is provided—in the short-term at least—by prospective results about ongoing program processes. This is why Cronbach believes that all evaluation should be formative.

In extending this argument, Cook [12] has noted another source of leverage that exists in program evaluation. After specifying both global objectives and procedures for fiscal accountability, programs usually leave to local discretion the particular activities that take place. This means that the Headstart center in one city is quite different from that in another, that the urban development bloc grant activities in one city are different from those in another, and that the form of crime prevention and drug abuse activities vary from site to site. Yet the variability is not infinite. Our guess is that many sites share a large number of common activities, perhaps because they are based on similar philosophies of professional practice or because there has been direct modeling. Some of these sets of related activities may be more effective than others. Given that local projects fade and die (even though the programs spawning them do not), leverage is provided in that the funding of new local sites can be made contingent on the provision of services of a form that seems to be effective. The argument, then, is that leverage is provided when evaluations compare the effectiveness and impact of different project *types* that exist within a program.

Definitions of Usage Based on Influencing Other Programs and Professional Practice

It would be naive to believe that evaluations are only used in debates about the program or local project for which the data were originally collected. Part of Weiss' [13] concept of the "enlightenment" function of social science data includes their use in contexts other than those for which they were originally collected. As evaluations accumulate about, say, early childhood learning programs, policymakers and policy analysts become more sensitized to what they can expect future programs in this area to accomplish, what they think are the major problems to be addressed, which forms of early childhood education seem superior to others, etc. In this perspective, an evaluation is merely one data point in a series that is continually being synthesized by interested professionals. The implication is that, in addition to providing input into debates, evaluations can function to raise the consciousness of managers about both classes of programs and general policy.

Evaluations are used in a different way by professionals, albeit in a way that also depends on synthesis and long time lines before utilization is apparent. Evaluation results are appearing more and more in textbooks aimed at teaching future professionals the skills they will need on the job. Leviton and Cook [14] have reviewed recent textbooks in social work and education. Most of them contain pages of text synthesizing the results of evaluations in order to infer practices that are empirically supported and seem effective and those for which there is little support. This analysis of introductory level textbooks suggests that evaluations function as one of the devices that disciplines professional practice by screening out actions that do not seem effective and justifying actions that do seem effective. In this we can see the utility of analyses of project elements or project types, for most of the textbook discussions attempt to infer the characteristics of projects that are most associated with bringing about desirable outcomes. Such characteristics are what local practitioners can adopt or adapt in their daily work.

The Implications of the Multiple Criteria of Usage

In the previous discussion the question: "Do evaluations get used?" is shown to be overly simple, with the answer depending on what one means by "used". Moreover, an alternative question is forwarded as being potentially more fruitful: "Under which conditions are evaluations of different types of object (policy, program, project element, or project type) used (1) to form or to contribute to decisions; (2) in debates about policy; (3) to raise policymakers' consciousness about the questions worth asking; and (4) to modify professional practice through the results being incorporated into textbooks and in-service training?"

The previous discussion also implies that several widespread generalizations about the use of evaluation results are oversimplified. The contention that knowledge of effectiveness and impact at the program level is never used, and so should not figure in the formulation of evaluation questions, fails to consider the case where evaluations of several related programs are synthesized and used in future discussions of how effective certain policies or classes of program can be in a given substantive area. The contention that evaluations of specific professional practices are not important to most senior managers—because they prefer results at the program level where global mixes of services are involved that are usually imperfectly implemented—fails to consider that feedback about effective practices slowly filters into consciousness of present and future managers, influencing their conception of what they think it is feasible to do and desirable to fund. To be sure, in each of these cases longer time lines are involved than those typically considered in discussions of the utilization of evaluation results. Yet such long and indirect paths of causal influence are almost certainly indicated by analyses of the sources from which senior managers currently get their information and cognitive structures for defining and analyzing problems. Some of their sources go all the way back to their formal training. (Think of the senior managers trained in economics who, 20 years after graduation, still talk with a distinct University of Chicago or MIT flavor). Other sources come from newspaper reports of social science, from academic consultants, and from cocktail party talk. Evaluation results filter into all these sources as specific findings and as general conclusions about programs, types of programs, and broad policy stances.

CONCLUSIONS

Evaluation is a new field of interdisciplinary applied social research that aims to shed light on the processes and consequences of policies, programs, local projects, project types, and project elements. The evaluations can be oriented towards retrospective accountability (i.e., what has been achieved?); prospective modification (how can the program or project be improved for the future?) and prospective formation (what programs shall we introduce in the future?).

Irrespective of the entity being evaluated and of the retrospective/prospective thrust, some combination of seven types of questions is likely to be asked. The questions deal with the number and characteristics of clients, the nature of the services actually implemented, their effects on clients, impact on the social systems of which clients are a part, the costs of the program, the causal processes that mediate or impede effects, and the "meaning" of the pattern of obtained results.

It is rare for all of these questions to be answered well in any evaluation, whatever the entity under study. This is partly because of resource and time constraints; but it is also due to the fact that different questions require different methods, and so choosing methods in order to answer one type of question reduces the quality of answers to a different type of question. A pressing issue for evaluation, therefore, is: "How does one choose the questions most worth answering?"

The answer seems most clear when an evaluation is Congressionally mandated and the legislation is clearly written. One answers the questions outlined. But even here the difficulty arises that many different groups have a stake in most programs, and not all of them would define the major evaluation questions in the same way as Congress. How should these other interests be represented in the evaluation, if at all? This difficult question does not arise often, for most evaluations are not individually mandated. The more typical state of affairs is that the issues to be explored in an evaluation are less clear, and it falls to agency officials to define them and incorporate them into a Request for Proposals. Yet even so, stakeholder groups differ in the issues they want probed. Senior managers tend to prefer effectiveness and impact questions tailored as closely as possible to what Congressional intent is presumed to be; officials in operating agencies are often more concerned with issues of program-level administration or with evaluating outcomes in contexts where the services are demonstrably implemented at a high level and the outcome variables are proximally related to the services; administrators at the local level rarely want to move beyond head counts; practitioners at the local level take for granted the effectiveness of the services they provide, and seek low cost ways to improve them through analyses of implementation and causal processes; and consumer groups typically worry about the costs, availability, and quality of services. The evaluator has "somehow" to juggle all these information needs, mindful of the fact that whoever funds the evaluation will probably have the major say in question-formulation. Yet meeting some of the information needs of other groups may not only increase the chances of utilization, but under some conditions at least, may also increase the commitment of stakeholder groups to cooperating with the evaluation.

Once the priority of stakeholder groups has been assessed and the overlap of different groups' information needs is clear, the evaluator has to think hard about whether all the desired types of information tend to be used in the short term, for some types of feedback are not. Foremost among these is feedback restricted to the effects and impacts of programs and local projects, nearly all of which are so politically impacted that major decisions about funding are not likely to be made on the basis of evaluation results. Nonetheless, such evaluations are often called for, particularly by Congress and senior managers who have a responsibility for "acountability". Though program-level outcome-oriented results are rarely used in the short term, they are often used later in broader policy contexts that transcend the program under evaluation. But such delayed usage in novel contexts obscures the reality that evaluation was initially promoted to enhance short-term decision capabilities. Thus, to make evaluations maximally useful great consideration has to be paid, not only to the types of questions that facilitate use, but also to other factors that increase use; e.g., keeping major stakeholder groups continuously involved, writing results simply, and discussing them face-to-face with interested parties.

One important factor we have not touched upon in suggesting how to prioritize research questions is needs analysis. It would be desirable if programs and local projects were only funded after an extensive needs analysis that specified just exactly which services were needed by a particular group. In the world of policy, needs analyses are often informal and place a heavy weight on the political needs of Congressmen as well as on the social or economic needs of citizens; or they place a heavy emphasis on Congressional interpretations of social and economic needs which may or may not closely match what these needs are. Nonetheless, where a needs analysis exists, it should be critically consulted as another input into prioritizing.

If no analysis is available the evaluator should conduct one. Indeed, should he or she interview stakeholder groups, this is likely to generate considerable information from professional groups about presumed needs and from client groups about felt needs. When related to background knowledge about the problem from scholarly sources, a firmer grasp of needs should ensue. It may, of course, be an understanding that is more complex than the one with which the evaluator began his pre-evaluation planning, perhaps because the evaluator discovers that different groups define the needs differently and that this very definition is a source of political dispute. This happened, for instance, in the field of compensatory education where some persons defined the problem for educationally disadvantaged children in terms of (1) increasing their absolute level of knowledge in major areas of the school curriculum; (2) decreasing the relative difference in knowledge between economically advantaged and disadvantaged children; (3) increasing the academic self-concept of economically disadvantaged children; (4) decreasing the differences in skill and enthusiasm between teachers in economically advantaged and disadvantaged areas; (5) increasing the involvement in schooling of parents who are economically disadvantaged, etc.

It is not easy to prioritize research questions, and issues of budget, time lines and staff capabilities are involved as well as issues relating to stakeholder interests, program objectives, and needs analyses. Yet prioritizing questions is vital if one believes that evaluation results are often used (albeit in many different ways), that not all the issues worth probing can be probed in a single study, and that the choice of evaluation issues has therefore a potential to further some groups' interests over others.

REFERENCES

1. Becker, H. S. Do Photographs Tell the Truth? *Afterimage*, 1978, 9-13. (Also reprinted in Thomas D. Cook and Charles S. Reicherdt (eds.). *Qualitative and Quantitative Methods in Evaluation Research*. Sage Publications, Beverly Hills, CA, 1979.)
2. Patton, M. Q. *Utilization-Focused Evaluation*. Sage Publications, Beverly Hills, CA, 1978.
3. Riecken, W. H., and Boruch, R. F. *Social Experimentation: A Method for Planning and Evaluating Social Interventions*. Academic Press, New York, 1974.
4. Scriven, M. Pros and Cons about Goal-Free Evaluation. *Evaluation Comment*, 3: (1972): 1-4.
5. Wholey, J. S. Using Evaluation to Improve Program Performance. In Robert A. Levine, et al., (eds.). *Evaluation Research and Practice: Comparative and International Perspectives*. Sage Publications, Beverly Hills, CA, 1981.
6. Chen, H. T. and Rossi, P. H. The Multi-Goal, Theory-Driven Approach to Evaluation: A Model Linking Basic and Applied Social Science. *Social Forces*, 1980, 106.122.
7. Hill, P. *Evaluating Education Programs for Federal Policy Makers*. Lessons from the NIE Compensatory Education Study. J. Pincus, (ed.). *Educational*

Evaluation in the Public Policy Setting. Rand Corp., Santa Monica, CA, May 1980.

8. Scanlon, J. and Walker, J. Program Evaluation and Better Federal Programs. *Journal of Health and Human Resources Administration*, Vol. 1 (Feb. 1979); 278-292.
9. Scanlon and Wholey
10. Lindholm, C. E. and Cohen, D. K. *Usable Knowledge*. Yale University Press, New Haven, CT, 1979.
11. Cronbach, L. J. and Associates. *Toward Reform of Program Evaluation*. Jossey-Bass, San Francisco, CA, 1980.
12. Cook, T. D. An Evolutionary Perspective on a Dilemma in the Evaluation of Ongoing Social Programs. In Brewer, M. B., and Collins, B. E., (eds.). *Scientific Inquiry and the Social Sciences: A Volume in Honor of Donald T. Campbell*. Jossey-Bass, San Francisco, CA, 1981.
13. Weiss, C. H. *Using Social Research in Public Policy Making*. Lexington Books, Lexington, MA, 1977.
14. Leviton, L. C. and Cook, T. D. *The Use of Evaluation in Education and Social Work Textbooks,* Evaluation Review, 1983.

14
A Survey of the Program Evaluation and Evaluation Research Literature in Its Formative Stage

Albert C. Hyde / *School of Business and Public Administration, University of Houston at Clear Lake City, Houston, Texas*

THE NEED FOR EVALUATION

> *All social institutions or subsystems, whether medical, educational, religious, economic, or political, are required to provide "proof" of their legitimacy and effectiveness in order to justify society's continued support. Both the demand for and the type of acceptable "proof" will depend largely upon the nature of the relationship between the social institution and the public. In general, a balance will be struck between faith and fact, reflecting the degree of man's respect for authority and tradition within the particular system versus his skepticism and desire for tangible "proofs of work." [1]*

The above quotation, taken from Edward A. Suchman's landmark book *Evaluative Research*, marks the starting point for a literature that now almost defies compilation. Suchman's study, eminating from his seminars in the mid-1960's at Columbia University, is especially significant for two reasons. First it is Suchman who advocates that evaluation be studied as a generic concept–i.e. that evaluative research and practice can and must be studied in a seperate context distinct from evaluation applications in such fields as medical, educational, legal or other social sciences. Secondly, there is the acuity of Suchman's predictions on the issues that confront evaluation and the expected direction and course of evaluation research as a field of study and a professional practice. More than anything else, as the opening quotation attests, Suchman's work sets the agenda for future discussion and research about evaluation, how it is to be conducted and how it is to be used.

This overview article addresses the literature of program evaluation concentrating for the most part on the parts of it that originated within the last two decades. The phenomenal size (there has literally been a deluge of books and articles on evaluation) of the literature parallels the growth of a large profession of evaluators in a number of organizations and institutions to include legislatures, public sector agencies and departments, consulting and research firms, public and private interest groups, educational and business organizations. The amount, quality, and impact of the evaluations they produce are only now being systematically measured, reanalyzed and evaluated. Still to be assessed is how the evaluation literature has aided and supported the development of evaluation theory and practice. But evaluation is obviously here to stay and the body of literature that has emerged reflects this confidence.

The sheer size of the literature in the last decade alone has also necessitated that this overview be divided into two parts. A subsequent article now being developed will focus on the literature that has emerged since 1975. One of the tasks of that particular article will be to compare evaluation insights provided by significant evaluation theorists before and after this 1975 demarcation. The choice of 1975 as break point for this article represents a belief that the evaluation literature made a pivotal transition at this point in time. Prior to 1975 the evaluation literature pursued a course designed to establish itself as a legitimate field of study. While Edward Suchman's work was one of the first treatises to advocate this there were numerous other highly significant writers and practitioners. They can not all be covered but an attempt will be made to represent enough of them to show the course and pace of evaluation in its developmental period.

Finally, since the literature is so large and still quite new, a truly comprehensive assessment of impact is beyond the scope and space limitations afforded here [2]. The approach that will be used is that of a benchmark concept where stages of growth in the literature will be studied through representative works. Again, using Suchman's work as the example—this has been chosen as a starting point, but it is necessary to first look backwards (for example, at the sources Suchman cites) and then forwards to see what has come in the post-Suchman period.

ANTECEDENTS: THE DEVELOPMENT OF PRACTICE AND LITERATURE

In Suchman's book one of the more minor (though rather fascinating) contributions traces the development of the eras of public sector development. The argument is made that the growth and development of evaluative research parallel the history of the public sector movement. Spanning several centuries, Suchman's history depicts several stages beginning first with a period of "Authority or Benevolent Despotism" [3] where autocratic officials gained responsibility for providing services and used empirical, trial and error evaluations to assemble a "valid body of operational procedures even in the absence of knowledge of underlying processes" [4].

A second period, entitled "Revolution and Enlightenment" follows where research, experimentation, and program development are central to assembling both knowledge about social conditions and professional processes. Scientific evaluations begin with the collection of vital statistics about the general populace. These early crude statistical indices are followed by comparative ratings of programs or community areas, usually conducted by some form of self-study.

A third period, originating after World War I, marks the first era of serious evaluation. Although Suchman himself didn't title this period, it can be labeled the period of "Standardization and Professionalism." Evaluation efforts were largely centered on "attempts at uniformity and the establishment of standards if public service was to advance as a professional field" [5]. In this period, evaluation guidelines that were essentially self-imposed professional standards were distributed for performance self-appraisals and program documentation.

It can be hypothesized that there is now a fourth period of development. In fact, its development was heralded by Suchman's work although he was perhaps too close in time to see the impact of the Great Society programs in the 1960's or his own impact in advancing the case for generic evaluation. This last and still current stage would be the period "Social Intervention and Systems Development." The impetus provided by the Great Society programs of the 1960's, the developments in the art and science of administration, and the impact of systems approaches and technology made evaluation a critical component of public service activity. Evaluation was fused as a prerequisite for funding into new programs that relied heavily on social experimentation [6]. Evaluation was also a critical facet of administrative planning, budgeting, and policy analysis processes. Finally, the form of generic evaluation Suchman proposed was essentially part of the same systems concept that would revolutionize administrative theory and professional practice. Partly responsible for the development of the systems approach to public service effort was the emergence of a highly advocatory literature in evaluation which argued that evaluation was the critical step that transformed processes into real systems of management.

As mentioned, the early literature of program evaluation prior to Suchman's work emphasized application. The sources used by health, education, and other social science practitioners were largely from scientific methodology or early social science action research. Kurt Lewin's *Resolving Social Conflicts* [7] was used extensively as were early works by Lazarsfield and Rosenbert [8], Cohen and Nagel [9], Donald Campbell [10], and R. L. Solomon [11]. The resulting meld produced articles or monographs in the 1950's and early 1960's that explored how more systematic evaluation could be used to assess current professional practices or new experiments and mildly innovative programs in these various fields of health or education.

In this early stage of literature development, evaluation was either viewed generally as a fact-finding exercise tied to program actions and results ('a la Lewin) or as a series of steps designed to establish more control for validating and assessing experiments. What was emerging however was a more cohesive statement about evaluation principles that would summarize some of the methodological and assessment advances realized. While there are several articles and reports in the 1980's that anticipate a statement of general principles, perhaps the most thorough exposition is found in Herbert Hyman, Charles Wright, and Terence Hopkins' study of the encampment for citizenship [12] a summer camp program for young men and women that started in 1945. With the camp program in its tenth year, the Bureau of Applied Social Research at Columbia was given the task of evaluating whether the program had achieved its objectives. The resulting study was appropriately titled Applications of Methods of Evaluation and its significant contribution to the development of the program evaluation literature is its first chapter, subtitled "Principles of Evaluation" [13].

The campers are largely forgotten as one might expect. What Hyman, Wright, and Hopkins make clear is that knowledge about evaluation is what is important, or as they state:

> *Effective application of the principles to the particular case, special modifications of procedure within the general framework—this is what must be learned. It is to this end that our work is presented. It consists of two parts, a general statement of principles of evaluation, and a detailed exemplification of the principles in a series of evaluative studies conducted in one action program. Even if the program studied were a rare and exotic one, the presentation would still have the virtue of showing the translation of the method into operative research. [14]*

Their treatment of evaluation principles rests on the premise that there are five planes of the evaluative problem: conceptualization of objectives; research design; instruments of measurement and research procedures; index construction for weighting effectiveness; and understanding findings on effectiveness. Each plane then is developed to illustrate basic principles and rules; the premise being that "it is difficult to develop the method for its solution" [15].

The student of program evaluation will find the encampment study interesting for its development of general evaluation principles and its somewhat unique applications of methods to the study in question. One might conclude that the field of evaluation was finally ready for a general statement about methodologies and objectives that would fuse both the many applications of evaluation tried in many social science fields and the principles of evaluation and social research methodology that has emerged. In short, the need was for a general treatment of evaluation as a field of research and professional practice that was undergoing radical change. It should also be remembered that the mid 1960's marked an important transition for public service programs with the advent of the Great Society programs [16]. While a detailed treatment of how the new emphasis on planned social change through government programs is beyond the purview of this article, it is sufficient to state that there was a phenomenal increase in the scope, level, and objectives of social programs in this period.

Evaluation was expected to be a central component in the search for effective social reform. Interestingly, the response from the developing evaluation community was two-fold–first, that knowledge and research capability on evaluation would have to be considerably enhanced to play such a role and secondly, that evaluation would have to recognize that favorable political circumstances were responsible for this current "commitment" to social programs which would affect both the use of evaluations and the long range continuity of the social programs themselves. Hopefully, one will not miss the irony of how this original context for evaluation has changed dramatically under the less than favorable political circumstances that now abound.

"GENERIC" EVALUATION AND SUCHMAN'S *EVALUATIVE RESEARCH*

Edward Suchman's landmark book *Evaluative Research*, first published in 1967, was and remains the first benchmark for the field of evaluation and evaluative research. It shows evaluation at a critical juncture in development–from trial and error to professional practice to principle to body of knowledge and/or field of study. This doesn't mean that evaluation was now totally developed. Indeed, Leonard S. Cattrell's foreward to Suchman's book warns: "Out of all this one gets the impression that what passes for evaluative research is indeed a mixed bag at best and chaos at worst. There are many reasons for this sad state and most of them, strange to say, are nonpejorative, as the present volume makes quite clear"[17].

Evaluation Research marks an arrival point, in that consensus or acceptance has been reached that evaluation does include a number of applicable methodologies for either operationalized research or ongoing program assessment; and that evaluation is a professional field of study with conceptual, methodological, and administrative dimensions that must be continually reassessed and developed. In addition Suchman makes clear that the political dimension to evaluation and social program effects can not be ignored. In fact, this may well be one of the most significant contributions in that recognition is given to the complexities of of the "evaluation problem" and its inherent political and economic dimensions.

One need only compare Table of Contents between Suchman's work and the first chapter from the encampment study (as illustrated in Table 1) to see the development from evaluation as a codification of principles to a complete field of study. But *Evaluative Research* is more than a clarifying overview textbook on a

Table 1 The Development of Evaluation from Principles to a Field of Study: Comparing the Subject Content of the Encampment Study to Suchman's *Evaluative Research*

The Encampment Study[1]	Evaluative Research[2]
I. Principles of Evaluation	I. An Introduction to Evaluative Research
a. Introduction	Social Change and Social Action
b. Conceptualization and measurement of the	The Need for Evaluation
objectives of the program and other	
unanticipated relevant outcomes	II. The Growth and Current Status of Evaluation
Conceptualizing the objective of the	Background of Evaluative Research
program	A Critique of Evaluation Guides
Conceptualizing unanticipated consequences	Current Problems of Evaluative Research
c. Research design and the proof of the	
effectiveness of a program	III. Concepts and Principles of Evaluation
Controlling for extraneous sources of change	Concepts of Evaluation
by experimental designs	Evaluation and Values
Controlling for effect of repeated testing	Objectives and Assumptions
Workable alternatives to the classic	
control-group design	IV. Types and Categories of Evaluation
d. Research procedures and the reduction of error	Statement of Evaluative Objectives
Quality of response	Levels of Objectives
Biases resulting from nonresponse	Assumptions of Validity
e. Problems of index construction and the proper	Categories of Evaluation
evaluation of effectiveness	
Weighing effectiveness in the light of	V. The Conduct of Evaluative Research
restricted ceilings for change	Evaluative versus Nonevaluative Research
Weighing effectiveness in terms of	Methodological Approaches to Evaluation
individual changes versus net changes	Formulating the Evaluative Research Problem
Weighing effectiveness by combining	
discrete aspects of change	VI. The Evaluative Research Design

Weighing the amount of effectiveness and tests of significance

f. Understanding the findings on effectiveness
   - Describing the program
   - Describing the subjects
   - Differential effects among contrasted types of subjects
   - The contribution of different aspects of the program
   - Inquiry into the processes by which the program produces effects

Variations in Evaluative Research Design
The "Placebo" Effect
The Longitudinal Study Design
The Three Main Conditions of Evaluative Research

VII. The Measurement of Effects
   - Reliability
   - Validity
   - Differential Effects

VIII. Evaluation and Program Administration
   - Evaluation and Administrative Science
   - Research
   - Planning
   - Demonstration
   - Operation
   - Resistance and Barriers to Evaluation

IX. The Administration of Evaluation Studies
   - Relation of Public Demand and Cooperation
   - Resources for Evaluative Research
   - Role Relationships and Value Conflicts
   - Definition of Evaluation Problems and Objectives
   - Evaluative Research Design and Execution
   - Utilization of Findings

X. The Social Experiment and the Future of Evaluative Research
   - An Evaluation Model for the Social Experiment
   - Evaluation and Social Causation
   - Applications of Intervening Variable Model
   - Conceptual and Methodological Considerations
   - Conclusion

---

1. Adapted from the Table of Contents of Ref. 12
2. Adapted from the Table of Contents of Ref. 1

new field of endeavor. Suchman continually focuses attention on problems in both past and future contexts. Much of the conceptual logic of his work follows his criticisms of these three general evaluation areas [18]:

- Problems with subject matter or objectives;
- Problems with methods of procedure for evaluation;
- Problems with administration and evaluation expertise.

These three categories constituted the heart of Suchman's classification system which also represented evaluations major deficiencies. Subject matter or objectives dealt with the "What" of evaluation, or the *problems of applications* in that evaluative research focused too narrowly on past performance, past methods, past objectives and priorities, past standards, and past assumptions about how programs should be carried out. Method of procedure, on the other hand, involved *methodology* problems as evaluative research emphasized various issues of measurement and operationalization. Essentially this second category was about the "How" of evaluation concerning research designs, measurement indexes, social indicators, control groups, descriptive statistics, and methods of comparison and causal measurement. Finally, administration dealt with the "Who" of evaluation or the *professional/implementation* questions, to include training, expertise, bias, ethics, planning, managing, and reassessment of evaluative resources, efficiency, and impact.

Subsequent chapters in Suchman's book are developed to deal with each of these areas specifically but his conclusions are really more predictors of anticipated difficulties that will have to be faced as the field advances. In fact, these three areas essentially constitute the loci of most of the current literature from 1970 onwards. One can classify most evaluative books or articles according to a subject matter, methodology, or administration orientation (See Table 2). Suchman's treatment of the problems in these areas is as relevant today as it was 15 years ago, which is an interesting reflection on the field. Either Suchman was an astonishingly accurate prophet or the field has simply not been able to make much progress in resolving these critical problems. Regretfully, the latter seems the more appropriate explanation.

Before turning to the Post-Suchman phase, several observations are in order. There are current problems with evaluation that Suchman didn't foresee. While his observations on political commitment and societal support for programs as pressures on evaluation are highly relevant, his emphasis on a generic research evaluation concept downplays the behavioral or bureaucratic dimensions to evaluation as a negotiated, interactive process; a theme greatly emphasized in the 1970's. A second development was also unanticipated in that the increasing intergovernmental relations context of social programs with mixed funding, management, and evaluative responsibilities has added a new and different political dimension to

Table 2 Categorizing the Evaluation Research Literature in the Post-Suchman Period Representative Works Published in the 1970's

Focus on Subject Matter of Objective (Politics)	Focus on Methods/ Procedures for Evaluation (Methodology)	Focus on Administration/ Evaluation Expertise (Administration's)
Rivlin (1971) *Systematic Thinking for Social Action*	Weiss (1972) *Evaluation Research*	Wholey et al (1970) *Federal Evaluation Policy*
Rossi and Williams, ed. (1972) *Evaluating Social Programs*	Weiss (ed) 1972 *Evaluating Action Programs*	Hatry et al (1973) *Practical Program Evaluation for State & Local Government*
Wildavsky (1973) "The Self Evaluating Organization"	Guttentag (1973) "Subjectivity and its use in Evaluation Research"	Poland (ed) 1974 *PAR* "Symposium on Program Evaluation"
Weiss (1973) "Between the Cup and the Lip"	Riecken & Boruch (1974) *Social Experimentation*	
Mushkin (1973) "Evaluation: Use with Caution"	Guttentag and Struening ed. (1976) *Handbook of Evaluation Research* (2 vols.)	
	Caro, ed. (1971, 1977) *Readings in Evaluative Research*	

evaluation. Lastly, Suchman only tangentially addresses the relationships of evaluation to planning, budgeting, policy analysis, economic analysis, and other facets of the administrative practice. However, in fairness to this remarkable work, the literature has yet to address this latter dimension or the intergovernmental context of evaluation in any comprehensive fashion.

PRESCRIPTIVE EVALUATION: THE FIRST STAGE (THE EARLY 1970's)

Three equally remarkable works followed Edward Suchman's *Evaluative Research* in the next half decade. Although each work had a distinct point of origin in one of the three aforementioned loci, these works covered general issues and provided a comprehensive assessment of evaluation. First to appear in 1970 was *Federal Evaluation Policy*, a landmark study by Joseph W. Wholey, John W. Scanlon, Hugh G. Duffy, James S. Fukumoto, and Leona M. Vogt, all with the Urban Institute [19]. This book begins with a review of what evaluation is and why it has come to such prominence in the federal government. The most significant contributions are about *administering evaluation*, the various roles of participants in evaluation, and the resulting organizational relationships. It discusses methodology and subject matter applications, but is most definitive in explaining how the administration of evaluation affects its use and value. *Federal Evaluation Policy* is emphatically prescriptive offering a number of major recommendations for formalizing, systematizing, and improving evaluation in the public sector.

In 1971, a second benchmark work, (this time illustrating a subject matter–objectives perspective) was released–Alice Rivlin's *Systematic Thinking for Social Action*." Rivlin, then at the Bookings Institute and formerly Assistant Secretary for Planning and Evaluation at the Department of Health, Education, and Welfare, delivered the third Gaither lecture series at Berkeley in 1970 and *Systematic Thinking for Social Action* was the published result. It is an exceptional work beginning with evaluation's origins in PPBS–and then using a series of insightful questions–analyzing what had been learned about various social program outcomes as a result of evaluation and policy analysis techniques. High marks are awarded for evaluation's ability to measure "who wins and loses" but less laudatory grades follow for evaluation on a more important set of questions involving what we know that works, why and what it may mean for the future. Her concluding note - "Put more simply, to do better, we must have a way of distinguishing better from worse" [21] recognized both the need for improved performance measurement and underuse of social experimentation. Rivlin saw evaluation as a significant force in effecting positive change but recognized that methodological and administrative difficulties would be considerable.

Alice Rivlin's assessment of the state of evaluation focused principally on political issues and lessons learned in administering the large scale social programs launched during the 1960's. A more comprehensive work eminating from a subject matter/objectives perspective was published in 1972 by Peter Rossi and Walter Williams. *Evaluating Social Programs* [22] was an anthology of essays by a number of the most significant evaluation research theorists and social scientists at the time discussing various problems of theory and practice of evaluation as it was being applied. While the work is neatly divided into theory and practice halves, there is no real line of demarcation. Essentially the book is political in that its premise is keyed to three related questions:

> *First; why have the quantity and quality of evaluation actively to date been so low?*

> *Second; What are the problems and risks associated with developing more evaluation research and using results in the social policy process?*
> *Third; What steps should be taken by the government and the social science research community to increase significantly the level of soundly conceived and executed evaluative studies and to reduce the dangers attendant in the use of results? [23]*

Although *Evaluating Social Programs* in comprehensive and considers the methodological and administrative issues, it is prescriptive in its recommendations that social research/evaluation be better organized and that organizations need to develop capacities to conduct large scale evaluation research efforts.

Completing Suchman's issues triad, there is Carol Weiss's classic methodological study *Evaluation Research* [24], released in 1972. Acknowledging the influences of Suchman, Hyman, Peter Rossi, and Howard Freeman at Columbia University and methodologist Donald Campbell, [25] Weiss's point of origin is method of procedure. While her work covers administration and subject matter areas, it provides a superbly ordered and balanced assessment of methodological questions to include purpose, structure, research designs, measurement questions, and relationships to other administrative practices. Weiss's excellent grasp of the political context is also apparent as she discusses a number of issues involving the dynamic environments of programs and the politicization of evaluation results. She concludes that evaluation has a long ways to go before it achieves its potential but the potential is strong. Weiss's work remains one of the great classic statements about the generic evaluative field that the serious student must read and absorb.

At this point, 1972, the evaluation literature was still in a formative and unified stage. Of the books mentioned, Federal Evaluation Policy (134 pages) *Systematic Thinking* (150 pages) and *Evaluation Research* (160 pages) represented comprehensive yet surprisingly terse and spare assessments of a field on the verge of specialization and fragmentation. An edited work *Readings in Evaluation Research* [26] by Francis G. Caro was released in 1971 as a companion volume to Suchman and fall, 1972 marked the birth of *Evaluation*, a journal on evaluation published under the support of the Minneapolis Medical Research Foundation. But the early 70's were bringing a series of new concerns about evaluation as well. As Susan Salasin, *Evaluation*'s editor wrote in a lead editorial entitled "What is Evaluation Good For?"

> *I believe that a more fundamental issue is at stake here than the mere effectiveness of evaluations. Rather, this questioning of evaluation seems to lead back to each person's expectations for evaluation. I*

> *think we used to expect program evaluation to provide us with answers about what to do, and when it didn't in our frustration we attached the process of evaluation itself. To ourselves, we said, "Since evaluation doesn't provide answers, evaluation is no good."*
>
> *If instead we try to ask ourselves what evaluation has given us, aside from a lack of answers, we can see a new role for evaluation. Instead of talking about what evaluation doesn't do, we can talk about what it does do. The experiences reported herein seem to indicate that evaluation does lead to a discovery of what some of the problems with our human service programs are. Evaluation does highlight the fact that we think we can accomplish more for people than we can, in fact, accomplish. Viewed from this perspective, evaluation is a valuable and effective tool that can help sense out the problems in our programs, and keep us honest in making promises to people about how we can help them. [27]*

THE SECOND STAGE (1973-1976)

Following in the same path as Wholey et al. in *Federal Evaluation Policy*; the Urban Institute released a second study in 1973 by Harry Hatry, Richard Winnie and Donald Fisk entitled *Practical Program Evaluation for State and Local Government Officials* [28]. Essentially, a "how to" guidebook for evaluation, the work focused on evaluation applications for state and local government urging that a substantial evaluation effort be undertaken. The book provided a superb case study on evaluating solid waste collection in the District of Columbia providing a number of methodological insights on how to conduct evaluations. Yet the heart of the work was in the administrative area. Hatry et al. discuss in depth who should shoulder the evaluation burden, how evaluation relates to local government management practices and policy decisions, and what are appropriate federal and local government roles in evaluation.

Completing the administrative dimension, *Public Administration Review* (PAR) issued a symposium on program evaluation in July/August 1974 [29]. The symposium was edited by Orville Poland, a superb choice given that Poland was one of the first significant public administration scholars to advocate that evaluation be incorporated with administration theory and practice. Five articles were included in the symposium: four of which examined how evaluation was practiced; in federal government agencies [30], the Office of Management and Budget [31], State Legislatures [32], and the U.S. General Accounting Office [33]. The fifth article was an excellent definitional piece by Poland himself on the relationship between evaluation and administration [34]. Updating Suchman's concerns,

Poland addressed three principle themes: (1) evaluation problems in social experimentation and objectives definition, (2) problems with evaluation in cost-effectiveness analysis, and (3) the lack of a theoretical framework for systematic management of evaluation efforts. But the central thrust remains integrating evaluation into administrative practice and Poland concluded that while the need is high, prospects for accomplishing this task are probably low.

But the Hatry work and the Poland - *PAR* symposium demonstrate a recurrent thrust in the literature in this final part of the Post-Suchman phase. These works recognized that political, methodological, and administrative issues are intertwined and that generic evaluation must address various issues in all three areas if theory and practice are to advance. Perhaps no where is this clearer than in the second phase of the politics-focused literature which began to address the complexities of evaluation and management processes and values interrelated within highly political environments. This political "environmental" dimension presented several major dilemmas for evaluation:

> *The problem of accomplishing "objective and realistic" evaluation of multi-purpose, complex, and often highly subjective, unrealistic, and necessarily ambiguous public programs;*
> *The problem of implementing the results/recommendations of evaluations so that meaningful program change occurs within a highly political, technical environment;*
> *The problem of maintaining the creditability of the evaluation process, both as an internal management tool and an external review/control/change mechanism. [35]*

These problems were greatly complicated by various perspectives of different evaluators and the reluctance or inability of evaluators to assay their own impact. While evaluation methodologies, and criteria of assessment were often subjected to rigorous review in planning various studies, very little progress was being made in ascertaining the failures of evaluation in either of two important aspects—political feasibility or facility of implementation.

Of course, Suchman had identified these issues earlier; thus they were not new concerns. In one of the first re-articulations of this problem Aaron Wildavsky, perhaps public administration's foremost critic, wrote an article in the 1972 *Public Administration Review*, "The Self-Evaluating Organization" [36]. Wildavsky examined what he described as "obstacles" to evaluation as organization problems. These are highlighted in Table 3. All of Wildavsky's obstacles focused in one way

Table 3 Evaluation as an Organizational Problem: Political Obstacles to Evaluation – A Comparison of Criteria

Aaron Wildavsky	Carol Weiss
Emphasis of Evaluation on Change which is in conflict with the Emphasis of Organizations on stability.	Uncertainty about the Purpose of the Evaluation
Difficulty of Separating Program from Clients being Served/of Distinguishing between Program Objectives and Clientele.	Lack of Clarity and Uniformity in Evaluation Methodologies.
Preponderance of Multiple, Vague, Conflicting, and Fast-Changing Objectives for Programs.	Ambiguity of Evaluation's Role in Organization.
Conflict between Evaluation Goals on Changing Allocation of Resources/Efforts in Whole Units Among Programs to Management Goals on Changing Allocations in Fractional Units within Programs.	Personality/Professional Differences between Evaluators and Program Operators.
Lack of Agreement between Managers and Evaluators on "Best" Time, Criteria, and Methodology to Conduct Evaluations.	Instability and Inconsistency in Evaluation Staffing.
Conflicts between Objectivity-Expertise-and Credibility.	Questions/Uncertainty about the Roles of Consultants –How Selected, What Purposes.
Insufficient Attention given Evaluation to Costs of Change or Anticipation of Problems of Change.	Difficulty with the Timing of Evaluations.
Political Rivalries between Competing Evaluators and Competing Programs.	Questions on Use of Evaluations–Who's Responsible for Implementation.
Predominantly Negative Nature of Evaluations in Conflict with Generally Positive Reinforcement Mode of Organizational Management.	Uncertainty about Follow-Up/Re-Evaluation Phases.
Source: Adapted from Aaron Wildavsky "Evaluation as an Organizational Problem." *Public Administration Review*, 1972.	*Source*: Adopted from Ref. 37.

or the other on how evaluation affected the organization or created organization dysfunction. At the heart of Wildavsky's critique was a premise—that evaluation emphasized *change* while organizations sought *stability* - hence organizational managers would naturally (ie. politically) resist evaluation. While Wildavsky's treatise was general, another analysis of the political problem was provided by Carol Weiss in a 1973 *Evaluation* article [37]. Weiss, also focused on the political failings of evaluation. (Her constraints are juxtaposed against Wildavsky in Table 3 as well). In arguments based on several select studies of evaluation projects, she concluded that the primary causes of failure were various organizational constraints that impeded the evaluator's ability to apply results, but were the responsibility of the evaluator to rectify. In a sense, both argued that evaluation wasn't working because of serious political faults. Wildavsky saw possible solutions lodged primarily in the organization—Weiss saw them in evaluation itself.

Two other articles appeared in what was to be a rather remarkable 1973 second volume of *Evaluation*. One, by Selma Mushkin, provided a critical reexamination of methodological issues. Mushkin's article—appropriately titled "Evaluation - Use with Caution"—essentially argued the proposed uses for evaluation findings were too far ahead of the primitive state of the art methodologies developed to date [38]. Her concluding message was aptly "To use evaluation results for policy-making we need to know what goes into the formulation of an evaluation study, what its limitations are, and what its findings mean" [39].

The other article was by Marcia Guttentag who confronted the classical research design model inherent in social experimentation and evaluation research. In an article entitled "Subjectivity and its Use in Evaluation Research." Guttentag argued that evaluation research to be useful had to be based on a more subjective model of decision theory and not out of the classical social science research paradigm [40]. She urged that evaluation research go its own way and refocus on relevance, subjectivity and political values.

All of the aforementioned articles show the focusing of evaluation issues across categories - i.e. political, methodological, and administrative. What remained to be accomplished for the evaluation literature at this junction in 1974-75 was the production of a major volume that could accommodate a number of significant theoretical, viewpoints documentations of evaluation efforts, and speculations on political, administrative and methodology problems. The field of evaluation research was significantly large enough, the level of evaluation effort sufficiently developed such that the time for a comprehensive approach at some form of encyclopedia or handbook was right. Marcia Guttentag and Elmar Struening produced such a work in a 2 volume set of, 1432 pages entitled *The Handbook of Evaluation Research*, published by Sage Publishers in 1975 [41]. The Post-Suchman period was complete.

There were, of course, other significant works produced on evaluation research in this period. The Brookings Institution issued a series of works in 1975 on Social experimentation including a highly regarded conference proceeding report edited by Alice Rivlin and Michael Timpane (*Ethical and Legal Issues of Social Experimentation*) [42] which added several new perspectives bridging administrative and methodological issues. Social Experimentation was an important theme of the evaluation research literature and a number of works constitute important bench marks in understanding this dimension of evaluation. The most notable work in this vein was Henry Riecken and Robert Boruch's *Social Experimentation* [43]. Further, Peter Rossi and Katharine Lyall produced another significant volume for the Russell Sage Foundation critiquing the Negative Income Tax experiment [44].

But these works anticipate a new series of developments in evaluation envolking increased specialization. As an illustration, Francis A. Caro completed a revised edition of his edited volume *Readings in Evaluation* in January 1977 [45]. While Caro's work addresses evaluation generically, it quickly turns to "social programming" and examines in depth what he terms "basic issues, the organizational context, and methodological issues" [46]. These issues are more than a simple refinement of Suchman's political, methodological, and administrative dimensions. In fact, they constitute a far more intense and comprehensive review of all of the issues involving evaluation research as applied to social programs and design of social program experiments. Caro's excellent introductory article in the book - traces a different (almost a more regional), history of evaluation research beginning with Lester Ward [47] in 1906 and F. Stuart Chapen [48] in 1917–two pioneers in the social sciences who argued for sociological experimentation. The history stops with the large-scale federal social experimentation efforts of the 1960's and early 1970's.

It is in this sense that the post-Suchman phase is complete. Evaluation, as Suchman advocated, had to be taken out of its substantive context - i.e. educational, health, evaluation, etc. and developed as a *functional* or generic concept. The 1975 *Handbook of Evaluation Research* represents in a sense the accomplishment of this objective - evaluation was to be considered as evaluation. But from the second half of the 1970's to the present, the evaluation literature would be focused more *professionally* representing the specialized needs of a number of evaluation sub-areas - (administration, legislative oversight, policy analysis, social programming, etc.) and the reemergence of substantive evaluation for various social science areas (health, education, law, medical, etc.)

REFLECTIONS OF EVALUATION'S FIRST PHASE

The post Suchman era of the literature essentially ends in 1975. It is as this juncture that the evaluation literature "takes off", going beyond the generic concept that Hyman, Wright and Hopkins or Edward Suchman had advocated. Evaluation was ready for more specialized foci and more extensive and intensive treatment of specific issues, areas, methodologies, and practices. Unfortunately as is bound to happen in a field of endeavor where there is considerable activity and resources, the literature of program evaluation virtually exploded.

The resulting deluge of literature is characterized by published evaluation studies released by numerous agencies, legislative commissions, consultants, etc. This formal documentation of "evaluation output" paralleled an equally prestigious quantity of books, monographs, articles, review annuals, anthologies and readers. While the quality level of many of these later works was somewhat questionable, the even more important question of direction was being highlighted.

What the literature explosion seems to have done that is most harmful to evaluation is mask its current identity crisis. There is little doubt as to the increasing sophistication of evaluative "technology" or the overall growth and acceptance of evaluations' role in social research and administrative management. The evaluative literature since 1976 certainly reflects these tendencies–growth, specialization, and differentiation. However, the dilemma for the field of evaluation for the 1980's is that in an era of "different assumptions"–decreasing resources, less central control, more intergovernmental "cooperation" and "slowth" (slower growth) –evaluation may have *less utility* and *social relevance*. As one practitioner lamented, evaluation may be pricing itself out of the public market. Whether this result will occur, and how evaluation will respond remains to be seen.

REFERENCES

1. Suchman, E. A. *Evaluative Research*. Russell Sage Foundation, New York, 1967, p. 2.
2. Rather, I have chosen 1976 as a demarcation line between the first (generic development) phase and a second (specialization) of literature development. Although a somewhat arbitrary division, 1976 does mark an explosive point of the literature's growth where the emphasis shifts from a generic, centralized perspective to a more specialized and decentralized perspective. Interestingly, arguments about the emergence of a 3rd phase entitled reform are now emerging. See Cronbach, L. J. et al. *Toward Reform of Program Evaluation*. Jossey-Bass, San Francisco, CA, 1980.
3. For an interesting historical interpretation of this development, see Dorwart, R. A. *The Prussian Welfare State before 1740*. Harvard University Press, Cambridge, MA, 1971.
4. Suchman, *op cit*. pp. 12-13.
5. *Ibid*. pp. 14-15.
6. Rivlin, A. M. *Systematic Thinking for Social Action*. Brookings, Washington, D.C., 1971.
7. Lewin, K. *Resolving Social Conflicts*. Harper and Brothers, New York, 1948.
8. Lazarsfeld, P. F. and Rosenburg, M. (eds.). *The Language of Social Research*. Free Press, Glencoe, IL, 1955.

9. Cohen, M. R. and Nagel, E. *An Introduction to Logic and Scientific Method*. Harcourt Brace, New York, 1934.
10. Campbell, D. T. Factors Relevant to the Validity of Experiments in Social Settings. *Psychological Bulletin*, 54 (1957): 297-312.
11. Solomon, R. L. An Extension of Control Group Design. *Psychological Bulletin*, 46 (1949): 137-150.
12. Hyman, H. H., Wright, C. R., and Hopkins, T. K. *Application of Methods of Evaluation*. University of California Press, Berkeley, CA, 1962.
13. *Ibid.* pp. 3-85.
14. *Ibid.* p. 4.
15. *Ibid.* p. 6.
16. A superb analysis of this is found in Schultze, C. H. *The Public Use of Private Interest*, Brookings, Washington, 1977, which is developed in a program evaluation context in Hyde, A. C. and Shafritz, J. M., *Program Evaluation in the Public Sector*, Praeger, New York, 1980.
17. Cottrell, L. S. Foreward. In Suchman, E. A. *op cit*. p. vii.
18. Suchman, *op cit*. pp. 16-18.
19. Wholey, J. S., Scanlon, J. W., Duffy, H. G., Fukormoto, J. S., and Vogt, L. M. *Federal Evaluation Policy*. The Urban Institute, Washington, D.C., 1970.
20. Rivlin, A. M. *Systematic Thinking for Social Action*, The Brookings Institution, Washington, D.C., 1971.
21. *Ibid.* p. 144.
22. Rossi, P. H., and Williams, W. (ed.). *Evaluating Social Programs*. Seminar Press, New York, 1972.
23. *Ibid.* p. XIV.
24. Weiss, C. *Evaluation Research*. Prentice Hall, Englewood Cliffs, NJ, 1972. It is somewhat unfair to neglect Howard E. Freeman's contributions to the development of evaluation. His *Social Research and Social Policy*, co-authored with Clarence C. Sherwood, provides one of the first methodological works and contains a superb, albeit brief, chapter on evaluation tasks and roles. See Freeman, H. E. and Sherwood, C. C. *Social Research and Social Policy*. Prentice Hall, Englewood Cliffs, NJ, 1970.
25. An earlier reference was provided to work by Donald Campbell but the classic statement of his influence on methodology remains *Experimental and Quasi-Experimental Designs for Research*. (co-authored with Julian C. Stanley), Rand McNally, Chicago, 1966.
26. Caro, F. G. (ed.). *Readings in Evaluation Research*. Russell Sage Foundation, New York, 1971.
27. Salasin, S. What is Evaluation Good For *Evaluation*, Fall 1972, p. 1.
28. Hatry, H. P., Winnie, R. E., and Fisk, D. M. *Practical Program Evaluation or State and Local Government Officials*. The Urban Institute, Washington, D.C., 1973.

29. Poland, O. F. (ed.). Symposium on Program Evaluation. *Public Administration Review*, July/August 1974: 299-339.
30. Horst, P., Nay, J. N., Scanlon, J. W., and Wholey, J. S. Program Management and the Federal Evaluator. *Public Administration Review*, July/August 1974: 300-07.
31. Lewis, F. L. and Zarb, F. G. Federal Program Evaluation From the OMB Perspective. *Public Administration Review*, July/August 1974.
32. Brown, R. and Pethel, R. D. A Matter of Facts: State Legislative Performance Auditing. *Public Administration Review*, July/August 1974: 318-26.
33. Marvin, J. L. and Hedrick, J. L. GAO Helps Congress Evaluate Programs. *Public Administration Review*, July/August 1974: 327-33.
34. Poland, O. F. Program Evaluation and Administrative Theory. *Public Administration Review*, July/August 1974: 333-338.
35. Hyde, A. C. and Shafritz, J. M. op cit. p. vi.
36. Wildavsky, A. The Self-Evaluating Organization. *Public Administration Review*, September/October 1972: 509-20.
37. Weiss, C. H. Between the Cup and the Lip. *Evaluation* 1 (2): pp. 49-55.
38. Mushkin, S. J. Evaluations: Use With Caution. *Evaluation* 1 (2): 30-35.
39. *Ibid.*
40. Guttentag, M. Subjectivity and Its Use in Evaluation Research. *Evaluation* 1: 2: 60-65.
41. Guttentag, M. and Struening, E. *The Handbook of Evaluation Research*. Sage Publishers, Beverly Hills, CA, 1976.
42. Rivlin, A. M. and Timpane, P. M. (eds.). *Ethical and Legal Issues of Social Experimentation*. The Brookings Institution, Washington, D.C., 1975.
43. Riecken, H. W. and Boruch, R. F., *Social Experimentation–A Method for Planning and Evaluation Social Intervention*. Academic Press, New York, 1974.
44. Rossi, P. H. and Lyall, K. *Reforming Public Welfare: A Critique of the Negative Income Tax Experiment*. Russell Sage Foundation, New York, 1976.
45. Caro, F. G. revised edition, op cit.
46. *Ibid*. p. xii.
47. Ward, L. *Applied Sociology*. Ginn and Co., Boston, 1906.
48. Chapin, F. S. *Experimental Designs in Sociological Research*. Harper and Brothers, New York, 1917.

15
Evaluation on Demand: Two Congressionally Mandated Education Evaluations

Beryl A. Radin / *Washington Public Affairs Center, University of Southern California, Washington, D.C.*

The *raison d'etre* for the enterprise called policy analysis/policy evaluation has, without dispute, focused on decisionmaking. Producers and consumers of various forms of policy research agree that somehow the information produced via the analytical process will have the ability to drive out inferior or "bad" ideas and set forth reasonable recommendations for action.

Despite this belief in an inevitable link between information and decisionmaking, there are few examples of application of social science concepts and methods to issues on the public policy agenda. Carol Weiss has noted that "Over the years, it has been the object of grandiose hopes and doleful disappointments" [1].

The literature is replete with diagnoses of solutions to address the problem; that is, the failure to use social research—particularly that called policy analysis and policy evaluation—in the decisionmaking process. For some, the dilemma is inevitable, stemming from the basic differences between the kind of knowledge needed by a decisionmaker and that which is produced by the domain of social science [2]. For others, the problems are derived from an unrealistic image of political decisionmaking and the relationship between "knowledge" and action [3]. Still others focus on the scope and organization of the analytic activities. Wholey has argued that the key to better decisions and better government programs is the "establishment of realistic measurable objectives and measures of program performance and the use of program performance information to bring about changes in program activities that will enhance program performance" [4]. Changes in the reward structure and organizational context of analytic activities have been detailed by a host of writers [5].

While the diagnoses of causes may vary, there are a number of persistent descriptors of the problem. Decisionmakers are not interested in our findings, say evaluators and analysts. Decisionmakers argue that evaluators/analysts do not prodata which addresses the questions they find relevant. According to evaluators, the incremental nature of the decision process does not allow "real" questions to be asked. Evaluators search for single goals of programs; they are not sensitive to multiple goals that emerge from any political process, argue decisionmakers. Conversely, analysts perceive that decisionmakers can't describe what they had in mind in establishing a program; how can evaluators proceed without specification of goals?

The distance between an analyst and a decisionmaker has often been noted as a functional attribute of the gap between production and use of analytic work. Meltsner has noted that propinquity—or the lack of it—can significantly affect the communication between client and analyst and, hence, the use of analysis [6]. Distance can be expressed in terms of vertical relationships (e.g., the multiple levels in an organization between the top official and a mid or lower level analytic staff) or horizontal relationships involving analysis performed by one organization and decisions made by a separate organization.

Meltsner places the relationship between the analyst and the client in the context of four central factors which are conceptualized as a set of concentric circles of influence. The analyst is found in the innermost circle, surrounded by the immediate client, the organizational situation and the policy area (in order of distance from the client).

The evaluation and analytic literature has tended to emphasize the importance of the relationship between the client and the analyst and to focus on the difficulties that develop when analysis is not anchored in real decisionmaking environments. There has been much less attention to the effects of either the organizational situation or the policy area involved in the analytic activity.

This article reviews two analytic efforts that involved analysis undertaken by one organization—the National Institute of Education—to serve the decisionmaking imperatives of the U.S. Congress. These examples, the first an evaluation of the federal compensatory education programs and the second a scrutiny of the vocational education programs, illustrate an increasing "urge" within the legislative branch to request and—hopefully—use evaluative information produced in a systematic and sensible fashion as a part of the intrinsicly political decisionmaking legislative process.

In both instances, Congress asked the National Institute of Education (NIE) via specific legislative language to conduct multi-year, large scale evaluations that would be completed in time for legislative reauthorization. These requests were timed to match a natural life cycle stage when legislation expires and programs must be reauthorized in order to continue. This part of the legislative process creates the closest thing to a feedback loop in the various stages of the policy process (that is, reopening an agenda setting stage which leads to formulation, adoption, implementation and, once again, evaluation and oversight).

In addition to the reauthorization cycle, both evaluations shared several other attributes in their basic construct. Both were asked to focus on large scale, on-going federal programs but while asked to determine various measures of program effectiveness, it appeared that neither evaluation was expected to recommend all-out termination of the program. Thus while seemingly open to modification and change, neither analysis had to deal with the ultimate summative evaluation question: is this program really a good idea and should it survive?

The two evaluations were also designed as activities undertaken by a research enterprise within NIE which functioned within a larger departmental hierarchy. However, both evaluations were to be exempt from all bureaucratic clearance within the Department. The results of the studies were to be communicated directly from NIE to the appropriate Congressional committees. For all intents and purposes, the hierarchical superstructure surrounding the evaluation institute did not exist. The normal supervisory line in the Department would receive the results of the study only when the formal client—Congress—was given its information.

Finally, in both cases the NIE evaluation groups received a combination of overly specific and quite vague instructions via the statutory language and relevant committee reports and floor debates. The mandate to conduct both studies included a specification of questions to be asked (and answered) by the evaluations. But the mandates tended to avoid many of the complexities and conflicts implicit in the multiple goals of the federal program areas.

Within this context, this article reviews and contrasts the process of organizing and conducting two large scale federal education policy evaluations. While not exhaustive (indeed, Congress has subsequently made several additional requests of NIE to conduct studies in the education area), these two examples illustrate a number of persistent evaluation issues.

THE STUDIES

The Compensatory Education Study [7]

At the same time that Congress enacted the Education Amendments of 1974 to make substantive changes in the federal education programs, it also directed various agencies to conduct studies and surveys that would provide up-to-date and accurate information for future legislative development. It specifically directed NIE to conduct a study of compensatory education, including programs financed by states as well as those funded through Title I of the Elementary and Secondary Education Act.

NIE chose to focus most of its attention on Title I, the largest federal education effort, providing more than $2 billion in 1977 for educational programs for low-achieving students in school districts serving children from low-income families.

The legislation instructed the Institute to conduct a study that included:

- An examination of the fundamental purposes and effectiveness of compensatory education programs
- An analysis of the ways of identifying children in greatest need of compensatory education
- An exploration of alternative ways of meeting these children's needs, including the use of written educational plans
- An examination of the feasibility, cost and consequences of alternative ways of distributing federal compensatory education funds
- Not more than 20 experimental programs which would assist NIE in examining the other issues.

The statute directed the presidentally appointed National Advisory Council on the Education of Disadvantaged Children to advise the Institute on the design and execution of the study. NIE was directed to submit interim reports to the President and Congress on December 31, 1976; on September 30, 1977; and to submit a final report in September, 1978.

The specific request to NIE reflected a number of concerns articulated during the 1974 Congressional consideration of the extension of ESEA Title I. These concerns were defined as:

- The effects of altering the definition of poverty used in the Title I allocation formula
- The feasibility of using measures of student achievement rather than numbers of low-income children in the formula
- The possibility of requiring individualized programs of instruction for each student participating in a Title I program
- The merits of requiring school districts to spend as much as 85% of Title I grants on basic skills instruction in reading and mathematics
- The relatively narrow focus on most prior efforts to evaluate the effectiveness of Title I.

NIE described its evaluation as one which adopted a "wide focus" for its examination of compensatory education. It interpreted the directed as constituting two major requests: the first required an assessment of the effectiveness of programs in meeting their fundamental purposes; the second required an examination of alternatives which might improve the effectiveness of programs.

Thus NIE developed a strategy which was "designed to produce a complete understanding of how the Title I program operates in practice as well as how it might change if any of several alternatives were adopted." Four major areas were examined: funds allocation, service delivery, student development, and program administration. The first three of these areas were defined as the "fundamental purposes" of the program while the fourth focused on the relationship between administrative structure requirements for achievement of those purposes.

The study group determined that three "broad philosophical concerns" were discernible in Congressional "intent." First, to provide financial assistance to school districts in relation to their numbers of low-income children and, within those districts, to the schools with the greatest numbers of low income students. Second, to fund special services for low-achieving children in the poorest schools. And third, to contribute to the cognitive, emotional, social, or physical development of participating students.

While noting that these three goals of Title I are consistent with one another, the evaluation acknowledged that each was not equally important to all members of Congress. It commented:

> *Congressional debates, and even the language of different parts of committee and conference reports, suggest that Members of Congress differ among themselves about the relative importance of the respective purposes. Some Congressional statements imply that the purposes form a hierarchy in which Title I delivers funds and provides services on to increase children's academic achievement (thus making the third the most important). Other statements, however, make it clear that the allocation of funds and delivery of services are important ends in themselves and may, in fact, define the practical limits of Federal action to promote the development of children.*
>
> *The evaluation of Title I must start from the recognition that the program has several goals, and to focus exclusively on one, improperly ignores the others. Evaluators must also acknowledge that Title I operates through the Federal system and that state and local governments determine what it will be in practice. Although there is only one Federal Title I program, i.e. only one basic framework of laws and policies, it operates differently in every State, in 14,000 school districts, and in countless classrooms. Thus, to understand and evaluate Title I it is necessary to consider the ways in which Federal policy interacts with the actions of States and local educational agencies (LEAs) that actually implement the program.*
>
> *The early national evaluations of Title 1 considered only the third goal—contributing to children's*

> *development—and often rendered judgments on the efficacy of the program without accounting for the diverse ways in which LEAs had implemented it. These evaluations overlooked some important truths about Title I: it has several objectives, and under it LEAs deliver a range of services with a variety of aims and emphases to a diverse set of beneficiaries. In contrast to earlier evaluations, therefore, NIE's strategy is designed to (1) provide clear information about what Title I is accomplishing toward achievement of each fundamental purpose and (2) examine the implications of alternative ways of organizing the efforts of the Federal, state and local governments to achieve these purposes.*

The final report of the study included attention to administration of compensatory education; the compensatory services delivered by local educational agencies; the effects of using counts of low-income children in allocating funds; the feasibility, costs, and consequences of using counts of low-achieving children in allocation funds; the effects of using student achievement to allocate funds; and student development in compensatory programs.

The information that was made available through the study was generally perceived to be the driving force behind the Title 1 reauthorization process in Congress in 1978. The reports became the basis for specific changes (e.g. shifts in allocation formula) as well as contributing to a much more sophisticated understanding of the strengths and limitations of the Title I approach.

The Vocational Education Study [8]

The Education Amendments of 1976 directed the National Institute of Education to undertake "a thorough evaluation and study of vocational education programs conducted under the Vocational Education Act of 1963, and other related programs conducted under the Comprehensive Employment and Training Act of 1973 and by the State Post-Secondary Commissions authorized by the Education Amendments of 1972." The legislation specified that the inquiry should include:

- A study of the distribution of vocational education funds in terms of services, occupations, target populations, enrollments, and educational and governmental levels and what each distribution should be in order to meet the greatest human resource needs for the next 10 years.

- An examination of how to achieve compliance with, and enforcement of, the provisions of applicable laws of the U.S.
- An analysis of the means of assessing program quanity and effectiveness.
- A review and evaluation of the effectiveness of programs funded to support Consumer and Homemaking Education and to make recommendations for the redirection and improvement of these programs.

The mandate called upon the study to make findings and recommendations pertaining to changes in existing legislation or for new legislation. To support the analysis, the Institute was authorized to attempt to secure funds from other federal agencies (Education and Labor) to conduct three "experimental programs" related to the first three required studies. (As it turned out, such funds could not be secured.)

The legislation provided for up to $1 million a year to be made available to NIE through transfers from the Basic Grant and Program Improvement and Supportive Services monies in the Vocational Education Act. Ten percent of these monies was to be directed to the study of consumer and homemaking education programs. Additional resources were developed through funds from NIE itself, the Bureau of Occupational and Adult Education, the National Advisory Council on Vocational Education, and the National Center for Research on Vocational Education at Ohio State University.

Three products were specified by the statute: a plan for the study to be submitted by the close of 1977; an interim report transmitted on September 30, 1980; and a final report due on September 30, 1981.

The first product—the study plan— gave primary emphasis to the areas of inquiry specified by the legislation: (1) the distribution of vocational education funds; (2) compliance with applicable laws; (3) the means of assessing program quality and effectiveness; and (4) review and evaluation of consumer and homemaking education programs. At the same time, however, the plan noted that "other lines of inquiry would have to be pursued in order to assure that the Study would be attentive, first, to the policy issues that would surface with the forthcoming reauthorization of the Vocational Education Act and, second, to the place of the public school vocational education enterprise within the larger domain of organizations and institutions providing occupational education and training."

The research strategy adopted by the study was built around a conceptualization of the task as a "policy inquiry," rather than a conventional program evaluation. It centered on the purposes, structure, implementation and consequences of federal policy and the degree to which the 1976 amendments "influenced changes in the Nation's decentralized and high diversified public school vocational education enterprise."

> *In Federal law, that enterprise which is formally defined as "organized educational programs which are directly related to the preparation of individuals for paid or unpaid employment, or for additional preparation for a career requiring other than a baccalaureate of advanced degree." . . . The scale and characteristics of the enterprise are shaped by policies made at each level of government–local, State, and Federal. Localities and States are responsible for operating educational programs and providing related services, as well as for the governance of the larger public educational system of which vocational education is a part. Even though it is national in scale and reflects national purposes, the vocational education enterprise is not a single system. It is a collection of different State systems and is characterized by diversity.*

The study was released in late 1981. At this writing it is difficult to ascertain the impact of the study on the reauthorization process. However, Congress has been responsive to the findings through requests for information and testimony in the reauthorization development activities.

TWO EVALUATIONS: A COMPARISON

As these descriptions of the two enterprises suggest, the two studies had a number of similar as well as strikingly different attributes and experiences. Among the areas that seem worthy of comparison are the following: the origins of the study; the construct of the program to be evaluated; the constituency organizations related to the program; the evaluation strategy; the development of a framework; interaction with the Congress; availability of resources; relationships with other parts of the federal bureaucracy; the evaluation staff; and the reports themselves.

Origins of the Study

Although both evaluations were requested and shepherded by many of the same Congressional members and staff, the two efforts were rooted in quite different bases. The Compensatory Education effort was placed in a legislative and policy context in which the issues of dispute had already been joined. As the study director noted, the "changes of interest were quite narrowly circumscribed." [9] While the legislative history of the program dating back to its creation in 1965 suggested that there were diverse perceptions of the basic thrust of the program, the dimensions of that diversity were already known and even reflected in existing legislative proposals for changes in the statute. The mandate for the study, for example, directed NIE to investigate an existing proposal to change the methods of allocating Title I funds on the basis of counts of low-achieving rather than low-income children. The study group perceived that its purpose was to help Congress do its own evaluation [10]. Rather than choose from among those identifiable purposes of the program, the study accepted the multiplicity of goals and, as the study director has commented, "it soon became clear that we did not have to produce a single 'bottom line' measure of the worth of Title I" [11]. That assumption of diversity in goals pushed the evaluation group to depart from the pattern struck by prior evaluations of compensatory education in which single measures (usually student achievement outcomes) were used to assess the worth of the effort. In this case, the task of the study group was to organize an evaluation that would be responsive to the existing and often debated set of perceptions about the compensatory education program.

The Vocational Education study was set in quite a different context. During the formulation of positions during the 1976 reauthorization process, a number of members of Congress found themselves frustrated by the lack of information and lack of compliance with the prior amendments of 1968 to the vocational education program. Visits to states, testimony and a General Accounting Office report supported a perception that failures to comply with the 1968 amendments were widespread and serious [12]. By the end of the reauthorization process, it appeared that Congress perceived that the "existing legislation had not served to realize Federal goals; that the vocational education enterprise had not been an effective partner in implementing Federal policy and had even been resistant to change; and Federal monitoring and oversight were sorely inadequate" [13].

The call for an NIE conducted study of the program was a response to the criticisms which were voiced during the reauthorization process as well as the objections to those criticisms. The GAO report, especially, evoked a controversy within the vocational education community as state officials argued that the compliance point of view expressed in the volume was misleading. Thus, when the study was organized, although there was some sense of a perceived problem in the administration of the past amendments to the program, there were not really well developed alternative formulations about methods of addressing these problems. In this case, the major task facing the evaluation group was to organize a conceptual framework that would be conducive to the development of alternative formulations of change. Unlike the Compensatory Education effort, those alternatives did not already exist in either the political or research environment.

Program Construct

Both evaluation efforts were directed toward large scale federal programs (Title I funds in 1977 totalled more than $2 billion dollars while Vocational Education monies in 1980 reached nearly $800 million) and both were constructed on complex intergovernmental relationships in which funds flowed through a set of allocation decisions at the federal, state and local levels. Despite these similarities, however, the two programs were quite different. The two efforts illustrate the differences between a categorical program design and a grants-in-aid approach to the allocation of federal monies and requirements. The Title I program was always conceptualized as a categorical program even though its early implementation indicated some tendency for it to be viewed as a source of general funds by local school authorities [14]. The iterative process of program refinement that had taken places in the years subsequent to its creation in 1965 moved the effort to an increasingly categorical posture. Although discretion continued to be vested in decisions of state and local agencies, that discretion was delimited to a set of federally prescribed mandates. And while the federal goals for the program were diverse, they were largely consistent with one another.

By contrast, the Vocational Education program was historically constructed through the Smith-Hughes Act of 1971 as a classic grant-in-aid intervention. that is, federal funds were made available to state agencies to provide unspecified types of services within a broad policy arena. The program had moved via the amendment process to become a potpourri of both specific and nonspecific federal requirements. As the evaluators found, it was possible to explicate ambitious and intertwined social and economic goals that were not always consistent with legislated means for realizing those goals or resources available to accomplish those ends [15]. In addition, the amendments that had been enacted during the last reauthorization process had moved the program toward some categorical elements. However, the law was enacted in 1976; additional amendments were passed in 1977; and regulations were not developed until 1977. The study was asked to look at a program in which significant elements would be in operation for less than three years at the time that the report was due. The intergovernmental map which could be conceptualized to depict the Vocational Education program was hardly the narrowing or funneling process that was in place for Title I (where general federal purposes were further refined at state or local levels). The study described the nation's public school enterprise as "pluralistic and diversified in structure and governance and constitutes a multiplicity of different systems which have key characteristics in common" [16]. The diffuse nature of the program, thus, had to be acknowledged in the design and conduct of the evaluation enterprise.

Constituency Organization

While both programs had articulate and well organized constituencies, each of the constellations of interest groups surrounding the separate programs operated somewhat differently. To some degree, this reflected the difference in the design and construct of the program at hand. The constituency groups around Title 1 could be described as making up a broad based coalition of multiple and quite diverse actors. Although they did not always agree with one another on specific characteristics of the program, the base of support was constructed on agreement about the general goal of providing federal funds for something defined as compensatory education. Differences, thus, revolved largely over the means of attaining that goal. Specific groups and actors were identified with specific positions, reflecting the broad political context of a program in which major issues were already joined. As such, the response of specific interest groups to various elements of the evaluation were largely predictable and the evaluation team could consciously avoid aggravating sensitivities of groups. The study director has noted that the group was able to "identify 'loaded' words and phrases that could elicit suspicion and opposition whenever they were used" [17]. It appeared that, with a few exceptions, such sensitivity was adequate to stave off general criticism of the study process. However, there were instances in which specific determinations about the study organization and the emphasis taken were criticized by various groups but the study staff appeared to be protected by their close relationships with Congressional members and staff.

The constituency organization around the vocational education program was different. Although it had declined in power and status in recent years, the large organization representing vocational education interests—the American Vocational Association—had been an extremely powerful lobby in Washington. Over the years, the AVA had developed close relationships with the federal career administrators of the program, concentrating much of its lobbying energy on administrative as well as legislative lobbying. The 1976 amendments to the program represented, to a significant degree, dissatisfaction with the values and priorities of state and local vocational programs and attempted to redirect at least a part of the federal support to other program priority areas, particularly those with equal educational opportunity attributes. Some members of Congress attributed the problems in vocational education to two sets of "villains"—the state directors of the vocational education program and the federal bureaucrats who administered the federal program. The field itself was characterized by a small number of networks with close communication linkages. The field, according to one observer, responded to the Congressional attacks with a clear expression of paranoia. When the study was included in the reauthorization statute, the traditional constituent groups were extremely unhappy (and reportedly, were responsible for cutting the study's appropriation in half). Some of the program defenders argued that the program was one of the most overstudied pieces of education legislation and believed that the NIE evaluation represented additional forms of harassment. This perception was one of the realities with which the study group had to contend. They realized that they had no sanctions or leverage to demand data from state or local program administrators if these individuals wanted to resist requests for information. Throughout the course of the study the NIE group found it necessary to strike a delicate balance between the need to maintain good relationships with the constituent groups and the imperative of maintaining enough distance from the groups to assure Hill people that the study would not be coopted by the field.

Evaluation Strategy

Both evaluation groups approached the job of devising a strategy for the research process in a very self-conscious fashion. Each group also devised a strategy that maximized consultation with its various audiences—Congress, interest groups and other researchers. The Title I effort was built around the centerpiece of Congress as the "client" of the study. The eclectic methodology that was developed for the task had a logical base in the primary importance of meeting Congressional needs. It was constructed around a strategy that acknowledged the supremacy of Congress—and not researchers—as evaluators of federal programs [18]. Interest groups and other researchers were consulted to elicit advice about research issues, largely at the beginning of the process. Continual consultation was undertaken with Congressional staff members throughout the course of the study.

Although a consultative strategy was employed in the vocational education study, it was organized in a somewhat different fashion. Interest group communication was not only viewed as a measure of good politics; it was also essential in order to elicit their cooperation in obtaining information. Information via the consultative approach became a quid pro quo—without formal contactual relationships or other resources, data availability to the relevant interest groups became a negotiable resource. In addition, a group of consultants was developed as a mechanism for access and expertise. The group was an ad hoc collection of individuals who represented the various viewpoints in the program arena and served as a sounding board and review mechanism for the study staff as well as outside contractors. This study appeared to maintain a more distant relationship with Congress than had the Compensatory Education effort. While maintaining regular informational contacts with Congressional staff, this study group perceived the importance of maintaining some distance from the Congressional clients.

The Development of a Framework

Both study directors have emphasized the importance of developing a conceptual framework around which the evaluation could be organized. The Title I study chose between two approaches: the first would be based on the different levels of government that had administrative responsibilities for the program; the second approach would follow the chain of administrative actions involving the program across the various levels of government and involving fund allocation, administrative decisionmaking and delivery of services to children [19]. The latter approach appeared to the study group to be more sensitive to the issues that would concern actors in the reauthorization process. This approach was believed to affect the work of the group profoundly and reinforced their view that Title I was a program with many features.

The establishment of a conceptual framework for the vocational education study was perhaps even more important to the effort because there were so few conceptual underpinnings to the task that could be intuitively generated by either the study group or its audiences. The articulation of two types of goals–social and economic–helped give form to what seemed to be a conceptual morass. In addition, the specification of the interplay between goals of programs, means for realizing them, and available resources helped to label the forces that defined the program and its environment. The framework was also used to mitigate against staff "tunnel vision"–to provide a context for individual staff members as they were working on specific and somewhat narrow pieces of research and analysis.

Interaction with Congress

As noted earlier, each study group defined its interaction with Congress in a somewhat different context; Congress was clearly "the" client for the Title I enterprise while Congress appeared more peripheral in the organization and operation of the vocational education study. Both groups, however, did go through a similar set of interactions with Congress as they redefined the questions that were handed them via the statutory mandate. The structure of the basic relationship between the researchers and the Congress allowed–indeed even encouraged–a set of interactions and redefinitions of the task at hand. Each group was asked to submit a plan for the evaluation study early in its operation and to complete an interim report midway through the effort. This structure provided the opportunity for the NIE staffs to scale down, modify and rethink the evaluations as they developed.

Both evaluation teams defined their task in a way that balanced a sense of compliance with the formal mandate of the legislative directives with an opportunity to view the statute as illustrative rather than as exhaustive. In the case of Title I, staff formulated possible research problems and issues and presented Congressional staff members with options [20]. Redefinition for the Vocational Education group became important because the team felt that there were more important questions than the ones posed by the statute and because there were important and troubling ambiguities in the directives transmitted through the legislation. For example, it was not clear what Congress meant when it called for examination of compliance with other "applicable laws"; the specific laws envisioned in that requirement were not spelled out. The Vocational Education group devised a procedure in which it made suggestions and Congressional staff commented when they had objections. Both study groups found that consultation with Congressional staff elicited an additional set of expectations about study context that went beyond the normal set of directives.

When they began the study, the NIE Title I group perceived that a number of prominent Congressional staff members were "openly skeptical about the utility of any further research on Title I" [21]. One of the problems to be faced, thus, was Congressional distrust of researchers—their belief that researchers did not take legislators' information needs seriously nor did they understand the policy process. NIE staff believed that adopting the client relationship with the relevant members of Congress was the appropriate antidote to the original Congressional distrust [22]. Indeed, it has been argued that the Congressional decision to include subsequent mandates for evaluations in other legislation was firm evidence of the success of the Title I group's approach.

The staff director of the Vocational Education effort did not perceive that Congress registered a distrust of the evaluation process. Rather, it was noted that few Congressional staff members were able to deal with researchers in research terms. Communication between the Hill and the evaluation team had to be sensitive to the reality that most of the relevant Congressional staff members were lawyers and conceptualized issues in legal rather than research terms. The vocational education group sometimes found it difficult to command the attention of members or their staffs but, nonetheless, persevered in maintaining communication through individual contacts as well as regular status reports.

Availability of Resources

The availability of resources—particularly fiscal resources—was an important factor in both studies. The Title I study group believed that its resources were clearly adequate for the task at hand. These resources, according to the director, gave it ability to resist pressures [23] and to mount a large number of relatively small projects with backup studies for protection. The availability of generous contract funding amounts gave the group confidence to mount some ambitious and somewhat innovative work in areas where few research activities had been previously directed. The experience led the project director to observe that, contrary to the belief that overlap and duplication are evidence of bad research management, "that redundant research on the core problems of a mandated study can be essential to the study's success" [24].

The Vocational Education study did not enjoy such abundance. When the bill mandating the study went to the conference committee, it called for an appropriation of $2 million a year; it emerged from the conference at half that figure. The attempts to increase the allocation were frustrated by Carter administration austerity moves, despite some Congressional interest in increasing the available funds. The strategy for increasing the monies was directed toward cultivation of relationships with other governmental bodies who would contribute dollars or in-kind resources to the study—a strategy which further reinforced the necessity of maintaining good relationships with a broader audience beyond the relevant

Congressional committees. The limited resources necessitated a decision to give out a few, large scale contracts, without any opportunity for commissioning redundant or backup studies. In addition, personnel ceilings limited the size of the staff that could be hired to be available to manage whatever contracts were let. This study team felt constrained by the limitations and delays in hiring processes as well as the complexity of letting contracts within the "normal" Request for Proposal process.

Relationships with Other Parts of the Federal Bureaucracy

The unique relationship between both NIE staffs and the Congress was bound to fan a conflict with regular bureaucratic expectations within the broader set of organizational relationships. For both studies, however, there were better relationships between the NIE teams and the relevant program staffs within the federal education bureaucracy than had been anticipated. The Title I program staff found that the evaluation would be fair and was not directed toward an evaluation of the performance of specific administrators [25]. While suspicious at the early stages of the evaluation, the program officials in the vocational education bureaucracy became quite cooperative, providing some funds for the NIE study and adopting some of the NIE-identified research priorities for their own Research and Demonstration agenda.

Because there were reauthorization planning groups at work within the executive level department at the same time that both of the studies were underway, there was some inevitable tension between the two activities. Staff in the Secretary's office wanted both the data and the advice of the study groups but it was clear that the Congressional mandated prohibited the release of data to those individuals before the reports were submitted to Congress. At least one incident was reported between NIE staff and top Department officials that illustrated the difficulty of maintaining those relationships within a hierarchical setting.

The Evaluation Staff

To some degree, the operating style of each of the NIE study groups reflected the orientation of the respective study director. The Title I study was directed by a political scientist who had just begun to make a name for himself in the education policy research field. The Compensatory Education study gave him increased status and visibility. By contrast, the Vocational Education study was directed by an individual who had passed official retirement age and who had great stature and extensive experience in the manpower and employment fields. The independent stance that was adopted by this group was possible largely because of the past contacts and personal relationships that this individual could draw on for support.

The Reports Themselves

Both of the studies produced a series of reports that stand as commendable examples of clear, concise documents written for a broad but relatively informed audience. Each study produced a final report as well as a series of supplemental papers on specific topics. Both study groups operated with a close eye on the clock. Deadlines were taken seriously and drove the production schedule as well as contributed to a sense of policy urgency for the task. The Vocational Education group was pushed to complete its final report before the final reports of all of its contractors were completed.

The Title I study did not contain recommendations for action. Arguing that few of their results led unambiguously to clear prescriptions [26], they believed that they had no grounds for selecting among the diverse policymakers objectives for the program. The Vocational Education group did not make recommendations as such but did offer a set of multiple options for change that were driven by diverse assumptions about the primary goal or intent of federal policy.

CONCLUSION

There are a number of observations that can be drawn from these two evaluation experiences. These examples suggest that specification of a client does not resolve or drive away all evaluation problems. Even when relationships between producers and users of analysis are structured (and in both of these cases, the structure was very formal), the separate roles and imperatives of evaluator and decisionmaker provoke different perceptions of priorities and clearly affect the level of attention and content of the evaluation experience. These examples suggest also that the subject matter of the evaluation or analysis drives both methodological and conceptual design issues. These two cases illustrate the differences between an evaluation of a grants-in-aid program and a categorical program. In addition, this experience informs us that any program or issue is brought to analysis with a history and constellation of past intra and interorganizational relationships. These components of the policy environment are a part of the baggage that any evaluator must carry.

When one reviews these experiences in the context of Meltsner's characterization of factors that influence the production of analysis, it is clear that relationships between all four factors (analyst, client, organizational situation and policy area) are essential [27].

These two experiences indicate that even when one can structure relationships between the client and analyst, the broader contextual characteristics of organizational pressures and the policy arena itself cannot be ignored in determining the design and modus operandi of the evaluative or analytic enterprise. It is this four tiered set of relationships that must be considered in the quest to link analysis and decisionmaking.

REFERENCES

1. Weiss, C. H. Ideology, Interest and Information: The Biases of Policy Positions. In Callahan, D. and Jennings, B. (eds.). *Ethics, the Social Sciences and Policy Analysis*. Plenum Press, New York, 1982.
2. Lindblom, C. and Cohen, D. K. *Usable Knowledge*. Yale University Press, New Haven and London, 1979.
3. Weiss, p. 8.
4. Wholey, J. S. *Evaluation: Promise and Performance*. Urban Institute, Washington, D.C. 1979, p. 3.
5. For example, Williams, W. *Social Policy Research and Analysis*. American Elsevier Publishing Company, New York, 1971; and Zweig, F. M. (ed.). *Evaluation in Legislation*. Sage Publications, Beverly Hills, CA, 1979.
6. Meltsner, A. J. *Policy Analysts in the Bureaucracy*. University of California Press, Berkeley, CA, 1976, pp. 3-7.
7. This section of the article draws heavily on the introductory material found in the NIE volume, *Administration of Compensatory Education*, NIE, DHEW, Washington, D.C. September 1977, pp. ix-xiv.
8. This portion of the article draws on the NIE reports, *The Vocational Education Study: The Final Report*, NIE, ED, Washington, D.C. September 1981, pp. xiii-xvi; I-1 to I-6; and *The Vocational Education Study: The Interim Report*, NIE, ED, September 1980.
   In addition, the author is indebted to Henry David, the director of the Vocational Education Study, for his willingness to share both his experience involving the project and his prudent and wise assessment of the experience.
9. Hill, P. T. Evaluating Education Programs for Federal Policymakers: Lessons from the NIE Compensatory Education Study. In Pincus, J. (ed.). *Educational Evaluation in the Public Policy Setting*. Rand Corporation, Santa Monica, May 1980, p. 55.
10. Hill, p. 57.
11. Hill, p. 57.
12. Frohlicher, J. S. The Education Amendments of 1976: Their Evolution in the Senate: Their Direction in the Future. Paper prepared for NIE Vocational Education Study, 1981.
13. NIE, *Vocational Education: Final Report*, p. IX-2.
14. See McLaughlin, M. W. *Evaluation and Reform*. Ballinger Publishing Company, Cambridge, 1975.
15. *Vocational Education: Final Report*, p. I-2, I-3.
16. Ibid, p. xxi.
17. Hill, p. 62.
18. Hill, p. 57.
19. Ibid, p. 52.
20. Ibid, p. 53.

21. Ibid, p. 50.
22. Ibid, p. 73.
23. Ibid, p. 65.
24. Ibid, p. 67.
25. Ibid, p. 64.
26. Ibid, p. 70.
27. Meltsner, p. 3.

16 Education Evaluations: More than Business As Usual

Lois-ellin Datta* / *National Institute of Education*[1], *Washington, D.C.*

First, a true story. About a year ago, some school superintendents in a large western state were grousing. They were ticked off about an achievement test the state department of education wanted administered as part of the state accountability system. Their plaint was the test's inappropriateness for this purpose.

The superintendents were at a workshop in which a keynote speaker was an expert on testing. His theme was the close relation among what is taught, what is learned and what is tested in measuring instructional effectiveness, vividly illustrated by his analysis of the strengths and limits of the recently mandated state test.

The superintendents were impressed and decided to pool some resources for him to write up the analysis for their appeals to the State legislature and to the Governor. He, intrigued with the idea, involved some of his colleagues, including an evaluator. The first paper reached its mark and the superintendents' consortium is a going concern. The superintendents choose the issues, and pool their funds to support a first rate analytic team. So far, they use the reports like gangbusters to inform themselves and, where appropriate, make a powerful case for their views with State authorities.

Among the points of this story are:

- action is shifting from federal vs state debates to state vs local views of what should be happening in education

---

**Present Affiliation:* Institute for Program Evaluation, United States General Accounting Office, Washington, D.C.

[1]Opinions expressed are the author's in her private capacity. Endorsement by the National Institute of Education should not be inferred.

- new coalitions are likely to arise to solve the problems of negotiating interests between the often unified central government (the state groups) and the usually fragmented periphery (local interests). The western consortium, for example, may be a forerunner of other, similar means of pooling scarce local resources to influence state decisions through evaluations. Such pooled resources could attract the best minds to those local agencies who individually can not afford an evaluation establishment of the size and quality state agencies or the federal government can muster.
- the issues these evaluators address probably will differ in substance from those with which the *ancient regime* was concerned, although the grand themes of educational access and instructional effectiveness may continue to sound.
- the policy-informing role of educational evaluation may predominate over the program improvement role, perhaps to the discomfort of educational evaluators who increasingly may need to call upon their approximation skills.

These points are argued at greater length in the next sections of this paper.

Where the Wild Things are in Educational Evaluation

Large scale support for educational evaluation began about 1964 with the Elementary and Secondary Education Act. The intent, at least of Senator Robert Kennedy to whom these provisions are attributed, was local empowerment. In general, he didn't often get it. Each local demonstration project *did* have an evaluation component. The federal evaluation offices, however, commissioned the big national studies of the categorical education programs that until recently have held the center ring (Title 1, Follow Through, and bilingual education evaluations). Also, following Congressional requirements for data that can be aggregated nationally from hundreds of local demonstration grant evaluations, federal views have driven local evaluation models and data collection systems. Examples are the National Vocational Education Data System (NVEDS) required by the Education Amendments of 1976, and the Title I evaluation models and evaluation technical assistance centers, also required in the 1976 Amendments.

The former, (NVEDS), has emphasized collection of compliance data on enrollment of women, minorities and the handicapped in various vocational education programs, follow-up of placement in training related work, and employer satisfaction (as required by Congress in the 1976 Amendments). The latter (Title I) has emphasized ways of estimating gains on standardized tests, and is credited (or blamed) for what is seen as a fixation on testing-as-evaluation in local school districts [1, 2, 3].

The federally commissioned national evaluations initially addressed summative questions: did the program work, why, and how. The most troublesome aspects of these evaluations have dominated evaluation journals and texts: whether statistical band-aids can be put over nonequivalent comparison groups for national samples, interpreting results when variance between sites presumably implementing similar treatments is greater than variance between sites implementing different programs, selecting measures for national studies when local program purposes shade differently, non-utilization of findings for policy making, and the merits or limitations of the different models proposed by the government for assessing student gains associated with program participation.

To be sure some local educational evaluators have received national attention for their efforts. Kean in Philadelphia, Rankin in Detroit, Pechman in New Orleans, Frankel and Frechtling in Montgomery County and Holley in Austin have written often and surpassingly well about local uses of evaluation. The flourishing Evaluation Network and equally burgeoning Division H (Local School Evaluators) of the American Educational Research Association, the increased participation of local educational evaluators on national commissions and on the editorial boards of refereed journals, the circulation of well-known evaluators among federal offices, national research organizations, state and local evaluation offices all indicate a coming of age of local educational evaluation. By and large, however, until recently the Big Time has been national.

Much of this national dominance has depended on concentration at the congressional and federal agency level of power to decide who is eligible for what services using federal money. The power may remain, but the will to use it has diminished as staff favoring the old federalism are replaced by those favoring the new federalism. Furthermore, the legislative and regulatory mechanisms which sustain the federal influence are being replaced through both deregulation and consolidation.

The eventual extent of both is uncertain: some governors and mayors are leary of being gifted with much more responsibility but much less money, however fewer the attached strings. Consolidation also could threaten unacceptably power distribution within Congress as Committees responsible for oversight of various categorical programs are less needed. Also, both deregulation and consolidation may smack too much of loss of a federal commitment to needy groups who otherwise might not be aided easily to go down some congressional throats. Already, however, there are some consolidations of categorical grant programs. Steps have been taken toward reallocation of power to state and local authorities in the withdrawal of proposed federal regulations, and in less stringent interpretations of regulations still on the books, particularly those associated with desegregation. These are noted in court decisions (for example, the California and Texas rulings on bussing and desegregation) and in such federal actions as the February 1981 withdrawal of the August 1980, Notice of Proposed Rule Making implementing the Lau (bilingual education) Supreme Court decision with regard to federal educational funds.

The uncertainties begin with the extent to which federal, state and local responsibilities in education will be reshuffled. Even more significant may be what shakes out within the states with the authority gained by State Education Agencies versus *other* state agencies, and possibly versus local governments. The United States seems, however, to be in the early stages of a notable shift of power from the federal government to others, particularly the private sector and the states. This shift is occurring in many sectors, of which education is only one, albeit a prominent, instance.

In part following broad decentralizing trends already evident, and in part due to specific shifting of federal roles in education, the wild things—the action—in educational evaluation increasingly will be at state and local levels. This shift is likely to affect how evaluations are organized and what the substance of evaluations will be.

Evaluation for Whom and by Whom: Organizational Impact

In the past, evaluation power became balanced more or less between federal and state offices when the states, through the Chief State School Officers, negotiated clearance authority over what data could be collected. All federally initiated evaluations, even those mandated by Congress, must be reviewed by the Committee on Evaluation and Information Systems (CEIS) of the Chief State School Officers before the federally funded evaluators can approach any state or local agency to participate in a study. This CEIS review is in addition to the reviews required internally by the Education Department's Federal Educational Data Acquisition Committee (FEDAC) group and by the Office of Management and Budget's (OMB) independent review of all data collection activities requested by federal agencies. A school may be eager, for example, to participate in a study but if CEIS approval is withheld, the federally funded contractor cannot collect the data. Congress can mandate a National Vocational Education Data System, but until it is approved by CEIS (and FEDAC and OMB), Congress can go whistle for its data [4, 5].

This institutional mechanism for negotiating interests (CEIS review of all federally funded educational evaluations) has a certain elegance as a way of assuring federal officials do not have too free a hand in proclamations on educational program effectiveness. Many states do not have the funds or apparently the desire to conduct their own evaluations on anything like the scale required by federal compliance and effectiveness evaluations. Review authority not only protects local and state groups from undue data burdens (the overt purpose); it neatly balances (or imbalances, depending on one's views) power.

As action shifts from federal to state and local levels, the tensions already evident between states[2] and localities on many issues, ranging from testing man-

---

2. Use of "states" rather than State Education Agencies (SEAs) and "localities" rather than Local Education agencies (LEAs) is a reminder that the state and local governments are no more monolithic than the Federal government. The educational agencies have to negotiate their places in the sun at these levels.

dated by states through state required bilingual services to state dictated resource reallocation decisions, may be heightened. To the extent that federal funds available for educational activities are given to states with little restriction on how the funds are spent, federal evaluations may be primarily of the broadly defined accountability varieties [6], rather than the categorical program impact type because there may be, in effect, no programs. States are likely to expand their evaluation and policy analytic offices, as education struggles for its share of a state's resources in competition with other sectors, particularly if states assume greater acacountability for how well funds are spent. The number of evaluators in state offices and the quality of these staff thus should increase. Some state evaluation offices already exceed many federal evaluation offices and evaluation consulting organizations in staff competence and number.

As examples, the Education Department has proposed changing the Management Evaluation Review for Compliance/Quality for vocational education from proof of compliance on 150 items to a new system involving a state self-assessment form reporting only 40 or 50 "most troublesome" items. Plato [7] notes that the Omnibus Budget Reconciliation Act of 1981 bans issuance of regulations related to planning, implementation and evaluation in a law whose purpose is to provide financial assistance to local education agencies with high concentrations of low income children. She anticipates increases in suits against school districts by parents disagreeing with local choices among groups formerly served by separate funding sources. These suits may lead to more elaborate procedures than at present to document needs of children. Small school districts in particular, Plato predicts, will need state evaluation help to fill the void in evaluation technical assistance and guidelines left by the phasing out of federal evaluation efforts. Such state "assistance" may or may not be perceived by local schools as benign [8].

What will the localities do to avoid being steam rollered by state evaluation "guidance" and requirements? The states may be willing to grant localities the same evaluation review rights that the federal government has negotiated with the states. As seen from the federal level, this review mechanism can be an inexpensive but mighty equalizer. Local evaluators already have flexed their muscle in recent agreements among them not to cooperate with test publishers in field testing measures without money for their time and effort from the publishers, and they may make this stick [9]. The local evaluator organizations are considering similar arrangements with states and the federal government. Another tactic could be for the local evaluation offices to preempt, through state legislatures, evaluation authority while the state evaluation programs are still relatively weak. Millsap [3] paints a fairly dismal picture of the competence and impact of many local evaluation offices, however, and reports that few localities even have such organizations. Nonetheless, there are notable exceptions, and where there is a very strong local evaluation organization in a state with weak evaluation leadership, the evolution in such a state well may reverse power concentration from that of states with few or no strong local evaluation units and a competent state education office.

At some point, however, this defensive posture may not be enough. There are many more small school districts than large ones, and even large ones may be hard pressed to support the evaluators needed to publish first and better on substantive issues, such as the impact of state bilingual education regulations on local practice. Pooling resources through a consortium may be an organizational solution which other superintendents may try out as word of the western state activity gets around. Strengthening intermediate service agency capacity for evaluation may be another. A third may be turning to cooperative arrangements with nearby university-based evaluators who come cheaper (usually) than either reliance on contract research firms or building up in each locality evaluation and policy analytic capacity for high quality work.

Whatever the mechanism, and there probably will be many, the best and the brightest evaluators increasingly may be attracted to state or local service where they are likely to meet some unexpected substantive challenges.

Not Business as Usual

States, constitutionally, always have had a far greater range of power in shaping education than the federal government. Increasing access to education and increasing opportunities for groups that may have been too few in any locale or too weak to influence educational decisions long have been the major federal concerns. Congress may seek to encourage localities to desegregate by providing Emergency School Assistance grants. It may encourage better planning to mesh curricular offerings with labor market opportunities through requirements in Vocational Education grants. It may stimulate improvement in the quality of television for young children by funding *Sesame Street*. Congress has not touched, however, the gut educational issues such as requirements for teacher certification, minimum hours of schooling each year, high school graduation requirements, promotion standards, retention in grade policies, school organization and services, which schools are opened or closed, or the content of tests and curricula–to name only a few matters. And in many instances–education for the handicapped, student loans–Congressional action often has followed and been less demanding than legislation in some states and than lower or state court decisions.

Kennedy, Apling and Neumann [1] report that all of the sample of 18 school districts they visited in which evaluation information was used successfully had a norm referenced testing system, at least one federal grant requiring evaluation, and enrollment files; several routinely conducted surveys such as follow-up studies of graduating classes or community attitudes toward proposed changes in district programs; and several had carried out such special purpose studies as comparisons of the cost effectiveness of various means of supplying schools and transporting of students, such as immediate and long-term consequences of fueling buses with regular versus premium gasoline. Many of the examples reported as being most useful are similar to business management studies, a point evident in the approach to evaluation underway in the Montgomery County (Maryland) school system under Frankel's leadership [10].

The range of educational issues on which state and local views may differ is greater than the range of issues federal and state educational authorities have debated. Declining enrollments everywhere; aging school facilities; minimum competency testing mandated by states such as Florida and New York; teacher recertification examinations being required by Louisiana and North Carolina; and school finance reform underway in California and Massachusetts involve substantive concerns touched lightly at best in federal programs and in evaluations of these programs initiated by federal offices.

Through research and Congressionally mandated policy studies, some of these areas have been examined by federal agencies: there have been no evaluations, however, by federal officials of such matters as state teacher certification programs or local school closings which were undertaken to influence state decision making.

Are the differences between state and local evaluation concerns and those prominent in federal evaluations exaggerated? Educational access and instructional effectiveness plausibly could be considered common denominators in many of these questions, denominators which have driven many Federal evaluations. California, for example, has conducted evaluations of the immediate and long-term effectiveness of its state legislated preschool programs. Many of the issues of design and measurement in this study would be familiar to evaluators remembering the early Head Start evaluations. The Illinois descriptive study of the implementation and impact of the state mandated bilingual education programs had elements well known to those involved in the federal studies of bilingual education. Most evaluators, however, working on federal projects would be less familiar with the issues involved in evaluating state reviews of schools of teacher education; of the requirements set by states of teach certification prior to practice; of state certifications for school principals and administrators; or of state established curriculum requirements and guides. They may be less familiar also with how evaluation findings will be used.

Never Mind the Question: What's the Answer?

The distinction between summative and formative evaluations, once made fairly seriously in federal educational evaluations, has been blurred in more recent theory and practice. Among evaluation researchers, educational programs first were seen as being specified (and hence close to replications of the same treatment), then were interpreted as requiring time to implement (but eventually, evaluable as replications of the same treatment), and now seem regarded as continually evolving (and thus never evaluable as instances of the same treatment, so describing the evolution becomes the end itself of study). Gradually, studies of implementation have taken precedence over program outcome assessment. Since the Office of Economic Opportunity's voucher studies and performance contracting experiments, there have been few national experiments in education involving a structured research design and summative impact, except for those funded through the Department of Labor Office of Youth Programs, and such "natural opportunity" evaluations as those of *Sesame Street* and the Emergency School Assistance Act.

Cumulatively, using evaluation for program improvement has seemed a better circuit for evaluators than expecting evaluation findings to trip go/no switches. Such an approach has characterized many recent national studies. Perhaps the most visible distinction between an educational evaluation of the 1970 vintage and one of the 1980 pressing would be the attention to program context, history, purposes, expectations from many views, and implementation descriptions. Even evaluations whose penultimate chapters deal with what happened to students devote much space to qualitative, ethnographic views of program process. How much of this change reflects riper evaluation wisdom, and how much avoidance of the clearance procedures required for summative and quantitative studies could be an illuminating analysis.[3] What is evident now is that although the social experiment/summative concerns certainly are continued by some evaluators and in some outstanding analyses (e.g. [11]), in national educational evaluations, stylistically descriptive, process oriented, program improvement studies predominate.

What will happen as educational evaluations informing state and local issues come to the fore is uncertain. Resources for such studies may be scarce. States usually do not fund demonstration grants, as the federal government does, with built-in evaluation. State legislators meet less frequently and constantly than federal legislators; they must get through many authorization and appropriation bills in each session, and the action can be rough and tumble, and fast. This may influence what kinds of evaluations will be supported, tipping the emphasis to does-it-work, who-gets-served, what-does-it-cost, what-happened summative studies, with fewer resources available for the in-house evaluator, program improvement roles [7]. To the extent that states can mandate what data will be collected without having to negotiate reviews and clearances among localities, more quantitative studies, with more interpretable summative designs may be possible. If so, evaluators may need to shift gears from the descriptive, qualitative, individual client mode that has characterized many local demonstration program evaluations into one that extrapolates from imperfect data for summative purposes, and one which integrates more fully

3. The impact of FEDAC, OMB and CEIS reviews on the rise of case studies, qualitative and ethnographic methods (and other methods which do not currently require such clearance because they do not involve forms or a quantifiable data collection load on individuals) has not been analyzed systematically. Much of the educational evaluation literature could lead to the impression we all got wise simultaneously about the limitations of tests and of planned variation experiments of the performance contracting type and it is the intrinsic merits of qualitative approaches that have led to the shifts in evaluation strategies. Perhaps so, but at almost any meeting of evaluators, anecdotal evidence suggests otherwise.

findings from diverse studies to inform the summative conclusions of the study at hand.

The work of Holley [12] may be a forerunner of such local evaluations. In her studies on engaged instructional time in the Austin schools, much of the conceptual framework for the inquiry, the methodology and the convincingness of her results came from integration of her local findings with a larger diverse body of research. At present, few evaluations refer to the findings of other evaluations: often the state and local studies—and some federally funded research—seem free-standing.

Integrating findings from new studies with the results of similar evaluations and of fundamental research perhaps can be among the strategies evaluators can use to sustain quality when time and resources diminish, and as the state/local client wants more decision-oriented, summative information. The evaluations funded by the Office of Youth Programs of the Department of Labor to a considerable extent may be better paradigms of such work than Department of Education funded evaluations. As an example, the Office has supported a planned variation comparison of the effectiveness of ten different ways of improving youths' basic skills, ranging from peer tutoring through computer-based instruction, with analyses that are strongly quantitative and cost/effectiveness oriented. The reports also draw heavily on related prior work, supplementing methodological and measurement limitations in the study itself by integration of findings from prior efforts.

Past Lessons in New Schoolrooms

The creation of the Education Department in 1980 stimulated Representative Holtzman to ask for a report on what evaluation should be like in the new Department. By 1981, three reports on this topic joined the analyses of educational evaluations commissioned earlier by the General Accounting Office.

Two of the Holtzman related reports [5, 11] assume continuation in the 1980's of the federal, state and local education roles of the 1960's and 1970's, and continuation of a federal social experiment role. Their analyses, while attentive to conditions needed to improve the quality of state and local educational evaluations, are concerned more with the quality and utilization of federally conducted experiments, program management studies, and impact assessments.

In contrast, Pincus and his colleagues [13] assume a loose coupling of federal, state and local interests, and are sympathetic to changing roles to ensure greater state and local autonomy. Their evaluation recommendations seek what they view as more realistic expectations, under these circumstances, for what evaluations can do, and argue for greater support for descriptive, illuminative, program improvement oriented studies.

All three reports seem, however, to consider lessons learned in a classroom of federal, state and local responsibilities the likes of which we may not see again quite as they were in the 1960's and 1970's, evaluation's own formative period. The shapes of the new classrooms are yet unclear; transferrability of the lessons is uncertain. Some elements of the 1960's education programs, such as concentration of federal resources on neediest students, may remain. And for some programs, federal, state and local relationships may be unaffected. In such instances, there now are many good guides to achieving effective, high quality evaluations, thanks to such thorough reviews as Boruch and Cordray [11] and Raizen and Rossi [5].

Circumstances may be so different, however, that evaluation almost begins anew, particularly with regard to organizational features balancing power between localities and states, the substance of what is evaluated, and the purposes of evaluation. Whatever else the new federalism future may hold for educational evaluation, business as usual for evaluators and those who train them, is unlikely.

REFERENCES

1. Kennedy, M. M., Apling, R. and Neumann, W. F. *The Role of Evaluation and Test Information in Public Schools*. Huron Institute, Cambridge, MA, August 1980.
2. Lyon, C. D., Doscher, L., McGranahan, P. and Williams, R. *Evaluation and School Districts*. Center for the Study of Evaluation, University of California, Los Angeles, CA, December 1978.
3. Millsap, M. A. *Towards Renewal and Reform: Evaluation and Testing in School Districts*. National Institute of Education, Washington, D.C., (in press).
4. Carter, L. F. Federal clearance of educational evaluation instruments: Procedural problems and proposed remedies. *Educational Researcher*, 6 (5) 1977: 7-12.
5. Raizen, S. A. and Rossi, P. A. (eds.). *Program Evaluation in Education: When? How? To What Ends?* National Academy Press, Washington, D.C., 1981.
6. Chelimsky, E. Program Accountability Evaluations. In Datta, L. *Evaluation in Change: New Government Roles*. Beverly Hills, Sage Publications, Beverly Hills, CA, 1981, 89-120.
7. Plato, K. C. Block grants: Implications for state and local education agencies. *Politics of Education Bulletin*. 10(1) Fall 1981: 6-9.
8. Stecher, B. M., Alkin, M. C., and Flesher, G. Patterns of information use in school level decisionmaking. UCLA Center for the Study of Evaluation, Los Angeles, CA, December 1981.
9. Kean, M. (chair). *Symposium on the School System/Test Publisher Uniform Testing Agreement.* American Educational Research Association meeting, New York, March, 1982.
10. Frankel, S. *Communicating the results of school system based management studies*. Paper presented at the American Educational Research Association meeting, New York, March, 1982.
11. Boruch, R. F. and Cordray, D. E. *An Appraisal of Educational Program Evaluations: Federal, State and Local Agencies*. Prepared for the U.S. Department of Education. Northwestern University, Evanston, IL, 1980.

12. Holley, F. M. How the evaluation system works: the state and local levels. In Raizen, S. A. and Rossi, P. A. (eds.). *Program Evaluation in Education: When? How? to What Ends?* National Academy Press, Washington, D.C., 1981., Appendix C. 246-274.
13. Pincus, J. (ed.). *Educational Evaluation in the Public Policy Setting*. Rand Corporation, Santa Monica, CA, 1979.

17
Evaluation of Human Services

William J. Page, Jr. / *Departments of Public Administration and Social Work, Florida State University, Tallahassee, Florida*

INTRODUCTION

The high rate of expansion of human services during the period 1930 to 1980, especially in the two decades from 1955 to 1975, was not matched by gains in relevant evaluative competence. The lag is attributable to a variety of interrelated factors, including rapid growth of resources for services but not evaluation, constraints on the application of classical experimentalism to human services, and societal and professional norms relative to delivering services without a commensurate concern for objective measurement of consequences of policies, programs, and techniques of service delivery.

An expanding economy during the 1960's permitted generation of increasing amounts of dollars and human services staff without intolerable cost to other national purposes. Description and particularized advocacy of human needs were sufficient to gain great increases in the portion of national resources allocated to human services. The incremental pattern minimized concern for efficiency and effectiveness. Educational curricula for human services professionals placed greater emphasis on needs and methods of service delivery than on measurement of consequences. Service was provided in each specialty mainly because it was "the right thing to do" and belief in the efficacy of current methodologies of large human service systems contained multiple variables which were beyond the evaluative capability or interest of most specialized service providers. Concepts and behaviors commonly observed in other complex systems, such as the exploration of space, were not dominant in professionally parochialized human service systems.

Economic and political perceptions of resource limitations, which began to arise in the late 1960's, were not sufficient to curb the momentum of human service expansion. Even during the early and mid-1970's increasing resource allocations were required to fulfill policy commitments made in earlier years. Inflation and personnel costs, the latter being especially significant because human services are labor-intensive, were factors in increasing demands for accountability and consideration of the relative merits of social investments and other sectors of the national economy. Human service advocates and providers lacked unassailable proof of the efficacy and worth of their realm.

The gradual ascendence of the political ideology which gained national dominance in 1980 stimulated in the 1970's increased demands for evaluation of human service policies and programs. Advocates and opponents alike raised questions about policy choice, program design, management, service methods, efficiency, effectiveness, and worth of human services. Some or all of these concerns produced questions in all sources of social policymaking, including the judiciary.

This paper explores the development, status, and prospects of human services evaluation in the United States. The principal focus is on "program evaluation", although presumptively policy, as the authorizing framework for programs, importantly affects program choice and design. To measure efficiency, effectiveness, or impact of programs is to gain intelligence for policy formation, revision, or termination. Rigorous policy and program evaluation may vary less in methodology than in unit of analysis and primary audiences. Neat differentiation is difficult to justify because of substantial involvement of administrators in policy formation as well as interpretation, implementation, and revision.

Human services, within the present context, will include most of the personal services which are intended to enable individuals and families to function in a complex world. Evaluative practice in these systems ranges from informal appraisal to highly formalized processes. Edwin A. Suchman has provided a usable definition of evaluation. To him, as to many administrators and evaluators, evaluation is ". . .the determination. . .of the results. . .attained by some activity. . .designed to accomplish some valued goal or objective. . ." [1]. Suchman's definition implies but does not explicate the quantitative and analytical dimensions of evaluation. Bruce L. Gates provides a definition which explicitly mentions measurement and purpose:

> *Program evaluation is a formal analytical process that entails the comparison of measurable outcomes with defined standards of performance. Its purpose is to provide both policy and program decision makers with information useful for program improvement. [2]*

Gates' definition provides adequately for formative evaluation, which usually characterizes the appraisal effort of continuing programs. Intentionally or not, this definition omits summative evaluation, which is a one-time appraisal of a program which has been terminated or marked for radical change. Success or failure of a program, or major changes in its environment, can dictate summative evaluation.

Carol Weiss, a widely published authority on evaluation research, is more rigorous in definition, as follows:

> *In its research guise, evaluation establishes clear and specific criteria for success. It collects evidence systematically from a representative sample of the units of concern. It usually translates the evidence into quantitative terms. . .and compares it with the criteria that were set. It then draws conclusions about the effectiveness, the merit, the success of the phenomenon under study. [3]*

Definition of evaluation should reveal distinguishing characteristics of focus, methodology and function. One definition, seemingly limited to formative evaluation, satisfies these criteria:

> *Evaluation (1) assesses the* effectiveness *of an* on-going *program in achieving its objectives, (2) relies on the principles of research design to distinguish a program's effects from those of other forces working in a situation, and (3) aims at programs improvement through a modification of current operations. [4]*

Much of the work performed in appraisal of human services cannot meet the scientific and technical standards which are explicit or implicit in these definitions. Aggregated activity counts obviously do not qualify. Scientific design and rigorous quantitative methods tend to disqualify prevalent and powerful information-seeking and judgmental behaviors frequently demonstrated by persons other than professional specialists in evaluation. Such behaviors include legislative oversight and high-level executive decisions which frequently are influenced by nonquantitative data from the political realm.

DEVELOPMENT OF HUMAN SERVICES EVALUATION

The development of evaluation in human services lagged the major expansion of human services in the second and third quarters of the Twentieth Century. As recently as 1969, Wholey and his associates at the Urban Institute found that from a federal perspective "(t)he art and techniques of evaluation are indeed underdeveloped" and that "substantial work in this field has been almost nonexistent" [5].

Wholey's team at the Urban Institute further observed that "(t)he most clear-cut evidence of the primitive state of federal self-evaluation lies in the widespread failure of agencies even to spell out program objectives" [6]. Absent precise objectives or clearly stated programmatic goals and unambiguous statutory language evaluators are handicapped in developing the most generally acceptable bases for design and performance of programmatic or organizational evaluation.

It would be incorrect to assert or assume that federal program creators or operators were uninterested in evaluation. Nearly all research grants, as well as federal formula and project grants for delivery of human services, provided for evaluation. Circumstances which minimized the quality and utility of resultant evaluative products were as follows:

1. Design of each grantee's evaluative component was partly or entirely within the grantee's discretion, *i.e.*, no systematic provisions were made for standardization and comparison of designs or results;
2. Persons with evaluative responsibilities frequently were prepared, educationally and otherwise, to practice roles other than evaluation; the most charitable characterization of their collective performance is "variable";
3. In a period of policy expansion, rigorous evaluation did not receive high priority;
4. Legislative and executive policy-makers had the power but lacked specific knowledge and interest requisite to use of evaluative learning for creation, revision, or judgment of the merits of burgeoning programs; and
5. Thorough evaluation was costly; the relative propensity to invest in increments of services in preference to evaluation was very high.

The overall effect was a system with a dull and inconsistent learning edge, enormously active and well-intended but deficient in intelligent behaviors. Federal grantors had little control of expenditures or the evaluative process at service delivery points. Wholey and associates are quite credible in their description of the situation in the late 1960's:

> *After five years of operating and evaluating compensatory education programs. . .we are still unable to say with confidence what works and what doesn't." [7]*

Failure to plan systematically and perform consistently in the evaluative dimension of national programs was enormously costly to policy relevance and influence. One should not discount the importance of low expectations from policy-makers, special interests, and executives in the political environment as causes of poor evaluative performance. Persons who had power to require it did not provide for or insist on excellent evaluative work. A frequent practice of leaving evaluation to the evaluators also was costly to utility and influence, *i.e.*, in many cases they were neither adequately commissioned nor utilized by policy makers. Wholey's group found "four basic reasons" for low utilization of evaluative products:

> "*Organizational inertia*". The literature of organization theory is full of explanations of resistance to change.
> "*Methodological weakness*". Whether actual or only perceived by potential users, this is a major detractor.
> "*Design irrelevance*". This reason derives from minimal or no relation to perceptions of critical program and policy issues.
> "*Lack of dissemination*". Cognitive gain and consequent action are mimimized by failure to provide or interpret findings to persons with power to make policy or managerial decisions. [8]

A few landmarks of initiative were established in bringing focus and efficacy to the diffuse and often unproductive evaluative dimension of human services.

The beginning of a departmentwide effort in program evaluation at the Department of Health, Education, and Welfare (HEW) is well documented by James G. Abert and others [9]. In 1967 William Gorham, than an Assistant Secretary of HEW, proposed establishment of a program evaluation unit in the office of program coordination. The departmental executive response directed Gorham to develop comprehensive plans for evaluating program effectiveness.

Only modest progress was made until Gorham was given status, power, and resources to implement the function. A series of HEW chief executives enlisted the assistance of Congress in making additional resources available for evaluation. In addition to small direct allocations to the Office of the Secretary, Congress authorized the Secretary to utilize for evaluation stipulated portions of funds appropriated to operating agencies. The Secretary had the option of reallocating the funds to the operating components, contingent on an approved plan, or using the funds directly to support his own staff's work. It is difficult to estimate which the previously autonomous agencies (such as the Public Health Service) liked least, the set-asides or the new requirement of evaluation plans which were reviewed by Assistant Secretary Gorham. Despite predictable organizational resistance, a systematic beginning was achieved.

Hugh Heclo makes incisive and relevant observations about analytic and evaluative capability of the sort established in HEW. Perceiving the analysts as possibly "the most important residue of the planning, programming and budgeting movement in the 1960's," he asserts:

> *. . .such analysts are often the agency head's only institutional resource for thinking about substantive policy without commitments to the constituents, jurisdictions, and self interests of existing programs. [10]*

Heclo's observation squares with the strategy, recommended by Abert, to "treat evaluation as a program and. . .institutionalize an evaluation-planning procedure" for utilizing evaluative information in the decision process [11].

Public organizations frequently turn to the private sector for evaluation of human services, using not-for-profit and for-profit firms. The reasons are many, including the following:

- Shortage of staff, especially of staff with technical knowledge and skills appropriate to evaluation;
- Independent evaluators are presumably more objective or, at least, may be perceived as being so;
- Avoidance of negative criticism of in-house staff when proposed evaluations might alienate policy-makers or interest groups;
- Contractural personnel may be less constrained than in-house personnel by procedural delays and logistics;
- Contractors may be able to supply immediately specialized expertise which would exceed allowable government compensation rates and response times.

It is sufficient for present purposes to mention without detailed exploration the possibility that past, present, and prospective business relationships between human service entities and consulting firms might compromise any aspect of an evaluation. If the relationship escapes this hazard, the specification of quick delivery of the evaluation might compromise the firm's efforts of design or the rigor of the work. Whatever the risks or benefits, private organizations under contract have performed a substantial portion of human service program evaluation.

In a recent visit by this author to a state agency for services to the developmentally disabled, eight recent evaluation reports were displayed by the agency director. Two were products of "outside" contractors and six were prepared by in-house staff of two organizational units. Cursory review of the whole set revealed no methodological superiority on the part of the private organizations. On the other hand, the appearance of the private firms' graphics, paper, and bindings were decidedly superior!

Whether "contracted-out" or performed in-house, evaluation has become a significant element of public and private human service program management. Gains in information handling, legislative oversight, competition for scarce resources, and managerial informational needs are among the reasons for increased attention to evaluation. The real value attached to evaluation by state agencies might be revealed in the near future as this function competes with delivery of services for scarce dollars and the federal government demands less planning, monitoring of operations, and reporting of results.

It seems reasonable to assume that the quality of evaluations might favorably affect propensities of legislators and administrators to allocate resources to the function, assuming also that they are aware of and understand the content of evaluations. The literature referenced in this paper and direct experience create or reinforce doubts about substantial removal of both of these contingencies—awareness and comprehension. Three factors operate to reduce these negative constraints in the future. The study of quantitative methods, usually with emphasis on evaluation and research, has become a usual part of graduate education for human service professions and general management. The increasing educational attainment of persons in managerial roles suggests a greater probability to comprehend evaluative products and methods.

Current and prospective human service systems receive stronger environmental stimuli conducive to evaluation. More acute resource scarcity might cause administrators and policy-makers to use evaluation for improving productivity and choosing among programs to reduce or terminate.

A third change, which might be the most important of all, has occurred in the state sector of the federal system. Approximately three-fourths of the states have taken some steps toward consolidation of policies, organizational structures, and administrative processes in their human service systems. States vary widely in the degree of unification achieved. A few states have achieved sufficient unification to permit systemwide planning, budgeting, data systems, and evaluation. In fact, organizational design of these consolidated or integrated systems is considerably more progressive than their administration would suggest. A new dimension has been added to human services policy-making in every situation where a single executive has been assigned the responsibility for multiple programs in a single organizational entity. These executives, many of whom have had professional experience in various aspects of human services, are more likely than governors or state legislators to require and to use high quality evaluations. As their systematic capacities for handling information improve, they are more likely than any of the traditional sources of policy influence to insist on knowing what is intended, the extent of achievement, what difference it makes, and what improvements might be made in programmatic design or service delivery.

Evidence of such changes is readily available. For example, each of the eight evaluation reports mentioned above attempted to relate outcomes to program goals. Experimental design methodology was applied to staff training in addition to client services, yielding persuasive information on changes in productivity. Explication of design features—objectives, variables, assumptions, methods and instruments of data collection and analysis—in these reports facilitates understanding and reduces the possibility of misleading administrative decision makers and elected officials. Issues of service quality, quantity, and distribution are explored. Some of the conclusions and recommendations assail conventional wisdom. Reviews of pertinent literature usually were provided and were adequately referenced. Overall, they represent tremendous progress in the practices of evaluation over the past decade.

APPLICATIONS OF HUMAN SERVICES EVALUATION

This section of the chapter will present findings from the literature of human services, including selected applications, misapplications, and problems and successes of evaluation in human service policies and programs. Vignettes are offered as minicases, each intended to make a different point about evaluative practice in mental health, programs for handicapped persons, social services grants, income maintenance, child support, child welfare, Social Security, and evaluation systems management.

Mental Health: Ideology Displaces Rational Planning and Evaluation

California's radical revision of its state mental health policies and programs in the 1960's provides an excellent case in policy revision and in the competition of ideology with evaluation methods and products [12].

Traditional mental health programming, particularly residential care, ran afoul of the community mental health movement. Advocates of community mental health services stimulated and joined forces with legislative and executive policymakers in a movement to deinstitutionalize mental hospital populations in California. As in other states which followed the California model, state mental hospitals were overcrowded, understaffed, physically inadequate, and mainly custodial. Persons voluntarily or involuntarily committed to these institutions were perceived by community mental health advocates as being neglected personally and therapeutically, thus adding a moral issue in their bid for the mental health function. One of the real objectives, closure of state hospitals, was not an obvious part of the activists' strategy. The surrogate issue, readily joined by civil libertarians, became deprivation of personal liberty through involuntary commitments to mental hospitals. Alternatives to hospital care, except services to be provided by community mental health programs, and consequences of "deinstitutionalization" were not thoroughly explored. The enactment of new policy accelerated the stream of mentally ill persons returning to local communities without developing local capability to care for previously hospitalized patients and persons being diverted from admission to state hospitals.

Resource allocations followed the revised patterns of care. Between 1968 and 1973 local claims on the state mental health budget increased from 21 to 64 percent of the state mental health budget. Five state hospitals were closed. Unanticipated or unintended consequences abounded:

- local communities were not prepared for and, unlike the advocates, did not welcome returning patients;
- local facilities were inadequate and some were overloaded with outpatients, mainly the less severely disordered ones;
- persons recently discharged from state mental hospitals wandered around in the cities in great numbers, failing to utilize local services;
- the state agency lost systematic control and could not hold the counties accountable for the program;
- promised cost savings were not realized.

In retrospect, it is clear that use of an experimental approach might have offset the hazards and untoward consequences of a strategy based on ideology. Ideological fervor blocked learning which should and might have occurred under a carefully designed experimental strategy. Obviously, there was no shared definition of the problem which the California program sought to solve.

Education of the Handicapped: Conflict About Evaluation Methods

Education and training of handicapped persons involve a variety of social and educational services. Advocacy produced widespread public awareness in the early 1960's that 90 percent of handicapped children were not enrolled in public schools, although human service organizations provided learning opportunities to some clients. Judicial decisions to the effect that handicapped children, as other children, had a right to public education helped to set the stage for the Education of the Handicapped Act, which became law in 1966. Appropriations under the new legislation were a token, less than 10 percent of state and local expenditures [13].

The General Accounting Office (GAO), an independent unit of the federal legislative branch, under the leadership of Comptroller General Elmer Staats, had begun to shift its orientation away from strictly fiscal audit toward audits designed to measure achievement of statutory purposes [14]. GAO studied the program for educating handicapped children and issued a report in 1974. Meanwhile, the Bureau of Education of the Handicapped (BEH) in the Office of Education was debating internally about appropriate evaluation strategies. Much of the content of the GAO report was noncontroversial, especially portions dealing with the scope and severity of educational disadvantage among handicapped children. Methodological aspects of the GAO study generated high controversy. The principal BEH criticisms were:

- Little effort was made by GAO to tap the expertise of BEH staff;
- Generally accepted methods, *e.g.*, probabilistic sampling, were not used consistently;

- Certain findings were unsubstantiated and were used in making inaccurate and misleading generalizations;
- Qualifications of GAO staff were questioned; BEH believed that only specialists in education or behavioral science were qualified to evaluate the program;
- It was unreasonable to assume that nine BEH specialists could monitor and assist 50 states and 16,000 school districts;
- The GAO was preoccupied with negative aspects of the program and failed to perceive grossly inadequate funding as a fundamental cause of modest results.

This conflict between evaluators and administrators points to technical defects and a failure of interactive process. Such deficiencies tend to minimize the impact of evaluation. Learning from this experience, GAO in 1976 studied training of teachers and achieved a mutually acceptable outcome. The three key differences were in the use of probabilistic samples, a validated research instrument, and extensive consultation with BEH staff.

A broad issue in this case, Who is competent to evaluate?, frequently is raised as a smokescreen or skirmishing technique in professional parochialism. Legislative audit units of federal and state governments, concerned with programmatic performance as well as fiscal integrity, have greatly increased their evaluative activities in recent years. Most of these units do not employ persons who are specialists in the programs which they audit [15].

Social Services: Formal Evaluation Preempted by Political Factors

The *National Journal* reported in June, 1972 that the states had found an exceptionally large and accessible source of funds in the social services provisions of the Social Security Act [16]. Expenditures under the open-end financial arrangement doubled in one year and continuing increases were projected. The program was not financially controllable. Two documented research reports reveal reasons for the difficulties in evaluating this billion-dollar operation [17]. A third report reflects evaluation after substantial policy changes were made [18].

The authorizing statutory language and administrative regulations were general and ambiguous. Almost any activity of state human service agencies could qualify as a "social service." Regulations were similarly ambiguous and permissive. An even greater problem was political ambivalence in the Congress and the White House. California, Illinois, and New York had tapped heavily the apparently unlimited funds. A Republican occupied the chief executive position in each of these large states and all had good access to a Republican President, Richard Nixon. This fact was especially important in 1972, a presidential election year. Congressional behavior was affected by the same electoral reality.

In this situation, program evaluation was preempted by ambiguous statutory language, the absence of measurable goals, and partisan political coalitions. The long-delayed policy response (1974) was a change of statutory language and administrative regulation aimed primarily at fiscal accountability rather than outcome or impacts of social services. In pressing for statutory limitations, Secretary Caspar Weinberger imputed intention to an exceedingly ambiguous statute, saying that "...social services have always been intended to complement the programs of cash assistance" [19]. Neither goals nor other measurable criteria were mentioned by Weinberger or during legislative debates. Subsequent revisions of the legislation did not greatly improve definition or measurability of expected results.

Income Maintenance: Unintended Consequences

Advocates of income maintenance strategies in public welfare long have argued that a guaranteed income adequate for a (variously perceived) "decent" standard of living would enhance family stability and achieve other desirable outcomes. Opponents consistently raised issues of cost and work incentives. Experiments were begun in the 1960's in local areas of several states [20]. Several years of experience elapsed before patterns emerged. In addition to positive results, evaluators reported unintended consequences: comparatively high rates of family break-up and reduced employment among welfare recipients.

Advocates may argue that extraneous variables could have caused the unintended consequences but, whatever the causes, these consequences and costs made the income maintenance experiments vulnerable to termination by a new national administration with revisive notions about public welfare.

Child Support Enforcement in Michigan: Problems in Replication

Responding to environmental conditions which included scarce resources and demands for efficiency and accountability, Michigan has designed and implemented a new system of child support enforcement. A governmental office called the Friend of the Court in each county receives child support payments from absent parents and disburses the funds to the parent or other person who cares for the children. Special features of the program are systematic information and vigorous enforcement. Missed payments cause warning letters and, if the obligated parent fails to respond, court action and a jail sentence.

Two programmatic assumptions affect the design of the enforcement program:

- child support can be achieved only if government acts, even to the point of charging and jailing nonsupportive parents; and
- the known record of enforcement action influences the compliance by actually or potentially nonsupportive parents. [21]

The program was effective in Michigan and was widely reported [22]. Florida wished to replicate and implement the design, beginning with a demonstration in several localities. The first attempt of replication was frustrated because the handling of cases in substate localities in Florida varied widely in institutional process and performance, both within Florida and in comparison with Michigan. The program which was designed and implemented in Michigan would not have been evaluable in Florida without comprehensive state policy and administrative changes, which apparently were politically infeasible. A different design is being prepared for the demonstration program in Florida.

Child support enforcement, incidentally, is a program where simple arithmetic—dollars collected per dollar expended or collections per investigator—has been sufficient to gain strong political support. Such rudimentary data speak of efficiency, which is a widely owned societal value.

Child Welfare Services: External Evaluation and Change

Multiple and frequently counteractive statutes enacted over a century created a fragmented policy base for the child welfare system in New York. Nearly 50,000 children were in foster care, over half of them in New York City. Children averaged about five years in foster care because of legal and administrative barriers to permanent placement. Low performance and high cost of the system spurred concerted governmental action.

In 1974, state legislation created the Temporary State Commission on Child Welfare. The Commission members included legislators (one of whom served as chairperson), jurists, social workers and other professionals, and private citizens. The Commission was given a deadline of May 1975 for a preliminary report to the Governor and the Legislature. The summary judgment in the preliminary report was that the entire system was uncoordinated and unaccountable [23].

Four years and five major publications after its establishment, the Commission had identified a welter of policy and administrative barriers to adoption and other constructive action, recodified state laws affecting child welfare (1976), and produced a unified program of incentives for adoption. Although Commission reports frequently refer to goals of permanence and high quality care, overall system performance, statutory deficiencies, comparative agency evaluation, monitoring, and accountability, this effort probably would not have passed the usual tests of formal, technical evaluation. Portions of it might have met minimal requirements of observational methodology. Despite the inclusion of the ideas, knowledge, and skills of competent professionals, one probably could not have found a satisfactory quantitative model for continual evaluation of the Commission's work. Instead, an organic political approach was chosen and constant emphasis was placed on corrective action. This situation provides a clear focus on one of the essential truths about evaluation. It may help to inform but may not displace political process or judgments.

Policymaking for Social Security: No External Evaluation Allowed

The Social Security system of the United States probably is unique in several respects. One of its distinguishing features is that its policy base and administration received no serious external evaluative scrutiny for nearly 40 years after its establishment. Policy proposals were generated within the agency. Few persons outside the organization gained informational competence sufficient to evaluate policies of program management, even if they had been so inclined.

Martha Derthick's trenchant study reports three areas of policy controversy in the early 1970's, more than 35 years after creation of the program. The first "surprise" was the high volume and cost of disability claims, to which jurists and physicians seemed surprisingly sympathetic when initial denials of benefits produced appeals [24].

The second analytic misadventure was underestimation of the decline in the fertility rate, which translates as a shortage of workers supporting increasing numbers of annuitants in future years. The third misadventure was failure to anticipate persistent and adverse features of the economy, including inflation and high unemployment, both of which contributed to fiscal shortfalls in paying inflation-adjusted benefits. Policy-makers, habituated by this time to administrative evaluations and proposals for policy revision, were disinclined to mandate adjustments in program design or financing of a politically sensitive program.

In this program, the clarity of goals was not a problem. The administrators knew precisely what they wanted, generated and skillfully promoted enactment of policy proposals, demonstrating willingness to compromise as long as accommodations enabled an incremental strategy.

Two insights afforded by Derthick's analysis are relevant to evaluation. Planning for evaluation of high quality must precede and be concomitant with policy implementation. Evaluation should not be merely a sequel to program operations. Second, a massive human service program rarely may escape intensive external evaluation but unanticipated demands upon policy-makers for huge, additional amounts of resources will open a relatively closed system to external inquiry.

Human Service Systems Absent Systematic Evaluation: The King Has no Scepter or Clothes

Refined methodology and financial resources dedicated to evaluation avail little in the absence of systematic design and continuing integrative structure in large human service organizations. The U.S. Department of Health, Education, and Welfare (HEW), now Health and Human Services (HHS), is an instructive case in point [25].

The initial step toward systematic departmental evaluation in HEW began as a result of President Lyndon Johnson's order in 1965 to transplant the Program Planning and Budgeting System (PPBS) from the Department of Defense throughout the federal government. HEW historically had been aggregated but not integrated. Its "operating agencies," within minimal departmental superstructure, had a high degree of administrative autonomy, yet their programs concurrently affected millions of people. Secretary John Gardner established an organizational unit under the direction of William Gorham to coordinate policy formation and evaluation. In 1967, Gorham proposed to Secretary Wilbur Cohen the establishment of programmatic evaluation capability in the new office of program coordination. Cohen responded affirmatively, directing Gorham to develop comprehensive plans for evaluating program effectiveness.

The nascent evaluative function initially was handicapped by a historical departmental pattern of extreme functional decentralization, relatively miniscule funding of evaluation, and scarcity of persons with knowledge and skills appropriate to the tasks. Gradually, a leadership role was given to an assistant secretary for planning and evaluation, funds were appropriated or set aside by Congress, and the central unit acquired staff.

Major resource gains were made in the early 1970's. The budget for the new function increased from $4.7 million to $27.9 million in 1970-71, with increases for the agencies within the Department as well as for the central unit. Congress assisted the departmental effort with mandates in HEW statutory authorizations to set aside stipulated percentages of appropriated funds for evaluation.

The HEW evaluative subsystem has been hampered consistently by persistent resistance among autonomous operating agencies, special interests of programmatic constituencies, and both physical and organizational remoteness from a staggering array of national, state and local, public and private organizations who spend HEW (now HHS) funds. More than a decade after its establishment, one participant reports a combination of problems which negatively constrain the evaluative subsystem:

1. Four major loci of evaluative responsibilities exist within HHS: the Assistant Secretary for Planning and Evaluation; the operating agencies; 10 regional directors' offices; and regional units of the major programs;
2. The Assistant Secretary's office lacks effective process for converting the results of analyses into information for program agency planning and management;
3. Evaluative activities may or may not be linked to priorities for research and evaluation defined by the Secretary;
4. Regional directors' evaluative results are not linked to HHS central office policy research, planning, and evaluation; and
5. Regional program evaluation units are not linked vertically or horizontally to policy or planning loci. [27]

Thus, the largest collection of federal human service functions comprising the greatest source of intergovernmental influence in human services has acute problems of evaluation systems design and coordination. One consequence is a dysfunctional circularity: evaluators encounter extreme difficulty in demonstrating the utility of their products and low utility negatively constrains the allocation of resources for a function which might otherwise be a powerful learning instrument for policymaking and management. This situation might worsen as current policy changes are implemented.

Expanded use of block grants and concommitant devolution to states of responsibility for human services policy and evaluation promises to create a future in which HHS will be completely disabled for *national* program evaluation. States have customarily collected and supplied data, mainly activity counts, to HHS while designing separate evaluation systems to meet their own policy and administrative needs. Most of the data requirements of federal grants-in-aid have been geared to instrumental use of recipient state agencies for monitoring, rather than evaluation. Accordingly, the major HHS investment has been made in data on administrative *process control*, which is a poor substitute for evaluation and accountability. Process control mainly provides descriptive data, whereas empirical data demonstrating a causal relationship between policies or programs and consequences are required for serious evaluation. Realistically, sparsely staffed federal units consider that they have had a successful year when they have been able merely to transfer the money to state, local, and private users.

The pattern of federal practices draws sharp criticism from experts in evaluation. For example, Wholey calls attention to great expenditures for studies, few of which have significant results. Failure of evaluative impact, in Wholey's view, is due partly to lack of uniformity of design and lack of comprehensive, systematic evaluative process [28].

Criminal Justice: Conflicting Social Values and other Complexities

The criminal justice system is an unenviably difficult environment for evaluation. Complexities of the system are apparent from the moment a suspect is apprehended through sequential phases of adjudication, incarceration or release, and restoration of personal liberty after "serving time" in a correctional setting [29].

Conflicting social values are important variables in formulating public policy and administering criminal justice programs. The value of public safety might or might not be served immediately by denial of opportunity for pre-trial release. Justice for the individual might be better served by a liberal policy on bail or release on personal recognizance. Aside from the issue of relative priority for public safety and personal liberty, multiple questions arise. Can reliable judgments be made about whom to release and under what conditions? If bail is required, does a telephone or other communication capability enable the charged person to gain pre-trial release? Are persons released without bail more likely than persons under bond to appear for trial? What programs are effective and what risks are tolerable in rehabilitation and parole of different types of offenders?

Satisfactory answers to these questions, sometimes obtained in local experiments, have not greatly reduced controversy over practices which vary tremendously among political jurisdictions and judicial subsystems. For example, a juvenile offender may be detained without arraignment for repetitive breaking-and-entering while an adult charged with the same offense may be released immediately on bond. Practices may vary widely from one jurisdiction to another and within the same jurisdiction over time. Further complicating the evaluative task is difficulty of ascertaining the comparability of effects of different practices on a short- or long-term basis. Randomization in evaluative designs may be perceived as violating Fourteenth Amendment rights of equal treatment; longitudinal study of outcomes for individuals and broader social impacts (*e.g.*, crime rates) may not be feasible options. If defensible and conclusive findings are reported, the evaluator's product still might not pass the acid test of utility in influencing policy or practice. Belief systems can be nearly impervious to facts. Judicially ordered restitution or the offender's payment of damages to the victim would be socially acceptable in some localities and unacceptable in others.

The convicted person is faced with variables ranging from local system policies to judicial compassion (or lack of it), to availability of prison facilities or alternatives to incarceration. Punishment and rehabilitation are competitive social values. Both values are frequently subsumed under the rubric of "correction." Variance among the states in incarceration rates appears to be even greater than differences in the types and levels of rehabilitative efforts. No generally accepted proof of differential rehabilitative efficacy exists.

The "corrections" phase of criminal justice apparently is approaching another critical juncture—"another", because recurrent crises rather than careful planning characterize the pattern of change in prison systems. The principal precipitants of change have been prison riots, judicial mandates to remediate overcrowding and other unacceptable conditions, and rights of prisoners. Overcrowding of state prison systems is an obvious possibility for generating the next crisis. More than 300,000 Americans occupy prisons built to house approximately half as many. Florida, with less than 5 percent of the national population, accounts for approximately 10 percent of the American prison population. It is ironic, and probably indicative of deficient societal learning, that major capital expenditures for prisons are being budgeted by states during a period of severe retrenchment in other human services. These actions are grounded in temporal, local notions of public safety and punishment because there is no evaluative evidence of substantial rehabilitative influence owing to imprisonment.

Concurrent with increased incarceration are experimentation with restitution by offenders, diversion of juveniles from the criminal justice process, work-release, and judicial decisions which allow convicted persons to work during the week and live in jail during weekends. The local character and lack of comparability of evaluations of these options are deterrents to their utility. The demise of the national law enforcement assistance programs of the 1970's and, especially, the failure to replace such programs through new public policies based on learning from evaluated results, make new crises inevitable.

The future of evaluation in "corrections" remains uncertain. Conflicting values preempt systematic evaluation. Punishment and rehabilitation compete for ascendance as the dominant social value, and rehabilitation is an apparent loser. Escalating costs of confining and regulating behaviors of increasing numbers of prisoners tend to hinder appropriate investments in experimental study of rehabilitative programs. Extremely localized, discontinuous efforts will not solve this national evaluative double-bind.

SUMMARY, CONCLUSIONS, AND PROSPECTS

The prospects for evaluation of human services in the United States are a mixed bag of favorable and unfavorable possibilities. Some possibilities of each type and summary observations comprise the author's view of short-range and long-range prospects. Three aspects of evaluation are considered in projecting favorable and unfavorable influences: (1) level of resources and degree of institutionalization of evaluative effort; (2) technical quality; and (3) utilization of evaluative informational products.

Evaluative experience acquired nationally, in states, and in local jurisdictions during the past 10 to 15 years has become an improved resource for future use. The human service community and related interests have learned from evaluative misadventures and from successes. The base of relevant knowledge and skills has been broadened through trial and error as well as classical research methods. The volume and quality of evaluative work have increased, although current reductions in priority and resources allocated to human services tend to reduce the level of effort.

Experimental and quasi-experimental models, long used in the "hard sciences" have been adapted successfully for human service applications. Observational designs have been developed which are useful and do not require dependence on showing cause-effect relationships. The overall effect has been a relatively rapid gain of evaluative competence, rather widely distributed in the public and private sectors, which apparently has outpaced utilization. Thus, societal learning has produced and institutionalized an improved competence for use in the future.

The currently dominant conservative political ideology, viewed optimistically, could produce further qualitative improvements through scrutiny of and opposition to human service activities. Processes and products of evaluation which demonstrate high relevance and methodological quality might be highly valued in an adverse climate because they will be more difficult to discount by opponents and more useful instruments in the hands of human service advocates.

The scarcity of resources for human services will adversely affect delivery and evaluation of outcome of services. Advocates of human services might counter the adverse impact through integral, carefully designed, rigorously performed evaluations, sacrificing scope for quality. These qualitative gains would further enhance knowledge resources for the future.

Current and prospective scarcity of resources, coupled with qualitative improvement of evaluation, could stimulate greater use of evaluative products. This development might habituate policy-makers and administrative decision-makers to dependence on and comfortability in using information provided through evaluation. This possibility appears to be greatest in state rather than national settings in the near future because additional state investments will be required to maintain acceptable levels of service.

Unfavorable recent and prospective developments are distressingly plentiful. Assuming continuance of an inimical but dominant national political ideology, both evaluative and direct service opportunities will be further reduced. Persons opposed to the current level and scope of services might devalue evaluative evidence if it does not support their preconceptions and political goals. Methodological weaknesses of evaluations are likely to be exploited by critics. Recent but clear evidence of sharply reduced feedback from states to the national element of the federal system is discouraging. Deregulation, as a political goal, might have been achieved by shifting emphasis from intergovernmental procedural control to a developmental approach of setting national goals and standards for human service programs, while allowing for state and local variance.

Within the national governmental environment, evaluative competence gained and institutionalized since the mid-1960's is presently adversely affected and will continue to be at great risk in the near future. A realistic prospect is further reduction of resources for human services in general and evaluation in particular as a consequence of low policy priority and scarce revenues. With a relative and absolute decline in national interest, influence, and competence, the states might become the primary loci of evaluative practice and emphasis in the public sector.

What will be the net impact of favorable and unfavorable events? A key assumption is that extreme political ideologies are distinctly temporal in character. Macro-forces, such as service needs of increasing numbers of older persons and young families, might be expressed in demands for restoration of high priority of human services and concurrent resumption of serious evaluation. Severe and continued economic distress might intensify human service needs and might make pragmatists of current ideologues who seek reelection. The dominant political negativism about human services would moderate, at the minimum, under these circumstances.

The evaluation function has been institutionalized in most large governmental entities. Quantitative knowledge and skills are presently better developed and more widely distributed than at any time history. Policy-makers and administrative decision-makers, especially in state governments, might be more likely in the future than in the past to depend upon and use evaluative information. The changed political environment might encourage systematic integration of evaluative processes and products with policy formation and revision, administrative planning, budgeting, and program operations. Hard-earned competence in evaluation is not likely to be forever wasted and probably will be enhanced as the prevailing political ideology moderates or is displaced by another.

REFERENCES

1. Suchman, E. A. *Evaluative Record: Principles and Practice in Public Service and Action Programs*. Russell Sage Foundation, New York, 1967, p. 78.
2. Gates, B. L. *Social Program Administration: The Implementation of Social Policy*, Prentice-Hall, Englewood Cliffs, NJ, 1980, p. 211.
3. Weiss, C. *Evaluation Research: Methods of Assessing Program Effectiveness*, Prentice-Hall, Englewood Cliffs, NJ, 1972, pp. 1-2.
4. Wholey, J. S., Scanlon, J. W., Duffy, H. G., Fukomoto, J. F., and Vogt, L. M. *Federal Evaluation Policy*, The Urban Institute, Washington, D.C. 1970, p. 23.
5. *Ibid.*, p. 5, p. 15.
6. *Ibid.*, p. 15.
7. *Ibid.*, p. 40.
8. *Ibid.*, p. 50.
9. Abert, J. G. (ed.). *Program Evaluation at HEW: Research vs Reality, Part 1, Health*. Marcel Dekker, New York, 1969.
10. Heclo, H. *A Government of Strangers*, The Brookings Institution, Washington, D.C. 1977, p. 151.
11. Abert, J. G., (ed.). *op.cit.*, p. 27.
12. Cameron, J. M. Ideology and Policy Determination: Restructuring California's Mental Health System In May, J. V., and Wildavsky, A. B. (eds.). *The Policy Cycle*. Sage Publications, Beverly Hills, CA, 1978, pp. 301-328.
13. Deck, N. G. The Federal Programs for Education of the Handicapped. In Kloman, E. H. (ed.). *Cases in Accountability: The Work of the GAO*. Westview Press, Boulder, CO, pp. 43-52.
14. Mosher, F. C. *The GAO: The Quest for Accountability*, Westview Press, Boulder, CO, 1979, especially Chapters 6-11, pp. 169-333.
15. For an institutional perspective of the federal performance audit role, see Keith, E. M. and Hedrick, J. L., GAO Helps Congress Evaluate Programs. *Public Administration Review* 34 (July-August, 1974): 327-333; for a similar perspective of the state audit role, see Brown, R. and Pethel, R. D. A Matter of Facts: State Legislative Performance Auditing *Public Administration Review* 34 (July-August, 1974): 318-326.
16. Igelhart, J. K. Welfare Report: HEW Program Doubles in size as Officials Scramble to Check its Growth. *National Journal* 4 (June 17, 1972): 1007-1014.

17. Derthick, M. *Uncontrollable Spending for Social Services Grants*. The Brookings Institution, Washington, D.C. 1975.
For a different analysis of this social services case, see: Mott, P. E. *Meeting Human Services Needs: The Social and Political History of Title XX*, Columbus, National Conference on Social Welfare, 1976.
18. Benton, B., Field, T., and Millar, R. *Social Services: Federal Legislation vs State Implementation*. The Urban Institute, Washington, D.C. 1978.
19. Weinberger, C. Statement before the Committee on Finance, U.S. Senate , May 8, 1973 (Processed).
20. Rivlin, A. M. *Systematic Thinking for Social Action*. The Brookings Institution, Washington, D.C. 1971, pp. 94-101.
Reports of these experimental programs provide details of experimental design, data collection and analysis, and consequences. See, as examples: Kershaw, D.N. A Negative-Income-Tax Experiment in Nachmias, D. (ed.). *The Practice of Policy Evaluation*. St. Martin's Press, New York, 1980, pp. 27-41; and
Rees, A. An Overview of the Labor-Supply Results. In Nachmias, D. (ed.). *The Practice of Policy Evaluation*. St. Martin's Press, New York, 1980, pp. 41-63.
21. Boynton, G. R. *Mathematical Thinking About Politics*. Longman, New York, pp. 158-164.
22. Chambers, D. L. Men Who Know They Are Watched: Some Benefits and Costs of Jailing for Nonpayment of Support. *Michigan Law Review* 75: 900-940. (Reproduced, with permission of the author, by the Department of Health and Rehabilitative Services, Tallahassee, Florida).
23. Temporary State Commission on Child Welfare. *The Children of the State: A Time for Change in Child Care*, I, New York, the Commission, May, 1975.
Subsequent reports of the Commission:
Barriers to the Freeing of Children, March, 1976;
Children of the State II, October, 1976;
Incentives to Adoptive Placements, February, 1977; and
Foster Care Reimbursements: A New Approach, May, 1978.
24. Derthick, M. *Policymaking for Social Security*. The Brookings Institution, Washington, D.C., 1979.
25. Abert, J. G. (ed.). *Program Evaluation at HEW: Research vs Reality, Part 1, Health*. Marcel Dekker, New York, 1969.
26. *Ibid.*, p. 30.
27. Grossbard, S. Closing the Loop: A Critical Assessment of the Role of Evaluation in the Federal Bureaucracy , *Journal of Health and Human Resources Administration*, 1. (May, 1979): 538-556.
28. Wholey, J. S. *Evaluation: Promise and Performance*. The Urban Institute, Washington, D.C., 1979.
29. *Ibid.*

18
Evaluating Defense Programs in an Era of Rising Expenditures

Grover Starling / *School of Business and Public Administration, University of Houston at Clear Lake, Houston, Texas*

INTRODUCTION

Harold Brown recently delivered a lecture to the University of Michigan's School of Business Administration with the heretical title " 'Managing' the Defense Department–Why It Can't be Done." Brown argued that "the analogy with business, useful in some contexts and with respect to some parts of the defense management process, breaks down in others. . . . Indeed, overall operation of the Defense Department cannot even use the same management criteria as a private nonprofit, or even those appropriate to other parts of government." [1]

If management criteria are elusive, then the evaluative process obviously becomes more difficult. Accurately determining how much evaluation goes on in a federal agency is about as hard as pinning down the size of an agency's public relations effort. Nevertheless, a recent compendium of federal evaluations by the GAO might provide a crude measure of relative effort. It should be stressed, however, that Table 1 is based on neither a census nor a probability sample; rather, it relies on federal respondents who themselves used a variety of criteria to label something as evaluation and, in some cases, did not report because they lacked complete information.

Keeping these caveats in mind, a safe generalization is that given the size of the defense budget, DOD remains among the least evaluated of federal agencies. Moreover, some evidence suggests that even the handful of studies that do appear have little, if any, effect [2].

It is hard to think of a time in recent American history when evaluation of defense spending could be more needed. The Carter budget for fiscal 1982 had called for an average annual real increase in total obligational authority (TOA) of

Table 1 Ratio of Evaluative Studies to Budget Size of Federal Department

Department	Reported Studies per Billion Dollars
State	80.7
Commerce	41.9
HUD	20.1
Interior	20.0
Justice	9.9
Energy	9.2
Education	9.1
Transportation	6.6
Agriculture	5.4
Treasury	3.4
Labor	3.1
HHS	1.8
Defense	0.4

Source: Data from U.S. General Accounting Office, *Federal Evaluations* PAD-80-48 (Washington, D.C.: GPO 1980) and U.S. Office of Management and Budget, *The Budget of the U.S. Government, FY 1979.*

4.7 percent each year for the next five years. Cumulative obligational authority for the next five years, with the effects of estimated inflation removed, would amount to $1,085 billion. Viewing this amount as underfunding, President Reagan called for about $195 billion more. In fiscal 1985, if Reagan had his way, defense would take a little over 7 percent of estimated GNP (It was 5.6 percent in fiscal 1981.)

But, as Harold Brown suggests, merely accepting the premise that defense programs merit more frequent evaluation might not be enough. At least two more things are required: a wider recognition of certain errors that have plagued evaluation of defense programs in recent years and the development of an institutional setting in which the results of evaluative studies will actually affect decision making in defense.

Before considering what those errors might include and what that institutional setting might look like, some terminology distinctions are in order.

For purposes of this paper, "evaluation" means an assessment of the effects of past and present programs or projects. Simply stated, evaluation asks to what extent a program is achieving its objective. A major assumption of this paper is that the overriding objective of all defense programs is combat effectiveness. Military effectiveness is a function of three variables: readiness, i.e., the level of technical proficiency of unit and weapons plus logistical support; cohesion, i.e., commitment of individual soldiers to the unit of *esprit de corps*; and credibility, i.e., perception of others that the military has the ability and will to undertake action when necessary [3]. How to measure combat effectiveness–short of war–is what makes evaluation of defense programs a particularly challenging task.

Another overriding objective may be "deterrence," which is a shorthand way of saying "preserving the peace." But, if one accepts the premise that the U.S. is not an aggressive, expansionist power, then combat effectiveness becomes virtually synonymous with deterrence.

Evaluative research entails the idea of casuality. What factor or factors cause AWOLs? What factors affect most decisively the retention of pilots and physicians? How much does the frequency of overhauling affect the performance of a ship or aircraft? In this sense, even trying to answer the question of what effect U.S. expenditures for defense have on the Soviet Union is an exercise in evaluation [4].

Undoubtedly, this definition of evaluation will seem unduly restrictive to some. But, when we start asking questions about the costs and benefits of alternative programs, it seems to me that we have really moved into the realm of policy analysis, which is more future oriented. Because the two concepts, evaluation and policy analysis, are so closely linked, some confusion of realms will always be with us.

Evaluation should also be distinguished from auditing. The latter is more concerned with a program's internal administrative procedures, and especially the prevention of fraud. While evaluation often uses audit information (e.g., workload measures, cost data, and staffing levels), the ultimate purpose remains determining how well a program is attaining its overall objectives.

Ideally, evaluative research focuses not on outputs but outcomes. That is to say, the crucial question is not how many armored divisions a country has but rather what is the overall combat effectiveness of those divisions [5]. Similarly, the technical configurations of a weapon–e.g., low profile in a tank, high speed in a submarine, or maneuverability in a fighter–are less important than their combat usefulness. What can be overlooked in peacetime is even more likely to be forgotten in war. Thus, Pentagon officials evaluated the effects of the 1965-68 bombing campaign ROLLING THUNDER by output; namely, the number of B-52 sorties and damage to North Vietnam military installations–when the proper measure should have its outcome, such as the effect on VC/NVA force levels or activity rates in South Vietnam.

The importance of this output-outcome distinction cannot be over-emphasized. The Department of Defense has an impressive network for conducting research on manpower and personnel programs [6]. But the crucial question in evaluating these programs must always remain, how much does this contribute to combat effectiveness? It is all too easy for professionals trained in psychology, education, mathmatics, statistics, operations research, and economics to forget that.

One last term needs clarification. "Defense programs" means those programs and projects that are concerned with building greater military strength. Defense is, therefore, only one of several objectives and requirements in national security policy. Other objectives include arms control, collective security arrangements (such as NATO), and the U.S. economic and technological base.

Defense decisions may be categorized by level and by kind. For purposes of evaluation, it is useful to distinguish [7]:

- nuclear strategy and planning decisions
- conventional force strategy and tactics decisions
- procurement or force composition decisions
- research and development decisions

The analysis that follows is in two parts. The first part explores systematically the special problems of evaluating defense programs. To provide a convenient and easily understood framework for this analysis, eight leading fallacies that frequently appear in the evaluation of defense programs will be discussed. Understanding these fallacies not only will help us appreciate the problems whereof Secretary Brown spoke but also point us in the direction of a solution. In other words, only if we appreciate the special nature of defense management can we begin to generate better evaluative studies. To outline in a tentative sort of way an evaluative strategy in DOD will be the aim of the last part of this paper.

SOME ERRORS OF EVALUATION

In defense programs, and indeed in government programs generally, there is no universal methodology that tends to insure consistent, high quality evaluation. Since the translation of "defense" into some more concrete measure or criteria cannot be avoided, the prevention of even gross errors in the translation requires hard thought. Nevertheless, some of the mistakes that occur most frequently have special characteristics and can be put into categories.

Fallacies of Verification

The best evaluative studies are no better than the answers that they generate—true answers, which are the object of all empirical inquiry. It is no easy matter to discover the truth, pure and simple, about defense programs; for defense programs are never pure and rarely simple.

The following point should be stressed: In several respects, assessing defense programs is *more* difficult than assessing social programs. The overriding difficulty in evaluating defense programs is the absence of any direct measure of combat effectiveness, short of actual conflict. In contrast, if the Department of Education wants to evaluate a new reading program, it can readily measure increased reading skills among an experimental group of sixth graders and then compare the results obtained from a control group. This is not to suggest that randomized tests of education programs are commonplace in the Department of Education but merely that opportunities for such objective testing are more plentiful there [8].

But there is a crucial difference. Social programs seek to belong to the world of cooperative and constructive things and are guided by the pursuit of goals under benign assumptions. Military operations, by contrast, belong to the world of conflict where things must work under great stress and where, above all, there is an active will systematically seeking to undo all that one tries to achieve. Whereas the administrators in the Pressman and Wildavsky book, *Implementation*, had to contend with a multiplicity of decisions points, and perspectives, military commanders must contend with an enemy who follows an explicit strategy of "exploiting the line of least expectation." In other words, the enemy tries to manipulate the condition of the battlefield in order to increase the degree of complexity and unpredictability [9].

For this reason, such concepts as "overall effectiveness" and "bottom line" have less relevance in the military sector. Because an enemy seeks victory by exploiting the weakest link in an operation or weapons system, across the board effectiveness is a desideratum in war. In contrast, social programs may be considered successful if they attain just a few of their stated objectives.

In addition to the human factor, there are profound technological uncertainties. Could a high altitude nuclear explosion bathe the United States with a high voltage wave known as an electromagnetic pulse (EMP) and, in turn, knock out unprotected communications equipment from coast to coast and shut down the U.S. power grid [10]? How vulnerable are nuclear aircraft carriers to a determined Soviet missile attack? How advanced is Soviet research in particle beam weapons (PBW)? And, most of all, would a nuclear exchange inevitably escalate? A number of experts profess to know the answer to that last question. But only one thing is certain—there is absolutely no precedent for such a situation.

The technological factor also limits the utility of one of the most important analytical concepts in the evaluation of public policy, marginal (incremental) analysis. Following the principle of maximum social gain, we spend on a program until the point at which marginal social benefits equal marginal social gains. What makes this mode of analysis difficult in defense is the "lumpiness" of benefits. Increases in spending, which buy only slight increase in performance, can sometimes result in big jumps in combat performance [11]. See Figure 1.

Reductionist Fallacy

Given the kinds of complexity outlined above, it is not surprising to learn that those who evaluate defense programs are driven to simplify their causal models. While all models must be reductive to some degree, some are more reductive than others.

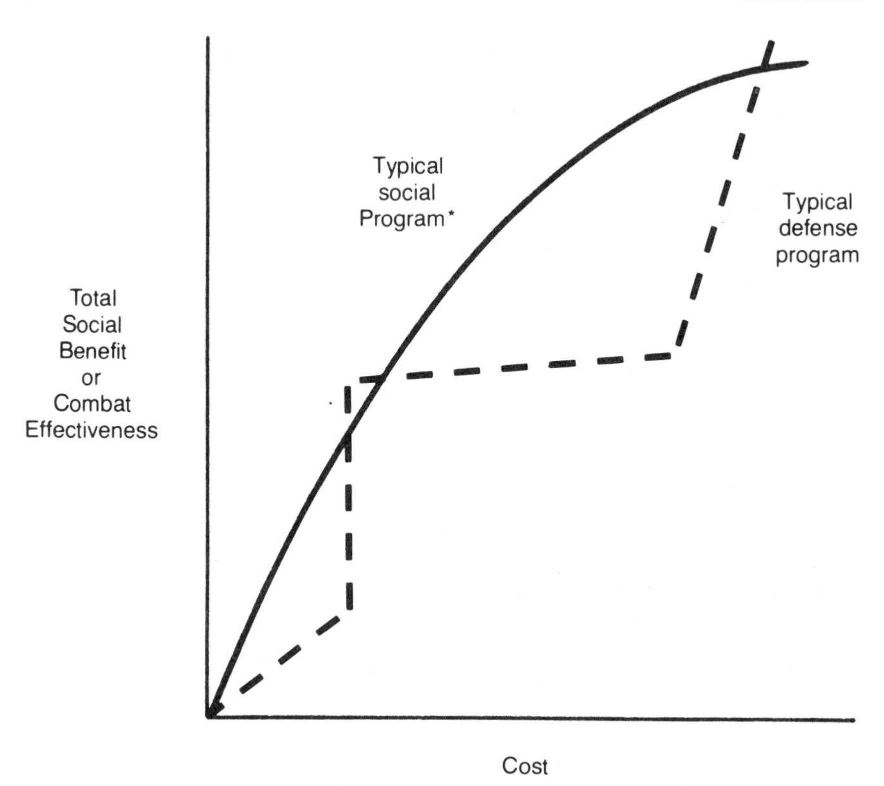

Figure 1 A comparison of the benefit schedules of social and defense programs. *This curve shows the value of total benefits derived from spending successive dollars on social programs. The assumption that program choices are finely divisible is, of course, more applicable to welfare or education programs than construction projects. In building a road between City A and City B such a smooth expansion of total benefits is not possible.

In June 1981, CBS-TV News broadcast a documentary entitled *The Defense of the United States*. The series ran for an hour of prime time on each of five consecutive nights, committing the reductionist fallacy several times. A case in point was CBS' assessment of the XM-1 tank: "so heavy, so complex, it gets only three gallons to the mile," and "it can't go nearly as far as our old tanks." The turbine powered XM-1 tank may or may not have been a wise investment, but surely no assessment of its effectiveness should be boiled down to m.p.g., as the television commentary seemed to imply. Other relevant factors might include capacity of armor to defeat Russian rockets, firing accuracy on the move, blast and fire protection for crew, ability to start in cold weather (as opposed to the more fuel efficiency diesel tanks), and detectability on the battlefield (turbine engine is quieter and smokeless).

In assessments of overall American combat capability, there is a tendency to reduce it to technological superiority. There is some basis for this in military history:

the invention of the stirrup had given impetus to cavalry warfare; the long-range infantry rifle, introduced during the Civil War, shattered the effectiveness of the rapidly concentrated attack of the Napoleonic era; and in the Battle of Britain, the decisive factor was the British radar early warning and fighter control system.

From the preceding discussion of the reductive fallacy, one conclusion is inescapable: an evaluation of U.S. defense cannot turn on any one factor—combat capability depends on several. In addition to leadership, technology, morale, and perception (discussed earlier) the following factors must also be weighed.

- *Readiness*; While modernization is important, existing forces cannot be left with insufficient funds for operation and maintenance. When they are, training must be cut back and some equipment cannibalized to keep other equipment operational. According to Caspar W. Weinberger, the most serious single readiness problem the U.S. has today is the shortage of experienced personnel, particularly in the senior enlisted ranks and in certain critical job skills [12].
- *Force structure*; that is, the numbers, size, and composition of the major units that constitute the armed forces.
- *Sustainability*; that is, the ability to support forces over time, allowing them enough time to win.
- *Operational doctrine*; that is, how commanders plan to use their men and materials. The French Army was decimated during World War I because its commanders—despite the lessons of the U.S. Civil War and the invention of the machine gun—had a mystical faith in the headlong offensive. The French army was routed by the German Army at the start of World War II because its commanders—despite a numerical superiority and the invention of the tank—maintained that illusion about defense. In both cases, French military leaders had not critically rethought their strategy and tactics [13]. They had committed perhaps the most insidious of all fallacies that plague the military mind, the didactic fallacy.

The Didactic Fallacy

Formally stated, the didactic fallacy is the attempt to extract specific lessons from military history and to apply them in the evaluation of present programs, without regard for intervening changes.

The traditional American doctrine of war, which crystalized during World War II, is to rely on mass production and the application of superior firepower. But U.S. defense planners may need to discover other ways to deter the Soviet armed forces. Many experts think a Soviet-American conflict might be a short and intense war; American productive capacity might not have sufficient time to gear up. Furthermore, even if it did, it is by no means an economic certainty that the U.S. could match the Soviet Union tank for tank, gun for gun, plane for plane.

Senator Gary Hart (D-Colo.) and others have asked how the U.S. can engage successfully in a firepower attrition contest with the Soviet Union. Soviet "allocation of resources to heavy industry and related technology, rather than consumer goods, gives her ample capacity to produce war material. Her population is larger than ours. Her deployed forces are significantly larger in most categories." An alternative theory of conflict, Hart thinks, is much more appropriate to our current situation. This theory embraces the "maneuver" style of warfare, which has historically often permitted the numerically inferior side to win and which has worked dramatically for the relatively small Israeli armed forces [14].

Fallacy of Composition

In avoiding the reductive fallacy, the defense analyst runs the risk of committing the fallacy of composition. It appears in a variety of forms. Here is one. The analyst recognizes that several factors contribute to combat effectiveness and tries to measure each. Then, he mechanistically adds them together for an overall assessment. The rub is that the whole is seldom the sum of its parts in any defense program. Analysts must consider how the parts interact.

For example, the combat effectiveness of U.S. Armed Forces is clearly dependent on the Services' ability to compete for qualified young men and women in the American labor market. The percentage of high school graduates declined to 68 percent in fiscal 1980 from 77 percent in fiscal 1978. But how adverse an effect this continuing decline could have on overall force readiness depends in part on how much more dependent the Armed Forces becomes on high-technology equipment.

Fallacy of Ethnocentrism

Closely related to the fallacy of composition is reasoning improperly from a property of one's own group to a property of other groups. Thus, it is committed by the defense analyst who exaggerates the role of his own culture and outlook in its interaction with other armed forces. According to Chaim Herzog, a major error of the Israeli general staff before the Yom Kippur War in 1973 was its assumption that the Egyptians would not cross the Suez Canal until they enjoyed air superiority in the Sinai, which would not be achieved until 1975. In their evaluation of Arab strategy, the Israelis failed to appreciate that the Egyptians would decide on a limited military solution to their problem based on the cover of a missile umbrella. Major General Herzog writes: "The mistake of the Israeli General Staff was to judge the Arab General Staff by its own standards of military thinking." [15]

Could American planners be committing the same fallacy with respect to Soviet military? It could be argued that a certain ethnocentrism, indeed a measure of arrogance, echos through the American defense community. They try to impose on Russian minds paradigms developed out of American thinking. These paradigms, rooted ethnocentrically in formal models and mechanical theories of strategic stability, are not derived from any study of Soviet views.

David D. Finley argues that the "conventional Soviet military build-up is best understood as a way to reinforce a tipping of the 'world correlation of forces' further to Soviet advantage, by fostering diplomatic, economic, and psychological gains consistent with Soviet desire to extend national influence." [16] But, because American military planners do not accept—perhaps cannot even see—the non-military functions of conventional military capability, this interpretation of the Soviet build-up is overlooked.

The Fallacy of Misplaced Precision

The distorting effect of statistics collected from operating agencies and their administrators, then used for comparative purposes in evaluating performance, is well known to students of policy analysis. In the military, it has been extensively documented. One general recalls his experience upon assuming command of a brigade in Europe. His superior counseled him he would find he had two regimental commanders—one "good," the other "mediocre." The good one had not had a case of venereal disease in his unit in six months [17].

During the McNamara years, this fallacy was committed at the Pentagon with a vengeance. Surely the apotheosis of these efforts was the infamous "body-count" measure developed during the Vietnam War.

Setting aside the question of how valid a measure of success body count could be in an essentially political war, let us focus only on the issue of accuracy. In armed conflict, estimating the number of casualties and amount of damage is common practice, but in Vietnam "estimated enemy casualties" became an all-encompassing measure of performance. Officially, it was the practice to claim as enemy dead only those bodies that had been physically counted by an American commander. Since this was impossible to implement (who wants to wander through a battlefield counting bodies?), combat units began to develop "estimates." Obviously, there was incentive for lower headquarters to falsify these numbers as they were passed on to higher headquarters. By the time they reached McNamara, they had taken on a reality of their own. (He should have known better: after World War II the U.S. Navy discovered that the amount of Japanese tonnage its commanders had estimated to have sunk was only one-third the actual amount.)

Today the most conspicuous example of misplaced precision is found in the system the Joint Chiefs of Staff use to evaluate the readiness of U.S. military forces. The basis of this system is the Unit Status and Identity Report (UNITREP), which focuses on the readiness of individual military units. In addition, each Commander in Chief of a unified or specified command assesses and reports the readiness of that command to implement the various operation plans for which he is responsible. According to an Army War College study, inaccurate reporting on UNITREP is rampant. Of those officers surveyed, 70 percent held the opinion that the report did not reflect the true readiness condition of their unit, they had been subjected to unjustified pressure to raise their units' readiness rating.

The Fallacy of Static and Absolute Power

Military programs must always be evaluated in relative and dynamic terms. The previously cited CBS presentation is a prime example of how this principle is ignored. In five hours given to examining the plans for a U.S. military build-up, there was no mention of the Soviet build-up which helped precipitate it.

In 1981, a study with a different ideological slant appeared, making the same mistake in reverse. The Department of Defense released a 99-page multicolored booklet, *Soviet Military Power*, that documented the expansion, modernization, and contribution to projection of power of the Soviet military machine. But the report contained virtually nothing on American forces and technology.

Like public opinion polls, comparisons of two armed forces might only provide a snap-shot in time. Clearly, a meaningful comparison must be dynamic, that is, offer some extrapolation of how relative strengths will vary over time.

Static measures compare only the physical characteristic of individual systems; they say little about the interaction between forces in conflict or the capability of forces to accomplish national objectives if employed. Dynamic analyses, which apply the two opposing arsenals against each other and against the opposing overall target systems, provide some insight into these concerns.

One type of dynamic analysis measures the effectiveness of opposing forces by an index called discretionary force potential (DFP). DFP indicates the extent to which an arsenal achieves—or exceeds—its targeting goals against the opposing target system. Figure 2 displays, for 1970 through 1989, the computed outcomes of one strategic force exchange between the U.S. and the USSR. In this scenario, the Soviet Union preemptively attacks the entire U.S. target system, and the U.S. retaliates in kind after riding out the Soviet attack. All strategic systems are assumed to be in a high state of readiness (bomber disperse, SSBNs on station, ICBMs at maximum alert).

The Fallacy of Microevaluation

The U.S. defense budget contains over 5,000 line items. There are over 1,500 different programs. Rigorously applying the criterion of economic efficiency to each item and program can distract civilian defense managers and senior officers from serious considerations of strategy and operational innovation. This phenomenon of making all the numbers look good on paper, while ignoring larger strategic issues, I call the microevaluation [18].

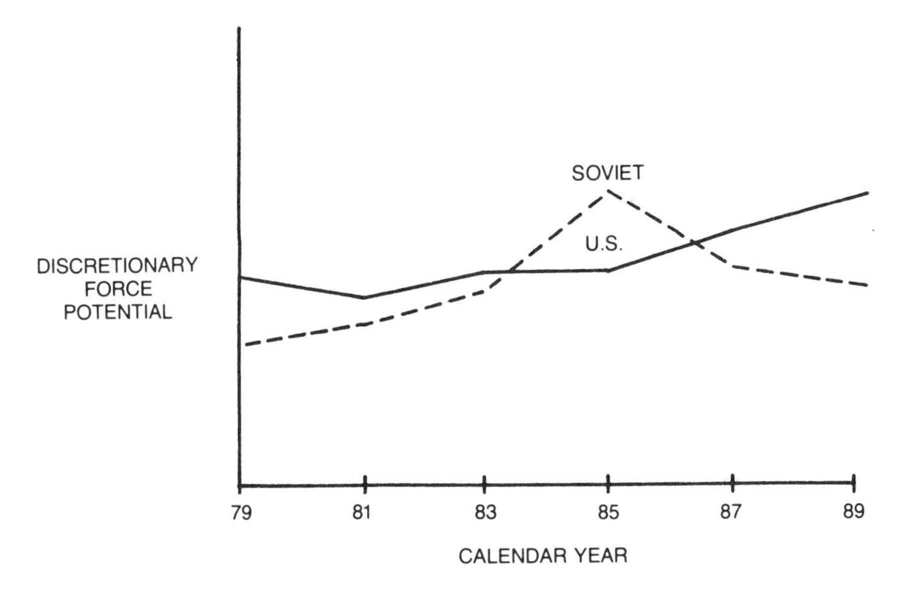

Figure 2 Dynamic measures of force effectiveness following counterforce exchange. (From the United States Military Posture for FY 1982, p. 28.)

One can save 10 percent in building fortifications, make sure that the most cost-effective guns are selected for the forts of the line, and thereby building another Maginot Line. To avoid such follies, decision makers need *first* to think through such strategic questions as whether a defensive orientation for any army is compatible with an unprotected northern flank and what Panzer divisions could do to the defensive network if they found a gap to penetrate in depth?

To see why good accounting practices often detract from such strategic considerations, one need only glance at the budget process in DOD. The mass of details swirling around the budget cycle monopolizes a great deal of the time of senior Pentagon officials to say the very least.

To prepare the budget, each service and defense agency must present its requests for scrutiny by a variety of internal bodies. After the budget is presented to Congress in January, Pentagon officials must justify each item in elaborate presentations to members of both houses and in even greater detail to Congressional staff. In short, the pressure to pursue efficiency and minimize "waste, fraud, and mismanagement" is quite powerful.

Unfortunately, defense issues can only be truly understood in a broad strategic context. But to avoid microevaluation may require neglect of lesser details. The politics of the Congressional budget process–with its emphasis on arguing points in minute details–make this difficult. Microevaluation may give the verisimilitude of business efficiency, but it does not necessarily lead to greater military efficiency—as the following three examples illustrate.

- Efficiency dictates that each individual serve where his skills are most productive. But this leads to constantly shuffling soldiers from over-strengthened units to under-strengthened ones; comradeship and small-group solidarity suffers.
- Efficiency dictates that contracts for weapons go to the company that can produce weapons at lowest cost. But if the nation is at war and needs the equipment in large amounts, decision makers may find themselves possibly wishing they had a less efficient firm to preserve a broad industrial base.
- Efficiency dictates standardization to avoid "wasteful duplication." But the pursuit of standardization makes American combat forces more vulnerable to Soviet countermeasures.

In sum, it is a fallacy to think that the criterion of business efficiency can always be applied to defense issues.

TOWARDS A SELF-EVALUATING MILITARY

In an influential article that appeared in 1972, Aaron Wildavsky wrote:

> *The ideal organization would be self-evaluating. It would continuously monitor its own activities so as to determine how well it was meeting its objectives or even whether these objectives should continue to prevail. When evaluation suggested that a change in objectives or programs to achieve them was desirable, these proposals would be taken seriously by top decision-makers who would institute the necessary changes without vested interest in continuing current activities. Instead they would steadily pursue new alternatives to better serve desired outcomes. [19]*

Given the eight fallacies outlined above, Wildavsky's concept of a self-evaluating organization might seem like too high an ideal to which the American military might repair. The problems are real enough. Freeman Dyson learned during his experience with the Operational Research Section that the official mythology of the gallant gunner defending his crewmates and the massive bureaucratic inertia of the Bomber Command prevented the removal of the gun turrets. Without these turrets the bombers would have flown faster and maneuvered better, but the turrets remained, and the gunners continued to die uselessly until the end of World

War II [20]. The planners of the Vietnam War maintained their mystical faith in strategic bombing–despite the finding by the U.S. Strategic Bombing Survey that allied bombing had little effect on German industrial production during World War II. They also refused to learn from the British successes in counterguerrilla warfare in Malaya. Examples like these are limitless.

But there is nothing inherent in a military organization that precludes self-evaluation. Significantly, the most incisive criticism of the Israeli Army during the Yom Kippur War comes from Israeli generals such as Herzog (quoted earlier). Dan Horowitz has pointed out how the Israeli command, control, and communications system provides the capacity for "on the spot" utilization of feedback on the battlefield [21]. And, in his history of German military leaders, T. N. Dupuy reveals the extraordinary effort German generals devoted to finding ways of getting realistic, accurate, first-hand information [22]. German field commanders were also instructed to be willing to experiment and not to stick to rules in old order books. As Liddell Hart himself wrote, the blitzkreig or lightning war was "one of the world's most striking examples of the decisive effect of a new idea carried out by a dynamic executant." [23]

Nor is there anything with the American military organization that precludes self-evaluation. In the first place, as numerous investigations have shown, the Defense Department and the armed forces are subject to much tighter auditing than any other department. Altogether DOD employs 18,000 people to perform audits and investigations [24]. As indicated earlier, auditing is not evaluation; but these data do seem to suggest that DOD has institutional capacity for self-examination.

By way of conclusion, I shall make two tentative recommendations on how the U.S. military might move–and, in some instances, is moving–a little closer to the ideal of a self-evaluating organization.

Primacy of the Empirical

As every student of evaluation knows, causal inferences should not rest on intuition or theoretical projections; they must be grounded on empirical data that systematically link the program variables to desired outcomes. Similarly, as every sergeant major knows, if you want to know how a unit or weapon will perform, put it in the field and find out.

Pentagon planners and politicians do not always subscribe to such ideas. Since 1960, there were some 20 incidents in which surface ships were hit by missiles. In nearly every case, the damage was considerable. Yet, during the same period, there was a tendency to reduce armor protection. And today several members of Congress are calling for a "streamlined" Navy with smaller carriers, like the two Britain sent to the Falklands, in place of more large-deck carriers. In light of experience, it would seem unlikely that small carriers could survive attacks by Soviet cruise missiles or Backfire bombers.

How then would Nimitz-class-carriers fare against a determined Soviet attack? While experience cannot answer that question directly, it points us in the direction of an answer. In 1969, for instance, an explosion wrecked the flight deck of the *U.S.S. Enterprise*. Although the explosion had the force of six Soviet anti-ship missiles, the carrier was able to resume flights in a few hours. Four years later during the Yom Kippur War, Israel demonstrated that the cruise missile could be stopped with a combination of electronic warfare, gunfire, and evasive maneuvers. In war, nothing is certain. But given past experience and the number of cruise missiles that the Soviet Union could send against American carriers (and their six concentric rings of defenses), the exchange rate of Soviet naval power for American naval power would not appear to be worth it.

In 1978, the GAO surveyed the practices and procedures for operational evaluation of weapon systems by the military services. It found some operational tests, which should have been performed before a production decision, but had been deferred by the Army and Air Force until after the production decision was made. This occurred on the AN/TPO-37 Radar, the Tactical Fire Direction System, and an air defense system. For example, the Army suspected, on the air defense system, that the total system, including its associated radars, had little ability to withstand electronic countermeasures. Yet, it did not test against this threat. Instead, the Army approved a low-rate of production without testing the entire system, including the radars, to electronic countermeasures. The system has since undergone two phases of a follow-on operational test and evaluation and has been approved for full-scale production. The system has been scheduled for deployment, yet it has not successfully demonstrated the ability to perform its mission in an electronic countermeasures environment [25].

Military exercises (as opposed to annual reviews like UNITREP) can provide good evaluations of plans, systems, and procedures. Exercises allow assessment of force readiness in a real world environment.

In 1977, the U.S. Air Force conducted the biggest fighter aircraft performance test in peacetime history. On one side were the newest fighter aircraft in the Air Force and Navy; on the other, American pilots trained in Soviet air-combat doctrine flying planes that looked and performed as Russian MIG-21s. The year-long, 70 million dollar test produced a wealth of knowledge about what actually happens in aerial combat. The details of hundreds of dogfights were preserved by computer for future study.

The largest test of U.S. war alert capabilities in recent years was NIFTY NUGGET in 1978. The operation, which assumed a sudden conventional attack on NATO forces in Europe had taken place, was designed to evaluate the American logistics system. The results were disappointing but did lead to the creation of several senior level task forces to correct a wide range of problems. In 1980, PROUD SPIRIT verified the correction of some of these and highlighted uncorrected deficiencies.

Recently the U.S. Army has taken steps to make war games more convincing. In January, 1982, it opened its National Training Center in the Mojave Desert near

Barstow, California. Using something called "experimental training," the Army hopes to come closer to simulating war's stress and friction (in the Clausewitz sense) as never before. Weapons on both sides are equipped with lasers. When soldiers or vehicles are struck by a beam, button-sized electronic sensors on them indicate they are "killed." Brigades coming for training are pitted against a special, resident 1,000-man armored force trained to act and look like a Soviet motorized rifle regiment. In short, the Army should get a better assessment of how effective the modern, all-volunteer force is [26]. Judges can score a large number of activities, if they wish: How long does it take a unit to road-march 20 kilometers? Were the vehicles properly spaced while moving? Was an adequate aircraft watch maintained during the march? Was the route properly scouted for enemy ambushes and mines? Was camouflage adequate? And so forth.

The greatest weakness in war games is that these evaluations can be distorted by lower level officers to give senior level officers what they want to see. When promotions and reputations ride on these evaluations, the pressures for distortion mount. These considerations bring us to the second recommendation.

Incentive Structure

The idea of the self-evaluating organization must mean more than a few high-level Pentagon officials trying to force evaluation on 2,000,000 other men and women. The spirit of the self-evaluating organization, Wildavsky suggests, is that the entire organization should be infused, in some meaningful way, with the "evaluative ethic."

The existing incentive structure in the armed forces is not conducive to such an ethic emerging. The primary problem is one common to virtually all military establishments: the very characteristics needed for successful leadership in war—the ability to tolerate uncertainty, spontaneity of thought and action, an open mind, capacity to be innovative, moral (as well as physical) courage—are not always appreciated in peacetime. Since promotion in peacetime is usually quicker for those who easily fit into the military routing and are not overly critical of the status quo, the system is biased against those who might be most likely to share Wildavsky's ethic. American officers are not stupid. The fact that Billy Mitchell's advocacy of air power led to his court martial and resignation in 1926 is not lost on them. Mitchell's ideas were not adopted until World War II—seven years after his death.

Thus, virtually all senior officers today refrain from advocating conscription. Although many firmly believe that high quality volunteer forces are too small and expensive, they know such advocacy is institutionally unacceptable. Similarly, Congress and the White House have in recent years offered few rewards for rethinking operational procedures. Procurement procedures are a prime example.

Procurement horror stories like the purchase of Black Hawk helicopters are not unusual. In the early 1970's, planners projected an average per-unit procurement cost for the Army of $951,000. By the 1980 fiscal year, the price had risen to $2.63 million. In the 1982 budget, with only minor engineering improvements, the helicopters will cost $5.26 million each [27].

There are several reasons for such increases. Ever since passage of the Defense Production Act of 1973, DOD has usually contracted for weapons systems one year at a time. While this allows Congress to maintain tight fiscal control, it has a devastating effect on productivity. Pentagon officials recognize that industry's willingness to make capital investments is enhanced if companies can look forward to sufficient continuing production to get payback. But they also do not want to upset Congress by pressing for a change in the 1973 Act.

(While the Reagan Administration may not have provided a sympathetic ear to conscription, it has initiated reassessments of defense procurement policies. In addition to backing multi-year contracting bills, it has placed renewed emphasis on programs under which the services provide seed money to contractors to develop advanced production methods.)

CONCLUSIONS

The present discussion has highlighted some of the major evaluation issues that have risen in the area of defense policy. Obviously, there are many other important issues that could–perhaps should–have been emphasized. For example, much of the applied research, surveys, and tests undertaken by the Army Research Institute, Army Training and Doctrine Command, and the Office of Naval Research, which might be regarded as evaluation, is ignored. Because of this research ranges from estimating drug use through controlled trials of training regimens, and overlaps to a large degree evaluative studies performed in civilian agencies, it seemed more useful to focus on the larger aspects of defense policy that are truly unique. The issues of procurement, research, and nuclear strategy have been raised only tangentially here. The first two issues are not unique to defense; the third is so vast, so complex, so rapidly changing, so riddled with uncertainties, that it really seemed better explored in a separate paper.

Several concluding–and hopefully not too obvious–observations can be made about the issues we have reviewed here.

First, the eight fallacies of evaluation noted earlier might involve lessons of interest to students of evaluation in other areas of government. Because military nomenclature tends to be relatively clear-cut and military history runs back so far, it is sometimes easier to understand certain features of domestic policy by considering military examples [28]. For instance, these principles of war, *mutatis mutandis*, seem applicable to the formulation and implementation of many public policies: maintenance of the objective, economy of force, security, flexibility, and entropy.)

Second, self-evaluating organizations probably need to be supplemented with institutional arrangements. As students of evaluation in organizational settings like Joseph S. Wholey and others [29] have recognized and our discussions of UNITREP and ROLLING THUNDER have reconfirmed, some valid program evaluations cannot be done by organizations charged with implementing them. The conflict of interest, whether recognized by the monitoring officers or not, is too great. Therefore, in certain areas of the command structure, program evaluation should be accomplished by different individuals and sub-units from those involved in implementation. Perhaps this will require, in turn, the development of a general staff type arrangement [30].

Third, evaluation cannot be considered outside the context of policy analysis. The best cure for the microevaluation noted earlier is a more carefully thought-through defense policy. And this must come from the top down—not vice versa.

The following examples should show why a full-fledged strategic analysis must precede the evaluation of any defense program [31].

- *Evaluating the right mix between complex weapons systems and more conventional forces must be governed by certain strategic considerations. If American forces fought, say, in Korea, it would be the allies who could best provide the numbers. What they would expect from the U.S. is precisely the smaller high-quality force of special capabilities.*
- *Evaluating the right mix of nuclear weapons must likewise be governed less by the cost-effectiveness of each system than by how well it fits into the big picture. Performance parameters of a new strategic bomber are important, but never more important is the effect it will have on Soviet behavior. (Will it require them to cut back on global naval developments in order to expand defensive systems?) Performance parameters and marginal cost savings of new ICBMs are important, but even more important is how they "match" Soviet strengths and weaknesses.*

Fourth, and finally, it is impossible to overstate the importance of good evaluation in the area of defense. Its importance transcends the gross budgetary figures cited at the start and even goes beyond the projected growth rates over the next several years. To really appreciate the importance of good evaluation—which presumably measures combat effectiveness—one must consider the costs of war. One month of heavy combat in Europe would cost the U.S. a quarter of its 1982 defense budget. If operations were carried out under total mobilization, the cost could be over $1100 billion a year [32]. That is nearly six times the 1982 defense budget. That great loss of human life would occur goes without saying.

The point is this: If evaluation can help assure that a nation has adequate forces, then the chances of that nation using them and spending even greater sums may be reduced.

REFERENCES

1. Brown, H. *Managing the Defense Department–Why It Can't Be Done*. William K. McInally Memorial Lecture delivered at University of Michigan, 25 March 1981.
2. The General Accounting Office, according to Brown (Ibid), "offers many suggestions every year–some practical and some not, some useful and some not, some adopted and some not. Unfortunately the correlation among sense, practicality, and adoption is imperfect."
3. Sarkesian, S. C. *Combat Effectiveness*. Sage, Beverly Hills, 1980, p. 11.
4. Harold Brown in U.S. Department of Defense, *Annual Report Fiscal Year* 1980 (Washington, D.C.: G.P.D., 1979), p. 13. provides this answer to the question:

   > *As our defense budgets have risen, the Soviets have increased their defense budget. As our defense budgets have gone down, their defense budgets have increased again. As U.S. forces in Western Europe declined during the latter part of the 60's, Soviet deployments in Eastern Europe expanded.*
   >
   > *As U.S. theater nuclear forces stabilized, Soviet peripheral attack and theater nuclear forces increased. As the U.S. Navy went down in numbers, the Soviet Navy went up. . . .*

5. In an effort to overcome such difficulties, the Department of Defense uses "armored division equivalents" to measure the capabilities of ground forces. The use of this analytical tool for calculating force ratios is not universally accepted. Nevertheless, it is DOD's standard measure of combat potential. See Congressional Budget Office, *Strengthening NATO: POMCUS and other Approaches* (Washington, D.C.: G.P.O., February 1979), pp. 52-53.
6. For a good summary of evaluative research done by DOD in the area of human resources management, Office of Personnel Managements' see *Public Management Research* (Spring 1981).
7. Cf. Hitch, C. J., and McKean, R. N. *The Economics of Defense in the Nuclear Age* Harvard University Press, Cambridge, 1961, pp. 131-33.
8. Achievement testing is routine but randomized tests are not. See, for example, the Department of Education's Holtzman Report (1981).
9. Hart, L. Strategy of a War, *Encounter* (February 1968), p. 17.
10. See Broad, W. J. Nuclear Pulse: Awakening to the Chaos Factor, *Science* (29 May 1981), pp. 1009-12.
11. See Merritt, J. N., and Sprey, P. M., "Negative Marginal Returns in Weapons Acquisition" in Richard G. Head and Ervin J. Rokke's *American Defense Policy* John Hopkins University Press, Baltimore, 1973, p. 486-95.

12. Caspar W. Weinberger's written statement submitted to House Committee on Armed Forces. Reprinted in U.S. Congress, House of Representatives, *Hearings of Military Posture and H.R. 2614 and HR 2970* (Washington, D.C.: GPO, 1981), p. 1000.
13. For a good discussion of the French generals' mystical faith in the *offensive a l'outrance* (that is, the headlong offensive)—despite the lessons not only of the U.S. Civil War but also the Russo-Japanese War—see Montrose, L. *War Through the Ages* (1960).
14. Hart, G., Statement on FY81 Defense Authorization, released on 1 July 1980, pp. 2-3.
15. Herzog, C. *The War of Atonement* Little Brown, Boston, 1975, p. 276.
16. Finley, D. D. Conventional Arms in Soviet Policy. *World Politics*, XXX111 (October 1980), p. 23.
17. Story told by Lewis Sorley. Prevailing Criteria; A Critique. In Sam C. Sarkesian, *Combat Effectiveness*, Sage, Beverly Hills, 1980, p. 69.
18. The term microevaluation is mine, but the discussion which follows draws heavily on Edward N. Luttwak, Why We Need More 'Waste, Fraud, Mismanagement' in the Pentagon, *Commentary* (February 1982).
19. Wildavsky, A. The Self-evaluating Organization. *Public Administration Review* (September-October 1972), pp. 00.
20. Dyson, F. *Disturbing the Universe*. Harper & Row, New York, 1979, pp. 21-30.
21. Horowitz, D. Flexible Responsiveness and Military Strategy: The Case of the Israeli Army. *Policy Sciences* 1 (1970), p. 191.
22. Dupuy, T. N. *A Genius for War: The German Army, and General Staff. 1807-1945*. Prentice-Hall, Englewood Cliffs, N.J., 1977.
23. Hart, L. *The Strategy of Indirect Approach*. Faber and Faber, London, 1946.
24. See U.S. General Accounting Office, *Who Is Watching the Defense Dollars*? AFMD-82-26 (5 February 1982).
25. Letter to Harold J. Brown from J. H. Stolarow, Director, Procurement and Systems Acquisition Division, G.A.O. (19 October 1978).
26. *Wall Street Journal* (4 November 1981), p. 25.
27. Miller, W. H. Pentagon Sows Seeds of Defense Productivity. *Industry Week* (13 July 1981), pp. 48-53. See also Pierce, A. C. Issues Facing the New Administration. *AEI Foreign Policy and Defense Review*, v. 3, nos. 4 and 5 (1981), pp. 47-70.
28. For an illustration of this point, see Starling, G. *Politics and Economics of Public Policy*. Dorsey Press, Homewood, Il., 1979, pp. 170-76.
29. Wholey, J. S., et al. *Federal Evaluation Policy*. Urban Institute, Washington, D.C., 1973, pp. 69-70.
30. A general staff is a group of officers, rigorously trained, that assists a commander by performing detailed duties of planning, administration, supply, intelligence, and coordination. "While this institution is peculiar to Prussia,

it does possess that American political quality of checking and balancing while enjoining a moral constraint upon chief of staff to restrain any tendencies to irrationality by commanding general". (Gabriel and Savage, op. cit., p. 120) Another organizational devise worth considering is the form of an Inspector General divorced from command control.

31. These examples suggested by Luttwak, op. cit., pp. 20, 24, and 29.
32. Estimates from Dunnigan, J. F. *How to Make War: A Comprehensive Guide to Modern Warfare*. Morrow, New York, 1982, pp. 357-58.

19
The Evaluation of Social Action Programs Involving Minorities

David Lopez-Lee / *School of Public Administration, University of Southern California, Los Angeles, California*

INTRODUCTION

In the last several decades, two interrelated observations may be made with respect to social action programs. First, social action programs (particularly those in education, human resource development, crime and delinquency, and health), are *usually legislatively intended to serve those most in need* [1]. Second, *such targeted populations are overrepresented by minorities and women*. Since there is much current public debate on the usefulness of such social action programs, it is important that various threats to the validity of procedures used to evaluate such efforts be clearly identified. Boruch, Rindskopf, Anderson, Amidjaya, and Jansson, make a similar point, but conclude that the state of the art is " . . . not sufficiently well-developed to predict them [these threats] accurately and to accommodate them." [2] While one may not be able to strictly quantify some of the threats to the validity of nonrandomized design efforts, a range of research design controls is feasible. Further, these may be buttressed with empirical findings from the broader over-arching social science research literature.

This chapter is believed to be a useful aggregation of evaluation issues of particular importance to those in the public policy arena who are, or will become, engaged in social action programs which have within their targeted populations sizable numbers of minorities and women [3]. It should also be instructive for those social science researchers who have little familiarity with the needs of those in the public policy arena. The following topics will serve as the basis from which the various issues will surface.

1. Nonrandomization
2. The heterogeneity problem

3. Covariate adjustments, reliability, and validity
4. False positives and false negatives
5. Classical experimental designs
6. Funding: the program versus the targeted population

NONRANDOMIZATION

Campbell states that:

> *The political stance furthering social experimentation . . . is the recognition of randomization as the most democratic and moral means of allocating scarce resources (and scarce hazardous duties), plus the moral imperative to further utilize . . . randomization so that society may indeed learn [the] true value of the supposed boon. This is the ideology that makes possible true experiments in a large class of social reforms. [4]*

It must be emphasized that the foregoing opportunity for randomization occurs primarily in those instances wherein the number of "needy" persons is known and is larger than the number of openings. This was true, for example, of the Job Training Corps, and is the case during the early demonstration phases of most programs. In those remaining instances wherein the number of such persons is typically equal to (or less than) the number of openings, appropriate control groups cannot be randomly created from the same pool from which the experimental group(s) are created because the only remaining potential controls are not as much in need. Indeed, such controls are on the average "superior" (in terms of experience, aptitude, and so on) to their experimental counterparts. This is not a minor problem, since the opportunity for a randomized evaluation design is not always taken during a program's demonstration phase. Moreover, even if one took every randomized evaluation opportunity during a program's demonstration phase, there are any one of at least three contextual dynamics which might add to the extensiveness of the problem:

1. The cultural groups comprising the "needy" category being serviced by a program may substantively change. For example, some smoothly running programs designed largely for "needy" Blacks and/or Hispanics are having considerable difficulties in assisting "needy" Vietnamese and Cambodians.
2. During economic bad times, sizable numbers of characteristically different "needy" persons are added to the existing pool of "needy" persons.
3. During times of declining government resources, program resources may

> have to be spread more thinly to help the same number of people, possibly more people. Or, those who fit the "needy" category may be redefined thereby shrinking the pool of people who are served by a program. [5]

All of these contextual dynamics change a program's targeted population considerably; so much so, that the evaluative data associated with a program's early demonstration phase may not be very useful. Under these conditions, "new" evaluation efforts are called for within a program setting not conducive to a randomized design.

When randomization is not possible, one may not readily employ analysis of variance (ANOVA) techniques without an unusual qualifying and/or delimiting contextual interpretation. There are other techniques that are frequently used to deal with such a situation. Those commonly suggested in the literature include: matching (blocking), analysis of covariance (ANCOVA), standardization, and multiple regression. It should be noted that the first two of these techniques were developed primarily for use in randomized settings as well. Also, when dealing with model misspecification and/or measurement errors in a nonrandomized setting, employing any one of these techniques may still produce large biases. For example, all of the techniques thus far mentioned, are susceptible to regression effects. Such effects are more likely under nonrandomized conditions and can lead to the conclusion that program effects are small even when actual effects are large, or to a conclusion that a program is harmful when actual program effects are negligible because scores between treatment and comparison groups are regressing toward different means [6].

There are some other less commonly used techniques or approaches which one might consider in evaluating social action programs: the "Dry-run Experimentation" or multiple pretesting approach, the adjusted covariance analysis technique, and the use of regression in a simultaneous equation system.

In the *multiple pretesting approach* one obtains data (T_0) from the treatment and control group members prior to the usual pretest (T_1) to posttest (T_2) format. Boruch and Rindskopf suggest collecting data over at least two time points prior to T_1 if possible [7]. By so doing one may analyze these double pretest data employing the same statistical technique to be applied on the main evaluation (T_1-T_2), and thereby assess the extent of bias in the latter. This approach, however, is weaker than a long time series approach. To quote Boruch and Rindskopf: "It is a kind of weak time series though it does not deserve the dignity of the phrase." [8]

Campbell and Erlebacher [9] have suggested using Lord's [10] and Porter's [11] *adjusted covariance analyses* when pretests are similar to posttests, and where homogeneity and other assumptions have been met [12]. It should be noted that Lord's technique is restricted to a single covariate setting (not unusual), and that it yields results similar to Porter's method for estimating true covariates for any number of groups.

Referring to the regression approach used by econometricians as the *structural equation models approach*, Boruch and Rindskopf [13] characterized it as the most powerful (and correspondingly technically demanding) one yet devised to analyze nonexperimental designs. Nonetheless, they noted that no approach existent, guarantees unbiased estimates of program effect. This is apparently no longer true. Due to recent ingenious econometric developments [14] we have *regression analysis within a simultaneous equation system* which seemingly does give an unbiased estimate. The econometricians argue: (a) that this simultaneous equation system includes regression adjustments which control for the important variables, and (b) that these important variables are sufficiently correlated with variables which have been excluded, thereby trivializing any differences that further adjustments might make. Yet there are some problems or difficulties with this approach including:

- The potential for misspecification of the original model (i.e., nonlinear terms may be proxying for omitted variables or nonlinearities)
- The choice of several estimation procedures which are available
- An assumption of bivariate normality for the error terms
- The potential for a high degree of collinearity in the second-step regressions

This approach is also particularly sensitive to minor violations of functional form and distributional shape. This is not the case for analysis of variance (ANOVA) and analysis of covariance (ANCOVA) procedures—they are both very robust. In addition, multi-variable designs pose few problems for ANOVA, while posing serious problems of multicollinearity for such regression approaches. ANCOVA, which includes adjustments by way of regression, is somewhere in between. Perhaps the most serious problem with regression approaches is that of model specification, i.e., the relatively precise specification, usually stemming from the empirical literature, of a manageable mathematical model and its associated measures of uncertainty which allow one to predict outcomes stemming from attributes of a program [15]. Such model specification in program evaluation efforts is often concerned with assessing how people got into (or did not get into) a program, i.e., self-selection. In nonrandomized efforts, model misspecification, by definition, is always, to whatever minor extent, present—and as previously noted, econometricians trivialize the "corrective" effect any minor adjustments might make. The trouble with this approach is that one is always at risk in having overlooked important variables. Unless one adequately addresses the three contextual dynamics previously described, the potential for misspecification could be considerable [16]. Because of the foregoing, problems associated with the simultaneous equation system, not to mention the unusual time and technical demands, ANOVA (often employed to assess matching designs) and ANCOVA approaches are "pragmatically" equal to the task in program evaluation. One must, of course, be fully apprised of those aspects of the social action program which may mitigate or enhance the bias of such analyses [17]. Whatever approach used, "guesstimates" about the magnitude of bias might be taken from the social science literature and be brought to bear on the results. Statistical technique is only one of many tools available to the decision maker; common sense should always supplement whatever tool is used.

THE HETEROGENEITY PROBLEM

Even if one goes to great lengths to assure for similarities between treatment and comparison groups, there is the potential problem of excessive group heterogeneity within one or more of the subsets comprising minority groups with regard to the dependent measure(s) taken. For example, suppose we have a sampling of self-selected (by whatever device) of Anglos, Blacks, and Chicanos participating in a social action program. A competent program evaluator would no doubt recognize that these groups will vary in income and educational levels. To account for such variations, evaluation specialists often build such variable disparities into their experimental design(s). However, evaluators often are not cognizant of the need to provide similar controls for other variables which may be directly or indirectly affected by the social action program in question. What type of variables are these? Consider the following: Minorities by contrast to the majority have historically had more emotionally trying experiences within our society's institutions—our schools for example [18]. Minorities then will tend to differ from the majority in such emotion relevant areas as anxiety, stress, alienation, self-esteem, need achievement, need affiliation, need power, and so on [19]. More broadly speaking, *minorities will typically be different from, and, depending upon their within group acculturation differences, will be more heterogeneous than the majority along dimensions specifically addressed or implied by social action programs.*

Thus, if one is providing a social action program whose outcomes are expected to be cognitive or skill oriented, one should carefully and comprehensively scrutinize the targeted population with respect to the affective variables described above. For example, if one is involved in a college program for improving test taking behaviors of minorities by contrast to the majority, an evaluator would be well served by attempting to control for anxiety by either equalizing (matching) both groups' anxiety levels or by using analysis of covariance (ANCOVA) to make their anxiety levels more comparable. Otherwise, a very likely result would be a biased estimate of the program's effect. (ANCOVA, which gives rise to other problems, is discussed in the next section.)

It is not clear how much bias is introduced when such "corrective" efforts (e.g., covariate adjustments by way of ANCOVA) are overlooked. Nonetheless, the potential for bias may be considerable. Consider the following. Anxiety level has been consistently related to measures of academic performance throughout the elementary, secondary, and college years [20]. Differences in anxiety level have been noted between ethnic minorities and nonminorities [21]. For example,

Hernandez found Chicanas (Mexican-American women) more anxious (statistically significant) than Anglo-American women in terms of *state anxiety* (situationally affected); parallel differences in terms of *trait anxiety* (stable) were found, but were not statistically significant [22]. What is interesting about Hernandez's finding is that she controlled for both acculturation and socioeconomic status—both of these measures are not only frequently used as indicators of successful "mainstreaming" within this society, but are also (it may be reasonably argued) useful as modest indicators of (certainly correlates of) anxiety. The evaluator should note, with perhaps some relief, that some of these variables, e.g., anxiety and need achievement, are positively correlated. By simply being prudent with regard to this heterogeneity issue, the evaluator may successfully address a large number of potentially problematic variables by considering a minimal number of such variables (e.g., two or three).

The above described minority/majority group differences will also correspond, essentially by definition, with differences in regression lines and associated error variances in prediction equations. That is to say, there is not only the potential for biased estimates of program effect, but also for poor predictions of performance on the basis of screening and selection tests (in personnel decisions, parole decisions, clinical prognoses, academic access decisions, and so on). How these are particularly addressed by covariance approaches are described next, along with the attendant problems of reliability and validity.

COVARIATE ADJUSTMENTS, RELIABILITY, AND VALIDITY

Consistent with what was previously implied, Winer makes the point that "At best, covariance adjustments for large initial biases on the covariate are poor substitutes for direct control." [23] For an excellent summary of cautions in the use of ANCOVA outside the experimental study setting, i.e., in program evaluation, one should refer to Di Costanzo and Eichelberger [24] and Proper and St. Pierre [25].

Consider now the example of the preceding section which addressed improving the test taking behaviors of minorities by way of a training program. A dependent variable (variate) in such a program most likely would be test scores. The covariate might be anxiety level (as measured by an instrument). Further, we could employ the same minority vs. majority group design. However, a better design would be to have both the treatment and comparison groups from the same ethnic groups, e.g., Chicano (or Black) students who meet "normal" college admission requirements versus those who do not. Since it is not unreasonable to assume that the former group has been more successful in "mainstreaming" within this society, it is reasonable to anticipate a higher degree of anxiety for the latter group. By way of ANCOVA, the contribution of anxiety to a difference between each group's test scores is eliminated, at least to the extent that the variate and covariate are correlated. This is a better design because it attempts to statistically equate groups experientially. Also, and consistent with Winer's point, it is a better design because initial biases in the covariate are more likely to be smaller than would be true for a cross-ethnic design.

Winer [26] cautions us, however, that "when the covariate is actually affected by the treatment, the adjustment process removes more than what can be considered an error component from the variate [the dependent variable]. It also may remove part of the treatment effect on Y [the variate]." To guard against this, he states that "if the measurements on the covariate are made before the treatments are administered, the covariate cannot be affected by the treatments." [27] Effecting the implied pretest is easier said than done. How to translate "before the treatments are administered" is no small operational task. For example, in a study contrasting *laboratory training stress* with *college examination stress*, Lubin and Lubin [28] reported obtaining covariate measures of stress (anxiety, depression, and hostility) just prior to the opening of laboratory training sessions and on a nonexamination day. This study is perhaps a good example wherein the one treatment (laboratory training) probably affected the covariate, whereas the other treatment (a college examination) did not. The moment subjects approached either treatment setting, their levels of stress were differentially affected. It is clearly more reasonable to expect "anticipatory responses" to affect stress tests (the covariate) which are given just before a laboratory session than it is to expect such a consequence from a nonexamination day (the latter condition not being immediately before the administration of an examination). Adjustments on a variate by the former type of affected covariate would remove more than just error from the variate. It would give misleading results. Therefore, the Lubin and Lubin Study is confounded. They incorrectly concluded that stress is lower for a laboratory training situation as opposed to a college exam setting. More importantly, what the researcher should be cautious of, in a setting such as that of the Lubin's, is an even more heightened differential between minorities and the majority in affective areas. It is reasonable to expect, for example, that anxiety begins earlier, and increases at a faster rate, for minorities as "treatment time" approaches. And further, that such increases occur at an even faster rate for less acculturated minorities (i.e., those having less success "mainstreaming"). The parallel implications of such heightened differentials in affective areas as between men and women is rather direct. The error then, about which Winer warns us, is potentially greater in affect-laden settings when minorities and/or women are involved.

As indicated in the previous section on heterogeneity, minority/majority group differences (particularly in affective areas) give rise to the potential for biased estimates of program effects and differential predictions of performance between such groups based on screening and selection tests. Campbell and Boruch note (in the following passages) this potential for biased estimates of program effects as well as the associated reliability differences corresponding with such minority/majority group differences:

> *It is a common experience in research on compensatory education that the disadvantaged group (usually the experimental group) has lower reliabilities than the advantaged group on both pretest and posttest. [29]*
> *. . . in a nonrandomized study, where the disadvantaged group receives the treatment, the lower reliability of the disadvantaged group has the effect of making the treatment look harmful. [30]*

Similarly, in the area of differential validity with respect to personnel decisions, Bobko and Bartlett conclude:

> *It is clear. . . , that differential prediction is found often enough to create concern for possible unfairness when a common regression line is used for selection. [31]*

Arriving at much the same conclusion with regard to differential validity, Katzell and Dyer express their concerns for measurement validity. They note that any rigorous effort to address the null hypothesis implicit in the question of differential validity, requires (among other things) that each sample or group " . . . be tested with a test shown previously to be significantly correlated with a relevant and unbiased criterion of performance on the job in question." [32]

While Campbell and Boruch have already provided a rather lengthy discourse on ways to correct for measurement reliability variations by either covariance or regression adjustments [33], questions of measurement validity (in either the predicted or predictor variables) have not been adequately addressed in the evaluation literature in instances involving minorities or women. For example, Rossi and Lyall observed that in the New Jersey-Pennsylvania Negative Income Tax Experiment, there were racial differences in average income reported—spurious positive wage rate effects were initially larger for Blacks and Puerto Ricans than for Whites. The reporting error was so strong that it was decided to drop earnings response from many of the final analyses [34]. Littlefield reports that women generally tend to *disclose* more to counselors and therapists than men [35]. Similarly, Schwartz and McDonald, in the evaluation of federally funded family-planning programs, noted that despite all efforts to minimize the "demand characteristics" of the interviews conducted, " . . . an indeterminate amount of exaggeration, misrepresentation, and sheer lapse of memory persist." [36]. Such problems of measurement validity translate rather directly into differences in reliability, since changes in factorial complexity imply changes in either test-retest or internal consistency measures of reliability.

To address these validity and reliability problems within nonrandomized settings, it would appear that one would be well served if the groups involved were made very similar with respect to those characteristics being addressed, in the sense described by Sherwood, Morris, and Sherwood [37]. Two other general approaches are recommended. The first approach is implied in an observation made by Campbell and Boruch–they make the point that test publishers usually do not publish group specific measures of internal consistency or test-retest reliability [38]. It would seem that in the short run, evaluators should assess such data sets for each program they evaluate. In the long run, they should consider aggregating and sharing such data sets as a professional body. The second approach involves an insistence that the criterion used to assess validity be the actual behavior itself and not any self-report nor any approximation. A brief review of a study by Gael and Grant makes clear the need for such an insistence [37]. In their study, employment test bias was examined by comparing regression line slopes and intercepts between minority and nonminority telephone company service representatives. They found no significant differences and concluded that their composite predictor was unbiased. Their composite predictor consisted of a general learning ability test, five clerical aptitude tests, and a specially developed role play interview. Performance criteria consisted of a Job Knowledge Review test (70 completion and 40 multiple choice items) and an individually administered work sample test (the Job Performance Review), composed of typical calls in which service representatives engage plus associated clerical work. *Actual on-the-job performance was not a criterion in this study*. It is conceivable that the individual administration of the work sample test may have raised the anxiety and stress of the minority group (for reasons earlier described) to such an extent as to obviate any real differences.

FALSE POSITIVES AND FALSE NEGATIVES

It is generally known by now that one should not make value, attitudinal or behavioral contrasts between people from different cultures, without taking economic dimensions into account, because any differences found may be just as reasonably ascribed to economic as well as cultural dimensions. To deal with such potential confounding, research methodologists will make cross-cultural comparisons, but only for those of similar socioeconomic backgrounds (e.g., contrast the lower economic class of one culture with the lower economic class of another).

In a similar vein, if we wanted to make value, attitudinal or behavioral contrasts between males and females, we may not only want to be sure that they are of the same socioeconomic level, but in addition, of the same cultural background. We would then be controlling for both socioeconomic level and culture. In the initial culture contrast example provided, one could similarly control for two variables–sex and socioeconomic level–depending on our objectives.

Unfortunately, when one compares cultures along some attitudinal or value dimension and controls for, say, socioeconomic level (e.g., compare the middle class of two cultures), the analyzed data all too frequently will still give rise to specious inferences, particularly if we are only looking at one socioeconomic level. This point was previously made in an article dealing with the incidence and treatment of alcoholism among third world women [40]. Provided as an example was the relatively minor, but substantive difference in alcoholism levels between middle-class Hispanics and middle-class Whites. Such a minor difference seemed very easily attributable to cultural variations and, only as an afterthought, to some minor level of societal discrimination. One might conceivably conclude that Hispanics and Whites of the same socioeconomic class are actually somewhat similar in alcoholism patterns; and as a result, erroneously provide similar psychotherapy. The fact that minority ethnics are grossly overrepresented in the lower socioeconomic ranks (some of which likely would be middle class were it not for the discriminatory treatment of the dominant society) probably will be missed, and the therapy inferred and applied, ineffective. To fully address this sort of problem, and of course similar difficulties, a two-fold approach is appropriate: (1) control for socioeconomic level, and (2) provide an aggregate picture of both cultures without regard to socioeconomic level. By so doing, one is then in a position to not only *assess cultural differences within one socioeconomic level, but also within the context of the total cultural picture*. In sum, it is important that both approaches be employed since what goes on at one socioeconomic level is very probably related to what is occurring at another level (at least for minorities). Such joint analyses should minimize errors with regard to causal inferences made.

The need for the foregoing types of analyses may be more widely understood in terms of the "false positives/false negatives" notion implicit in selection strategies. Those cut-off points selected for predicted success in whatever context, through levels within school, college, or careers, typically do not acknowledge the earlier described minority/majority group differences in regression line slopes and intercepts which favor the majority [41]. Not acknowledging such differences has the consequence of producing fewer "false positives" (those passed or selected when they should not have been) among minorities than for the majority population, and more "false negatives" (those failed or not selected when they should have been) among minorities than for the majority population. This is what one would expect to find with tests designed specifically for one ethnic group, i.e., they tend to result in an equal number of "false positives and negatives" for the majority, but not so for the various minorities. This 'lopsidedness" in outcomes has been observed in the "formula" allocation laws–monies from programs designed largely to help poor areas have instead gone to rich areas.

CLASSICAL EXPERIMENTAL DESIGNS

It must be remembered that the elegant experimental design models, of which we generally speak in the evaluation literature, were derived from highly controlled settings, i.e., laboratory studies on animals and vegetation whose life support systems were highly controlled. It is not surprising then, that as late as 1972, Rossi observed that, with respect to social action programs, "there are almost no examples of evaluation studies . . . which have followed these models with any degree of fidelity." [42] Since that time, many more randomized programs have been successfully evaluated [43]. However, effecting randomized program efforts remains a difficult task. There are at least three reasons for this. First, there is of course the nonrandom nature of the participant selection process discussed earlier. Second, as both Apsler [44] and Guttentag [45] point out, often the *evaluation of one program is tantamount to evaluating several programs under one administrative umbrella* (e.g., Headstart and Special Programs for the Disadvantaged). Thus *"good" programs are frequently drowned in a sea of data*. This habit of lumping good and bad programs (some of which also have differing theoretical bases) is, in part, why some evaluators have not felt comfortable using classical approaches. With regard to such heterogeneity, Apsler speaks of "conceptual integrity." When the "conceptual integrity" of an umbrella program is "low" (i.e., when variation between its individual programs is great), it makes no sense to treat the umbrella program as it if embraced a common independent variable. The results may be misleading. Apsler's request for high "conceptual integrity," however, overlooks a basic problem. As Guttentag points out, low "conceptual integrity" is *typical* of social action programs. They differ radically site by site and, of course, over time. Indeed, a *key objective of current social action programs is that they adapt to local conditions. To deal with this obvious diversity*, Guttentag suggests that *inferences should be aggregated*, not data. Because programs change, or are modified, over time, Guttentag contends it is essential that continuous information-gathering and associated feedback to decision-makers be built into evaluation efforts. And third, even if the various programs under one administrative umbrella have high "conceptual integrity," whether the programs are aggregated or looked at separately, *one is not evaluating the effects of one independent variable, but rather a host of variables* (a point not broached by Boruch, et al.). Moreover, in such situations the presence of one or more variables may enhance or inhibit another. And, if one is restrictive in the number or types of measures taken, overall program impact is not fully assessed. Harm may thereby be incurred by the social body, depending on the inferences made. Indeed, some programs emphasize only cognitive measures and neglect affective measures. In evaluating social action programs, it is considered by now a maxim that the greater the number and type of measures taken, the less likely the misinterpretation of program impact [46]. To maximize the likelihood that relevant (rather than all) variables are included, particularly those related to minorities and women, these groups should be included in the early design phases of social action programs. Such inclusion should also help address some of the previously mentioned problems. The types of variables mentioned in the heterogeneity section would be more likely to surface, and one would be better equipped to piece together the type of total cultural picture mentioned in the preceding section.

FUNDING: THE PROGRAM VERSUS THE TARGETED POPULATION

Cautions emphasized in this article with respect to social action programs do not solely pertain to the statistical or methodological aspects of program evaluation. With regard to program continuation/funding, for example, there have been some recent political pronouncements, largely precipitated and fueled by a public constituency, that we must lower our expectations of government. The contention is that the many social action programs, initiated in the 60's, generally have not worked and should be terminated. Basically, this public constituency says they want less government. What they mean is less government for *some* segments of the citizenry. What is often overlooked, however, is the fact that government programs have always addressed *targeted* populations. These are invariably segmented by region, income, age, and so on. Wheat subsidies, for example, serve states of varying wheat productivity levels, fuel subsidies go to persons of low income, and government loans assist students at different levels of income. Thus, we may have before us a given program that looks good in Oregon, but looks bad in Mississippi, not so much because of the program, but because segments of the targeted populations served in those states are so different. We need to distinguish then between *program* (good or bad) on the one hand, and funding of segments of the *targeted population in need*, on the other. With such a distinction, one might then insure that a "targer" segment will not be made to suffer a loss of funding because of an inefficient program. Instead, the government might require the proposal of a substantively different and/or more defensible program. The following example should clarify the need for such a distinction. In 1970, Assembly Bill 938 (a compensatory education effort) was finally implemented in the State of California (the bill was passed in 1966). The intent of the bill was to provide funding for compensatory educational program activities for those most academically in need. Accordingly, the schools initially targeted by this bill were the 16 poorest academically performing schools in the state. Curiously enough, on the basis of first year performance data, the state planned to continue funding the top performing 13 of the 16 initially funded schools. However, it was pointed out by a contingent of people from one of the "to be excluded schools" that, consistent with the intent of the law, the top 13 *programs* should be refunded, but only if implemented in those 13 *schools with the poorest absolute level* of academic performance. This point was translated into a motion which was passed by the California State Board of Education.

Developing policies that fund programs with the foregoing distinction in mind should minimize the likelihood of "apparently better" programs being refunded simply because a segment of the targeted population is "superior" (i.e., less in need) to begin with, or because that segment had a superior proposal writing team. To deal with both of these points, a weighting system is needed. Also, certain proposal writing teams could be recruited to work with specific population/

geographic areas. It should be noted that under the Emergency School Aid Act, Title VII (of the Education Amendments of 1972 and 1974), a proposal evaluation format is used which gives more weight to those areas which suffer more from the ills associated with racial isolation in their school.

CONCLUDING REMARKS

A number of statistical, methodological, and conceptual approaches have been suggested to deal with problems associated with nonrandomized evaluations of social action programs which involve in their targeted populations sizable numbers of minorities and women. Among the more prominent of these problems were:

- The great amount of heterogeneity (e.g., affective variation) to be expected from minorities and women for some settings
- The potential for sizable errors in the reliability and the validity of measures taken from minorities and women
- The "false" overrepresentation of minorities at the lower socioeconomic levels and their "false" underrepresentation at the upper levels.

Of the problems noted in this article it was suggested that the inclusion of minorities and women with evaluation expertise in the early design phases of such programs would go a long way toward minimizing threats to the validity of procedures used in evaluating such efforts. Because of the apparently small number of minorities and women with such expertise, it would perhaps be most fruitful to have them on appropriate governmental decision-making bodies. This should be particularly useful to those specific programs which may be unable to locate minorities and women with the relevant expertise. It is understood that such inclusion would entail changes in power relations, not to mention institutional practices and policies. It should be emphasized that without such changes and accommodations, social problems will no doubt continue to exist (at least in the foreseeable future) and the established wisdom will continue to wonder why "their" social action programs do not work.

REFERENCES

1. Eyestone, R. *From Social Issues to Public Policy*. John Wiley and Sons, New York, 1978; Jones, C. O. *An Introduction to the Study of Public Policy*. Wadsworth Publishing Company, Belmont, CA, 1977; Langbein, L. I. *Discovering Whether Programs Work: A Guide to Statistical Methods for Program Evaluation*. Goodyear Publishing Company, Inc., Glenview, IL, 1980.
2. Boruch, R. F., Rindskopf, D., Anderson, P. S., Amidjaya, I. R., and Jansson, D. M. Randomized Experiments for Evaluating and Planning Local Programs:

A Summary on Appropriateness and Feasibility. *Public Administration Review* 39 (January/February 1979): 36-40.

3. This paper did not address those research and ethical difficulties associated with gaining access to illegal aliens, nor how one might protect such persons from any negative consequences, research or otherwise. It was believed that this would have involved an endeavor considerably beyond the scope of this paper.
4. Campbell, D. T. Reforms as Experiments. In Struening, E. and Guttentag, M. (eds.), *Handbook of Evaluation Research* Vol. 1, Sage Publications, Beverly Hills, CA, 1975, p. 87.
5. Ms. Ruby Aguilar, Chairperson of the Mexican-American Education Commission, Los Angeles Unified School District (LAUSD) reports that there has been a considerable influx of Vietnamese, Cambodians, and other Asians in the LAUSD, resulting in increased needs for bilingual instructors. As a consequence she states that bilingual programs have deteriorated (also, an increasing "English as a Second Language" orientation is occurring), and that non-English speaking children are being pushed into regular classrooms with increasing lower levels of English competence (personal communication, May 10, 1982). Mr. Robert Medina, a specialist in substance abuse prevention programs, similarly notes that both the cultural and socioeconomic character of populations served in the Southern California area (whether in hospitals or community agencies) have changed and are creating problems in both delivery and evaluation (personal communication, April 29, 1982).
6. See: Campbell, D. T., and Boruch, R. F. Making the Case for Randomized Assignment to Treatments by Considering the Alternatives: Six Ways in Which Quasi-experimental Evaluations in Compensatory Education Tend to Underestimate Effects. In Bennett, C. A. and Lumsdaine, A. (eds.). *Evaluation and Experiment: Some Critical Issues in Assessing Social Programs*. Academic Press, New York, 1975. pp. 263-264.
7. Boruch, R. F. and Rindskopf, D. On Randomized Experiments, Approximation to Experiments, and Data Analysis. In Rutman, L. (ed.), *Evaluation Research Methods: A Basic Guide*, Sage Publications, Beverly Hills, CA, 1977, p. 159.
8. Ibid., p. 161.
9. Campbell, D. T. and Erlebacher, A. Reply to Replies. In Hellmuth J. (ed.). *Compensatory Education: A National Debate* Vol. III of *The Disadvantaged Child*. Brunner/Mazel, New York, 1970.
10. Lord, F. M. "Large-sample Covariance Analysis when the Control Variable is Fallible." *Journal of the American Statistical Association* 55 (June 1960): 307-321.
11. Porter, A. C. The Effects of Using Fallible Variables in the Analysis of Covariance. Unpublished Ph.D. dissertation, University of Wisconsin (Madison), 1967.

12. Cf., Cronbach, L. J. 'Notes on Temptress and Campbell-Boruch. unpublished memo, Stanford University, Department of Education, January 18, 1976.
13. Boruch and Rindskopf, op. cit.
14. Barnouw, B. S., Cain, G. G., and Goldberger, A. S. Issues in the Analysis of Selectivity Bias, *Evaluation Studies Annual Review* Vol. 5, Sage Publications, Beverly Hills, CA, 1980, pp. 43-59; Heckman, J. J. Sample Selection Bias as a Specification Error. *Evaluation Studies Annual Review* Vol. 5, Sage Publications, Beverly Hills, CA, 1980, pp. 61-69; Houseman, J. A. and Wise, D. A. Social Experimentation, Truncated Distributions, and Efficient Estimation. *Econometrica* 45 (May 1977): 919-938.
15. See: Mosteller, F. and Tucker, J. W., *Data Analysis and Regression*. Addison-Wesley Publishing Company, Menlo Park, CA, 1977, pp. 21-22.
16. Ibid.
17. A set of procedures for selecting samples matched on a profile of carefully selected variables which result in the creation of experimental and comparison groups having very similar characteristics which appear not to suffer from such bias problems has been devised by Sherwood, C. C., Morris, J. N., and Sherwood, S. A Multivariate, Nonrandomized Matching Technique for Studying the Impact of Social Interventions. In Struening E., and Guttentag, M. (eds.). *Handbook of Evaluation Research* Vol. 1, Sage Publications, Beverly Hills, CA, 1975, pp. 183-224.
18. Lopez-Lee, D. An Assessment of Pluralism and Universalism: Their Implications for Local and Central Controls. *Journal of Comparative Cultures* 1 (Fall, 1972): 3-10; Lopez-Lee, D. The Identification and Socialization Process. *Journal of Comparative Cultures* 2 (Winter, 1974): 73-86.
19. Alvarez, R. The Unique Psycho-historical Experience of the Mexican American. *Social Science Quarterly* 52 (1971): 15-19, Baughman, E., *Black Americans*, Academic Press, New York, 1971; Fabrega, H., Mexican Americans of Texas: Some Social Psychiatric Features in E. Brody (ed.), *Behavior in New Environments: Adaptation of Migrant Populations*, Sage Publications, Beverly Hills, California, 1970; Grier, W. and Cobbs, P., *Black Rage*, Basic Books, New York, 1968; Ramirez, III, M., Identification with Mexican-American Values and Psychological Adjustment in Mexican-American Adolescents. *International Journal of Social Psychiatry* 15 (1969): 151-156; Ramirez, III, M., The Relationship of Acculturation to Educational Achievement and Psychological Adjustment in Chicano Children and Adolescents: A Review of the Literature. *El Grito* 4 (1971): 21-28; Sommers, V. S., The Impact of Dual-cultural Membership on Identity. *Psychiatry* 27 (1964): 332-344.; Torrey, E., The Case for the Indigenous Therapist. *Archives of General Psychiatry* 20 (1969): 365-373; for the female vs male dimension, see: Baefsky, P. M., Self-sacrifice, Cooperation and Aggression in Women of Varying Sex-role Orientations, unpublished

doctoral dissertation, University of Southern California, 1974; Horner, M. S., "Sex Differences in Achievement Motivation and Performance in Competitive and Noncompetitive Situations" unpublished Ph.D. dissertation, University of Michigan, 1968; Maccoby, E. E. and C. N. Jacklin, *The Psychology of Sex Differences*, Stanford University Press, Stanford, California, 1974.

20. Spielberger, C. C. The Effects of Manifest Anxiety on the Academic Achievement of College Students. *Mental Hygiene* 46 (1962): 420-426; Ruebuch, B. K. Anxiety. In H. W. Stevenson (ed.). *Sixty-second Yearbook of the National Society for the Study of Education, Part I, Child Psychology*. University of Chicago Press, Chicago, 1963; and Sarason, I. G. "Empirical Findings and Theoretical Problems in the Use of Anxiety Scales." *Psychological Bulletin* 57 (1960): 403-415.
21. Barabasz, A. F. Galvanic Skin Responses and Test Anxiety among Negroes and Caucasians. *Child Study Journal* 1 (1970): 33-35; Glenn, P. *Anxiety and Ethnicity of Fourth-Grade Children*. Unpublished master's thesis, the University of Texas at Austin, 1969; Phillips, B. N. *An Analysis of Causes of Anxiety Among Children in School*. (Final Report, Project No. 2616, Cooperative Research Branch, United States Office of Education), University of Texas at Austin, 1966; and Tseng, M. S. and Thompson, D. L. "Need Achievement, Fear of Failure, Perception of Occupational Prestige, and Occupational Aspirations of Adolescents of Different Socioeconomic Groups." Paper presented at the annual meeting of the American Educational Research Association, Los Angeles, February 1969.
22. Hernandez, A. R. A Comparative Study of Fear of Success in Mexican-American and Anglo-American College Women, unpublished doctoral dissertation, California School of Professional Psychology, Los Angeles, California, 1976.
23. Winer, B. J., *Statistical Principles in Experimental Design* 2nd Edition, MacGraw-Hill, New York, 1972, p. 755.
24. Di Costanzo, J. L. and Eicherberger, R. B. Reporting ANCOVA Results in Evaluation Settings. *Evaluation Review* 4 (1980): 419-450.
25. Proper, E. C. and St. Pierre, R. G. Reporting ANCOVA Results: A Response to Di Costanzo and Eichelberger. *Evaluation Review* 4 (1980): 451-459.
26. Winer, op. cit. p. 754.
27. Ibid., p. 755.
28. Lubin, B. and Lubin, A. W. Laboratory Training Stress Compared with College Examination Stress. *The Journal of Applied Behavioral Science* 7 (1971): 502-507.
29. Campbell, and Boruch, op. cit. pp. 263-264.
30. Ibid., p. 265.
31. Bobko, P. and Bartlett, C. J. Subgroup Validities: Differential Definitions and Differential Prediction. *Journal of Applied Psychology* 63 (1978): 1-11.

32. Katzell, R. A. and Dyer, F. J. Differential Validity Revived. *Journal of Applied Psychology* 62 (1977): 137-145.
33. Campbell and Boruch, op. cit. pp. 224-248.
34. Rossi, P. H. and Lyall, K. C. *Reforming Public Welfare*, Russell Sage Foundation, New York, 1976.
35. Littlefield, R. P. Self-disclosure Among Some Negro, White and Mexican-American Adolescents. *Journal of Counseling Psychology* 21 (1974): 133-136.
36. Schwartz, J. and McDonald, S. L. Evaluation of Federally Funded Family-Planning Programs, in James G. Abert (Ed.), *Program Evaluation at HEW: Research versus Reality* (Part 1), Marcel Dekker, New York, 1979, p. 277.
37. Sherwood, et al., op. cit.
38. Campbell and Boruch, op. cit. p. 266.
39. Gael, S. and Grant, D. L. Employment Test Validation for Minority and Nonminority Telephone Company Service Representatives. *Journal of Applied Psychology* 52 (1972): 135-139.
40. Lopez-Lee, D. Alcoholism Among Third World Women: Research and Treatment, in Vasanti Burtle (ed.). *Women Who Drink*, Charles C. Thomas, Chicago, Illinois, 1979, pp. 98-115.
41. For examples of such differences, see: Edgerton, R. B. Arthur Performance Ratings of Mexican and American High Grade Mental Defectives. *American Journal of Mental Deficiency* 63 (1963): 372-385; Mercer, J. R. "IQ: The Lethal Label." *Psychology Today* 6 (1972): 44-47, 95-98; Reyes, R. H., "Examinations and Minority Students," unpublished manuscript Testing and Admissions, San Francisco State College, 1970; Semler, I. J. and Iscoe, I., Comparative and Development Study of the Learning Abilities of Negro and White Children Under Four Conditions. *Journal of Education Psychology* 54 (1963): 38-44; Shotwell, A. M., "Arthur Performance Ratings of Mexican and American High-grade Mental Defectives." *American Journal of Mental Deficiency* 49 (1945): 445-449; Stodolsky, S. S. and Lesser, G., "Learning Patterns in the Disadvantages." *Harvard Educational Review* 37 (1967): 456-593; Watson, P., "IQ: The Racial Gap." *Psychology Today* 6 (1972): 48-49, 97-99; Bobko and Barlett, "Subgroup Validities . . . "; Katzell and Dyer, "Differential Validity . . . ."
42. Rossi, P. H. Testing for Success and Failure in Social Action. In P. H. Rossi and W. Williams (eds.). *Evaluating Social Programs*, Seminar Press, New York, 1972, p. 29.
43. See: Boruch, R. F., McSweeny, A. J. and Soderstrom, E. J. Randomized Field Experiments for Program Planning, Development, and Evaluation. *Evaluation Quarterly* 2 (November 1978): 655-695; and Boruch, et al., "Randomized Experiments . . . ."
44. Apsler, R. In Defense of the Experimental Paradigm as a Tool for Evaluation Research. *Evaluation* 4 (1977): 14-18.

45. Guttentag, M. On Quantified Sachel: A Reply to Apsler. *Evaluation* 4 (1977): 18-20.
46. Cf., Webb, E. J., Campbell, D. T., Schwartz, R. D., and Sechrest, L. *Unobtrusive Measures: Nonreactive Research* in the *Social Sciences*, Rand McNally and Co., Chicago, 1972.

20
Evaluation for the Training and Development Function

Enid F. Beaumont / *Academy for State and Local Government, Washington, D.C.*

INTRODUCTION

We live in a time of great irony for training and development. Most large companies and government agencies invest a great deal of effort in providing educational programs for managers and executives. Every serious writer in the field of management asserts that professional development programs are an integral part of the management function. The national organization for training and development is growing, and it has been estimated that total training and development expenditures for all government and industry probably exceed $100 billion annually [1]. Yet professional development programs, particularly in the public sector, are easily stopped when money resources are tight. If training and development could be demonstrated to increase productivity, which in many cases it does, it should not be reduced when financial resources go down.

As long as professional development efforts are not measured in terms of tangible outcomes, they will be subject to the vagaries of financial cycles. This is not a new problem; training and development efforts have long needed an effective research component. Development programs will continue to be vulnerable to changes in leadership and fiscal crises until they are proven essential to organizational results.

The premise of this article is that establishing the link between training and development and organizational outcomes is one of the most important challenges facing the social science research community and that such efforts cannot be avoided. For the purposes of this article, professional development encompasses executive development, management training, education, supervisory training, etc. While many of the arguments made here concerning evaluation apply to all types of training and development, training in specific non-management skills, e.g., specialized occupational skills, is excluded. Professional development ranges from management skill building to the highest levels of broadening horizons. The difficulty in measuring results from such programs increases as the subject matter becomes more general.

Four Levels of Evaluation

Research efforts designed to measure the results of professional development can be conducted at four levels. These four levels are called reaction, learning, behavior, and results [2]. One level of effort has been the measurement of the reaction of participants with the formal program. Almost all of those who provide professional development programs obtain such responses. They can be useful in improving future programs and in determining whether the planners and the participants are in agreement on the program objectives.

A second level of evaluation measures knowledge, skills, or abilities learned during a training program. In this type of evaluation, what is to be learned is spelled out in advance, and participants are measured on the amount that they have learned. Such measures are excellent evaluation tools in skills programs and should be used when appropriate. However, the skills learned are not linked to their usefulness at work by this level of evaluation.

The third level of measurement attempts to look at changes in the behavior of individuals on the job or the use of the training material on the job. This is most often done by self-assessment or by interview with superiors after the end of the formal training experience. Except when the training is for concrete skills, such measures are difficult to obtain, and are rarely conclusive because so many variables interact in human behavior that the effects of training are easily masked and distorted.

The fourth and most important effort for professional development evaluation is that of assessing the link between formal training and organizational performance. When researchers can show that training effort improves the performance of the organization, development will be less likely to suffer during decreases in budgets. Little has been accomplished in this level of evaluation in the past because the constraints of research make the effort costly and frustrating. However, if professional development is to be bought by tough managers in a time of scarcity, then the attempt must be made. This article, however, reviews some good designs that begin to address this problem.

Evaluation Use

Both top management and the staff who provide training and development need to use evaluation as an aid in decisionmaking. Evaluation can aid managers in deciding:

1. Who needs what kinds of training and development experiences? In organizations with adequate performance appraisal systems, the decision could pinpoint needed opportunities.
2. Which of several training and development alternatives would be most cost effective? Even given the limitations on the state-of-the-art, some evidence of useful cost/benefit research is available which will be discussed later in this report.
3. What types of training should be conducted internally and which should be purchased outside the organization?
4. What types of training have the greatest impact on the organization?
5. What kinds of training and development activities can be reliably and validly measured and what cannot?
6. What can managers reasonably expect training and development to do?

Having said that evaluation can be useful, however, there are many constraints that need to be taken into account.

In using evaluation data and in authorizing evaluation research, one recent author calls for rigor, relevance and economy. Rigor refers to the reliability, validity and precision of measurement. Relevance connotes a link to organizational goal. Economy analyzes the relationship between costs and benefits. Zenger and Hargis cite some recent evaluations of training in the private sector that show promise [3]. By raising the above questions and deciding in advance what kind of evidence is needed, evaluation can be helpful in decisionmaking.

A Conceptual Model

Evaluations, which prove results in overall organization performance, are costly and difficult and, in some situations, impossible to obtain. Facing this problem, Kirkpatrick argues that we obtain satisfactory evidence while still working toward proof. Evidence of results is easier to obtain than proof. He notes that "our superiors would be more than satisfied with evidence, particularly in terms of behavior or results. It is certainly a lot more than most of them have been getting now." [4]

Managers should expect training and development to contribute to improved organizational performance. And those who supply training need to provide more information for decisionmaking. This means that the training and development professional should integrate evaluation into the overall process. However, it must be recognized that there are differences in the types of training and development and that these differences have implications for what is measureable and what is not. The highest objective is to obtain proof that training and development achieves organizational results and this is the most difficult and sometimes unachieveable goal.

Regardless of evaluation results, it must be recognized that decisions about training and development in public agencies are tied to macro-economic and political forces which are less likely to be influenced by evaluation. Evaluation is more likely to influence decisions about the internal management of training and development than the policy/budget decisions that allocate resources for training and development, a reality in a constitutional democracy.

Placing this into perspective means that the profession needs to increase its sophistication about evaluation and help increase the range of decisions guided by scientific information.

The more specific the training and development program in scope the easier is the measurement problem. The more difficult to determine results, which is related to the level of subject matter and participant, the more difficult it is to obtain the higher types of measurement. These factors, presented on the chart below, show the possible reasons why decisions about higher-level executive development are most often subject to the political/budgetary decision model rather than the scientific evaluation decision model. The more the program deals with high levels of discretion, the more difficult it is to measure scientifically in terms of both behavior change and results for the organization and thus the more subject to political rather than scientific decision.

REVIEW OF RECENT EVALUATIONS

Following are summaries of some recent research efforts in the public sector which attempt more sophisticated linkage between professional development and organizational performance.

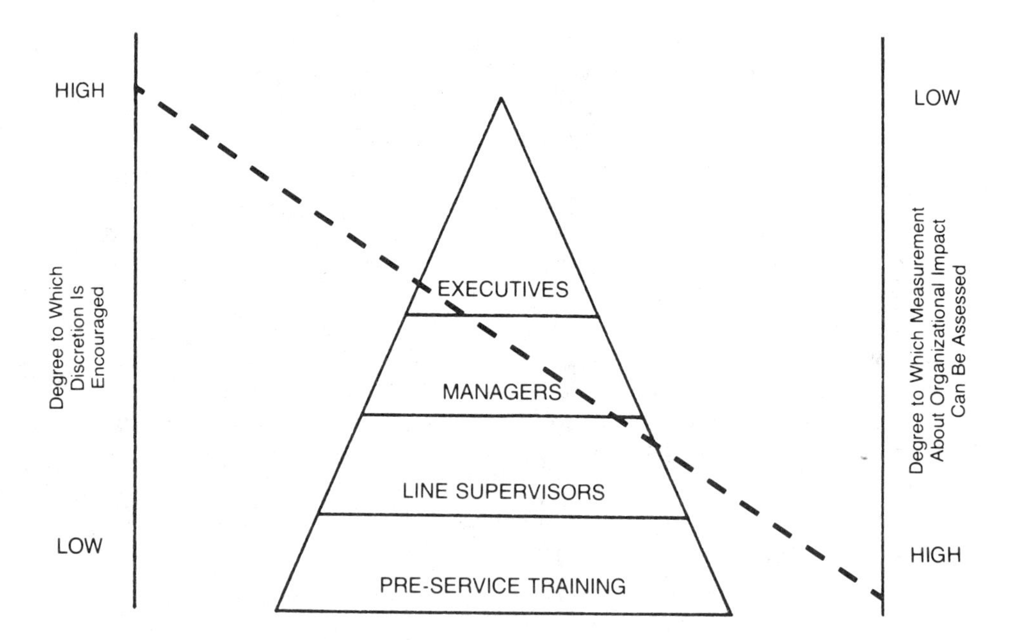

Two recent cost/benefit evaluations of professional development programs deserve serious consideration. Sauter studied a public sector executive development program by asking for the impressions of both the executive and the supervisor who had sent this executive to the Federal Executive Institute (a residential program for senior Federal executives). Based upon a written survey and follow-up interviews with a random sample of pairs of participants and supervisors, Sauter found cost/benefit ratios that were highly favorable in terms of organizational return for the cost of the program. Participants reported benefits to the government amounting to 9.3 times the cost of the training. Their supervisors estimated that post-training savings on the job were 2.5 times training cost. While both ratios were favorable, the disparity shows the need for more refined analysis. Sauter concludes that while the data may not appear as convincing as would be desired, it is reassuring that the benefits were probably well in excess of costs. He does note several qualifications that should be considered in utilizing cost/benefit analysis for a specific development program. These qualifications include the difficulty of finding pairs of supervisors and participants and the costs of a very large sampling. He also notes that he did not apply a discount rate to the benefits as is often done in this type of analysis because there is a flow of benefits over time from such a program which would make the application of a discount rate seem to be an unproductive refinement. He also notes that the fact that these particular participants and supervisors chose this program over other alternatives could have favorably biased the results of the study [5].

There is obviously a need to find a way in such studies to control the tendency of decisionmakers to rationalize the positive aspects of their decisions. In addition, the problems of the lack of a test of reliability between supervisor/subordinate perceptions and the potential bias for respondents to justify their choice of executive development in the first place limit the findings of this study.

Cascio and Gilbert studied the costs and benefits of one management development program for Florida's Department of Health and Rehabilitative Services (HRS). In this study, interviews of a random sample of participants were conducted to gather specific information concerning (1) competencies learned during the training, (2) the extent to which these competencies were later applied on the job, and (3) the dollar value to the organization of the newly acquired knowledge, skills and attitudes. The findings suggest that the benefits to the organization outweighed the costs by a ratio of 6 to 1. The researchers attempted to be as rigorous as possible in requiring documented evidence to support the anecdotal reports of participants. However, many improvements reported by the trainees, such as revised long-range strategy plans for the organization or changed policies that resulted from training, could only be documented over long periods of time. Cascio and Gilbert also note that the flow of personnel among various jobs as well as into and out of the organization, compound the problem of measurement of long-term payoffs from training. In spite of such constraints they recommend further use of such techniques to prevent organizations from basing their training program selection upon beliefs rather than upon evidence [6].

The General Accounting Office (GAO) has conducted several evaluation studies of Federal professional development programs that suggest some useful avenues of methodology. While GAO's approach is basically at Level 2–learning– rather than Level 4–results–their eclectic approaches to evaluation suggest ideas that can help in decisionmaking about training.

Two GAO studies determined by interview whether formal courses were utilized on the job. Based on a sampling of employees, they estimated that 39 percent of the material in one study and 50 percent of the material in the second study was utilized as compared to 56 percent in five comparable agencies. GAO noted that although most employees used part of their training on the job, there were instances of little or no utilization. They reported that the reasons for not using the training were that employees were not authorized to do so, the course material did not apply to the job and that employees had not reached the level in which the course material could be used. They recommended that the relevance and effectiveness of training courses should be evaluated and that employees with the greatest needs should be trained. They concluded that non-utilization of training results in inefficient use of training funds and salary costs for the time employees are away from the job and potential decrease in morale of employees who cannot use their training [7].

GAO is beginning to evaluate its own use of executive development programs for staff by estimating the degree to which program content is perceived as needed or useful by participants. While still primarily in a descriptive phase of this project, GAO has some practical recommendations that are useful for our purposes:

1. Improve recordkeeping;
2. Better identify competencies, knowledge, skills, and abilities desirable for managers and executives;
3. Design a development program to provide the identified competencies recognizing that formal training is likely to be only one part of the overall program;
4. Match individual needs with a variety of executive development experiences; and
5. Integrate the executive development programs into the agency and the individual jobs. [8]

DUAL REQUIREMENTS FOR IMPROVED PROFESSIONAL DEVELOPMENT EVALUATION

There is an imperative need to experiment in the evaluation of professional development to prove its legitimacy and usefulness as a management strategy [9]. It is also apparent that such an evaluation strategy must be useful to decisionmakers. Most of the thoughtful arguments about training evaluation have emphasized improved rigor and methodology. Some recent studies can be categorized as both useful and methodologically well done. However, such studies are not numerous nor does there appear to be tremendous interest in or support for continued evaluation efforts. For example, a recent sample of nearly 100 American academic programs designed to provide a map of contemporary public management research reports only one study that is relevant in the evaluation of professional development programs [10].

Improved research is not the only answer. What is needed is a dual approach: one that moves toward greater sophistication from a measurement standpoint; the other that uses a common sense approach to help decisionmakers decide about professional development programs. These efforts, while related, are not the same.

Methodological Rigor

To obtain reliable and rigorous evaluative research results in this field is very difficult in most circumstances. "The ideal methodology requires measuring change from before training to after; identifying to the extent possible cause and effect; and using statistically equivalent, randomly selected experimental and control groups" [11]. Other strategies, when random selection is not possible, include precourse and postcourse testing of two groups to determine the influence of training. Other argue that training reliability is not sufficient. Internal validity must also be established which measures the effects as a result of the instructional program. Goldstein concludes that most efforts at evaluation are afterthoughts. The establishment of internal training validity must still consider the evaluation components, including pre- and post-tests, control groups, and random assignment of trainees [12].

A Common Sense Approach

In contrast to the requirements of methodological rigor mentioned above, there is need to find a more practical, common sense approach. One example of this was used in a development program designed to institutionalize a productivity improvement program. Four questions were used to guide an observational evaluation:

1. Does the overall training strategy appear to be appropriate for the city organization and for the purpose of institutionalizing a productivity improvement program?
2. To what degree have the participants become committed to the productivity effort?
3. Are the trainees taking responsibility for the progress of the productivity improvement program?
4. Have productivity gains been achieved? [13]

In this case, the training effort is considered to have succeeded because a great deal of effort was put into it and it had the support of the top leadership. While the evaluation strategy was not methodologically pure, the program has acceptance.

Measuring Behavioral Change

Level 3, behavioral evaluation, shows the complexity of this field. If one simply defines the behavior change that one desires and measures that change, whether or not such change can be scientifically measured to show impact on the organization (Level 4) is another matter. We do in fact purchase training that is designed to create behavior change. However, sometimes the desired behavior change does not occur. Some possible reasons are suggested in that the employee is not encouraged to use the new behavior on the job or the new performance is not valued by the organization and others. In addition, confusion abounds about behavioral change and morale and attitudes. Often training and development increases morale, but this benefit is rarely measured.

Rensis Likert suggested that management should measure an organization's morale as often as it measures its fiscal strength. This lesson has long been ignored in the United States. Yet, we are now rushing to adopt quality circles as applied in Japan and many are arguing their worth simply on the grounds of improved morale. Presumably, our new acceptance of such soft factors is not unrelated to the conspicuous competitive success of Japanese industry. Researchers need to find ways to prove the value of such attitude factors in training evaluation.

One reason why this effort has been so frustrating is that managers have had difficulty in accepting the worth of the soft side of professional development programs.

CONCLUSION

Even if professional development evaluation were further advanced, it is possible that the training dilemma would remain: the dilemma that trainees are satisfied with the training but their skills are not utilized or not needed on the job, or organization leaders are dissatisfied.

It would appear that ways must be found to engage organizational decision-makers in this area. It is often said that the best managed companies in the private sector are committed to extensive professional development. While correlation does not prove causation, it is probable that such efforts have a considerable impact on organizational profitability. The lack of the profit factor in government may account, in part for the problems of funding professional development activities in the public sector. Until the link between organizational performance and professional development can be estimated in the public sector, development will continue to experience growth and retrenchment based on fiscal cycles. Those who argue for professional development must face its cyclical nature or prove to decisionmakers that it is more than an extra fringe benefit.

The recent emphasis on cost/benefit analysis of professional development has been good. However, there are weaknesses inherent in any cost/benefit study. There are invariable disagreements over what is a cost and what is a benefit. There is also difficulty in measuring changes in attitudes and in accounting for very long-range benefits. Some caution must be exercised in too heavy reliance on this one technique in professional development evaluation.

Training professionals need to do more to determine in advance what constitutes evidence of the success of their efforts. Such clearly stated evidence must be agreed to by decisionmakers. Those in professional development must be willing to be objective about their own offerings and be willing to recommend elimination of weak programs. Equally they need to fight tenaciously when organization leaders base their decisions on intuition rather than fact.

In the case of the Federal Executive Institute, the program has been evaluated as excellent on the basis both of participant satisfaction and of favorable cost benefits. This is not preventing current Federal decisionmakers from seriously considering its abolition.

The situation is even more complex in government than in the private sector because of frequently changing top leadership. It may be that no matter what evaluations show, some top political executives will decide only according to their own biases. In spite of this possibility, it is imperative that the education community take evaluation very seriously and find ways to prove or disprove the value of professional development.

At this time, it will be necessary to stop short of exacting methodology. The dual approach to evaluation of professional development programs may help to improve the situation. On the one hand would be a continuing effort to improve evaluation methodology and embark upon major research efforts. The other would be to try to achieve in both the public and private sectors an estimate of the value of investment in professional development to organizational achievement. This latter approach should be practical, show common sense and take a long-range view. But it should attempt to determine why better managed companies in the private sector continue to commit extensive resources to professional development whereas the public sector shows ambivalence. It should also attempt to show the impact of training on retention, role modeling and competency building.

Such a strategy is in line with current trends in policy analysis research. Nagel points out that policy analysts are increasingly using pre-adoption projections rather than post-adoption before and after analysis. In addition, policy evaluation is developing increased precision in its methods, but at the same time, it is increasingly recognizing that simple methods may be enough for many policy problems [14].

In both types of evaluation strategies, it should be kept in mind that any formal development program is but a small facet of organizational life. So much occurs beyond the confines of development programs it might simply be too difficult to isolate executive development as one variable. However, with a regularized evaluation program, with top management in agreement on the evidence of success or failure, and with an estimate of the value of professional development to successful organizations, it might be possible to move from blind faith in or distrust of professional development to more rational decision models.

REFERENCES

1. Gilbert, G. R. (ed.). Symposium: Evaluation Management: Can We Improve Organizational Learning. *Journal of Health and Human Resources Administration*, No. 3, (February 1979): 274-316.
2. Kirkpatrick, D. L. Evaluating Training Programs: Evidence vs. Proof, *Training and Development Journal*, (November 1977): 9-12.
3. Zenger, J. H. and Hargis, K. Assessing Training Results: It's Time to Take the Plunge, *Training And Development Journal*, (January 1982): 10-16.
4. Kirkpatrick, op cit.
5. Sauter, J. Purchasing Public Sector Executive Development. *Training and Development Journal*, (April 1980).
6. Cascio, W. F. and Gilbert, G. R. Making Dollars and Sense Out of Management Development. In Huseman, R. C. *Proceedings of the Academy of Management*. 40th Annual Meeting Detroit, Michigan, 1980. pp. 95-98.
7. General Accounting Office. *Survey of Utilization of Training Received by Civilian Employees at the Army Materiel Development and Readiness Command*. FPCD 76-96 (October 1976) and *Survey of Utilization of Training Received by Civilian Employees at GSA*. FPCD 76-96A (October 1976).
8. General Accounting Office. *Evaluation of GAO's Executive Development Programs*. Evaluation Report No. 2, (April 1981): 27-28.
9. Beaumont, E. F. Training Evaluation: Opportunities and Constraints. *Southern Review of Public Administration*. 2 (4) (March 1979): 496-510.
10. Garson, G. D. and Overman, E. S. Draft, *Public Management Research Directory*. Sponsored by the National Association of Schools of Public Affairs and Administration. Vol. I (October 1981).
11. General Accounting Office. *Better Evaluation Needed for Federal Civilian Employee Training*. FPCD-75-120 (August 1975): 21.
12. Goldstein, E. L. The Pursuit of Internal and External Validity in the Evaluation of Training Programs. *Public Personnel Management*. 8 (6) (November-December 1979): pp. 416-429.
13. Lovell, C. Training for Productivity Improvement: Long Beach, California. *Southern Review of Public Administration*. 2 (4) (March 1979): 469.
14. Nagel, S. S. Policy Evaluation Methods. To be published. *Handbook on Public Organization Management*. In Eddy, W. B. (ed.). Marcel Dekker, New York, 1982. See also: U.S. Office of Personnel Management. *Report of the Training Evaluation Demonstration Project*, 1979.

21
Management of Evaluation: Implementing an Effective Evaluation Program

Joseph S. Wholey / *Washington Public Affairs Center, University of Southern California, Washington, D.C.*

INTRODUCTION

In large government agencies, it is often difficult to create an effective evaluation function, one that will assist policy and management decisions and contribute to improved program performance. Evaluation resources are always limited; managers and policy-makers have quite different information needs; evaluators tend to have difficulty meeting the needs of either group in the typical bureaucratic environment. In large agencies, evaluation staffs often become independent research offices, with little direct relationship to line managers or policy-makers.

This paper suggests actions that can be taken to redirect evaluation activities throughout a large agency. Four sets of activities appear necessary to implement an effective evaluation program: (1) establishing and communicating a clear evaluation policy; (2) mobilizing needed resources; (3) carrying out demonstrations of desired evaluation activities; (4) monitoring evaluation activities and results. A fifth set of activities is likely to enhance the effectiveness of evaluation programs: (5) linking evaluation to other management support functions.

The paper uses experiences in the U.S. Department of Health, Education, and Welfare/Department of Health and Human Services (HEW/HHS) to illustrate how these actions can be carried through in a complex environment. At that time, approximately 40 HEW/HHS organizations were carrying out evaluations, at an annual cost of more than $40 million [1].

ESTABLISHING A NEW EVALUATION POLICY

In many agencies, "evaluation" is an undefined term. The first step in establishing an effective evaluation program is to develop a clear policy on how evaluation resources are to be used, what types of evaluation activities are to be given priority, and what results are expected from evaluation. Since both managers and evaluators tend to be unhappy with past evaluation efforts, finding them time-consuming but seldom very useful, it will often be easy to get agreement that changes are in order.

In 1978, for example, the Department of Health, Education, and Welfare (HEW) set new directions that placed increasing emphasis on short-term management-oriented evaluations designed to improve the design and performance of HEW programs. (Before 1978, HEW "evaluation" tended to cover a multitude of long-term studies that were primarily undertaken to meet information needs of policy and planning staffs.) The new directions put particular emphasis on evaluation activities that would assist managers and policy-makers in setting realistic measurable objectives for their programs. The Under Secretary's guidance for fiscal year 1979 HEW evaluation activities stated that:

> *During FY 1979, I want the timeliness and usefulness of evaluation projects improved. The Secretary and I have been impressed with the value of the quick turn-around service delivery assessments conducted by Regional Offices under the general direction of the Inspector General. I have asked the Assistant Secretary for Planning and Evaluation to work with you to shorten the time duration of evaluation projects and to improve the utilization of evaluation findings. In my view, the most important initial step is the identification of realistic measurable objectives and outcome-oriented performance measures on which the program will be held accountable. . . .*
>
> *During the coming year, the Assistant Secretary for Planning and Evaluation will be working with you to begin to identify the realistic measurable objectives and important side-effects (indicators of program performance) on which the Department's programs will be held accountable. The Assistant Secretary for Planning and Evaluation will also be developing evaluation standards and providing training and technical assistance to agency managers and their staffs. [2]*

In subsequent years, the Department's evaluation planning system was modified to accelerate the desired types of evaluation activities, and subordinate agencies were directed to reallocate resources from research-oriented to management-oriented evaluations. The Under Secretary's guidances for fiscal year 1980 and fiscal year 1981 evaluation activities put increasing emphasis on the desired changes in evaluation focus:

> *Managers and evaluators are to give high priority to activities designed to clarify program goals, identify appropriate program performance indicators, and document what is known about program performance in terms of those indicators. To facilitate these activities, approval of certain evaluations is delegated to agency heads. [3]*
>
> *Principal Operating Components are to give high priority to program performance evaluations designed to clarify program objectives and to assess program performance in terms of those objectives [4]. In FY 1980, the Department made important progress in the initiation of these efforts. For FY 1981, each Principal Operating Component should develop a two-to-four-year schedule for completion of program performance evaluations for all its programs. At least 30% of POC/agency evaluation resources are to be devoted to such evaluations. To facilitate these activities, approval of evaluability assessments costing less than $100,000 is again delegated to agency heads. [5]*

In a large organization, policy-level guidances and directives are often dead letters. Informal efforts are needed to convince agency managers and evaluators that new evaluation directions make sense. Beginning in 1978, for example, staff in the HEW Office of Evaluation undertook an extensive missionary effort, which helped "sell" management-oriented evaluation and the concept of "demonstrably effective program" in many but by no means all agencies throughout the Department. In this missionary effort, three sets of activities were important:

- Presentations to line managers and executive staffs;
- Periodic meetings with evaluation staffs throughout the department; and
- Seminars and training sessions for in-house evaluators and evaluation contractors.

Important to the credibility of these missionary efforts were three changes in Department-level evaluation activities.

- Acceleration and compression of the Department's lengthy process of evaluation planning and plan review;
- Delegation to agency level (one or two levels below Department level) of approval of certain management-oriented evaluations costing less than $100,000; and
- Provision of assistance to agency managers and policy-makers. (The HEW Office of Evaluation provided assistance to Office of Human Development

Services managers, for example, when OHDS was under Secretarial pressure to develop appropriate program performance measures and an appropriate performance measurement system for the Head Start program. The Office of Evaluation provided assistance to Office of Education managers and policy-makers in setting new directions for the Follow Through program and in responding to a Congressional mandate to develop measurable objectives for all education programs.)

Such activities facilitated general acceptance and implementation of the new management-oriented evaluation policy by most of the Department's evaluation staffs.

IMPLEMENTING A NEW EVALUATION POLICY

Given a clear evaluation policy and management/staff understanding of that policy, implementation of a new evaluation policy requires mobilization of the necessary resources, staff training, and demonstrations of the desired evaluation activities.

In HEW, for example, the key initial step was the creation of a new evaluation staff in the Office of the Assistant Secretary for Planning and Evaluation (ASPE). Even before the new Office of Evaluation was formally established, actions were taken to assemble the best staff that could be quickly put together. With staff positions limited, the necessary evaluation staff were assembled through transfers within ASPE and within the Department, through details of two staff members from universities and two from State governments under the Intergovernmental Personnel Act, through use of temporary and term positions, and through use of contractors.

After the new office was created, the Department selected six contractors to carry out management-oriented evaluations under task orders that would later be developed for specific evaluations. The contractors were awarded two-year contracts, each of which provided for a series of short-term evaluations (evaluability assessments and rapid-feedback evaluations) under task orders developed for each evaluation. To facilitate timely initiation of evaluability assessments, the Office of Evaluation developed a generalized task order specifying activities to be undertaken and products to be produced. Information was included in each task order specifying the program to be evaluated and the time and resources available. To ensure the relevance of contract evaluation activities, each of these evaluations was guided by an Office of Evaluation staff member and a work group and policy group consisting of relevant program and policy staff.

When an evaluation approach is new to an organization, a good deal of training and technical assistance will be necessary to ensure that the approach is implemented effectively. In HEW, training and assistance were given to central Office of Evaluation staff, to agency staff, and to contractors through a monthly evaluation seminar and a series of one- and two-day training programs for agency managers, evaluation staff, and contractors. Staff from the Office of Evaluation were also available for informal assistance "as needed."

When introducing a new evaluation approach, it will be necessary to focus evaluation resources on a subset of agency programs. In HEW, the Assistant Secretary for Planning and Evaluation, Henry Aaron, decided to focus initial management-oriented evaluation activities on Public Health Service, Office of Education, and social services programs, where existing legislation provided that a small portion of program funds could be used by the Secretary for program evaluation. (At that time, and still today, the Office of the Secretary lacked resources for systematic evaluation of many of the programs funded under the Social Security Act.) Based on an agenda approved by the Under Secretary, the new Office of Evaluation undertook evaluations that provided assistance to managers of approximately 25 HEW programs.

In response to these efforts to demonstrate the value of management-oriented evaluation, the Public Health Service and the Office of Education/Department of Education have embarked on their own efforts to establish realistic measurable objectives for agency programs and increase the emphasis placed on management-oriented evaluation activities.

MONITORING EVALUATION ACTIVITIES AND RESULTS

"Evaluation of evaluation" has commanded increasing attention in recent years. In implementing a new evaluation program, evaluation of evaluation will be helpful at three points: at the planning stage, while the evaluations are under way, and when evaluations are completed. In HEW, the Department's Office of Evaluation monitored and assisted agency evaluators at the planning stage—and documented the extent to which evaluations were used in policy development and program management. Most ongoing evaluations were monitored at agency or bureau level.

As functional manager of the HEW/HHS evaluation program since 1967, the Assistant Secretary for Planning and Evaluation (ASPE) is expected to set standards for evaluation, to monitor evaluation activities throughout the Department, to review and approve agency evaluation plans and projects (most of which are undertaken under legislation authorizing use of up to 1 percent of certain program funds for program evaluation "by the Secretary"), and to encourage semi-autonomous agencies and bureaus to meet Departmental priorities [6]. As a result of its distance from most agency and bureau evaluation staffs and its having had relatively little evaluation staff of its own, ASPE's management of HEW evaluation was primarily a paper process prior to creation of the Office of Evaluation in 1978.

Since ASPE already had the power to review and approve agency evaluation plans and projects, it proved possible to bring the evaluation management function to life with the creation of a more adequately staffed Office of Evaluation within ASPE. At the evaluation planning stage, evaluation activities were monitored and given Departmental direction through a four-stage process:

1. Early meetings between ASPE and agency evaluation staffs, to exchange and discuss "Evaluation Strategy Statements" (plans for evaluations to be undertaken in the coming year);
2. Follow-up memoranda indicating which evaluation projects were likely to be approved;
3. A second round of meetings to review detailed descriptions of proposed evaluation projects;
4. ASPE memoranda indicating which evaluation projects were approved, which were disapproved, and which needed more discussion [7].

Review of HEW/HHS evaluation plans was intended to ensure the quality and relevance of proposed evaluations, and to avoid duplication or unnecessary overlapping of evaluation activities. By getting the evaluation planning process moving early, by undertaking joint (rather than sequential) agency evaluation plan reviews with the Public Health Service, the Office of Education, and the Office of Human Development Services, and by emphasizing the desirability of initiating projects early in the fiscal year, the new Office of Evaluation was able to accelerate the evaluation planning process. More importantly, the human interaction in the ongoing series of meetings allowed the Office of Evaluation to move agency and bureau evaluation offices in the desired direction—in this instance, toward management-oriented evaluation. (The availability of help from Office of Evaluation staff and contractors was also important in getting agency evaluation offices moving toward management-oriented evaluation.)

Sad as it may sound, it is often difficult or impossible to locate evaluations a short period of time after they have been completed. Since 1974, ASPE has solved this basic problem by operating an Evaluation Documentation Center, which collects, indexes, and disseminates information on completed and ongoing evaluations throughout the Department [8]. The Evaluation Documentation Center publishes abstracts of completed and ongoing evaluations, and operates a computerized indexing and retrieval system.

In July 1979, the Senate Appropriations Committee gave a very helpful prod to ASPE efforts to monitor the usefulness of HEW evaluations, stating that:

> *The Committee is unaware of any significant program improvements that have been brought about by the Department's large annual investment in evaluation contracts with consultant organizations. It seems as though, year after year, the same programs get re-evaluated, yet never change. [9]*

In response to the Senate Appropriations Committee report, which clearly indicated that the HEW evaluation program was perceived to be ineffective, the

Office of Evaluation challenged evaluation staffs throughout the Department to produce counterexamples that would show that the Committee was incorrect. By the time of the next appropriations cycle, key members of the Senate and House Appropriations Committees had been presented with a report on "Evaluation Utilization in the Department of Health, Education, and Welfare" [10]. This report presented 21 examples of HEW evaluations that had influenced legislative proposals, influenced program regulations, or helped bring about improvements in day-to-day program operations. In transmitting the evaluation utilization report to Congress, Patricia Roberts Harris, Secretary of Health and Human Services, noted that:

> *Several of the studies cited have influenced legislative proposals, and many have contributed to improvement in program design and management.*
>
> *As Part II of the report indicates, it is now Departmental policy to devote more of its evaluation resources to program performance evaluations. The objectives of these evaluations are to produce evidence on the extent to which the Department's programs are achieving the results intended by the legislation and to inject greater accountability for such results into the management of HHS programs. [11]*

The evaluation utilization report met its objective of convincing key appropriations committee staff that HHS evaluations were being used to redirect and improve HHS programs. The report also served as a vehicle for communicating the steps that had been taken to strengthen the Department's evaluation function and bring together the Department's management, evaluation and personnel administration systems.

Of probably greater importance were the Department's decisions to monitor utilization of evaluation on a systematic basis. In fiscal year 1981, the Office of the Assistant Secretary for Planning and Evaluation (ASPE) produced a second report presenting examples of recent evaluations that had been used to influence policy or program direction; in fiscal year 1982, ASPE decided to establish a system for ongoing monitoring of the results of completed evaluations.

LINKING EVALUATION TO OTHER MANAGEMENT SUPPORT FUNCTIONS

The activities outlined above would probably have been sufficient to establish and implement an effective management-oriented evaluation program. With the passage of the Civil Service Reform Act in 1978, however, there was an opportunity to bring new incentives to bear on federal managers–incentives designed to stimulate demonstrable improvements in agency management and program performance. The Civil Service Reform Act was intended to create an environment in which bonuses, merit pay, and other incentives would be directed toward:

- "providing a competent, honest, and productive work force,"
- "improving the quality of public service," and
- "improving the efficiency, effectiveness, and responsiveness of the Government to national needs."

Among the means to these ends were the establishment of a Senior Executive Service of top-level federal executives, establishment of a new system of performance appraisal for senion executives and middle managers, and provisions for cash bonuses for senior executives and merit pay for middle managers.

At the suggestion of the HEW Office of Evaluation, the U.S. Office of Personnel Management asked the Department to undertake an evaluation of the impact of Civil Service Reform on the management and performance of the Department's programs. This evaluation, which focused on the Senior Executive Service, gave the Office of Evaluation the opportunity to work closely with Thomas S. McFee, Assistant Secretary for Personnel Administration. The evaluation and related Office of Evaluation work focused on linkages among agency management, program management, performance planning, program evaluation, and personnel administration (including allocation of bonuses to high-performing managers). McFee used the Civil Service Reform evaluation to identify policy and management actions needed to improve the implementation and impact of Civil Service Reform in the Department.

In implementing Civil Service Reform, the Department was among the leaders in federal efforts to link management, program evaluation, and personnel administration in ways designed to stimulate improvements in management and program performance.

CONCLUSION

Those in charge of evaluation can stimulate creation of effective evaluation programs by setting clear policy, gaining the support of policy-makers and line managers, demonstrating desired types of evaluation activities, and monitoring evaluation activities and results. Desired management and evaluation activities can be stimulated by linking evaluation to other management support functions–in particular, to the personnel administration system. Given the necessary resources, including support from policy levels, evaluation managers can move even large organizations toward more effective evaluation, improved management, and improved program performance.

REFERENCES

1. Abramson, M. A. and Wholey, J. S. Organization and Management of the Evaluation Function in a Multilevel Organization." *Evaluation of Complex Systems, New Directions for Program Evaluation* 10 (San Francisco: Jossey-Bass, 1981): 31-48.
2. Champion, H. Guidance for Evaluation, Research, and Statistical Activities. Memorandum from the Under Secretary of Health, Education, and Welfare, July 28, 1978.
3. Champion, H. FY 1980 Guidance for Evaluation, Research, and Statistical Activities. Memorandum from the Under Secretary of Health, Education, and Welfare, April 9, 1979.
4. HEW Principal Operating Components included the Office of Human Development Services, Public Health Service, Health Care Financing Administration, Social Security Administration, and Education Division.
5. Stark, N. FY 1981 Guidance for Evaluation, Research, and Statistical Activities. Memorandum from the Under Secretary of Health, Education, and Welfare, February 27, 1980.
6. Abramson and Wholey, op. cit., 35-36.
7. Ibid., 38-39.
8. Ibid., 44.
9. United States Senate, Committee on Appropriations, Senate Committee Report 92-247, "Departments of Labor and Health, Education, and Welfare, and Related Agencies Appropriations Bill, 1980," July 13, 1979, 25.
10. U.S. Department of Health, Education, and Welfare. "Evaluation Utilization in the Department of Health, Education, and Welfare," April 1980.
11. Harris, Patricia Roberts. Letter from the Secretary of Health and Human Services to the Honorable Warren G. Magnuson, May 27, 1980.

Index

A

Absolute Power
fallacy of, 298 (*see also* Fallacies)
Abt Associates, 102
Academics, 69, 70, 73, 206, 207 (*see also* environment)
Accountability, 26, 34-36, 175
Accountants, 204
Administrative process
defined, 92
Aggressive Pluralism, 14-23 passim
Aging, 123
Agriculture
U.S. Department of, 103, 290
Air Force, 302
Airline deregulation, 59
Ambition
as a variable, 95-96
American Educational Research Association, 259
American Enterprise Institute, 28, 102
American Medical Association, 95
American Political Science Association, 118
American Society for Public Administration, 40
Amtrak subsidies, 61-62, 65
Analysis
adjusted covariance, 311
Analysis of Covariance (ANCOVA), 311-314
Analysis of Variance (ANOVA), 311-312
Anti-crime
crime reduction, 89
Anti-pollution policy, 93
Anti-Poverty, 26, 87, 88
Applied Social Science Research, 174
Arab oil embargo, 144, 176
Army Corps of Engineers, 63, 180
Army
U.S. Department of, 302, 303
Army Research Institute, 304
Army Training and Doctrine Command, 304
Army War College, 298
Ash, Roy, 4
Assembly Bill, 938
of California, 321
Association for Policy Analysis and Management, 103
Attitudes
and experimentation, 102

Audit, 25-42 passim
compliance, 35
economy and efficiency, 291
vs. evaluation, 291
financial, 35
management, 204
results or effectiveness, 35
Automobile
design standards, 141, 144, 148-149
energy consumption, 141, 144, 148-149
omissions, 144, 149
safety, 143-144, 148-149

B

Behavior
measurement of, 334
Behavioral Science and Evaluation, 40
Benefit-cost
of crime, 89-90 (*see also* cost benefit)
Bloc grants, 36, 197
Bolling, Dick, 28
Brookings Institute, 28, 102
Brownlow Committee, 154
Budget and Accounting Act of 1921, 25, 114
Bureaucrat, 2-3, 69
Bureau of the Budget, 26
Bureau of Education of the Handicapped, 277, 278
Bureau of Land Management, 181
Burns, Arthur, 39
Business, 2-5, 74-75
analysis, 96, 119
and evaluation, 40
vs. public administration, 3-5

C

California State Board of Education, 320
California State Legislature, 18-19
California
University of, Graduate School of Public Affairs, 102
Carter Administration, 18, 164
civil service reform, 68-83
national urban policy, 57
President Jimmy, 81-83
vocational education, 250
Case studies, 167
Categorial grants, 35-36, 254
Causation
causal flow model, 199
causal inference, 318
causality, 291
causal relations, 99-100, 198, 202, 205
Central business districts (CBD's), 59-61
Channel deepening, 64
Child support enforcement, 279, 280
Child welfare, 280
City managers, 4-5
Civil Aeronautics Board, 59
Civil rights, 87
Civil Service Commission, U.S., 68, 82
Civil Service Reform Act of 1978, 68-83 passim, 153-172, 343-344
Clean Air Act, 144, 149, 175
Client questions, 195-196
Columbia University
Bureau of Applied Social Research, 222
Combat effectiveness, 291
Commerce
U.S. Department of, 103, 290
Committee on Evaluation and Information Systems, 260
Compensatory education, 210-211, 216, 241-244, 316, 320
Composition
fallacy of, 296 (*see also* Fallacies)
Comprehensive evaluation, 183 (*see also* Evaluation)

Comptroller General, 26
Computer expertise, 40
Conceptual integrity, 319
Congress, 25-42 passim
budget process of, 299
as a decisionmaking body, 43-55
vs. executive branch, 71-72
interaction with, 251
mandator of evaluations, 51-52, 70, 205, 208, 209
oversight of, 112-113
political control of, 33
political efficiency, 52
vs. President, 112
as producer, 51-55
relationship to GAO, 26, 104
role of, 18, 25-27
use of evaluation and analysis, 104, 205, 246-248
voting behavior, 43-55
Congressional Budget and Impoundment Control Act of 1974, 27, 115, 117
Congressional Budget Office, 32, 55, 104, 115, 123
Congressional Budget Reform Act, 27, 28
Title Seven, 27
Congressional
Committees, 45
Hearings, 54
Congressional Research Service, 55, 104
Constituency organization, 248
Conviction
probability of, 101
rates of, 100, 101
Cost-Analysis, 200-202 (*see also* Cost-Benefit, Benefit-Cost)
Cost-Benefit, 7, 194, 202, 331, 335, (*see also* Benefit-Cost, Cost-Analysis)
Covariate adjustments, 310
Criminal Justice, 283
Criteria, 213-214, 289
distal, 199
proximal, 199, 200
public vs. private, 4
questions about, 197-199
Cultural differences, 317-318

D

Data
banks, 87
baseline, 165
processing equipment, 87
Davis-Bacon, 35
Decision-Making
incremental vs. rational, 7, 13-14
process of, 6-7
stages of, 3-7
techniques, 7, 40, 194, 197, 204
Decontrol
of gasoline prices, 59-61
Deductive approach, 101
Defense
U.S. Department of, 103, 104, 281, 289-308 passim
Defense Production Act of 1973, 304
Delivery system, 92
Delphi technique, 7
Democracy
positive constitutional, 1
American, 208, 211
Derwinski, Ed., 81
Deterrence, 291
Didactic fallacy, 294-295 (*see also* Fallacies)
Disaster Relief Act, Amendments of 1975, 178
Discrepancy analysis, 7
Discretionary force potential, 298, 299-300
Duke University, 91
Dynamic analysis, 298

E

Econometric analysis, 194, 197, 204
Economics, 71
  approach of, 102, 204
  associations, 103
  efficiency, 52
  optimizing analysis, 91f
  stagnation, 112
Economists, 92, 93
Education Amendments of 1972 and 1974, 244
  Emergency School Aid Act, Title VII, 321
Education, U.S. Department of, 103, 290, 293
Effectiveness (*see* Criteria)
Electric Power Research Institute, 181
Elementary and Secondary Education Act, Title I, 241-244, 258-261
Elites, 1
Emergency School Assistance Act, 264
Employee Attitude Survey, 166
Energy
  conservation, 176
  and environmental policy, 173, 174, 177
  as a policy problem, 69, 118, 176
  shortages of, 112
Environment
  academic/non-academic, 67-68 (*see also* Academics)
  contextual, 2-11
  as a policy field, 88, 92, 93
Environmental
  impact analysis, 180
  protection, 87
Environmental Protection Agency, 180
Equal Employment Opportunity, 4, 35
  records, 167
Equal Employment Opportunity Commission, 154
Ethnocentrism, fallacy of, 296 (*see also* Fallacies)
Evaluability assessment, 208, 339
Evaluation
  administration of, 228
  audiences for, 205-207
  comprehensive, 204
  contracted out, 273-274
  defense, 289-306
    vs. social programs, 292-293
  vs. customer, 56n
  definition of, 270, 271, 285, 287, 290
  evaluation of, 340
  external, 164, 281
  formative, 270, 271
  function, 337
  future of, 41-42
  historical background of, 193-194
  human services, 276-286
  in-house, 273-274
  levels of, 328
  managers of, 338
  manager's role in, 208
  methodology, 203-205, 333
  normative issues of, 207-210
  objectives of, 194-195
  people vs. place oriented, 57-59
  policy, 337
  political obstacles to, 232
  prescriptive, 227-234
  principles, 222-223
  and program planning, 175
  questions, 195-203
  retrospective, 191
  short term, 339
  strategy, 250
  summative, 270

Evaluation (continued)
of training and development, 330-332
of transportation policies, 59
utilization, 44-51, 210-214, 273, 343
in private sector, 274
utility, 329
Evaluation management, 337-345 passim
Evaluation Network, 103, 174
Evaluation research, 174, 177, 184, 219-220, 223-227, 271
Evaluation Research Society, 103, 174
Evaluation Review, 175
Executive branch, 28, 31
political control of, 33
vs. congress, 71-72
Executive Office of the President, 31
Executive Order 1229, 179
Experimentation, 102 (*see also* research)

F

Fallacies, 292-300
Feasibility
political, 99-100
Federal Aid Highway Act of 1962, 146
Federal Executive Institute, U.S., 335
Federal Highway Act
of 1921, 142
of 1962, 142, 146
of 1973, 143
Federal Highway Program, 58-59, 141-146
Federal Housing Authority, 94
Federal mass transportation, 141-143, 146-148
Federal personnel policy, 70-83 passim
Federal Reserve Board
GAO's audit of banking agencies, 39
Federal system, 33
Field research, 7
Fifty-cent gas tax, 61
Fiscal constraint, 21
Florida,
State of,
Health and Rehabilitation Services, 331
Force structure, 295
Ford Foundation, 103
Forecasting, 7
Functional health, 125
Funding
program vs. population, 320-321
as a research issue, 310

G

General Accounting Office, 11, 25-42, 45, 104, 156, 230, 277, 278
agencies, working with, 30-31
agency staffing, 40
audit
of banking agencies, 39 (*see also* Federal Reserve Board)
FBI, 39
IRS, 39
Compendium of GAO evaluations, 253
Comptroller General, 25-42
congressional committee
utilization by, 45, 49
as a congressional support agency, 55
education
evaluation of, 265

General Accounting Office (continued)
evaluation focus, 70
evaluation, results of, 30
Institute for Program Evaluation, 27-28
intergovernmental difficulties, 33-34
jurisdiction of, 39-40
milestones on evaluation, 25-28
Policy Analysis Division, 115-121
professional development
evaluation of, 332
self evaluation, 38-40 (*see also* Internal Evaluation)
service delivery
interest in, 49
testimony, 39
vocational education
report on, 247
weapons systems, 302
Georgetown University, 91
Goals, 87, 88-91
analysis of, 91
economic-oriented, 91
to evaluate policy, 98-99
maximization of, 91, 119
political science, 91
process-type, 92
setting of, 7
Goals and objectives
public vs. private, 3
within policy frameworks, 67
goal free, 198
Grants-in-aid, 240-254
Great Society (*see* Johnson Administration)

H

Harvard University
Kennedy School, 102
Health and Human Services
U.S. Department of, 103, 104, 119, 337, 341, 343
Maternal and Child Health, 194, 281, 282, 283, 290
Health care
available information, 131
framework for, 126-127
historical background of, 130
long term, 123-140
measurement of, 130
Hastings Institute, 91
Head Start, 26, 69, 212, 263, 319, 339 (*see also* Anti-poverty)
Health, Education and Welfare
U.S. Department of, 176, 273, 281, 337-339
Health maintenance organization, 124
Herzog, Major General, 296
Heterogeneity
Problem of, 309, 313-314
Highway finance, 142, 145-146
Hoover Commissions, 154
House Foreign Affairs Committee, 34
House Government Operations Committee, 34
House of Representatives, 26, 27
CSRA
Formulation of, 81-82
Government Operations Committee, 27
Rules committee, 27
Ways and Means committee, 35
Housing and Urban Development
U.S. Department of, 103, 104, 119, 176, 290
Housing policy, 93
Human services, 269, 270, 285, 290

I

Ideology, 276, 277, 285, 286, 287
Impact analysis, 179, 181, 182, 199-

Impact analysis (continued)
200, (*see also* Impact Evaluation)
Impact evaluation, 50 (*see also* Impact Analysis)
as a methodology, 89
vs. optimizing analysis, 91n
urban, 57
Implementation
objectives, 160
questions, 196-197
Impressionistic analysis, 88
Incentive structure, 18, 21
Income maintenance, 279
Incremental
policy making process, 13-14
Incrementalists, 2-3
Indicators
aggregate level, 200
Inflation, 87
Inspector General, 70
Inter-American Development Bank, 34
Interest groups, 1, 3, 18, 36-37, 74, 207
Intergovernmental relations, 33, 40, 226
Interior
U.S. Department of, 290
Internal evaluation, 34-36, 38-40, 50
Internal vs. external evaluations
conflicts and misunderstandings associated with, 29-30
Congress as external evaluator, 51-53
International competition, 116
Interstate highway program, 142, 145-146
Interviews, 167

J

Job Corps, 310
Job knowledge review
test of, 317
Job performance review
test of, 317
Johnson Administration
President Lyndon B., 26
Great Society, 18, 221, 281
Joint Chiefs of Staff, 37, 297
Jury size, 100-101
Justice
U.S. Department of, 103, 176, 290

K

Kennedy Administration, 17
Kennedy, Robert, 258
Keynesian economic theory, 16-18, 21

L

Labor
U.S. Department of, 103, 118, 290
Office of Youth Programs, 264-265
Language and theory, 19-20
Lasswell, Harold
policy making progress model, 5-6, 13, 67-68
Law Enforcement Assistance Administration, 97
Leadership in public sector, 75-76
Legal services, 90, 91-92, 94, 96-98
Legislative branch, 31
Legislative Reorganization Act of 1970, 26, 27, 28-29, 32, 115
Legislators, 18, 21, 43-55
Library of Congress
Legislative Reference Service, 32
Limited mobility, 123
Linear programming, 7
Line of balance, 7

Lobbyists, 37
Local education agencies, 260
Local interests
    in education, 258
Low cost/no cost program, 177

M

Macy, John, 169
Management
    decision-making process of, 5-7
Managers
    responsibility to evaluate, 41
Maryland
    University of, 91
Maximized, 90 (*see also* optimistic approach)
    goals, 91
    income, 96
Media, 211
Mental health, 276
Merit pay, 156, 162-163, 166
Merit Systems Protection Board, 154
Methodological questions, 209
Methodology
    Lasswellian, 68
Methods
    defined, 88-89
    and trends, 96-99
Microevaluation
    fallacy of, 298 (*see also* Fallacies)
Middle East, 87
Minneapolis Medical Research Foundation, 229
Minorities, 309-326 passim
Minority Business Enterprise, 4
Mitre, 102
Misplaced precision
    fallacy of, 297 (*see also* Fallacies)
Modeling
    deductive, 95, 106
    mathematical type, 95
    predictive, 100-101
Model mispecification, 312
Models
    mathematical type
        deductive, 95
    Lasswell, 67-68
Motivation
    federal employee, 70-83, passim
Motor Vehicle Air Pollution Control Act of 1965, 144
Multi-attribute utility analysis, 7, 167
    expected utility, 7
Multiple pre-testing approach, 311
Mumford, Lewis, 145-147

N

National Advisory Council
    disadvantaged children
        on the Education of, 240
National Environmental Policy Act, 175
National Health Insurance, 125
National Highway Traffic Safety Administration, 144
National Institute of Education, 240
National Institute of Mental Health, 103
National Planning and Resources Development Act of 1973, 124
National Science Foundation (NSF), 103, 118
National Traffic and Motor Safety Act, 143-144
National Urban Policy, 57
National Vocational Education Data System, 258
National Water Quality Commission, 93
Naval Laboratories Demonstration Project, 154-156
Navy
    U.S. Department of, 64, 297, 301, 302

Navy (continued)
Naval research, 304
Ocean Systems Center, 153-172
Negative Income Tax, 95-96
experiment, 95, 316
New Deal, 14, 16, 19
Nifty Nugget, 302
Nixon Administration
homeownership, 94, 278
Non-randomization, 309, 310-313
Northwestern University
Research Evaluation Program, 102
Notre Dame,
University of, 91
Nuclear Regulatory Commission, 180, 181

O

Occupational Safety and Health Administration, 4
Office of Economic Opportunity, 26, 97, 264 (*see also* Anti-poverty)
Office of Management and Budget, 39, 82-83, 117, 230
Office of Personnel Management, 72-83 passim, 100, 118, 153-172, 344
Office of the President, 32, 112, (*see also* Executive branch Office of Management and Budget)
Office of Science and Technology Policy, 181
Office of Technology Assessment, 32, 55, 104, 115, 181
Ohio State University
National Center for Research or Vocational Education, 245
Operational doctrine, 295
Operations research, 89
associated with optimizing analysis, 91n
Opportunity-cost, 90
Optimizing approach
and deduction, 102
impact analysis, 91f
in policy analysis, 89
Optimum
mix, 100
policy level, 100
Outcome measures, 197
Outcome objectives, 161, 164 (*see also* Goals, Goals and Objectives)
Outcomes, 291, 327
Outputs, 291

P

Paratransit services, 147-148
Participant observation, 194, 197
Passive restraint systems, 148
Pay administration, 153
Pendleton Act, 154
Pentagon, 37
Performance appraisal, 154, 155, 166
Performance evaluation
employee, 153
Personnel department records, 167
Petroleum taxes, 149
Pittsburgh
University of, 91
Planning
operational, 3
strategic, 3-4
Policies
defined as alternative government decisions, 88
Policy
research, 96, 105, 107
Policy/administration dichotomy, 1
Policy analysis
business analysis
compared to, 96-97
defined, 5-7, 87, 88
demand for, 113-115

Policy analysis (continued)
growth of, 87-90
as a profession, 88
research, 87, 88
Policy formulation
defined, 5-7, 89
Policy paradigms
aggressive pluralism, 14-23
New Deal, 14-23
progressive era, 14-23
Policy problems, 90-91
Policy scientist
defined, 68
Policy sources, 90
Policy Studies Organization, 103
Political ambivalence, 278
Political efficiency, 52
Political perceptions, 53, 54
Political science
and impact analysis, 91n
approach, 102
associations, 103
Political scientists, 203
Pollution
air, 141, 144, 148-149 (*see also* anti-pollution policy)
Pollution
water, 93
Pollution tax, 93
Port user charges, 63-64
Position classification, 153, 159-162, 166
PPBS, 28, 29, 229, 278, 281
Press
fourth estate, 37
role of, 37-38
Private sector, 2-5
Private vs. public sector, 2-5, 157
Probability, 90
Productivity measurement, 167
Professional development, 328
Professional Standards Review Organizations, 124
Program construct, 248
Progressive era, 14-19
Project reflex, 169
Proposition 2 1/2, 21
Proposition 13, 21
Prospective analysis, 174, 179-183, 212
Proud Spirit, 302
Proxmire, Senator William, 28
Psychology, 40, 89, 204
Public administration and evaluation, 40, 73, 208
Public Administrator
as bureaucrat, 2-3
as manager, 2-3
Public Choice Society, 103
Public Health and Evaluation, 40, 204
Public interest groups (*see* interest groups)
Public personnel administration, 70 (*see also* Federal personnel policy)
Public vs. private sectors, 3-5, 193
personnel practices, 71-72

Q

Qualitative techniques
participant observations, 194, 197
case studies, 194, 197
in-depth interviews, 194, 197
Quasi-experimental Research, 99 (*see also* research)
Quie, Congressman and Governor, 28

R

Rail transit, 147
Rand Corporation, 27
Rational
policy analysis, 100n

Readiness, 295
Reagan Administration, 19, 22, 36,
60, 118, 119, 155, 164
transportation policies, 146, 148
defense budget, 290
Reduction in force, 160, 161, 163
simulation, 168
Reductionist
fallacy, 293-295 (*see also* Fallacies)
Reformers and progressives, 14-18
Regression, 312 (*see also* structural equation models approach)
Regulations
government, 4
social, 4
Regulatory programs, 175, 177, 178
Reliability, 310, 316-317, 329
Replication
problems in, 279-280
Research
experimental, 7, 194, 197, 204, 285, 318, 319
non-experimental, 7
quasi-experimental, 7, 204, 285
Research and development, 176, 177
Residential conservation science, 176
Resources
availability of, 252
Resource scarcity, 111
Retrospective analysis, 178, 179, 182, 206, 212
Revenue sharing, 35, 197
Rhodes, John, 81
Ride sharing, 144, 147-148
Rockefeller Foundation, 103
Role model
bureaucrat, 2-3
manager, 2-3
Rolling Thunder, 291, 305
Roosevelt Administration, 16-17
Russell Sage Foundation, 103, 234

S

Samples
non-random, 99
Scaling
psychological, 7
Science and technology, 116
public accountability of, 117
Senate, 26, 27
Government Affairs Committee, 39
CSRA formulation, 81-82
Senate, 26, 27
Senate Appropriations Committee, 342-343
Senior Executive Service, 154
Sequential screening, 7
Sesame Street, 263-264
Smith Hughes Act of 1971, 248
Social construction , 19
Social experiments, 50, 198, 233-234
Social impact analysis, 181
Social psychology
associated with impact analysis, 91n
approach, 102
Social sciences, 95
Social security, 281
Social Security Act, 278
Social service programs, 175
Social services, 278-279
Social values:
sensitivity to, 91-92
Society for the Psychological Study of Social Issues, 103
Society for the Study of Social Problems, 102
Socioeconomic level, 317-318
Sociology, 89, 204
Special Programs for the Disadvantaged, 319

State
U.S. Department of, 290
State education agencies, 260
State Energy Conservation Program, 176
State legislatures, 230
Statistical methodology, 95
Statistics, 40
Stockman, David, 37
Structural equation
models approach, 312 (*see also* Regression)
Summative vs. formative evaluation, 263
Sunset legislation, 42, 120
Supply-side economics, 22
Supreme Court, 102
Survey research, 7, 194, 204
Sustainability, 295
Systems analysis, 40

T

Technology assessment, 179
Technology Assessment Act of 1922, 181
Temporary State Commission of Child Welfare, 280
Tenure, 164
Time-of-day pricing, 177
Time sampling, 197
Time series analysis, 204
Total obligational authority, 289
Trade-off, 7
Training
evaluation of, 327-336 passim
GAO, 40-41
public policy, 102, 118-119
Transit finance, 142-143, 147
Transportation
U.S. Department of, 57-67 passim, 103, 141-151 passim, 290
Transportation systems, 142-143
Treasury
U.S. Department of, 290
Truck deregulation, 62-63
terminal charges, 62
True experimental designs, 310, 318-320 (*see also* Research)
Twin Rivers project, 177

U

UCLA
Institute for Social Sciences Research, 102
Udall, Morris, 80
Unemployment, 112
Unintended consequences, 279
United Nations
proposal for, 34
United Nations Food and Agriculture Organization
GAO's audit of, 33-34
Unit Status and Identity Report, 297-298
University of Michigan
School of Business Administration, 289
University of Southern California, 164, 169, 170
Urban Institute, 27, 102, 271, 272
Urban Mass Transit Authority, 60
Urban Mass Transportation Act of 1964, 143, 147
Urban transportation, 141-142
planning, 142, 146
regulation, 146, 148

V

Validity, 314-317
differential, 316-317, 392

Variables
dependent, 199
Verification,
fallacies of, 292-293 (*see also* Fallacies)
Veteran's preference, 164
Vietnam, 87, 112, 291, 297, 300
Vocational Education Study, 244-246
Voting behavior of congress, 43-55

W

War on Poverty, 175
Watergate, 112
Weatherization Assistance Program, 176
Weinberger, Casper, W., 295
Welfare recipients, 95
Welfare Rights Organization, 18
Wilson, Woodrow, 25
Women, Infants and Children, 194, 203
Women's liberation, 87
Workforce data base, 167
World Bank
GAO's audit of, 33-34
World Health Organization, 34
World War I, 294
World War II, 294-295, 300

Y

Yale University
Institute for Social and Policy Studies, 102

Z

Zero Based Budgeting, 28-29